LAWRENCE & WISHART LTD.

LONDON

IRELAND HER OWN

by T. A. Jackson

Ireland her own,
and all therein, from the sod to the sky.

JAMES FINTAN LALOR

Ireland one, and Ireland free —
is not this the definition of Ireland, a Nation?

PATRICK PEARSE

Ireland Her Own

An Outline History of the Irish Struggle for National Freedom and Independence

BY T. A. JACKSON

EDITED AND WITH AN EPILOGUE
BY C. DESMOND GREAVES

1985
LAWRENCE AND WISHART
LONDON

First published by Cobbett Press, London, 1947
This edition is published simultaneously by
Lawrence & Wishart, London, International Publishers,
New York, and Seven Seas Books, Berlin, 1971
Second impression 1973
Third impression by
Lawrence & Wishart, London
in association with
Seven Seas Books, Berlin, 1976
Fourth impression by Lawrence & Wishart, London, 1985
SBN 85315 219 5

TO THE MEMORY OF
MY FRIEND AND COMRADE

CON O'LYHANE

one-time Secretary of the Cork Branch, Irish Socialist Republican Party; a representative of that long line of Irishmen who have done valiant service in the working-class, democratic, and socialist movement in England, Scotland, and the U.S.A. without ceasing for a moment their fight for Ireland's national freedom.

CONTENTS

EDITOR'S PREFACE   16

FOREWORD   18

PART ONE   THE ENGLISH CONQUEST OF IRELAND

I   ANCIENT IRELAND   23

Geographical Determinants–Gaelic Society–The Political Structure–Unity and Opposition in Gaelic Society–The Church in Gaelic Ireland–The Danish Invasion (795–1014)

II   THE SUBJUGATION OF IRELAND–I   36

Political and Economic Background–Submission of 1171–Progress of the Conquest–Statute of Kilkenny–The Prelude to the Tudor Conquest–Tudor Conquest: First Phase–Irish Chiefs, English Lords–Confiscation and Plantation–The Plantation of Ulster

III   THE SUBJUGATION OF IRELAND–II   54

Background: English Revolution, 1640–Ireland and the "Thorough" Conspiracy–Religion in the English Revolution–The Long Parliament; and the Rising of 1641–Rebellion and Civil War in Ireland–The Episode of the Levellers–The Cromwellian Conquest of Ireland–The Cromwellian Settlement–The Restoration Finale

IV   THE SUBJUGATION OF IRELAND–III   76

The Whig Revolution (1688)–Ireland and the Whig

*Revolution–The "Patriot" Parliament of 1689–The
Williamite War–The Treaty of Limerick–The Penal
Code–Protestant Ascendancy–The Penal Code and
Irish Nationality*

PART TWO   FROM GRATTAN TO THE
UNITED IRISHMEN

V   ENGLAND'S COLONY–IRELAND   93

*England's Colonial Policy–Restraints upon Irish
Trade–Administration and Parliament in Ireland–
Economic Conditions in Ireland (1690–1778)*

VI   GRATTAN'S REVOLUTION   100

*Urban Agitations–Agrarian Unrest and Revolts–
The Volunteers–Henry Grattan and His Leadership–Flood: and the Convention of 1783*

VII   THE RISE OF THE UNITED IRISHMEN   114

*Ireland in 1790-1–Theobald Wolfe Tone–The
Rights of Man in Ireland–Tone, and the Catholic
Committee–The Catholic Convention–The Catholic
Relief Act (1793)*

VIII   THE WAR UPON THE UNITED IRISHMEN   126

*The Programme of Reaction–The Convention Act
and the Volunteers–The Suppression of the
Volunteers–The Resistance to Militia Conscription–
The United Irishmen and the Defenders–The
Society of United Irishmen Suppressed–The Orange
Society Founded*

IX   "THE FRENCH ARE IN THE BAY"   146

*Wolfe Tone in France–The European Situation–
French Attempts to Invade Ireland, 1796-7–The*

Dragooning of Ulster–Waiting for the French to Come

X   THE RISING OF 'NINETY-EIGHT   161

The Case of William Orr–Curran's Indictment of the Government–Moving to a Crisis–Counter-Revolutionary Terror–Lord Edward Fitzgerald and the Rising–The Boys of Wexford–The Rising in Antrim and Down–Vengeance on the Vanquished–The French Expeditions of 1798

XI   THE UNION: ROBERT EMMET: SUMMARY   187

The Act of Union–The Catholics and the Union–Emmet's Conspiracy–What the United Irishmen Accomplished–The Falling-away of the North

PART THREE   FROM O'CONNELL TO YOUNG IRELAND

XII   AFTER THE UNION   205

Ireland's Place in England's Economy–Landlordism in Ireland–Poverty in Ireland: its Extent

XIII O'CONNELL AND CATHOLIC EMANCIPATION   210

Daniel O'Connell–Orangeism: the Tories, and the Whigs–The Revolt of the 40s. Freeholders–The Clare Election an ' Emancipation

XIV   THE TITHE WAR   217

The Tithe System in Ireland–The Tithe War: First Phase–The Tithe War: Second Phase–The Tithe War: Third Phase–Thomas Drummond

XV   THE TRANSITION TO REPEAL AGITATION   226

O'Connell's Political Standpoint–O'Connell and

the Chartists–The Nation *and its Writers–Thomas Davis*

XVI THE CRISIS OF THE REPEAL AGITATION 233

The Monster Meetings–Reactions to the Agitation–The Crisis at Clontarf–The Trial of O'Connell and others–O'Connell changes his front

XVII FAMINE: AND 'FORTY-EIGHT 243

The Great Starvation–The End of O'Connell–The Irish Confederation–John Mitchel: Duffy: the Chartists–The Rising of 'Forty-Eight

PART FOUR THE TENANTS' RIGHT LEAGUE TO THE FENIAN BROTHERHOOD

XVIII ECONOMIC CONSEQUENCES OF THE FAMINE 261

Free Trade in Land–The Encumbered Estates Act–Emigration and its consequences

XIX DUFFY'S TENANTS' RIGHT LEAGUE 266

The Persistence of Agrarian Terrorism–The Tenants' Right League–The Pope's Brass Band–The Great Betrayal

XX THE FENIAN BROTHERHOOD 275

The "Phœnix" Conspiracy–Revolutionary Affiliations of Fenianism–"Felon Setting"–Garibaldi and the Pope–The MacManus Funeral–The Civil War in the U.S.A. and Fenianism–The Irish People

XXI THE CRISIS OF FENIANISM 284

The Arrests of 'Sixty-five–The Trials of Luby, O'Leary, Kickham and Rossa–The Rising of 'Sixty-

Seven-The Manchester Rescue-The Clerkenwell
Explosion

XXII THE OUTCOME OF THE FENIAN MOVEMENT 290

The International and the Fenians-Gladstone's
Disestablishment Act-The Fenian Tradition

PART FIVE   FROM PARNELL TO EASTER
WEEK (AND AFTER)

XXIII   ECONOMIC DEVELOPMENTS, 1870-1960   299

Agricultural Development in Ireland-The Case of
Belfast-The Struggle for the Land, 1870-1909-
Lalor: and the Theory of Agrarian Struggle

XXIV   HOME RULE: THE RISE OF PARNELL   307

The Home Rule Movement Begins-The Home Rule
Party in Parliament-Scientific Obstruction: Biggar
and Parnell-The Crisis in the Home Rule Party-
The Parting of the Ways

XXV   DAVITT; THE LAND LEAGUE; AND PARNELL   318

The Famine of 1879-Davitt, Devoy and the New
Departure-Parliament and the Land War-The
Case of Captain Boycott-Gladstone Tries Coer-
cion-The Land Act of 1881-The Kilmainham
Compact-The Phœnix Park Murders

XXVI   PARNELL, THE "UNCROWNED KING"   333

Left-Wing Terrorism and the National Struggle-
Gladstone's Conversion to Home Rule-"Judas"
Chamberlain-The Plan of Campaign-Tory Anti-
Parnellite Propaganda-The Times Special Com-
mission-The English Masses and the Irish Party

XXVII THE BETRAYAL AND DEATH OF PARNELL   350

*The O'Shea-Parnell Triangle—The Nonconformist
Conscience—The Party Split—The Death of Parnell*

XXVIII THE YEARS BETWEEN   358

*Killing Home Rule with Kindness—The Land Acts,
1870–1909—The Degeneration of the Parliamentary
Party—Elements of National Revival outside the
Party—The Socialist Republicans*

XXIX THE HOME RULE CRISIS, 1912–14   370

*The Parliament Act, 1911—The Tory Opposition to
Home Rule—The Opposition in Ulster—Classes in
the Ulster Resistance—The Curragh Incident—The
"Larkin" Labour War—The Irish Volunteers*

XXX THE ROAD TO EASTER WEEK   382

*Redmond; the Nationalist Party and the War—The
Volunteer Split—The Struggle with the Authorities—
Preparing for Revolt—Easter Monday, Dublin, 1916*

XXXI THE EASTER-WEEK RISING   396

*The Battle for the Republic—The Blood-Fury of the
Reactionaries—Judgments on the Rising*

XXXII THE TRANSITION TO A NEW CRISIS   403

*The British Government and Ireland—The Fenian
Dead—The Emergence of a New Party—Lloyd
George's Circus—The Resistance to Conscription—
The General Election of 1918*

XXXIII ANGLO-IRISH WAR AND THE TREATY   410

*Dáil Eireann—The War with the Army—The Black-
and-Tans—The Government of Ireland Act (1920)—*

*The Belfast Pogroms–The Truce and Negotiations–
The Treaty of 1921–22–Pro- and Anti-Treaty Civil
War–The Civil War and the Six Counties–Partition
Consummated*

XXXIV ECONOMIC WAR: CONCLUSIONS TO DATE   428

*DeValera Returns to Power–The Evil of Partition–
To End Partition*

PART SIX   EPILOGUE   437

INDEX   485

Ireland Her Own was the last major work of Thomas Alfred Jackson, one of the most colourful figures of the working-class and socialist movement in England in the late nineteenth and twentieth centuries.

It was written in accordance with a promise made by the author to his friend Con Lehane (who then spelled his name Con O'Lyhane) when the two young men were active members of and propagandists for the "Left" group which broke away from the London Social Democratic Federation in 1904.

O'Lyhane was a lieutenant of Connolly, and Jackson met the Irish socialist leader during his visits to London in the first years of the century.

Born in London in 1880 Jackson became a "printer's devil" in Clerkenwell in 1893, making almost immediate contact with the socialist movement in an area where memories of the Fenians were still strong. As far as can be ascertained he had no Irish ancestry. But his strong radical background in the great days of Charles Stewart Parnell impelled him from his earliest years to sympathy with the Irish cause.

Throughout over sixty years of socialist activity his firm grip of fundamentals, his insistence on Marxist understanding, allied to the most lively and inventive imagination, found expression in a series of works, of which *Dialectics* is probably the best known. As a conversationalist he was unrivalled.

His autobiography (*Solo Trumpet*) was published by Messrs Lawrence and Wishart in 1953.

The work now re-issued deserves a word of explanation. It was originally cast at substantially greater length. I well remember Jackson's dilemma. Either he could publish a severely cut version or he could wait until the war-time paper restrictions were eased. "I am sixty-seven," he said, "and I have not much time."

He decided therefore to prune and compress his text, which was reduced to less than a half of its original length. The result may not give full evidence of the sprightly and elegant prose of which he was capable. But as he later remarked himself, "the story stands out stark and clear."

Ireland Her Own is probably the briefest, simplest and most precise statement of the international case for Irish independence that is available today. I have added a brief Epilogue dealing with the developments since Partition, with which T. A. Jackson's book ends.

C. Desmond Greaves.

FOREWORD

In this book I try to tell the story, first of how Ireland came to be a part of the British Empire, then of how the Irish people struggled to undo that conquest and so regain possession of the soil and the sovereign rule of Ireland.

The reason for telling this story is that, contrary to common belief, the process is not yet complete. I have thought it necessary to show the causes of the Anglo-Irish conflict, since only when these are known will the common people of England, the final arbiters, be able to tackle this long-outstanding Irish Question with a comprehension of the real issues involved.

The most valuable parts of this book should be those which show with what anxiety and diligence the rulers of England have had to labour to avoid being caught in a "pincer attack" between two distinct but converging emancipation struggles–those of the English and of the Irish common people respectively. The relations between the English rulers and the Irish ruled have been, throughout, imperialist relations, consequently, the history of the 800 years of Anglo-Irish conflict–with its examples of every variety of imperialist aggression and of every form of resistance thereto–supplies an invaluable introduction to the critical study of Imperialism in general.

The writings of Englishmen upon Anglo-Irish relations only too often call to mind an often-quoted remark by the Earl of Essex to Queen Elizabeth: "'Twere well for our credit that we had the exposition of our quarrel with these people and not they themselves."

Irish writers upon the subject have commonly been satisfied with destroying such shreds of credit the English expounders of the quarrel have contrived to save. Thus they have, usually, missed the real tragedy involved in Ireland's history–the manner in which the English and

Irish common people, each of them struggling for freedom, have been time and again jockeyed into becoming weapons used by the exploiters, each for the enslavement of the other.

The outstanding exception is James Connolly, whose work *Labour in Irish History* is a work of genius. This work I have taken as my guide; but Connolly, writing as an Irishman for Irishmen, could suppose that his readers knew many things which are not at all well known to the ordinary Englishman. I, who write as an Englishman, primarily for Englishmen, have to explain these things, as well as to continue the narrative beyond the point at which Connolly left off. If I have succeeded in what I have tried to do, my outline will provide English readers with an introduction to the study of Connolly's work, and that of other specialist writers on Irish History. It will, at the same time, provide Irish readers with an introduction to the history of the English democratic and labour struggle.

The English and the Irish common people, each with its own splendid record of unyielding resistance to oppression, should, by rights, understand each other better than they do, and be more ready than they have been to act in concert. Both together should find reasons for solidarity with the democratic and working-class struggles in other lands.

It was, as it chanced, on Wolfe Tone Sunday (June 22, 1941) that the Nazi-Reich launched its attack upon the Soviet Union. The spirit of Wolfe Tone and of the United Irishmen forms so fundamental an ingredient in Irish Nationalist tradition that one looks with confidence for an Irish enthusiasm for the Soviet Union parallel to that of Tone for the revolutionary people of France.

The very words with which Irishmen, in 1791, acclaimed the French, would apply with treble force to the people of the Soviet Union today: "Go on, then—great and gallant people! You are in very truth the hope of the world—of all except a few men in a few Cabinets who thought the human race belonged to them, but who, now, taught by awful example, tremble and dare not confide in armies arrayed against you and your cause."

Tone died struggling to win the Rights of Man for Ireland. Those who follow him could not honour him better than by claiming for Ireland her rightful place in the battle-line of those who fight to win the Rights of Man for the whole world.

I write frankly as a partisan. I have done my best to be candid; but impartiality is beyond my scope. My concern is to help forward the cause I uphold. If this book does that, even by a little, I shall have attained my object.

T. A. J.

PART ONE
THE ENGLISH CONQUEST
OF IRELAND

CHAPTER I

ANCIENT IRELAND

When they invaded Ireland in 1169, the Anglo-Normans found in being a Social Order—one radically different from their own—which resisted for centuries their efforts to break it up.

In this chapter we examine the nature of this Gaelic Social Order.

Geographical Determinants

Measured from the Mediterranean Regions in which modern civilisation arose, England and Ireland lay together at the end of the earth. Each was protected by the sea against mass migrations; but neither was impervious to cultural infiltration, or immune from conquest by a determined invader.

Each preserved the primitive social organisation which the West Mediterranean region had long outgrown. In England this was thrown into confusion by the Roman occupation, and into further disintegration, centuries later, by the barbarian invasions which followed the Roman withdrawal. During all these years Ireland developed without interruption. As the barbarians over-ran the Roman Empire, "saints and scholars", fleeing from their ravages, found a refuge in Ireland. And it was from Ireland that a large part of Western Europe was ultimately re-civilised and re-Christianised.

To its escape from inclusion in the Roman Empire and involvement in its collapse, Ireland owes its early differentiation from England's development; and this in turn caused Irela d to react differently to those experiences the islands went through in common.

England was better placed for communication with the Mediterranean over land; but Ireland was the better placed for communication by the long sea route. Ireland received Christian influences from Greece and Alexandria long before England received them from Rome; and at a later date Ireland through its southern and western ports was able to maintain trade contacts with France, Spain and Italy while completely cut off by England from contact with the over-land trade-routes.

A point of internal geography is that Ireland's mountain masses lie mostly upon, or parallel to, its coast-line. This is rocky except for a gap on the east coast where the great central plain reaches to the sea—which central plain is traversed by rivers and interspersed with bogs, some of considerable extent. This disposition of the mountains played an important part in the history of Ireland. In ancient times the central plain was densely wooded, so that the aboriginal settlements took place in isolated parts of the hill country. This delayed materially the development of a centralised state. Later on these separate mountain regions provided refuges from the Anglo-Norman invaders, and similarly checked their efforts at unification.

Gaelic Society

Of the racial origins of Gaelic Ireland little is known with precision though much is inferentially established. The Gaels, who reached Ireland in comparatively small parties, at different times, came from various points— Spain, Western France, and Belgium—after a prolonged period of wandering in the grassland-belt of Europe. Detached parties of their stock made their way into Greece and Asia Minor and also into Italy, France and Spain. It is quite inconceivable that they should have preserved their "racial purity" during all these, possibly, thousands of years; and very doubtful whether they had any to preserve. A federation of tribal-groups of mixed origin, which, through long association, had evolved a common speech, gives the most probable starting-point for the history of the Gaels.

In Ireland they found an aboriginal population which was likewise of mixed descent. The Gaels did not exterminate the aborigines; in time they fused with them. Any theory, romantic or fascist, which supposes a "pure" Gaelic "blood" as a determinant of Irish history, is completely worthless. Not only have the Irish people "racial" affinities, at one point or another, with most of the nations of southern and western Europe; the seemingly "unique" features of Gaelic-Irish society can be shown to be akin to those of the kinship society which everywhere in Europe preceded the establishment of the class-differentiated Territorial State.

The special interest of Gaelic society is that it preserved into modern times an archaic social organisation which had not changed, in principle, since the Bronze Age, but which, notwithstanding, proved compatible with a high degree of cultural development or "civilisation."

The economy upon which Gaelic society rested was basically a "natural" economy—production for immediate consumption by the producing community. Its principal feature was cattle-breeding, supplemented by tillage and handicrafts. There was, in general, a surplus of production in excess of immediate requirement which was disposed of to a limited extent in exchange, but more normally by the "ostentatious consumption" of the chiefs of *Septs* and *Clanna*.

The unit of exchange-value was the *cumhal* (coo-al) which means literally a slave-woman, but in practice denoted three cows. Wealth was reckoned in terms of cattle, and an aristocracy of wealth was replacing, where it had not already replaced, an aristocracy of descent. Milk and milk-products with oatmeal porridge and barley-bread constituted the staple diet, and this was supplemented from the game with which the country abounded.

In structure Gaelic society was hierarchical both in its economic and its political aspects. The economic unit was the *Fine* (finna) which resembled the *familia* of the Romans but was of wider scope. The political unit was the *Clann* which corresponded to the Roman *tribe*. Intermediary between the *Clann* and the *Fine* was the *Sept* whose functions were both political and economic.

The territory occupied by a *Clann* was deemed its collective possession; it was variable in extent, since an area of no-man's-land invariably separated the territories of adjacent *Clanna*. The upper limit of expansion was fixed for each *Clann* at the point where further advance would be regarded by its neighbours as an encroachment. Its limit of contraction was set by the fixed quantity of land possessed by the *Septs* of which it was composed.

The area belonging to each *Sept* was by undeviating practice fixed in extent and location. This area as a whole was an inalienable possession of the *Sept* collectively. The portions allotted to meadow and arable, and the share allotted to each *Fine* in each of these, varied in quantity and location. Thus, while the *Clann*-territory might vary in extent and the *Fine*-allocation might vary in location, the *Sept*land remained fixed in both respects; and this gave Gaelic society its stability through the fluctuations of circumstance and mischance. In the gradual break-up of Gaelic society under the impact of invasion and conquest the *Sept* was the last unit to succumb. A question which has exercised Gaelic scholars is whether this society was "communist" or "individualistic". The dispute has little relevance since in different aspects it was both, and neither. This is seen from the structure of the *Fine* and its relation to the *Sept*.

In its completest form the *Fine* consisted of "seventeen men" disposed in four grades. The *Geilfine* (or true family) consisted of a *Flaith* (Flah) and his four sons, or other males next of kin. These constituted, with their dependants and slaves, a single productive unit, and claimed a full member's share in the allocation of the *Sept* lands. The four males next of kin to the foregoing constituted the *Deirbhfine*, the four next the *Iarfine*, and the four next again the *Innfine*. These grades made a "family" for two purposes. They shared in the division of the disposable property of the *Flaith* at his death in a proportion which lessened with each succeeding grade. Broadly the "true family" took two-thirds, the second grade two-thirds of the residue, and so on. Similarly when the *Flaith* became involved in a feud, or liable to an *eric* or bloodfine, or other penalty imposed by judicial authority, the responsibility was *collective* but in a degree differentiated in a way which corresponded to the gradation of the family.

A cardial point, and a clue to its functioning, is found in the rule that as the sons of a *Flaith* reached manhood they entered the *Geilfine*. If it had previously its full quota, the new-comer automatically pushed out its senior member (under the *Flaith*). For economic purposes the senior so extruded became qualified to share in the *Sept* lands as a full member. For other purposes he descended to the next grade, pushed out its senior, who repeated the process so that with a full "seventeen" the arrival of a new-comer at one end released a kinsman from family obligations at the other.

Thus the *Fine* gives a fine example of an historically conditioned transitional stage between collective and "private" property and responsibility. It is remarkable as combining the maximum of stability with the maximum of fluidity.

The territory of a *Sept* was disposed of in three ways: (1) To each *Fine*, land was allocated as a permanent possession. On this *mensal* land the family dwelling was erected with the huts of the dependants, etc. Only if the *Fine* became extinct did this land revert to the *Sept*. (2) A portion of the land was cultivated in large open fields as arable or meadow, and in each field the *Fine*

27

shared in prescribed proportions. (3) The remainder was left undivided; but custom set limits to its use by each *Fine* according to its standing. Common affairs were decided upon by a Council of *Flaiths* who appointed one of their number Chief of the *Sept*. An old Gaelic law tract says: "It is one of the duties of a *Sept* to support every member, and the *Sept* does this when it is in a proper condition."

The Political Structure

Gaelic society on its political side never attained to the complete unity of a Territorial State. It approximated thereto but was more of a multiplicity than a unity despite the fact that a so-called "High King" (*Ard-Ri*) was recognised for centuries before the Norman invasion, as also was a number of subordinate but independent "province kings".

The unit of this agglomerate structure was the *Tuath* (too-ha) or petty-state, which comprised, under a common head, the *Ri* (ree), a number of neighbour *Clanna*.* The title *Ri* is cognate to the Latin *rex*, which possibly derives from it. Within recognised limits the office was elective, and the holder could be deposed by the Council of Chiefs whose sanction installed him in office. Even when at a later date the office became virtually hereditary this sanction was necessary and could be refused.

The right to depose a *Ri* was jealously guarded to the end. Its exercise provided a pretext for the Norman invasion; and later still occasioned one of the bloodiest of the Elizabethan wars in Ireland. The fact that a *Ri* became disqualified by physical blemish, congenital or

---

* The *Clanna* were also grouped in kinship aggregates called *Cineil* (kinnel) which occasionally coincided with the *tuatha* but were usually dispersed between differing *tuatha*. Here again a rudimentary transition from a purely kinship organisation to a purely territorial one is observable.

acquired, proves his function to have been basically magical—that of a public mascot. This is supported by the fact that the office of war leader, called *Taoiseach* (Tee-shock*) was quite distinct. A corollary of the elective nature of the office of *Ri* is seen in the appointment of a *Tanist*, a "next in succession", who could take over in an emergency.

The functions of the *Ard-Ri* and of the "province kings" are less clearly defined. Originally they represented a differentiation among the various *Ri-tuatha* of a regional or an All-Ireland predominance, based on the possession of some spot—generally a hill—deemed to be endowed with special *mana* or "sanctity". Thus the *Ard-Ri* was for long the *Ri* in possession of the hill of Tara. The term "province king" is a complete misnomer. They were not "kings" and they did not rule "provinces". The familiar territorial division of Ireland into four provinces was made originally by the Church for purely ecclesiastical purposes. The names attached to them are those of federations of *Cineil* or of *Tuatha*, with in three cases a Danish termination (*ster*–stand, or abiding place) added to a Gaelic tribal name. Thus *Ulaidh* (Ulla), *Laighin* (Lay-in), *Muman* (Moo-an) and *Connachta* were each originally the names of tribal federations, whose territories were liable to variation at their points of contact. In each case the *Ri-mor* who was accepted as the federal chief was vested with a ceremonial primacy rather than any authority to rule. Here again a transitional form in between kinship society and the territorial state is evident.

According to tradition Ireland was always divided between Five of these federations. In historical times the extra "province" was created by dividing *Laighin* into North and South. Later a portion of the territory of the Northern *Laighin*, with portions from *Ulaidh* and *Con-*

* The pronunciation of the initial "t" is approximately intermediate between an English "t" and "th" (as in "thin"). The "ch" resembles that in Scottish "loch" – Ed.

nacht, constituted the "province" of *Midhe* (Meath) with Tara as its centre.

Unity and Opposition in Gaelic Society

That an All-Ireland community-consciousness existed, which contrasted sharply with the political division of Ireland into scores of independent *Tuatha*, is testified by the antiquity and importance of periodical festivals at which, in theory, every free man and woman in Ireland attended. They bore notable affinities to similar assemblies among the Hellenic Greeks, and, like them, derived from collective rituals deemed of magical efficacy. They also served the purpose of a periodical market; and showed the learned professions (Brehons, Bards, etc.) as constituting each a species of guild which laid down rules, fixed an order of professional precedence, and admitted, or refused, candidates to the profession.

The only surviving function of the *Ard-Ri* was to preside at the magical-religious part of this ceremony, and to pronounce judgment in law-cases submitted for his final jurisdiction.

A basic social division was that between the "free" and the "unfree"–"freedom" in this case being that to share in the allocation of *Sept* land as of right. Originally this division corresponded to that between the conquering kindred and the conquered aborigines who were tolerated on the *Sept* land in return for the performance of servile functions. It became extended by the admission into the *Sept* area of "strangers", sometimes merchant-craftsmen, sometimes men ejected from other *Septs* for various reasons. Where these strangers possessed wealth they were admitted to the *Sept* land on payment of a "rent" to the Chief. Usually they occupied a portion of what had been unappropriated land; but they might on occasion be admitted to rent a portion of the *mensal* land of a Chief or other *Flaith*.

As distinct from household slaves—who were usually purchased as young boys and girls from English traders —the lowest grade of the unfree, the *Fuidhir*, supplied most of the heavy manual labour required by the *Fine* to which they were attached. They were paid with food for themselves and their families and with a small share in the *mensal* land of the *Fine*. A superior grade of "Old Retainers" was admitted to a share in the arable and meadow land allotted to the *Fine*; four of this grade usually received between them the share of a single member of the *Fine*.

There were provisions enabling a *Fuidhir* to reach the category of an Old Retainer, and for an Old Retainer to be admitted to the *Sept* by adoption into a *Fine*. Correspondingly there were provisions whereby a *Sept* member might lose his rights and become "unfree". This arose occasionally from the commission of a crime. More usually it arose from the practice of cattle-lending—a form of hire-purchase in which the rate of payment was fixed at one-third of the value loaned each year for seven years. If a cattle-borrower made default he was subject to distraint; and, in certain circumstances, to the loss of his *Sept* membership.

A point here is that cattle-borrowing would be resorted to only when a man's near kinsmen were unable, or unwilling, to make him a free gift. The cattle would be borrowed, therefore, usually from one of the wealthy strangers whom the Chief or the *Clann* had allowed to establish themselves on *Clann* land not the property of any *Sept*. When a *Sept* member lost his rights he did so very often by default to such a stranger, who, acquiring the defaulter's rights, thus acquired entry into the *Sept*.

Within the communal-collectivity of Gaelic society appeared therefore (1) inequalities of descent; (2) inequality of wealth; and (3) lines of class-division developed from the germinal forms of the employer-labourer, landlord-tenant, and debtor-creditor relations—all of which existed in Gaelic society as in the society of Greece and Rome on the eve of the transition to the Territorial State.

These tendencies were accentuated by two important historical impacts: (1) The Establishment of the Christian Church; and (2) the Danish Invasions.

The Church in Gaelic Ireland

The Christian Church was instituted in Ireland by Patrick the Saint in the thirty-three years which closed with his death in 461.*

There had been isolated Christians in Ireland long before the mission of Patrick. Like Augustine in England he *organised* the Church, and he did so with the approval and support of the *Ard-Ri* and of the "province" *Ri-mor*. The support of the Church and its authority was invaluable to them in their struggle to bring the *Ri-tuatha* into subjection. A parallel process went on in England, and indeed all through Europe.

"The Establishment of the Western State was curiously coincident with the triumph of a new type of religion, the chief characteristic of which was *universality*. It may sound at first hearing ridiculous to associate the meek religion of Christ with the aggressive military institution of the *State*. Yet it is quite certain that Christianity had a great deal to do with breaking down tribal prejudices and with establishing great political communities ... Though Christianity in its early days had been a mission to the poor and lowly, its great conquests in Northern and Western Europe were due to the conversion of Kings and Princes. The conversion of Aethelbirt of Kent was the signal for the conversion of England. Christianity passed from Court to Court. ... And Christianity well repaid the favour of princes. Under the

* An alternative date is 493 – Ed.

32

cry of 'One church and one King' the older tribal
divisions were ultimately wiped out and England
became one nation, with *Church* and *State* in intimate alliance."

Edward Jenks: *History of Politics*.

In Ireland a similar process was well-advanced when
it was interrupted and aberrated first by the Danish, then
by the Norman invasion. An interesting otherside of the
process is found in the manner in which the Church was
accommodated to, and itself modified by, *Clann* society:

"Each *clann* had its own bishop, and its own
priests, the diocese was merely the district occupied
by the *clann*. There was naturally a great number
of bishops ... and it was not until the 12th century
that the present system of definite dioceses, grouped
into provinces, was introduced. The *Clann* allotted
to its clergy for their support certain lands ... looked
after by an official who was generally a layman.
The clergy of a *clann* mostly lived in communities
under their bishop, so that the church was both tribal
and monastic."

Hayden and Moonan: *Short History of the Irish
People*.

These communities performed an important function by
becoming centres for the cultivation of arts and crafts,
for the development of industry as distinct from agriculture, and for the development of trading-relations.
The completion of this process was aided by two centuries
of Danish invasion.

The Danish Invasion (795–1014)

The forays of the Scandinavian pirates who are known
traditionally in Ireland as the "Danes" left indelible
marks upon the history of Ireland. They did not establish
themselves permanently as they did in Normandy, or
make themselves kings of the country as they did for a

time in England and in Sicily. They effected a great deal of destruction and completed the elimination of the *Tuath* as an independent entity–it being replaced by the enforced aggregation of *Septs* under a *Ri-Mor* or Chief of a composite *Clann*. The driving of many *Clanna* from their ancestral locations–their *Septs* being driven often in different directions–caused the *Clanna* in many cases to disappear as such; while the dispersed *Septs* of differing kindred united under a common *Ri-Mor* to establish new aggregates in the territory to which they had been driven.

A more positive effect was the establishment by the Danes of some of the chief sea-ports of Ireland. The Danes had been traders before they turned pirates, and continued to combine the occupations–piracy procuring the materials for a profitable trade. They had been farmers and fishers before they became traders; and the cities they established at the mouths of rivers and on inlets gave them first-class facilities for practising all their specialities at once. Dublin, Wexford, Waterford, Youghal, Cork, Bantry and Limerick were all founded and built up into walled cities by the Danes; and, in the intervals of peace during the two centuries of their era, they developed into permanent institutions the market relations which the Church had begun to establish. In their cities they provided a refuge for the individual craftsmen and traders scattered by their violent destruction of the monastic communities. On the other hand, some monastic communities survived–by means of the ingenious invention of the Round Towers–to become, when peace was restored, nuclei for trading towns in the interior.

Under the impact of invasion, the various *Ri-Mor* had to develop into military chiefs, with strong bands of trained men under their command, or go out of existence. They recruited professional soldiers–trained in war against the Danes–in England, and these *Galloglaich* (foreign-soldiers) survived as an institution to mystify later ages under the name of "Gallow glasses". Thus equipped with armed bands the rival chiefs commenced a furious struggle for the title and office of *Ard-Ri*.

The prize was won by a North Munster Chief, Brian called *Boroimhe* (bor-roo), meaning "of the Tributes", meaning again that he achieved the first step toward a unified state by extorting tribute from every *Ri* in Ireland.

A measure of peace had begun to emerge when (1014) the Danes made a final rally to come to the aid of the Danish King of Dublin from whom Brian the Brave had extorted tribute. A battle fought within sight of Dublin on the shore at Clontarf ended in the total rout and partial extermination of the Danes. Brian, then an old man, was killed by a fugitive Dane. As the *Njal Saga* says: "Brian lost his life; but he saved his Kingdom."

After Brian's death the anarchical strife for possession of the title of *Ard-Ri* was resumed. General exhaustion caused, in the end, the recognition, by most contenders, of the superior claims of Ruraidhe O'Connor, *Ri-Mor* in Connacht.

It was at that point, when all Ireland was settling down to enjoy a long-wished-for peace, that Diarmuid MacMurrogh, *Ri-Mor* in *Laighin*, fell into feud with the chief of the O'Rourkes—over some "trifle" of wife-stealing. The chiefs of the *Laighin Septs* promptly ejected Diarmuid from office. They wanted peace; and were not going to be mixed up in his family quarrels.

Diarmuid fled overseas to the court of Henry II, King of England, swore fealty to him as his vassal, and asked for aid to "recover his rights". Henry, for reasons explained in the next chapter, gave Diarmuid permission to recruit any of his vassals who were willing to try their luck.

All Ireland wanted was peace; all Ireland got was an Anglo-Norman invasion.

CHAPTER II

THE SUBJUGATION OF IRELAND-I

Reducing Ireland to the status of a fief of the King of England proved a tedious and an interminable business. It was "always a doing, yet never done". Centuries passed, the Middle Ages ended; but the struggle to conquer the still unsubdued Irish went on and on.

The Norman Conquest became a Tudor Conquest which continued into the reign of the first Stuart before it reached an approximate end.

In this chapter we outline the Norman Conquest from 1169 to 1485, then the Tudor-Stuart conquest from 1485-1610.

The Political and Economic Background

Henry's prompt compliance with Diarmuid's petition calls for some comment.

The basic explanation is that the feudal system was still in its ascendant phase and an equilibrium between the powers of the King, the barons and the church respectively, had not been attained. It was the Papal policy of the period to work for a settlement along the lines of "One Church and One King"; which meant in practice that the Papacy as a temporal power aimed at a political rule—effected through a few powerful monarchs acting as its vassals—which would form the complement to the unified authority it had already established in the spiritual sphere. With that object, the Pope had granted Henry II an authorisation to make himself Lord of Ireland, twenty years before Diarmuid appealed to him for aid.

Though a most powerful monarch in theory—being not only King of England, and Duke of Normandy, but also Lord of Brittany, Anjou, Maine and Aquitaine—Henry II was in practice faced with trouble arising from the predatory rivalry of the barons, his vassals, in every part of his dominions. These barons united only to resist his efforts to unite them into an ordered state.

What this had led to was described by a monkish scribe on the eve of Henry's accession: "It was a time when any rich man made his castle and when they filled them with devils and evil men. They were days when wretched men starved with hunger. In those days the earth bore no corn, for the land was all foredone by such deeds, and men said openly that Christ and his Apostles had gone to sleep."

Ireland was as good a place as any in which to dump that potent cause of mischief—the unemployed problem peculiar to feudalism—the problem of disposing of the younger (and the illegitimate) sons and the redundant dependants of the feudal lords.

The company Diarmuid recruited illustrated Henry's problem vividly. The leaders were most of them the bastard sons of Norman lords. The followers were all professional "toughs"—Norman, Welsh, French and Flemish mercenaries, greedy for pay and plunder. All were at a loose end in consequence of their failure to carve out lordships for themselves in Wales. Diarmuid must have appeared to them like a fairy godmother, while Henry must have been more than glad to see the backs of them all.

The Submission of 1171

The expedition had little difficulty in effecting its object. It got possession of Wexford and Waterford, advanced to Dublin and sacked it. Diarmuid was reinstated as "king" of Leinster. In gratitude he married his daughter to the leading gangster, Strongbow, and advanced a claim to the title and office of *Ard-Ri* of Ireland. At that moment (1171) he died; and Strongbow as his heir by marriage, claimed, along with Diarmuid's Kingdom, the reversion of his claim to the *Ard-Ri*-ship. There seemed nothing to stop him making this claim good.

This was anything but what Henry II wanted. In next to no time he was in Ireland with a strong army led by reliable supporters, and accompanied by a Papal Legate, who summoned a Church Synod, while Henry summoned every *Ri* and chief in Ireland to come in and make his submission. The clergy submitted to Papal authority, and persuaded most of the chiefs likewise to submit immediately. O'Connor held out for a bit, but came in later. Strongbow came to heel without a murmur.

Having installed himself as Lord of Ireland, Henry II proceeded to apportion his new dominion between his leading followers—leaving to them the job of effecting an actual occupation. The walled cities he retained as direct crown possessions. In each a castle was built and a royal seneschal installed. Dublin and the "County" around it he made into a special appanage of the Crown. He repeopled the city (which Strongbow had destroyed) with Englishmen—mostly from Bristol—who were given special inducements to restore the town and its trade; and he apportioned the County in small estates between minor "lords of manors" who were permitted to grant sub-tenancies only to actual tillers, on English-feudal tenures, mostly in villei age. Only those Irish were admitted who were willing to become "English" in dress, speech and allegiance. This was the first "English" plantation in Ireland, and the most nearly successful. The special area, surrounded by a dyke, or palisade, became known as "within the Pale", or for short "the Pale". Any Irish caught in the area were hunted with as little mercy as wolves.

Such was the Anglo-Norman Conquest of Ireland as feudal law envisaged it. It constituted the only quasilegal claim English kings had to Lordship in Ireland from 1171 until, in 1541, a hand-picked "Parliament" in Dublin invited Henry VIII to assume the title of King of Ireland.

The Progress of the Conquest

From this "submission" onwards, for three centuries, the history of Ireland outside the Pale presents a monotonous succession of variations on a single theme. The Anglo-Norman lords, with their private armies, advanced across the great central plain, and up (or down) the great river valleys. The Irish retreated with their cattle to the hills, the woods, and hiding places in the bog-country.

On the level plains the clansmen stood no chance against the armoured Norman spearmen and their professional archers. In the hill country the reverse was the case, and every defile was a death-trap. As for the bogs—the spearmen might as well try to charge from Wexford to Milford Haven.

Thus as a first result the Normans got possession of large tracts of empty land; but in nearly every case the Irish, hidden in their lurking places, were only a night's march away, ready to pounce on cattle, barns, or outlying parties. The expected flow of emigrants from England dried up early; thereafter, to get any profit from their lands, the Normans, willynilly, had to come to terms with the Irish *Septs*. Soon the Irish were back where they had been, paying tribute to the newcomer it is true, but in all other respects living as they did before he came.

This brought the second result. The backsliding Norman lords were impeached as "traitors" by the Lord Deputy, the King's seneschal or by those of their number who had contrived to import settlers and plant their estates on English feudal tenures. The result was a series of bloody feuds among the Anglo-Norman nobles, in the course of which their harried English tenants skipped off either to the towns, or back to England again. The

English kings could only at rare intervals give any assistance to their agents in Ireland; accordingly the feuds, in time, burned themselves out.

To get into good standing with the clan chiefs the Norman lords married Irish wives, or contracted marriages between their daughters and Irish chiefs or their sons. (Their followers, most of them, had done likewise already.) As the old generation died away they were succeeded by half-Norman, or quarter-Norman heirs. Brought up by Irish nurses, with none but Irish or part-Irish playmates, speaking nothing but Irish except on rare occasions, these heirs thought in Irish, and became "more Irish than the Irish themselves". From tolerating the Brehon law, they passed on to complying with it. Save for their titles they had become Irish clan chiefs.

The Pale and the towns held out against this. They drove a profitable trade with England, of which they had a monopoly, and it was to their interest that the demand for English products should not fail. But even their position was weakening, as the Irish steadily filtered in. The ruin and wastage of war produced a thin stream of refugee clansmen who, for convenience, were ready to comply outwardly with English usages. The Lords Deputy and the Pale Parliament (set up in imitation of the English original shortly after that was instituted) railed bitterly against the "Irish enemy"; but the process went on.

The Statute of Kilkenny

How far the process of Gaelicising the conquerors had gone was revealed in a Statute of the Parliament called by the Duke of Clarence, son of Edward III, then Viceroy, and held in Kilkenny in 1367. Among other things this Statute decreed that:

(1) Intermarriage with the Irish, and entering into binding personal ties with them, such as gossipred, incurred penalties as High Treason.

(2) Englishmen adopting Irish names, dress, custo
or speech, incurred forfeiture of all lands and
tenements.

(3) Tolerating the *Brehon* law, still more submitting
to it, was High Treason.

(4) Permitting Irish tenants to hold by Gaelic tenures,
or permitting Irish *Septs* to graze their cattle on
estates granted by the Crown incurred forfeiture.

(5) Anyone harbouring or encouraging Irish minstrels,
rhymers, or taletellers incurred heavy fines.

(6) Admitting Irish priests to benefices, or to monastic
establishments was forbidden.

(7) The practice of *coyne and livery* was declared an
abuse.

(8) Etc., etc., etc.

The correct way to interpret this historic Statute of
Kilkenny is to treat it as a Hymn of Hate by the Pale
against the Anglo-Irish lords. The Parliament had no
power to enforce a single one of these decrees. Nor could
the Viceroy enforce them without a large-scale war for
which he was not prepared.

The Statute recognised, in the language of the law-
lords of the Pale, the existence of a "middle nation"
separating the "English" Pale from the "Irish enemy",
a middle nation composed of "degenerate English" and
partly-anglicised Irish. It admitted that the Normans had
made only a formal conquest over some of the Irish,
while the Irish had made a real cultural conquest of most
of the Norman-English.

The Statute of Kilkenny gave itself away by making
it treason to make war upon the Irish, or to conclude
peace with them, without authorisation from the King's
Deputy.

Its' provisions were aimed at known and notorious
offenders. The descendants of Henry II's leading follower,
Hugo de Burgh (Gaelicised as "Burke") had "gone Irish"
so far that Richard de Burke had accepted the status of

a *Ri-Mor*, and his tenantry had reciprocated by becoming Clann Rickard. The sons of his son William had gone further. They had divided the inheritance and taken the name of MacWilliam. Theirs was far from being the only instance. The provision against harbouring minstrels, etc., was aimed especially at the Geraldines, both the Kildare and the Desmond Fitzgeralds, all notorious offenders.

The provision against *coyne and livery* arose from a then-recent incident. The Lord Deputy having reason to fear an Irish raid upon the Pale had called upon the Earl of Desmond* for aid. Desmond had come with 10,000 men, nearly all Irish or three-quarters Irish, and had quartered his troops upon the gentry and inhabitants of the Pale. He claimed it was an old Irish custom, *coinmed* (coyney) which the English translated as "livery" or board-wages. It was, as Desmond claimed, an old Irish custom, but with a qualification he was careful to forget. In Irish law the amount a chief might levy in this way was strictly limited. Not knowing this the Lord Deputy was left wondering whether it was worse to be ravaged by the Irish or saved by Desmond.

The final futility of the Statute was revealed less than twenty years later when Richard II, who had come to Ireland to enforce submission all round, suffered a crushing and ignominious defeat at the hands of the Wicklow clans—a defeat which sent him back to England, without an army, totally discredited and ripe for deposition.

Preoccupation with dynastic changes, French war, and the civil war of the Roses which followed, kept the English kings from paying attention to Ireland until after the accession of Henry VII in 1485.

The Prelude to the Tudor Conquest

The reign of Henry VII (1485–1509) was one of the major transition periods in English history. The transition

* Desmond = South Munster, Thomond = North Munster.

involved was that from feudalism as a system of graded local sovereignties to feudalism centralised and fixed in its final—and therefore ossified and degenerating—form of Absolute Monarchy.

The first essential of the change consisted in destroying the separate military powers of the great feudal lords and absorbing all their sovereignties into that of the King as sole sovereign and Lord. The change was necessitated by the anarchy into which the older system had degenerated, and by Henry Tudor's precarious position as technically a usurper. It was facilitated by the self-destruction of the nobles in the civil war of the Roses and by the support of the burghers, who gained from the change a much greater freedom to develop their bourgeois mode of production. The nobility accepted the change when they realised that the loss of their political independence gave them greater freedom to exploit their domains economically. As a rent-eating landocracy and as profit-grasping sheepfarmers they became less ostentatious but greedier than ever. Eventually they became slavish adulants of the New Monarchy when, to complete its Absolutism, it turned to rob and degrade (politically) the Church, and then to set sharp barriers before any further political progress of the bourgeoisie which had helped to bring the changes about.

An important technological factor in this transition was the possession by the Crown of the only train of heavy artillery in the country, and its ability—aided by the wealth of the burghers—to hire an army of continental mercenaries equipped with, and skilled in the use of, the new firearms.

The process as outlined falls into three stages: (1) The disarming of the territorial lords by the destruction of their castles and the dispersal of their private armies; (2) The Reformation struggle against the Papacy and the Church; (3) The imposition of restraints upon the bourgeoisie by the Crown and the landocracy in alliance. During the first of these phases the Kings of England

43

(Henrys VII and VIII) had to temporise in Ireland by tolerating there, in the persons of the Earls of Kildare, the political aggrandisement of the territorial nobility they were systematically destroying in England. During the second phase in England it became possible to carry through the first two stages simultaneously in Ireland. This constituted the Tudor Conquest which passed over into the Stuart conquest which involved the application of the third stage in both countries.

The Tudor Conquest: First Phase

While England was racked by the War of the Roses, the policy of the Norman Conquest in Ireland revealed its final bankruptcy. Its essential feature had been that of conquest through intermediaries. The Pale, directly under the control of the Crown, was established to supply a base for, and also to exercise control over, the Territorial Nobility, who, in turn, were expected to establish their sway over the Irish Chiefs, who were expected to carry through the actual subjugation of the Irish people.

The policy broke down because the Territorial Lords (by becoming largely Gaelicised) came to an understanding with the Irish Chiefs and so grew far too powerful for the Pale to control. In fact, with the English Kings draining away its man-power instead of adding to it, the Pale, ravaged by the Geraldine Lords and largely reoccupied by the clans, became reduced to its smallest dimensions, and kept itself in being only by paying blackmail both to the Clans, and to the Territorial Lords.

At the same time the Norman policy succeeded to the extent that the conditions it had brought about favoured a large degree of feudalisation of the Gaelic Nation. The Chiefs became in practice hereditary. They greatly increased their power over their Clansmen in consequence of the fact that the shifts and migrations impelled by centuries of strife had broken up the older clan *unities* and combined under the surviving Chiefs a somewhat fortuitous aggregation of unrelated *Septs*. Thus as the Territorial Lords grew Gaelicised the clans grew feudalised. A possibility was established for a re-union of Ireland into a frankly feudal state which, absorbing the Pale, would become completely independent of England.

Two things operated as a check upon this tendency.

(1) The Territorial Lords and the greater clan chiefs, each pursuing a policy of family aggrandisement, were perpetually at feud with each other. Their situation differed in fact from that of their English counterparts in the War of the Roses only in that there was a free-for-all fight instead of a simple Red-versus-White struggle.

(2) The trading towns in the Pale, and in the *Gaeltacht** were more concerned to develop intercourse with England than to interrupt it. Similarly, the Territorial Lords, who in many cases owned estates in England, gained as landlords from the changes introduced by the New Monarchy. Thus there existed a power to separate from England, but no will to do so. That alone saved English dominion in Ireland at this point.

The extent to which economic development had gone in the area outside the Pale was far greater than is commonly realised:

> "In all the Irish territories great fairs were periodically held, and were attended by Irish and foreign traders. So well attended were these fairs that the townspeople of the Pale complained of the injury they suffered because English and other traders deserted their own markets in favour of them. The records of European ports also show that Ireland carried on a great foreign trade ... from the Mediterranean to the Baltic."
>
> Hayden and Moonan: *Short History of the Irish People.*

* *Gaeltacht:* that part of Ireland in which Gaelic was (or is) the everyday speech of the people.

The cultural progress of Gaelic Ireland, though severely set back at first by the Norman invasion, made a recovery commensurate with this economic advance.

In these circumstances it was impossible for the English King to rule in Ireland except through the instrumentality of the leading family of the "middle nation"—the Kildare Geraldines. Three Earls of Kildare, father, son and grandson, held the position of Lord Deputy in succession, virtually monopolising between them the Government of Ireland from 1468 to 1533, with only temporary interruptions.

This virtual *Ard-Ri*-ship of the Geraldines, Thomas, Garrett Mor and Garrett Og, involved a virtual scrapping of the whole Norman policy turning upon the supremacy of the Pale.

The Geraldines were supreme over the Pale and as good as absorbed it into the "middle nation". At the same time they were intermarried with the O'Neills and the O'Connors (as their junior branch, the Desmond Fitzgeralds, was with the O'Briens) and so in part closed the gap between the "middle nation" and the "mere Irish". They were, however, closely related also to the leading Yorkist families and lent them assistance during the Civil War. Their power was so great that Henry VII on his accession recognised the need to ignore their Yorkist affiliations and confirm Garrett Mor in the post of Lord Deputy. But for the fact that the Henrys, VII and VIII, knew enough statecraft to play the Geraldines, Garrett Mor and Garrett Og, as a skilled angler plays a trout a break might easily have come.

When, however, the time was ripe, their virtual monopoly of office, and the zeal with which they had sought to bring Ireland under their rule as a single unit, were turned into weapons against them. All the rivalries and jealousies they had aroused—particularly their feud with the Ormond Butlers—were secretly fostered and then crystallised into charges. Garrett Og was summoned to London, but as he was allowed to appoint his son "Silken" Thomas to act as his substitute, and as he, his father, and his grandfather had all survived similar summons, he thought little of it. This time, however, the mine was sprung. Arrived in London, Garrett Og was arrested and thrown into the Tower. Silken Thomas was tricked by a bogus letter into believing his father had been executed. He accordingly renounced his allegiance and called out his supporters for war.

It was what was wanted. This was not a "national revolt": the Geraldines in the exercise of their office had made too many enemies for that, and the "mere Irish" were only indirectly concerned anyway. But it was onerous enough to call for the full strength of the Royal power. Once again the Royal train of artillery came into action, and a Royal army of German and Italian mercenaries. When the Geraldine stronghold of Maynooth was battered down and all its garrison exterminated, Silken Thomas surrendered. His father, Garrett Og, had died in the Tower. When Silken Thomas and five of his uncles were all hanged together at Tyburn on a single gallows, in 1537, the whole senior line of the Geraldines became extinct save for an infant who had by a fluke been over-looked in the sack of Maynooth.

With their central leadership destroyed the entire "middle nation" with their Irish allies were at the mercy of the Royal power. The Pale which a few years before had been all-but absorbed into the "middle nation" was now all-but liquidated in an opposite direction. Being now extended virtually to all Ireland—save for pockets of Gaelic clan-influence—it ceased to exist as a Pale and became "official" Ireland.

The technique which had been employed against the Geraldines was, from this point onwards, employed with modifications against the Irish clan chiefs. It was very simple. The Chief was first flattered with titles, honours, and a subsidy into becoming an agency of anglicisation. If he fell in with the plan he was made straightway, by a legal "magic", the owner of all the clan-territory; and his clansmen, if they submitted, became his tenants, either for life, on lease, or at will. If he accepted the title but did not introduce English-feudal tenures he was attainted as a traitor, his lands were confiscated and the English-feudal tenures were imposed on the clans by force. If the clans revolted either with the new lord-chief or against him, a punitive expedition achieved the same result. All through the process the one object was steadily pursued: as in England, every "lord" whether English, Anglo-Irish, or plain Irish had to choose between (1) becoming a rent-hungry landlord on the English model, or (2) being attainted as a traitor, hanged as a "rebel", driven into exile, or disposed of by private assassination.

The process continued with monotonous persistence from 1533 into the next century. The revolts involved grew bigger, the Irish lords involved more powerful, the repressions more wholesale and bloodier. Eventually toward the end of the "spacious days of Great Elizabeth" the local revolts so ran into each other that something near to general revolt raged all through the *Gaeltacht* and what was left of the "middle nation".

The issue was complicated by the quasi-religious war between England and Spain. The rebel lords appealed for aid to Spain and to the Pope, who sent small expeditions which landed at Dingle, in 1579, and at Kinsale in 1580. The only difference they made was to give the English commanders an excuse for ferocity to the limit of extermination.

In order to force the rebels to surrender, cattle were impounded, and the standing-crops were destroyed systematically. In one campaign alone crops to the value of £20,000 (equal in current values to £1,000,000) were destroyed. The result was a famine of appalling intensity. An Irish chronicler laments that "the low of cattle could not be heard fr m the rock of Cashel to Dingle Bay". An English observer, the "poet's poet", Edmund Spenser, describes what he saw:

> "Ere one year and a half they [the rebels] were brought to such wretchedness as that any stony heart would have rued the same. Out of every corner of the woods and glens they came creeping forth upon their hands, for their legs could not bear them; they looked like anatomies of death; they spoke like ghosts crying out of their graves; they did eat the dead carrions, happy where they could find them: yea, and one another soon after, insomuch as the very carcasses they spared not to scrape out of their graves; and if they found a plot of water-cresses or shamrocks, there they flocked as to a feast for a time, yet were not able long to continue there withal; that in short space there were none almost left, and a most populous and plentiful country suddenly left void of man and beast."

Edmund Spenser: *View of the State of Ireland (1595)*.

Confiscation and Plantation

Overlapping this culmination of Tudor policy was a development which continued into the reign of James the First Stuart, the policy of "clearance and plantation".

Impelling the policy of tricking Irish Chiefs into incurring the confiscation of their estates was the general desire to establish English Landlordism in Ireland. Impelling the particular policy of clearance followed by plantation was the same motive which gave the Reformation the

49

distinctive form it took in England—the desire for a reservoir of estates from which to reward the pliant tools of the Crown, which estates in turn would absorb as tenants some of the army of vagrants infesting the English countryside, as a result of "clearances" to make room for profitable sheep-walks owned by the new nobility.

All that Ireland ever saw of the Protestant Reformation was this aspect—of an excuse for robbing the Church of its treasures and its lands. There was literally nothing in Ireland to correspond to the popular ideological-political movement which on the Continent and in England made the Reformation "the first general uprising of the European bourgeoisie".

As if to point this difference, the first state experiment in large-scale clearance was made during the reign of Mary the Catholic. The lands cleared were made into "shire-land" and divided into Queen's County and King's County with Maryborough and Phillipstown as their respective county towns. The land was auctioned off in large estates for which there was no lack of bidders. When it came to planting them with new settlers a great lack was found of Englishmen ready to risk their lives and their capital in farms in Ireland. In the end the original clansmen returned, to occupy as tenants under a landlord (usually an absentee) the lands they had once owned without question or doubt.

A similar clearance was attempted in the same reign in South Wicklow and North Wexford; and here a few English Catholics were induced to settle—until the O'Dwyers, O'Faollains and MacMurroughs from the hills gave them a sufficient reason for returning to England. Thereafter the clans returned as before.

An exactly similar result attended an attempt to clear and plant the large area in Munster which had been desolated by war and famine. Here again large estates were granted, and they in turn were cut up into large-size farms. Walter Raleigh the "Empire builder" was one of the grantees; Edmund Spenser had one of the farms and was busily at work upon the *Faery Queen* when those of the O'Driscolls, O'Lehanes, O'Carrols and O'Donovans who had survived came out of the woods and burned his farmstead about his ears. Once again, the Clans came back—with a vengeance.

The Plantation of Ulster

At this time (1598) was planned the most-known Plantation of all, that of Ulster, which was, eventually, carried out in 1609.

All the estates of the Earls of Tyrone (O'Neill) and Tyrconnell (O'Donnell) and those of their chief supporters, comprising some half a million estimated acres of arable land (waste, woodland and bog thrown in uncounted) in the counties of Donegal, Tyrone, Fermanagh, Cavan, Coleraine (Derry), and Armagh, were confiscated:

"The land was divided into lots of 2,000, 1,500, and 1,000 acres, and these lands were assigned to be occupied by persons of three classes. The *Undertakers* on whom the largest lots were bestowed were ordinary colonists English or Scots. They were forbidden to take Irish tenants. The *Servitors* (those who had held office under Government in Ireland) who might, if they chose, let a portion of their land to the Irish. But if they did so, the rent which they themselves had to pay to the Crown would be increased from £5 6s. 8d. per 1,000 acres to £8. On the other hand, persons of the third class, the *Natives*, must not receive as tenants anyone but their own countrymen. ... As a rule only small estates were given to the Irish, and the total they received was scarcely one-tenth of the whole. They were required to pay ... £10 13s. 4d. per 1,000 acres."

Hayden and Moonan: *Short History of the Irish People.*

From the limited size of the holdings, and the fixed rents stipulated, it is clear that the object of this plantation differed from its predecessors in that the crown's greed for revenue was subordinated to its imperialist need for a reliable garrison of planted colonists who would hold the Irish nation in check. To get round the difficulty of finding suitable colonists, part of the problem was shifted to the Corporation of London which was asked to "undertake" the planting of the County of Coleraine (now called Londonderry) and the restoration of the cities of Derry and Coleraine.

The city undertook the work somewhat grudgingly. There was clearly little or no prospect of profit; but on the other hand it was good policy to oblige the King. A special company—the Irish Society—was formed to manage the plantation, and the actual planting was divided between groups of city companies in proportion to the amounts subscribed towards the cost. Farms of specified size were erected; Derry and Coleraine and their respective harbours were put into repair.

To find suitable tenants was not easy. Few Englishmen or Scots were willing to expatriate themselves unless for some reason, creditable or otherwise, they feared facing the wild Irish less than the risks of staying at home. Some were persecuted Dissenters: some were secretly Catholics. Many wished to bilk their creditors or the mothers of their illegitimate offspring, or for other reasons to get beyond the reach of "avenging justice". A contemporary Scottish writer said that the settlers were "generally the scum of both countries ... abhorred at home".

It is in fact a complete fallacy to attribute to this Plantation the peculiar characteristics of political "Ulster". That four out of the six counties planted were never part of "Orange" Ulster (until the Partition) and that the two most "Protestant" counties, Antrim and Down, were never included in this plantation are facts which destroy the myth.

Actually the difficulty of finding tenants caused even the London Corporation to wink at breaches of the terms of their grant. In 1624 they had 4,000 Irish tenants when they should have had none.

The Ulster Plantation—from whose area the clans were simply ejected—laid the foundation for an explosion and a new conquest. For the time being, however, the object of English policy seemed to have been attained.

CHAPTER III

THE SUBJUGATION OF IRELAND–II

The third great wave of conquest beneath which Ireland was submerged–the Cromwellian Conquest–differed from the preceding conquests in that it was less of a prolonged process, and more of a sudden, calamitous impact. For that reason it has left bitter memories which survive in popular tradition while the older conquests are remembered only vaguely.

Another distinctive feature of the Cromwellian Conquest is that it arose as a by-product of a revolutionary crisis and uprising in England into whose orbit Ireland became drawn on the counter-revolutionary side; with consequences disastrous both for England and for Ireland.

Background: English Revolution 1640

The Revolution of 1640 arose from a cause we have already indicated. The establishment of the New (absolute) Monarchy was bound to reach a point at which stabilisation could be brought about only at the expense of the bourgeoisie, and particularly of its freedom to trade and accumulate capital.

Identifying the English Revolution as a bourgeois revolution does not mean, as reactionaries and sentimentalists have supposed, that its motives were entirely selfish and base, or that the King and the Cavaliers fought to protect the common people from Capitalist exploitation. Very far from it!

> "The interests for which Charles' Monarchy stood were not those of the common people at all. It represented the bankrupt landowning nobles, and its policy was influenced by a Court clique of aristocratic-commercial racketeers, and their hangers-

on, sucking the life-blood from the whole people by various methods of economic exploitation... And free capitalist development was of much more benefit to the masses of the population than the maintenance of an outmoded unproductive and parasitic feudalism."

Christopher Hill: *English Revolution.*

The Tudor monarchy had been, on the whole, popular in England because it opened up (temporarily) new fields for expansion to the producing classes. The Stuart Monarchy dissipated this popularity because these classes learned at its hands that this expansion would be permitted only so far; that thereafter productive expansion would be tolerated only on condition that it yielded a "rake-off" to the King and also to the Court clique of racketeers.

Finding that this roused the bourgeoisie and the lower orders generally to a fury of revolutionary resentment, Charles I and his advisers cast around for ways and means of dragooning the Commons generally into submission, alike in England and in Ireland. The Revolution of 1640 was precipitated by the going astray of a plan concocted between the King and his chief advisers—Archbishop Laud and the Earl of Strafford (previously Sir Thomas Wentworth, and Lord Wentworth)—a plan for a counter-revolutionary *coup d'état* called by the conspirators among themselves the "Thorough" plan.

Ireland and the "Thorough" Conspiracy

As part of the project Strafford went to Ireland as Lord Deputy. Here his plan was broadly (1) to so reduce the country to disciplined submission to the Crown that it would yield the King a revenue which would make him independent of the English Parliament; (2) to placate the resentment of the Irish by making concessions to the Catholics and winning them over to the King's side;

(3) to raise an Army in Ireland (largely composed of Catholics) which could be used at a pinch to coerce the English into submission. In a word the plan was designed to do for its period what every variety of "fascism" has attempted in our own time; and the Irish Catholics were to be tricked into becoming the gangsters and thugs through whom the plan was to be imposed.

Strafford went to work in a businesslike style. He called a Parliament, but took care to pack it well beforehand by creating sixty new boroughs for each of which he nominated two members. These, with office-holders under the Crown whom he could dismiss at will, gave him a majority straightaway. A majority of the Lords thought it safest to stay away and send their proxies for Strafford to use at pleasure.

His next concern was to complete the conquest by planting Connacht—or, rather, threatening to plant it. He demanded that every landowner in Connacht should surrender "voluntarily" one acre in every four to create farms upon which he could plant reliable men. Simultaneously he "put the wind up" every landowner in Ireland by appointing a Commission to inquire into the validity of all titles to estates. It soon appeared however that the Connacht landowners could escape if they paid down a cash fine, and that a similar payment would "remedy" any defect in any title, however glaring.

He and his fellow-conspirator Laud worked the same trick on the City of London. The Court of Star Chamber, presided over by Laud, revoked the City's Ulster Charter on the express ground that they had failed to exclude Catholic tenants. A new Charter cost them £70,000.

The Dublin Parliament was "worked" by the trick of asking Catholics and Protestants to draw up statements of the "graces" they desired the King to grant (in return for a subsidy). The King got his subsidy: Catholics and Protestants were each told that the King would "consider" their petitions.

When any landowner would not submit to the "racket", a "defect" was found in his title. If he went to law Strafford either packed the jury, or, as in one instance in Galway, when the jury gave a verdict against the Crown, imprisoned the entire jury until every member had paid a heavy fine.

He is credited with having promoted the linen industry; but this is a complete error. What he did was to sell a Charter of Monopoly to a Linen Company which would have ruined all the domestic spinners and weavers in Ireland, if the Company itself had not gone bankrupt. It was part of the "Thorough" plan to establish similar monopolies for every industry in England as well as in Ireland. Being himself interested personally in the Yorkshire woollen manufacture Strafford set the example of banning the export of woollen cloth from Ireland, and subsidising the export of raw wool.

He paid particular attention to the raising, training and equipping of an Army. Its rank and file was almost exclusively Catholic, its officers were mostly English Protestant aristocrats. (The analogy to the "native" regiments in India is obvious.)

Finally he circulated diligently both by word of mouth and by ambiguously worded letters a rumour that, as soon as he had reduced the English Commons to "reason", the King would grant liberal concessions to the Irish Catholics.

At this stage Strafford was summoned post-haste to England. His fellow-conspirator Laud had "upset the apple-cart" by trying to impose the English liturgy on the Scottish Kirk.

Religion in the English Revolution

So much of the controversy attending the Revolution of 1640 turned on questions of Religion that a note or two on the issues really at stake is necessary. The crux of the matter is that, at that date, men understood by religion something much wider than a system of private belief and its expression in practice. They thought of religion as an indispensable public institution and function. The Church was part of the apparatus of the State. It was, in its local expression, a unit of local government and magistracy, as well as a dispenser of public assistance. It was also a revenue-yielding property; a property-owning corporation in itself, and a source of revenue directly and indirectly to the lay-impropriators of the tithes, as well as to the nobles and squires who had the right of presentation to Church livings. The Church in Ireland was, in this way, a valuable supplement to the revenues of the English landlord class which as absentee owners of land in Ireland "possessed" these Church emoluments, or the right of installing dependants to enjoy them.

From the point of view of the State, the Church not only provided a moral "police" and a supplement to the magistracy; it fulfilled the indispensable function of moulder and guide of public opinion. From the pulpit once a week at least the people were told what to believe, not only about Heaven and Hell but still more about earthly matters. It was self-evident that in such a crisis as was then brewing the Church would be an indispensable instrument for royalist and counter-revolutionary propaganda.

It is also self-evident that in such circumstances those who were opposed to the political policy of the Court and its clique would resent this use of the Church and denounce it. They would, in more advanced cases, make provision for pulpits through which their own anti-royalist views would find expression. In a word they would set up Nonconformist or Dissenting sects which would supplement their political hostility to the Crown and Court with a theological hostility to the Bishops, their doctrine and their ritual.

The Reformation, in England, as a popular movement,

had been basically a revolt against an alien Italian Church and its foreign propaganda. It had been an intensely Nationalist revolt, and the same spirit was carried over to and intensified in the Nonconformist sects.

From the point of view of the "Thorough" plan these Nonconformist sects had to be stamped out as rigorously as Hitler and his *gauleiters* stamped out all listening to unauthorised and enemy broadcasts. But Laud was hampered in this by the existence of the Presbyterian Kirk in Scotland which he could not control. As it was a State Church in Scotland he could not ban it in England, and the revolutionaries took full advantage of his dilemma.

He tried to get over the difficulty by persuading a section of the Scottish clergy to adopt the Anglican liturgy as the first step towards bringing the two Churches into conformity. The result was an explosion of Scottish revolt, the mass signing of the Solemn League and Covenant, and the march of the Scottish Army to, and beyond, the Border.

It was this revolt that Strafford was sent for to repress.

It may be added here that the Reformation passion of hostility to the Papacy and Papalism generally was still intense both in England and in Scotland. Laud's insistence upon liturgy and ceremonial seemed to the masses "Papistic", and, as the King was notoriously under the thumb of his ostentatiously Catholic wife, the popular opinion swayed to the conclusion that the Royal plans included a restoration of the Papal Church, and with it (of course) the Inquisition.

As the struggle developed, the more ultra-Protestant sects—those which most completely rejected all Authority in religion save that of the individual conscience—naturally came increasingly to the front, since they had most to gain from the defeat of the King and his reactionary schemes. In this way an anti-Papist element was introduced into the struggle from the outset, a sentiment which grew more bitter as the struggle progressed.

When Strafford reached England and faced the situation he saw that Laud had bungled badly. The King's soldiers were few, and none too ready to fight the Scots. The English militia were openly mutinous, and were more likely to join the Scots than to fight them. The best policy, as Strafford saw, was to play for time; to call a Parliament, fob it off with promises, get supply, and, when the excitement had died down, get to work another way. He, in the meanwhile, would push on the work of raising, quietly, a really powerful army in Ireland.

Strafford's advice was accepted. A Parliament was summoned in England, while Strafford himself returned to Ireland, summoned his packed Parliament, and got a vote of £180,000.

In England the matter was not so simple. All efforts to pack a Parliamentary majority failed. When Parliament met in November, 1640, its first Act was to decide that it could not legally be dissolved without the consent of both Houses. When Charles gave his assent to this Act—which he was in no position to refuse—the initiative passed to the revolutionaries, and the English Revolution had begun.

A few days later the Courts of Star Chamber and High Commission were declared unconstitutional and a grievance. Everyone connected with them, from Laud downwards, was ordered under arrest. When Strafford arrived from Dublin he too was impeached, arrested, and thrown into the Tower. Charles tried to save his fellow conspirators by arresting the five leaders of the Commons. Warned in time, the members escaped, and the Commons as a body took refuge in the City of London which called out its trained-bands and closed its gates.

Charles gave way. The Commons, finding Strafford might wriggle out of a formal trial, passed a special Act declaring him guilty and sentencing him to death. On the night of the day (May 12, 1641) on which Strafford was executed all England blazed with bonfires of rejoicing.

Optimists thought the struggle was over and the Revolution won: sceptics thought things were going too well to last. As if in answer to their doubts came the startling news that the Irish clans had risen *en masse* on the night of October 23, 1641, and "massacred every Protestant in Ireland".

Things were not, in fact, as bad as that; or as good as the Irish had hoped. The central pivot of the whole rising–the capture of Dublin Castle–had failed to materialise. But the O'Neills, O'Donnells, O'Dohertys, O'Cahans and Maguires had cleared the planted area of Ulster and driven the population in panic flight before them to take refuge in the towns and castles.

How many Protestants were killed, in fair fight and otherwise, and how many died of exposure during the flight and pursuit has been debated with partisan acrimony on both sides ever since. An estimate of those killed may be fixed, on a balance of probability, at under 3,000; perhaps as many as 7,000 died of exposure. This is bad enough in all conscience, and proved that the clansmen showed as little consideration as they had received. But contemporary estimates–the belief which determined the conduct of the English revolutionaries–put the figure at 300,000 and even 400,000 "massacred in cold blood". That John Milton, an experienced man of affairs, who stood in the front rank of the cultured of his time, and was in touch with the best-informed official opinion of his day, as also the last man to be swayed by any passing wave of popular credulity, should have accepted as a fact the highest of these estimates is decisive as to what was actually believed. Actually there were not so many as 300,000 Protestants in all Ireland in 1641; while the succeeding years showed the Protestant community in being without noticeable diminution.

The effect of the "atrocity" story upon English affairs was immediate and searching. The King reported the rebellion to Parliament and asked for supply and a Parliamentary authority to raise an army for the suppression of the rebels.

The Commons received the message with deep suspicion. An army he could rely upon was the one thing the King could rot be trusted with. Then there was the manifesto issued by the Irish rebels themselves which avowed they were not hostile to the King or his authority, but were only seeking a remedy for intolerable grievances.

Englishmen in 1640 had not been conditioned into the belief in "Handy Andy" as the norm of Irish National character, consequently they did not dismiss this manifesto as an Irish "bull". They took it at its face-value and argued that if assaulting the King's garrisons, capturing his castles, and chasing the King's officers and his Protestant subjects into places of refuge or out of the country was not done in defiance of the King it must have been done, if not by his authority, at any rate with his collusion. They remembered Strafford, and so much as had come to light of the "Thorough" plan; and with it that the Irish were Papists while the King was credited with a design to restore Papacy.

It all seemed to fit in. Accordingly, after deliberation, they passed an Act authorising the raising of an army, but they inserted into the Act the names of those who were alone empowered by the Act to recruit soldiers, to appoint officers, and to dismiss them along with the troops when they thought fit. The names they inserted were all those of men upon whom the revolutionary chiefs thought they could rely.

The King's reception of this Act confirmed their worst suspicions. If his desire had been, *bona fide*, to suppress the Irish rebels with no ulterior motive, he had no reason to object to the safeguards adopted by the Commons. If he objected to them, a probability was at once established that he wanted the army for some work nearer home than in Ireland. A great suspicion arose that the Irish Rebellion had been engineered to provide Charles with a pretext for raising just the army he required.

The King did more than object. He left London for Nottingham, and there raised his Royal Standard and summoned the nobility and gentry to aid him against his "rebellious" Parliament.

The English Revolution thus passed into the phase of Civil War.

The details of the Civil War in England do not concern us. It is sufficient to note that the course of the struggle necessitated the "new modelling" of the army in such a way that it became recruited wholly from sturdy petit-bourgeois, peasant and near-proletarian elements, all zealots for the revolution and fanatically hostile to royalism and episcopacy in all their forms—in short it became a democratic republican army.

Rebellion and Civil War in Ireland

While the Civil War raged in England (1641–1649) Ireland was the theatre for a succession of political combinations, divisions, and recombinations so tangled that it almost defies analysis.

Confusion began even before the Rising of 1641. Strafford had kept the threads of things so entirely in his own hands that his arrest—which took him completely by surprise—left nobody to make provision for the pay or the provisioning of his Irish Army. There is no doubt that he, and Charles I, had intended that this army should follow Strafford to England as soon as the weather was favourable; but the arrest and impeachment of Strafford made the ship-owners, Irish as well as English, unwilling to take the risk of transporting the troops. Left without pay or provisions the army took to plundering and had to be disbanded. Many of its elements took part in the

Rising; others provided nuclei for the various armies which contended in the later struggles.

The Rising itself was planned by a group of clan-chiefs who, although they had submitted to the English, and had accepted knighthoods and titles, were not comfortable in their new position of Anglicised landlords. The ultimate cause of the Rising was the discontent and anger of the clansmen who were constantly urging their chiefs on to recover possession of the clan lands. General dissatisfaction; the doubt and uncertainty excited by Strafford's administration; the hope that the King and Strafford would do something for them; the fear that they would do nothing, or worse, might carry out their threat of planting all Connacht; hopes and fears centred upon the King, and hopes and fears of a victory for the Parliament; all these combined to make an occasion for the Rising and to ensure at the same time that the objects of the rebels should be hopelessly in conflict. The only settled purpose was that of the clans and of Owen Roe O'Neill, then in effect the head of the O'Neill clan, a distinguished soldier in the service of Spain who had promised the conspirators that if they could get an army together he would come from Spain to lead it.

O'Neill and the clansmen were of one mind from the start. They wanted a restoration of the clan lands and of the independence of Ireland; and the example of the Scots seemed conclusive as to what might be achieved by a united nation. But a united nation was just what did not exist in Ireland, though a semblance of unity was forced upon the Catholic community by its common fear of both the contending factions in England.

The King through his officials in Dublin denounced the Rising of 1641 as a "Papist" plot, and threatened condign punishment on all concerned. The English Parliament proclaimed a long list of proprietors as "traitors" and raised money to fight the King on the security of their estates—which were declared forfeited. Threatened

by both sides the Anglo-Irish Catholics, led by their land-lords, and ex-chiefs, joined the original conspirators; but with many misgivings.

There were thus from the outset three distinct parties, each with its army in the field in Ireland—(1) The English Parliamentary Party held Derry City and part of the Counties of Derry, Antrim and Down; (2) The King's Party led by Ormond held Dublin, Louth, part of Meath, and, through Lord Inchiquin (Murrough O'Brien), part of Cork; (3) The Catholic Confederation, formed in Kil-kenny, in May 1642, held the rest of the country.

The Catholic Confederation set up an elaborate Council in which each province and every county was repre-sented, but from the start it disavowed any sort of separatism. It affirmed its allegiance to Charles; and struck his head on its coinage. It showed a tolerant spirit towards other religions, but it courted trouble from the Ormond Royalists when it decreed the restoration of Church lands to the Catholic Hierarchy. It refused to do the obviously correct thing and appoint Owen Roe O'Neill its Commander in Chief. Instead, it appointed Thomas Preston, nephew of Lord Gormanstown, an Anglo-Irish Catholic. Preston had served with distinction in Spain, but he was in every respect inferior as a soldier to O'Neill with whom he had quarrelled.

The Confederation, in short, took as its basic stand-point the landlordism which the English conquerors had introduced, and only tolerated O'Neill and his clansmen so far as they were necessary to their resistance to the Parliamentarians led by Coote and Munro in the North, to the Royalist Ormond in the Pale (who held the "Papis rebels" in the utmost abhorrence) and to the turncoa Inchiquin in the South—who joined and sold every par in turn, but who at the outset earned the name "Murrough of the Burnings" by the desolation he wor' in East Munster and South Leinster. But for Owen the Confederation would have been overwhelmed

than once; but all the time it bent its chief energies upon negotiating a treaty with Charles which would give satisfaction to Catholic claims. There, however, the Confederation split into fragments. The Anglo-Irish Catholics of the Pale would have been satisfied with toleration and a free parliament; the Clerical party wanted more than this—a restoration of church lands, the possession of all churches recaptured from the Protestants in the Rebellion, and so on.

The political confusion in the Catholic camp was increased by intrigues in the Royalist camp. While Ormond and Inchiquin in concert were campaigning fiercely against the Catholic Confederates, an emissary of Charles was negotiating a secret treaty with the Council of the Confederation. Charles was willing to promise anything in return for an Irish Army; but he dared not let it be known in England that he was negotiating with the Irish rebels. Half his English Army would have been ready to desert if they had known of it. When this secret treaty was discovered, Charles repudiated it, and imprisoned the man (Lord Glamorgan) who negotiated it.

Meanwhile Ormond for the Anglo-Irish Protestant Royalists was negotiating a peace of his own. The King had suffered the crushing defeats of Marston Moor (1644) and Naseby (1645), and Inchiquin had gone over to the Parliamentarians, when Ormond, in 1646, negotiated a peace which a majority of the Confederate Council agreed to. Those who opposed it were, however, the more powerful since they included the Pope's Nuncio and Preston (who both wanted a peace the Queen was negotiating on her own authority) and Owen Roe who wanted no treaty with the King at all.

Owen Roe and Preston marched on Kilkenny, scattered the old Council, and appointed a new one which repudiated the treaty. Ormond, in disgust, threw up the struggle, surrendered Dublin to the Parliamentarian General Michael Jones (1647) and retired to France.

The departure of Ormond simplified the situation somewhat by eliminating the Royalists as a separate force. Some of his followers joined the Catholic Confederation; some joined Inchiquin and the Parliament. Shortly afterwards (1647–8) Inchiquin, who had over-run all Munster, opened negotiations with the Confederates and made offers for a peace and an alliance. A majority of the Council accepted his offer; and Owen Roe, indignant, broke with the Council and took the field with an independent army. The Nuncio excommunicated everyone who had signed the treaty with Inchiquin, but Ormond at that moment came forward with fresh offers, and the second Ormond Peace was concluded January 17, 1649. The Nuncio in disgust sailed from Ireland a few weeks later, just after Charles I had been executed in Whitehall as "a man of blood, false to his word, and an enemy of the people of England".

Ormond returning to Ireland as the representative of Charles II, at once dissolved the Catholic Confederation, converting its followers into a Royalist party pure and simple. He had great hopes of Scottish assistance since the Scots had broken with the English Parliamentarians and a Scottish army was besieging the Parliamentarian General Coote in Derry.

Owen Roe would have nothing to do with Ormond, Preston, Inchiquin, or any of the Irish and Anglo-Irish gentry. He drove the Scots away from Derry and entered into negotiations with the English Parliamentarian General Monk.

This, which is passed over in orthodox histories as a mere episode of no significance, was in fact by far the most fateful moment in the whole struggl , as we shall see when we look at it from the English angle. Meanwhile we note only that the English Parliament issued peremptory orders to Monk to break off all negotiations instantly.

Owen Roe, there being nothing else for it, agreed to

a treaty with Ormond and prepared to march to his aid. He was, however, already a sick man, and in November 1649 he died. It was commonly believed he was poisoned; there is next to no evidence to support the belief, except the character of Inchiquin, who was, indeed, quite equal to anything.

Meanwhile, at the end of August 1649, Oliver Cromwell had landed in Dublin at the head of an army of veteran troops.

The Episode of the Levellers

The situation in which the newly-born English Republic stood in the spring of 1649 was highly precarious.

That the New Model Army and its supporters were only a minority of the population is probably true. But it is equally true that they were the strongest single political force in the country and the only united and organised body. That they had executed the King was not, as sentimentalists and reactionaries have argued, any sign or cause of weakness. On the contrary, it proved a thing that many then living needed to be taught—that a King's head would come off just as easily as that of any other man, and that a King could be in fact called to account for crimes committed in the exercise of his public trust.

It was because they taught the world that salutary lesson that the men of the New Model Army who brought the King to trial, and insisted upon their Parliamentary representatives executing justice upon him, were hated and reviled by the reactionaries in every court in Europe, and have been traduced, slandered, and misrepresented by sentimentalists and reactionaries ever since.

The real weakness of their position arose from a fact common to all bourgeois revolutions. Necessarily, to carry through its fight against feudalism and the Absolute

Monarchy, the bourgeoisie had to carry with it into the struggle all the virile elements in the lower ranks of society. The yeoman farmers, the small manufacturers, the independent craftsmen, journeymen, and so forth, who formed the rank and file of the New Model Army, had developed in their camp meetings and debates a high grade of political understanding and consciousness.

Up to the point at which the King was finally disposed of and the Monarchy and the House of Lords abolished, the interest of the progressive bourgeoisie coincided with that of its petit-bourgeois rank and file. Here, however, the turning point was reached, since here the bourgeoisie wished, in principle, to bring the revolution to an end and begin the work of conserving the victory won.

The rank and file wished to go further and complete the revolution by breaking the power of the squirearchy as well, and that of the parson also. They wanted at any rate a political levelling; and some of them wanted an economic levelling into the bargain.

The vital crux was the demand for the confiscation of the estates of the King and the royalist landowners and their distribution among the land-hungry in the army and the countryside. With this went a demand for the restoration of the people's rights in the commonland which the landlords had stolen. And it was just at this point, when the Leveller sentiment had spread to most of the rank and file of the army, and their kinsfolk and supporters among the civilian population, that Owen Roe O'Neill and George Monk—who was suspected of Leveller leanings himself—opened negotiations in Ireland.

Did Owen Roe know that a strong party in England entertained designs upon the estates of the aristocracy and gentry of England which were on all fours with his own designs for Ireland? He was too good a general not to be well-informed about what was going on in the enemy camp. And he was an experienced politician who could tell the way the wind was blowing as well as any man. We can only guess. But the promptness and vigour with which Monk was ordered to break off all negotiations with the "rebels" is very eloquent when read in conjunction with the equal promptness and vigour—not to say violence—with which Cromwell at the same time crushed the incipient mutiny of the Levellers before it had time to come to a head.

Moreover it is suspiciously suggestive of a deliberate side-track that Cromwell and the Parliament promised the Leveller Regiments ordered for service in Ireland that they would be rewarded with a share of the land confiscated from the Irish Royalists—who now as a result of Ormond's skilful intrigues and the political weakness of the Confederates—included virtually all the landowners in Ireland.

When the English Levellers let themselves be sidetracked; and when Owen Roe, stalled-off, succumbed to Ormond's temptations, both the English and the Irish revolutions were aborted. From that moment the Restoration of the Monarchy was merely a question of time.

The Cromwellian Conquest of Ireland

When Cromwell landed in Dublin he knew clearly what he had to do. The Irish armies had to be smashed utterly before either the Scots, or any Continental aid Prince Rupert and Charles Stuart the younger might muster, could get into action. Provided he could deal with these enemies one by one there was little reason to doubt the result. Therefore he acted with a speed and a ferocity that gave a measure of his estimate of the urgency of the situation.

The military details of the campaign need not detain us. Cromwell attacked Drogheda first, and ordered an assault as soon as the wall was breached. As is notorious, the order of "no quarter" was given and obeyed—the fact that the garrison consisted mostly or largely of English

Royalist troops did not incline the men of the New Model to show mercy anyway. The same process was repeated at Wexford. In each case a certain number of civilians got mixed with the garrison and were slaughtered along with them.* All "friars" and priests were "knocked on the head as soon as seen".

The business was barbarous, bloody, and inexcusable. And the fact that the Elizabethan conquerors had done equally barbarous deeds, or that giving "no quarter" to a garrison which refused to surrender on summons was a military custom of the period does not lessen the enormity. An Englishman concerned for the honour of the English Revolution, and the good repute of the New Model and its Leveller rank and file, has a right to protest that a standard set by the exterminators of the German Peasants' War, by Alva in the Netherlands, and by Tilly and Wallenstein in the religious wars in Germany is a standard of condemnation not of exoneration.

The only excuse for Cromwell's "frightfulness" was that he was genuinely pinched for time and, further, that the policy worked. Inchiquin, double-crossing to the last, deserted to the Parliament. Garrison after garrison surrendered at summons. A rump of the Anglo-Irish Catholic nobility sent an appeal for aid to the Duke of Lorraine. A few towns—notably Waterford and Limerick—put up a stout resistance. But the only real check the New Model met—apart from delays caused by weather and outbreaks of epidemic disease—was when they met and were repulsed by the O'Neills and their fellow-clansmen in the breaches of Clonmel.

In that mutual slaughter of the last representatives of the communism of primitive society and the first representatives of the communism of the future, lies the essen-

* The story of the "massacre of hundreds of women and children around the market cross at Wexford" is a fiction invented by counter-revolutionary Royalists, without a shred of contemporary evidence to support it.

tial tragedy of the English Revolution and of the Cromwellian conquest of Ireland.

Called away to meet and defeat the Scots, Cromwell left the completion of the conquest to his lieutenants Ireton, Fleetwood, and Ludlow. It was ended in May 1652, when the last Irish armies—mostly clansmen—accepted the Articles of Kilkenny. All who surrendered, and were not guilty of murder, were allowed to transport themselves beyond the seas. Thirty-four thousand Irish soldiers took the opportunity to take service in the Armies of Continental Kings.

The Cromwellian Settlement

In 1652 Ireland had been in a state of war for eleven years. With bloodshed, destruction, and the interruption of normal pursuits, plague and pestilence and famine had stalked hand in hand. "Whole counties had been depopulated," says one witness. "A man might travel twenty miles and not see a living creature, either man or beast or bird," says another, an English officer. "As for the poor commons," says a third, "the sun never shined upon a nation so completely miserable."

These were the conditions in which the English Parliament, moving with great deliberation, set to work to effect a "Settlement" of the population.

In principle they merely followed the clearance and replanting plan of their predecessors; but the scale upon which they did it would have taken Elizabeth's breath away—and she was "as tough as they make 'em". Cromwell must take his share of the blame—Royalist reactionaries have combined with Irish sentimentalists to put all the blame upon him—as must also the rank-and-file soldiers who made the Settlement possible and shared in the plunder. But it is only fair to point out that Parliament had decided in principle what it intended to do immediately after the Rising of 1641.

The principle of the Settlement was simple. The Commonwealth was in debt to sundry creditors, and to its soldiers for arrears of pay. Ireland, considered as a property, had to bear the whole of this burden.

In essence the whole of Ireland was deemed to be confiscated from its legal owners. Then a scale of degrees of criminality was drawn up. Those who had shown "constant good-affection" to the Parliament and its Cause, which meant those who had fought for the Parliament all through, or who had aided those that fought, were adjudged to be entitled to the number of acres they then held. Those who had organised the Rising of 1641 were to lose all the acres they possessed; if they were guilty of murder they were hanged also. Those whose criminality was less, were to lose two acres in every three. Those whose criminality was least were to lose one acre in three.

When every landowner who had possessed more than 50 acres had been classified, the Catholics among them were ordered on a certain date to betake themselves with their belongings beyond the Shannon into Connacht, where room would be found for them on the acres confiscated from the proprietors there domiciled.

The villainy of the business lay in a matter the Commissions had overlooked. It had not been intended to interfere with small leaseholders, tenant farmers, cottagers, or artisans. The Commissioners knew from experience that tenants and labourers from England were hard to get, and nobody wanted the land just to look at. What they had to face was that the Irish Catholic landlord in the majority of cases stood to his tenants in the relation of a chief to his kinsmen. In many instances this was actually the case. In others it was a tradition-based custom. In most cases where the landlord went, there his tenants followed, regardless of the fact that they might have stayed. In many of these cases the humble tenant had a purely customary tenure based on a verbal understanding; such a tenant feared to remain lest the new landowner should eject him as a trespasser or impose upon him conditions not to be borne.

In the end the authorities found the situation they themselves had created was an impossible one. Legal juggling was set to work and soon the tide was setting the other way. The "Transplanters" were allowed, in many cases, probably a majority, to creep back. It cost them dearly. They had to surrender more acres; or to pay a "rake-off"; or even to return as tenants to lands they had once owned. With them returned their dependants, and things were as before, except that virtually the whole Irish population now carried on their backs the burden of alien landlords.

This reshuffling was greatly to the advantage of a swarm of speculators who followed the Land Commissioners like vultures swooping over a battlefield. The army's claim for accumulated arrears of pay was met by a distribution of "tickets" entitling the soldiers to share in the allocation of land by lot. Speculators who had lent money to the Government received the equivalent in acres, but in scattered parcels. Many soldiers did not want to settle in Ireland. There was a grand opening for a speculator with ready cash to buy soldiers' "tickets" (at a liberal discount) and then negotiate exchanges until he had got together a fine compact estate of tens of thousands of acres. More than one "noble" family estate was thus thriftily got together.

An incidental by-product of the period was that swarms of orphan children, and youths of both sexes, were to be found on every hand. Their parents had died, their employers had cast them off, or they had strayed and got lost in the confusion. To get rid of them the Government rounded them up and sold them to agents who shipped them to the West Indies or to the Carolinas where they fetched a good price as indentured labourers. The profits were so great that the agents came back for more; and, when the supply of Irish vagrants ran out, took to kidnapping to supply their market. The agents got so bold that they kidnapped Englishmen, not only in Ireland, but also in England. Then the traffic was prohibited.

The Restoration Finale

When the Monarchy was restored in England there were great hopes among the dispossessed proprietors that their fidelity to the Stuart cause would be rewarded.

Some little was done in the case of a few Anglo-Irish lords whom the Commonwealth had deported, but little more.

The Irish found themselves up against the difficulty that virtually every one of them had been technically in rebellion against the Crown at one time or another. And as any real restoration of confiscated acres would have to be made at the expense of Englishmen of wealth whom Charles--not wishing "to go on his travels again"--had no intention of disobliging, he gave the Irish his blessing, and let it go at that.

CHAPTER IV

THE SUBJUGATION OF IRELAND–III

The fourth and final conquest of Ireland–the Williamite Conquest (1690-2)–grew, as its predecessor had done, out of a revolutionary conflict in England into whose orbit Ireland became drawn; again, on the counter-revolutionary ("loyalist") side.

This time the crisis was that of the Whig* Revolution (1688). Once again a revolutionary advance in England involved in Ireland a further subjugation and an intensification of enslavement.

The Whig Revolution (1688)

After the Restoration of the Monarchy (1660) the English common people had time in which to regret that they had been headed-off from their true line of revolutionary advance. They had thwarted the designs of Charles I, Laud, and Strafford; but the cream of the gains from their victory had been skimmed-off and enjoyed by an oligarchy of wealthy (and ennobled) bourgeois allied to aristocratic (and bourgeoisified) landlords and a clique of Court parasites.

In these new political circumstances even the great and growing advances in trade and commerce (for which the Revolution of 1640 had prepared the way) were no adequate compensation for their steadily intensifying dread of a new and more subtly-contrived attempt to re-establish the Absolutism they had fought to destroy, and with it, possibly, a return to "Papacy" also.

---

* Whig and Tory: These party nicknames came into use between 1660 and 1685 as denoting respectively those who wished to restrict the Crown and the succession by specific Constitutional law, and those who thought this a personal insult to the King and an illegitimate curtailment of the Royal prerogatives.

There were agitations, and insurrectionary conspiracies; but the main body of the bourgeoisie had been content (while grumbling) to pick up the material gains of trade while their aristocratic upper strata and the Court clique held the lower orders drastically in check.

The accession in 1685, of James II, a Catholic zealot, threw this tacit coalition entirely out of balance. It threatened a considerable section of the oligarchy with a deprivation of political power and a loss of the emoluments of public office, as well as of its monopoly of patronage. It threatened the Church with loss of status and of revenue; and it threatened the bourgeoisie with the restraints (and the parasitism) it had escaped from in 1640.

In these circumstances the common-people of the West of England—then the chief manufacturing area and where Leveller traditions were still strong—believed they could count upon support from the merchants of the City of London, and the Whig nobility and gentry in the North. Accordingly they responded to the call of James, Duke of Monmouth, a bastard son of Charles II, and rose in revolt; choosing significantly the sea-green of the Levellers, as their party badge.

Their rising was double-crossed in two ways. (1) The Whig lords and gentry fearing the strong Leveller element in the rebellion, held aloof. (2) Monmouth, to placate these Whigs, rejected the demand of his followers for an immediate proclamation of a Republic, and tried the compromise line of claiming to be the legitimate heir to the throne. Thus he alienated the Leveller elements in London who might have forced the hand of the City merchants. On the whole it paid the Whigs best politically to let James II incur the extra odium of suppressing the rebellion with ruthless ferocity, since this would destroy any hold he might have on the country at large, and at the same time minimise the risk of a Leveller Movement in the revolution they were contemplating on their own account.

Things worked out as the Whigs had planned. The West Country rising was suppressed with a barbarity that revolted all England. James, both obstinate and stupid, showed his intention to corner all the chief state offices and emoluments for Catholics—real and pretended—in so glaring a fashion that even a docile and subservient Church took alarm. A Whig junta representing an alliance of landowners, wealthy merchants, and ecclesiastics, sent an invitation to the ruler of Holland, William of Orange —who as a grandson of Charles I on the maternal side, and as the husband of James's eldest daughter had a direct interest in the succession—to come to England with an army to "restore the Liberties of England and the Protestant Religion".

Accordingly when William of Orange complied, and landed with an army at Torbay, on November 5, 1688, James II found himself confronted, not only with an invasion but a universal desertion by Army, Navy, Court functionaries, the Law, the Church, the City, and even his own family. Fearing for his life at the hands of a raging London mob, James fled for refuge to the Court of Louis XIV of France.

When a convention Parliament had formally installed William and Mary as joint monarchs, and they had given their assent to a Bill of Rights and an Act of Settlement, limiting the succession to the throne exclusively to Protestants (even marriage to a Catholic constituting a disqualification) the Whig or "Glorious" Revolution was accomplished.

Ireland and the Whig Revolution

In Ireland, the accession of James the Catholic had aroused intense excitement because of its possible bearing upon the Cromwellian settlement which Charles II had refused to upset, or to modify, except to a negligible extent.

The extent of the problem involved may be gathered from an estimate made after Charles II had modified the settlement (·lightly) in favour of the Catholics.

The categories named hereunder possessed (in 1665) the number of acres specified: (1) owners installed by the Cromwellian settlement, 4,560,037 acres. (2) Old English Colonists 3,900,000 acres. (3) "Innocent" Irish, including some Transplanted, 2,323,809. (4) Irishmen of "good affection" 600,000. This left, out of an estimated total of 12,208,237 acres, only 824,391 acres not appropriated by any large landowners, a good proportion of this category being town dwelling-sites, etc.

There were then some 200,000 Protestants in Ireland to over 1,000,000 Catholics, therefore if we ignore the unappropriated category, which was largely in the hands of planted Cromwellian soldiers or their Protestant descendants, we get the result that over two-thirds of the good arable and meadow land was owned by less than one-sixth of the total population, the large-owning minority being almost exclusively Protestants. The proportion of Protestants to Catholics in the various provinces was: Ulster 5 to 2; Leinster 2 to 13; Munster 2 to 20; Connacht 2 to 25.

From these figures can be estimated the height of Catholic expectation and the depth of Protestant fears excited by the accession of James II in 1685.

Hopes and fears were equally intensified when James appointed an Anglo-Irish Catholic, the Earl of Tyrconnel* (otherwise "Lying Dick" Talbot) Commander in Chief, and later, Lord Lieutenant of Ireland. And Tyrconnel,

---

* Tyrconnel: Talbot must not be confounded with the O'Donnell, who claimed this title. This Talbot Tyrconnel was alluded to in the song

> "There was an old prophecy found in a bog,
> That Ireland be ruled by an ass and a dog.
> Now is that prophecy come for to pass,
> For Tyrconnel's the *dog* and James is the *ass*."

unwittingly, contributed to James's downfall by raising Catholic regiments in Ireland, and sending some of them to England to support the Crown at the crisis of the trial of the Seven Bishops for sedition—the "sedition" being a written protest against James's attempt to suspend by arbitrary decree the laws against Catholic worship.

The Irish regiments arrived in the neighbourhood of London, just in time for the immense, popular rejoicing at the acquittal of the Seven Bishops (1688). Their coming excited a frantic panic when a rumour spread that they were marching to sack London and massacre the population. The rumour was baseless; but it indicated the state of feeling in the English Army as well as in the civil population. The attempt to introduce Irish Catholic regiments into England ensured that not a single English soldier would be ready to so much as fire a shot in defence of James. Bundling the Irish troops back to Ireland did nothing to better the situation.

Meanwhile the withdrawal of the troops from Ireland had given the towns of Derry and Enniskillen a chance to close their gates and defend themselves against the troops of Tyrconnel and James.

In 1689 Tyrconnel refused to accept the Settlement of the Throne enacted by the Convention Parliament. He declared for James, and invited him to come from France (with an army) to take possession of his "lawful" kingdom. James landed in March 1689, with some officers, French and Irish, a few troops, but little or no artillery. His concern for Ireland was small; his real hopes being fixed upon Scotland, where "Bloody Grahame of Claverhouse" (alias "Bonnie Dundee") was raising the clans on his behalf. Checked by the stubborn resistance of Derry and Enniskillen, James summoned a Parliament to meet in Dublin.

The Parliament which assembled on May 7 included six Protestant bishops among the Peers—James had thought it expedient not to summon the Catholic bishops—and something under a score of Protestants among the 232 members of the House of Commons. In the circumstances it was bound to be revolutionary; but once again revolution for Ireland clashed with and countered the revolution in England.

The "Patriot" Parliament (1) declared the English Parliament incompetent to pass laws for Ireland; (2) made the Irish House of Lords the court of final appeal in law cases; (3) declared for complete religious toleration; (4) enacted that tithes while remaining compulsory might be paid by the land-holder to the Church of his choice. So far even the English Whigs had little to complain of. But when it went on to (5) revoke the Cromwellian Settlement, and (6) threaten all emigrant land-owners with confiscation if they did not return to their allegiance (to James) by a specified date, it stirred up a nest of hornets some of which still buzz.

The chief failure of the Patriot Parliament—its willingness to leave the mass of Irishmen as landless as it found them—is seldom noted.

From James's standpoint the Patriot Parliament was disastrous. Revoking the Cromwellian Settlement alienated at a stroke all the Tory landowners in England upon whom he was counting for aid; and his worst fears were realised a week after the Parliament had adjourned, when, first, Dundee was killed in action at Killiecrankie, and then Derry was relieved after standing a siege of 105 days.

The Williamite War

Following the relief of Derry, William of Orange began (somewhat tardily) military operations to obtain possession of Ireland; but the war which followed was only in part an incident in the Whig Revolution.

Both England and Ireland were pawns in a balance-of-power game fought out on the Continent between Louis XIV and his Allies, on one side, and an European Coalition (which included the Pope, as a temporal monarch, as well as William of Orange) on the other. It was England's good luck that the maintenance of its independence coincided with William's continental interest. It was Ireland's bad luck that it stood to lose whoever won. James II and his backer Louis were even less concerned for the independence of Ireland than was William III. Apart from the incidental question as to which of two rival Kings of England should rule Ireland, the issue which the mass of Irishmen fought to decide was whether they would be robbed by an English protestant landlord, or a Catholic Irish one. Robbed they were certain to be either way.

It is illuminating to remember that the English Whigs were so loath to give William the army he needed–"he had plenty of Dutchmen anyway"–that when he did advance to force the crossing of the Boyne on July 1, 1690, William's army included–as well as a few English, Scottish, and Ulster regiments–Dutch, Danes, Swedes, Prussians, and French Huguenots. Incidentally, William's army wore green badges to distinguish them, some of the Ulster troops choosing the Leveller sea-green. James's army wore the white cockade of the Bourbons and the Stuarts.

As a battle the Boyne-crossing was an affair of little significance. William's army was slightly the superior in numbers, and much the superior in training, equipment and artillery. Patrick Sarsfield, the best soldier on James's side, advised against accepting battle at the Boyne. Knowing the relative strength of the two Armies Sarsfield advised a retreat behind the line of the Shannon until the Irish troops had become better trained and equipped. James over-ruled Sarsfield's objections and insisted upon a battle, which he promptly proceeded to lose by massir; his best troops to face what proved to be a feint on his left, and so leaving his centre and right too weak to prevent the forcing of the fords. The only dash and skill shown by James was in securing the lead of the retreat to Dublin! The total casualties on both sides were under 2,000.

A story, probably true, runs that Sarsfield, covering the retreat, exchanging banter with English officers whom he knew personally, shouted: "Change kings with us, and we'll fight it all over again!" Incidentally also, we note that a Pontifical High Mass and *Te Deum* were sung in Rome in th nksgiving for William's victory at the Boyne.

After the Boyne, with James out of the way, the Franco-Irish army fell back, as Sarsfield had advised, to defend the line of the Shannon. The year closed with Sarsfield's successful defence of Limerick, which was set off somewhat by Marlborough's capture of Cork and Kinsale from the sea.

In 1691 the line of the Shannon was forced at Athlone by a desperate Anglo-Dutch assault upon a weakly-guarded ford. The French general, St. Ruth, decided to risk a stand (July 12, 1691) at Aughrim, near Ballinasloe, Co. Galway, but in the middle of a bloody struggle St. Ruth was killed and a pass for the English advance was treacherously deserted by an English-Jacobite cavalry commander Henry Luttrell. Taken in the flank and rear, with no one in command, the Irish were routed in confusion.

After Aughrim only the cities of Galway and Limerick were left to be conquered. Galway surrendered early in August, and Limerick, seeing the situation hopeless, accepted terms.

The Treaty of Limerick

The articles of Capitulation, commonly called the Treaty of Limerick, signed on October 13, 1691, derive importance from the difference revealed between the attitude of William III who approved them and that of the Irish Parliament which rejected them.

There were two treaties. Under one the Irish soldiers who surrendered were given the option of taking service with the King of France (which some 10,000 of them did) or of returning to their homes unmolested. Under the other the civilian Catholic population was promised, in return for taking an oath of allegiance to William, "not less toleration" than they had enjoyed prior to the accession of James.

The Dublin Parliament, from which all Catholics were excluded, refused (1692) to ratify the Treaty, until in 1697 a number of laws penalising Catholics had been passed, and a legal stipulation had been accepted that the Treaty meant that the least favourable conditions for Catholics prior to 1685 were to become the most favourable condition for Catholics in the future.

The Treaty of Limerick became in this way a classic instance of "English" bad faith.

In 1692, along with its refusal to approve the Treaty, the Dublin Parliament adopted an English Act which imposed confiscation upon all Irish landowners who had taken part with James. The Catholics appealed to William on the ground that this involved a flagrant breach of the Treaty of Limerick. Eventually the matter was compromised by the surrender of some three quarters of a million acres by the incriminated Catholics. Those who lost entire estates were mostly English Jacobites. The estates of James II in Ireland were granted by William to his mistress, the Countess of Orkney.

Beginning in 1692, a number of Acts were passed by the Dublin Parliament, all levelled against the Catholics, which are known collectively as the *Penal Code.*

Catholics were debarred from the vote, and from entry into Parliament, the municipal corporations, the learned professions (except medicine) and from commissions in the Army, Navy, and Civil Service. No Catholic might open or teach in a school; or take any part in the sale or manufacture of arms. No Catholic might possess or carry arms without a magistrate's licence, nor might one own a horse worth more than £5. Except in the linen trade, no Catholic might have more than two apprentices. Protestants might not take Catholic apprentices at all. Catholics were barred from the manufacture and sale of newspapers and books. Marriages between Catholics and Protestants were prohibited as far as possible.

Catholics were subjected to special taxes, and to special restraints if they were landowners. No Catholic estate could be entailed: it must be divided at death between all the children. Catholics could not take leases for longer than thirty-three years and a Catholic's profits from subletting might not be more than one-third of the rent he paid. A Protestant landowner lost his civil rights if he married a Catholic; a Protestant heiress, marrying a Catholic, lost her inheritance.

By conforming to the Protestant Church, a Catholic son could make his father a mere tenant for life on his own estate, which the son could inherit entire. Catholic orphans must be brought up as Protestants. A Catholic wife by conforming to the Protestant Church acquired the right to live apart from her husband and make him support her.

With regard to the Catholic Church itself all archbishops, bishops, etc. were ordered to leave the country under the penalties for high treason if they remained or returned. Only one priest was permitted per parish, however large, and he must register, and might not set foot outside his parish except with special permission. No priest might enter the country from anywhere.

These provisions were designed to make the work of the Church, and its continued existence, impossible. They had the effect of turning it into an "underground" organisation endeared to the people. Unregistered priests and banned ecclesiastics carried on the work in the huge country parishes in which only one priest was permitted by law. Mass was celebrated in secluded spots, in all weathers, while scouts watched for the approach of enemies.

English trade-unionists who know how firmly the tradition of trade-unionism was laid in England when the unions were banned as "seditious conspiracies" by law, can understand why adherence to the Catholic Church came to be a point of honour with the common people of Ireland.

Protestant Ascendancy

An aspect of this iniquitous Code which has survived into our own time is that it conceals the political subjection of a distinct people to special super-exploitation, combined with social segregation and humiliation, all under a cloak of zeal for a particular religion. That this religion was the Established Religion of the imperial country shows this pretended zeal as the imperialist hypocrisy it was.

In England the Anti-Papal tradition, since it arose in the course of national struggles against an alien church, and counter-revolutionary kings, had at first a strong revolutionary content. It is not noted as often as it should be that for analogous reasons the Catholic tradition in Ireland has always had (despite the Hierarchy) a strong democratic and revolutionary content likewise, and that it is against this revolutionary democratic content that the malice of the Protestant Ascendancy faction was, and still is really directed.

In England, the "No Popery" tradition as it lost its revolutionary significance degenerated into the equivalent of the reactionary slogan "Down with the Jews". In Ireland from the days of the Penal Code it has equated with the imposition of the colour bar and the "Jim Crow" laws of the Plantation States of the U.S.A.

The reactionary political essence of the Protestant Ascendancy slogan is proved by the fact that at that period, and for long after, the term "Protestant" included only adherents to the established Church, and excluded the Dissenters who were likewise subjected to special penalties as the politically suspected descendants and representatives of the revolutionaries of 1640, and especially of the Leveller element in the New Model army.

The Dissenters were mostly located in North-Eastern Ulster where they were small farmers, merchants and manufacturers. On a most favourable computation the Dissenters and Protestants together were never more than one-third of the total population, and the Protestants were seldom, if ever, equal in numbers to the Dissenters. Thus the Penal Code was designed and imposed as an instrument for the aggrandisement of a privileged caste, which with its flunkey and sycophant hangers-on never totalled more than one-sixth of the population of Ireland. In their interest the Pale, which had ceased to exist as a territorial division, was revived as a line of social-economic and political exclusion.

The Penal Code and Irish Nationality

Such a policy as that embodied in the Penal Code was bound to have far-reaching effects, most of them evil, especially upon the characters of the respective categories of rulers and ruled, superiors and inferiors. Irish writers of our own time have summarized its consequences thus:

"The Protestants developed the vices of slave-owners, becoming idle, dissipated, and neglectful of their duties. The Catholic population grew, as a serf-population always does grow, cringing, shifty, untruthful. They were lazy because they had nothing to work for· lawless because they knew the law only as an enemy to be defied or evaded wherever possible. Not such had been the Irish of the old times, praising truth as the highest of virtues; obeying strictly a law supported by no force save that of public opinion. Nor were such qualities observed in the soldiers and statesmen whom Ireland at this very time was giving to the nations of Europe and of America.

"That bad effects must have followed from these pernicious enactments as regards proficiency in professional and artistic work, in industry and in agriculture is evident. The Catholic's abilities were lost to the country, since he had no means of exercising them. The tenant whose improvements the landlord might confiscate at the end of his short lease, if indeed he had a lease at all, naturally did not improve. If a tenant at will he did not dare even to show any sign of prosperity in his dress or in the equipment of his house or farm. The purchase of a new coat or a new plough might result in a raising of his rent next gale day."

Hayden and Moonan: *Short History of the Irish People.*

This summary, though true as a generalisation, needs qualification. The Code had a different effect upon different classes of the subjected Irish population. For the Catholic landowners there were ways of escape. They could make a formal submission to Protestantism. They could convey their estates in trust to sympathising Protestants who could as the nominal owners shelter them from the law while leaving them in continued possession in fact. With Protestant connivance they could provide education for their children in England or on the Continent. A sense of class-solidarity made the bulk of the Protestant landowners collaborate with them in evading all the more offensive personal restrictions of the Code.

From any such easy way out the great mass of the Irish people were debarred by their poverty. The immense majority of them were small-scale tillers of the soil whom necessity kept tied to scanty holdings and conditions of tenure which could have no result but one or other form of wretchedness. For their children, the only education available—apart from a few ill-intentioned and worse-managed institutions designed to turn Catholic children into monstrosities of sycophantic servility, miscalled Protestants—was such as they could pick up from wandering scholars who taught the children of the poor under hedges in the fields, while scouts watched out for spies and informers.

The penalty for these hedge-schoolmasters, if caught, might be hanging, or transportation on a charge of treason, or a flogging on the charge of vagabondage. The payment for their labour was—a seat by the fire, a lodging in the hay, a share in the family meal, and such oddments in the way of clothing and ha'pence as the neighbours could scrape together. But they were sure of a welcome at any time in any thatched cabin because they were the last survivors of an integral feature of the old Gaelic social order. Many of them were the actual descendants of the hereditary chroniclers, pedigree-keepers, brehons, bards, and tellers of legendary tales of one or other of the clans; and it is due entirely to them and those who sheltered them that the living stream of Gaelic culture never wholly failed. With the parish priests, who remained faithful to their vocation in circumstances which make the lot of a missionary to cannibals luxurious by comparison, the

89

hedge-schoolmaster, and the wandering poet or musician kept glowing a spark of Gaelic fire among those humblest tillers of the soil who seemed in English eyes less to be regarded than the beasts of the field.

These tillers, the lowest strata of the conquered Irish –segregated by poverty, by language, by creed, by law, and by the supercilious arrogance of the class which, in Grattan's phrase, "knelt to England on the necks of their countrymen"–these people of the thatched cabins had one inestimably precious compensation. Around their turf fires they could hear retold again and again the legendary stories of the Gaels, and be solaced by poem, song and music preserved from days which far out-dated the oldest of their miseries–far-off days when the sun always shone and the blackbird's whistle never failed in the glen.

It was thus, and in these cabins, that the seed was kept alive which in due time would burst forth in the rich profusion of a regenerated Irish Nationality.

PART TWO

FROM GRATTAN TO THE UNITED IRISHMEN

O may the wind of Freedom
   Soon send the Frenchmen o'er
To plant the Tree of liberty
   Upon our Shamrock shore.
O, we'll plant it with our weapons
   While the English tyrants gape
To see their bloody flag torn down
   To Green on the Cape.
        O, the wearing the Green!
        Yes! the wearing the Green!
God grant us soon to see that day
      And freely wear the Green.

Antrim's Defenders' Song, 1796.

CHAPTER V

ENGLAND'S COLONY–IRELAND

So far we have traced the English Conquest: from now on we are concerned with the Re-Conquest of Ireland by the Irish Nation. And first of all this entails considering how a new Irish Nation was evolved historically in the developing process of struggle against the agencies and consequences of English Rule. In Part Two we deal with the first epoch in that process–one which begins with the rise of Grattan and the Volunteers (1778-82) and ends with the rise and fall of the United Irishmen (1791-98). In this chapter we deal with the economic and political relations which led to the rise of Grattan, and the Volunteer episode.

England's Colonial Policy

English official policy in the 17th and 18th centuries treated a colony as a child which had a claim upon, but also owed a duty to, its parent country. This policy originated in the Navigation Acts designed to break the Dutch mercantile monopoly and to make London the chief centre of the commerce of the world. Goods were refused entry to England unless carried in English ships, or in those of their country of origin. Exports were permitted only in English ships or those of the country to which the goods were invoiced.

In effect this policy restricted the Colonies to producing raw materials in exchange for English manufactures, all the carrying being done in English ships. Applied strictly, it would have prevented all sea-borne trade between one American colony and another except in English ships; and, though laxly enforced, it remained a rule that the American Colonies must not trade directly with foreign countries or with the possessions of foreign powers in

America. In the end the friction these rules generated was the basic cause of the revolt of the American Colonies, and the War of Independence (1776-82).

Restraints upon Irish Trade

In America this policy restricted manufactures and trade as they arose. In Ireland it involved destroying deliberately trade and manufactures that had already arisen and were competing successfully with English rivals. A few examples will illustrate the process.

In the 17th century a profitable Irish trade in fat cattle exported to England grew up. English graziers protested; the trade was prohibited. Irish cattle-breeders exported, instead, lean cattle for English graziers to fatten. English cattle-farmers protested; the trade was stopped. Ireland exported slaughtered carcasses; English butchers protested, and the trade was banned. Finally, salt beef (and pork) in barrels became the outlet for Irish live-stock breeders; and this trade, being useful to the English Navy and the mercantile marine, was allowed to pass without protest. It became one of Ireland's staple industries.

Irish-grown wool was of exceptionally fine quality, and the manufacture of Irish woollen cloth developed rapidly after 1690. It was of sufficient importance to induce the Irish Parliament to tax woollen exports to produce a revenue. The English Parliament placed a prohibitive import-tax upon woollens imported from Ireland. Finding that continental buyers bought Irish woollens in preference to English, the English Parliament prohibited all woollen export from Ireland, including raw wool, except to England and Wales—where the cloth had to pay a prohibitive duty. The raw wool useful to English manufacturers was admitted duty-free.

Irish manufacturers, unable to support themselves upon Ireland's internal market, emigrated and set up woollen manufactures in Germany, Holland, Belgium, France, and Spain—relying in each case largely upon raw wool and woollen yarn smuggled from Ireland.

These are type examples; similar restraints were applied in every branch of Irish industry, with the solitary exception of linen manufacture. This was fostered by royal and State subsidies because Irish manufacturers were better able than the English to compete successfully with French and Dutch producers. It was, as it happened, fostered in a Protestant area; but equivalent encouragement would have established it equally well in a Catholic region.

A contributory motive for this trade policy was that it diverted to investment in English manufactures all the capital accumulations wrung by the Anglo-Irish landlords from their Irish tenantry.

Administration and Parliament in Ireland

The Irish Administration consisted of the Viceroy, the Chief Secretary, and Ministers appointed by the Viceroy. The Viceroy and the Chief Secretary were, in practice, nominated by the English Cabinet to which the Chief Secretary was directly responsible. From this followed a radical difference between the English and Irish Parliaments. Changes in Irish administration were initiated in London. An adverse vote of the Dublin Parliament did not affect them, but an adverse vote at Westminster did so at once.

As in England, but in a greater proportion, many of the seats in the Irish Parliament were for Boroughs which had no real existence. With Catholics debarred from voting, most of the counties were also controlled by territorial magnates. The borough franchise was usually so restricted that most of them became, virtually, nomination boroughs. Out of 300 seats, it was estimated, in 1778, that 219 were the property of patrons. Of the 81 "contested" seats many were shamelessly corrupt.

Four great landowners by combining their interest could command a majority of the House, even against Crown influence. The management of the House thus became merely a business of awarding places, pensions, etc. Nearly two-thirds of the Members were placemen, pensioners, or both. And this state of things had endured for more than fifty years.

The Irish Parliament was still held to be restricted by "Poyning's Law" (1494). No Bill might be introduced until its "heads" had been approved by the two Privy Councils, either of which might delete clauses from Bills after they had been passed. In addition, by an Act of 1720 the English Parliament claimed the right to pass laws for Ireland at its pleasure. This arose from the desire to prevent the use of Ireland by the Crown as a base for resistance to the people and Parliament of England, which was an additional reason for checking the growth of trade and manufactures in Ireland. Collaterally, the Irish Civil List was a convenient means of making provision for Court favourites (King's mistresses, etc.) whom it was inadvisable to saddle upon the English establishment.

The Irish landed oligarchy, who could invest their revenues in England, had no direct interest in promoting Irish trade or manufactures. As they controlled the Irish Parliament, there was little or no resistance from that quarter to English legislation against Ireland's trade and manufactures.

Economic Conditions in Ireland (1690-1778)

England in 1690-1760 was passing through the mercantile-manufacturing prelude to the Industrial Revolution Ireland's economy was being arrested in its development and turned aside into producing, as well as subsistence for the Irish population, food-stuffs for English workers and raw materials for England's manufactures.

The bulk of Irish land was owned in large estates by titled landowners, many of them English absentees. A large proportion was leased on long terms either to resident gentry or to speculators who sub-let in smaller estates. There was a fair number of substantial freeholders, mostly Protestants of planted stock; and a fair number of Catholic leaseholders on short terms. Much the most numerous class was that of the cottagers whose position was a compromise between that of a wage-labourer and that of an allotment farmer.

When a labourer was hired he was allotted a plot (an acre or half-acre) upon which to erect a cottage, sometimes with materials supplied in part by his employer. From this "potato-ground" he produced the subsistence for himself and family. In addition he was allotted grazing for a cow or cows. He paid rent for both potato-ground and cow's grass by deductions from wages due. Any surplus was paid in cash or kind.

The tenant of a small farm frequently needed to supplement its yield by wage-labour for the landowner. Thus his position approximated to that of the cottager-labourer, while the landlord stood to both much as a tribal chief stood to his clan-kinsmen. The practice of permitting the labourer and the smaller tenants the free services of the landowner-employer's bull or stallion was another vestigial relic of the clan relation.

The main productive activity of the Irish population (1690–1760) was subsistence tillage. The diet-staple of the peasantry of every grade was potatoes and butter-milk, supplemented in the off-season by oatmeal. Bread-corn was grown primarily for sale to the towns. Barley was grown for brewing and distilling; which, in this period grew rapidly from domestic crafts into important manufactures. Dairy products—butter, cheese, poultry, eggs and bacon—were too valuable as articles of exchange for them to enter, more than occasionally, into the dietary of the peasantry.

Certain consequences followed: (1) The Landlord's rent was provided not by advancing production beyond the point at which the tillers' wants had been satisfied; it was provided by depressing the consumption of the tillers to the lowest level compatible with continued existence. (2) The grass-farmer who needed a minimum quantity of labour for a maximum number of acres was the natural enemy of all tillage-farmers and especially the cottagers. (3) Any failure of the potato crop brought immediate disaster to the mass of the population. (4) If such a failure coincided with a rise in grass-farming, a trade slump, or any other curtailment of the demand for labour, literally the only choice for the peasantry was between begging, stealing, and absolute starvation.

In that masterpiece of blazing indignation disguised as smooth-faced irony—his *Modest Proposal* to use the children of the poor as butcher's meat for the rich—Jonathan Swift envisages just such a state of things:

"I have already computed the charge of nursing a beggar's child *(in which list I reckon all Cottagers, Labourers, and four-fifths of the Farmers)* to be about two shillings per annum, *rags included*, and I believe no gentleman would repine to give Ten Shillings for the carcass of a good fat child, which as I have said, will make four dishes of nutritive meat when he hath only some particular friend or his own family to dine with him. Thus the squire will learn to be a good landlord and grow popular among his tenants, the mother will have eight shillings net profit and be fit for work till she produces another child."

Swift, it will be noted, so defines the "Beggars" as to include five-sixths of the rural population. He goes on to drive the point home: "I grant this food will be somewhat dear and therefore *very proper for landlords* who as they have already devoured most of the Parents seem to have the best title to the children."

He turns the point against England: "This kind of commodity will not bear exportation, the flesh being of too tender a consistence to admit a long continuance in salt, although perhaps *I could name a Country which would be glad to eat up our whole nation without it.*"

Swift, no doubt, exaggerated; but not so much—only enough to make his thrust go right home.

CHAPTER VI

GRATTAN'S REVOLUTION

English Colonial policy begot an inevitable result in the revolt of the American colonies, who declared themselves Independent, July 4, 1776. The war which resulted gave the Anglo-Irish colony its chance to enforce (1) Freedom to Trade (1780), and (2) Legislative Independence (1782). This enforcement constitutes Grattan's Revolution.

The crisis was led up to by popular agitations (1) among the urban trading community, and (2) among the rural population.

Urban Agitations

In the first third of the 18th century, no combined action including both the Anglo-Irish colony and the subjected Irish agrarian community was conceivable. Within the colony there was furious discontent among the manufacturers and traders at the restraints upon trade, and at the acquiescence therein of the oligarchy. The agrarian (Irish) community was, at first, too disorganised by defeat to offer any general resistance. Struggle began in spontaneous local protests at particular hardships. Since, however, both the urban and rural struggles were, in practice, directed against one and the same ruling oligarchy, their continued development begot in the end a sense of community in struggle against a common enemy.

Much experience had to be gone through before the champions of the colony and of the *Gaeltacht* could think of each other as "fellow-countrymen". The champions of the "colony" against the English Government no more thought of themselves as "Gaels" when they called themselves "Irish" than Benjamin Franklin or George Washington identified themselves with the Sioux or the Iroquois when they called themselves "Americans". As a proportion of the Gaelic Irish became drawn into trade and manufactures by the penal obstructions to land-owning by Catholics, they became drawn likewise into echoing the traders' protests against English exactions and interference.

One of the earliest champions of the "colony" was Jonathan Swift (1667-1745), then Dean of St. Patrick's, Dublin. He joined in the protest against a flagrant job —the giving to an English iron-founder of the job of mint-ing a new copper coinage for Ireland—and helped to work the agitation up to fever pitch.

Writing ostensibly as a "Drapier", Swift in his first *Letter* attacked the project on utilitarian grounds—adopt-ing the (fallacious) popular belief that the currency in Ire-land would be permanently debased. In his second *Drapier's Letter*, Swift attacked those who granted the patent on public grounds—that it was a "job". He excited so much agreement that the Dublin Parliament was forced to join in his protest. When the English Parliament scorn-fully refused to take notice of clamour, Swift in his *Third Letter* took patriotic ground and asked—would anyone in England dare so to describe a protest by both Houses of the English Parliament? "Are not the Irish people, then, as free as the English? Is not their Parliament as repre-sentative?"

This raised the issue from a squabble about the relative values of two brass farthings into a question whether the Irish Parliament did or did not possess the right to control and mint its own coinage. In his *Fourth Letter*, addressed to the whole people of Ireland, Swift took a definitely Nationalist ground: "'Tis true indeed that within the memory of man the Parliaments of England have some-times assumed the power of binding this Kingdom by laws enacted there, wherein they were first opposed openly (so far as Truth, Reason, and Justice are capable of opposing) by the famous Mr. Molyneux, an English gentleman born here, as well as by several of the greatest patriots and best Whigs in England. But the love and torrent of power prevailed.

"Indeed the arguments on both sides were invincible. For, in Reason, *All Government without the consent of the Governed is the very definition of slavery;* but, in Fact, eleven men well armed will certainly subdue one single man in his shirt."

The issue is joined squarely: Ireland has the Right, but England has the Might. The logical deduction was too obvious to need statement.

Swift's *Modest Proposal* written a year later openly identified the landlord class with England and stigmatised both jointly as the implacable enemy of Ireland. Swift's Nationalism was exclusively "colonial"; but he cannot be denied his title of Father of Nationalism in Ireland. From the time of his *Drapier's Letters* a patriot opposition was never lacking in the Irish Parliament.

Agrarian Unrest and Revolts

We have noted earlier the complete dependence of the peasant upon his potato patch and cow. A word is necessary about the operation of the "middleman"—the speculator who leased land only to sub-lease it. An extension of this system begot a hierarchy of landlords broadening down from the great owners-in-chief at the apex to a mass of tenants at the base, all holding tiny plots as yearly tenants, tenants by labour service, or plain tenants at will. The wretched peasantry at the base carried on their backs a hierarchy of middlemen, three and four deep, with the great lord himself to cap all.

To add to their miseries a practice was introduced of putting tenancies, as they fell in, up to auction. The insecurity this created was a powerful lever for exacting the last possible farthing from the tenantry. And if, as frequently happened, the middleman saw a chance to let his land in large parcels for grass farming, the resultant eviction of the occupiers, and loss of employment, made the change-over as disastrous to the poor man as was the death of his cow or the failure of his potato crop.

Such a change-over on a large scale produced the first-recorded general uprising of the peasantry (1761) known as the White-boy conspiracy.

It first appeared, near Limerick, as a reply to an attempt by the landlords to enclose stretches of waste land which had been treated as common from time immemorial. This "waste" was indispensable to scores of peasants as grazing for their cows, sheep, goats, etc. Faced with this calamity the peasants turned out by night, threw down the walls, filled the trenches, ploughed up the meadows and restored the whole "waste" to its original condition. The landlords abandoned their attempt. From this successful beginning the Whiteboy movement spread through Munster into Connacht and Leinster.

From sporadic and occasional resistance to attempts to substitute grass-farming for tillage, the movement developed into a permanent resistance to rack-renters, evictors, land-grabbers, and tithe-proctors. Finally it offered resistance to landlord-employers who offered (and labourer-tenants who accepted) employment at less than a standard rate.

The methods of the Whiteboys were frequently terroristic. Threatening letters were followed up by domiciliary visits and physical vengeance. Murder was rare; but bludgeoning, and such punishments as being flung naked into a pit filled with thorns, were common. More highly-placed offenders suffered the maiming of their cattle.

Whatever might be said against the barbarity of their methods, it remains a fact that the Whiteboys (so called from wearing shirts outside their garments as a disguise) did function as a Tenants' Protection Society and an Agricultural Labourers' Union, and did establish a code of agrarian solidarity which became generally observed.

From the circumstances in which they operated, the Whiteboy organisation never advanced far beyond a loose aggregation of self-contained local secret societies. They developed in time a species of free-masonry with signs and passwords whereby the members of one local society could make themselves known as confederates to those of other localities; and, in the form of a dispersed aggregate of Ribbon Lodges, the organisation survived down to the end of the 19th century.

From 1761 to 1778 the landlords and the Authorities waged perpetual war against the Whiteboys. Military expeditions were led against them. Suspects were taken and hanged in scores. Acts were passed imposing frightful penalties—including death—for administering or taking the Whiteboy oath of fidelity. All of them failed. As often as Whiteboyism was reported "exterminated" in one locality it reappeared in another. Even the cynical Lord Chesterfield, when Viceroy, was moved to observe that if the military had shot half as many landlords as they had hanged Whiteboys it would have been twice as good for the peace of the country.

The spontaneous origin of the Whiteboy movement from economic causation is proved by the appearance of parallel movements in Ulster. As a Protestant tenantry was involved these were usually less ferociously repressed than were the Whiteboys.

The Oakboys appeared in Monaghan in 1762—spreading thence into Tyrone and Armagh—as a revolt against the exaction of forced labour for the repair and upkeep of roads. Catholics and Protestants joined in this movement which was finally suppressed only after a bloody battle in Armagh in which the Oakboys were defeated. This notwithstanding, they won their point. Thereafter a money-rate was levied instead of forced labour.

The Steelboys were Protestants of Antrim and Down who put up (1764) a mass resistance to fines for the renewal of tenancies, to rack-rents, to tithes, and to an attempt to introduce grass-farming. They were strong enough to march into Belfast, break open the gaol, and liberate some of their number who had been captured. Juries in Belfast refused to convict Steelboys and, when the venue of trial was changed to Dublin, juries there also refused to convict.

In the end, however, the landlords were strong enough to drive most of them to emigrate to America.

These Agrarian struggles testified to an unrest which gave added force to the opposition waged in Parliament against the landed oligarchy on other grounds. They prepared the way for a National movement.

The Volunteers

In the American War of Independence the sympathies of Irishmen were almost unanimously on the side of the Americans, whose grievances were very similar to those of the "colony". The war, too, brought distress to Ireland by automatically cutting off a profitable linen-trade, and this was intensified when the English Government banned all exports of provisions (barrelled beef and pork). When the Irish Parliament agreed to place all the troops in Ireland at the disposal of the Crown, and voted money to raise regiments specially for service against the Americans, it brought a hailstorm of indignation about its ears.

This indignation was given its lever to work with when France and Spain took the opportunity (1778) to join in the war on the side of the Americans; and when the Administration had to warn Belfast that a descent by a combined French and American fleet upon the North of Ireland might be anticipated at any moment. The Administration confessed that, as it had sent all its troops to England or to America, it had none to place at Belfast's disposal. It recommended the citizens to provide for their own defence.

The citizens of Belfast rose to the occasion. Within a surprisingly short time several regiments of Volunteers were raised. All were uniformed, armed, equipped, and supplied with cannon by public subscription. The Volunteers elected their own officers and started intensive training at once.

Belfast's example proved contagious. Town corporations and County Grand Juries took the lead and by the middle of 1779 fifty thousand volunteers were embodied; by the end of the year there were a hundred thousand with 130 pieces of cannon.

This Volunteering enthusiasm transformed the political situation. The will and ability of the citizens to defend themselves contrasted sharply with the confessed inability of the Administration; and, in turn, it derived added significance from the failure of the English Government to hold its own against the American Colonies. The war being nearly as unpopular in England as it was in Ireland, the possibility of the Irish Administration's getting military support from England could be disregarded.

The altered situation gave an opening for the free expression of every Irish grievance. In imitation of the Americans, "non-importation associations" began to be formed, whose members were pledged neither to use themselves nor to associate or trade with those who used, or traded in, goods imported from England. Every meeting to raise recruits for the Volunteers became an agitation meeting; every meeting of Volunteers to elect officers became an organisation meeting; every meeting of officers to plan drills, parades, etc., became a caucus meeting of the mass opposition party in which the Parliamentary leaders of the Patriot Opposition figured prominently from the start.

The Government could do nothing. It tried to start a scare that, under cover of Volunteering, the Catholics were securing arms. The Opposition leaders countered this by requesting the Catholics to refrain from Volunteering. The Catholics complied; and in addition raised large sums of money to buy equipment for the Protestant Volunteers. The Government thus, in trying to divide Protestants and Catholics, promoted their union. The laws which debarred the more well-to-do Catholics from large-scale landowning and from the professions had caused the more well-to-do Catholics to put their sons to trade and manufacture, and when the test came bourgeois class-solidarity overrode sectarian divisions. This enthusiasm of the Catholic bourgeoisie for the common cause—for the common struggle against the restraints upon trade, and against the English Government and Parliament which imposed them—communicated itself to the Catholic countryside; and so was created the ground-plan for a united Irish Nation in modern form.

In places, the ban upon Catholic entry into the Volunteers was disregarded. In Dublin, a popular small proprietor and trader, James Napper Tandy, a Protestant democrat, whose championship of the Catholics on the Dublin Corporation had earned him the title of "Tribune of the Plebs", got round the difficulty ingeniously. He formed a corps of Volunteer Artillery into which he recruited Catholic artisans freely, arguing that they could not be said either to possess the cannon (which legally belonged to him as Treasurer) and still less to carry them. Tandy's humorous ingenuity was a joke enjoyed by all Ireland outside Dublin Castle.

Henry Grattan and his Leadership

Henry Grattan (1750-1820), a young Dublin barrister and small proprietor, had risen by his eloquence and zeal for the Volunteers to the recognised leadership of the Patriot Opposition in Parliament. In October 1779, he voiced the growing National demand by moving an amendment to the Address demanding a free export trade.

The time was well chosen. The disastrous course of the American War had reduced the power and political credit of the English Government to a minimum. All England was a ferment of discontent. With no possibility of aid from England the Irish Administration was totally unable to face a front-to-front trial of strength with the Opposition. Several of the leading borough-mongers had deserted them. The lower ranks of the aristocracy and most of the gentry were on the popular side. Consequently the debate on Grattan's motion resolved itself into a competition, in which placemen joined, to see who could best amend the amendment into the strongest possible expression of the popular demand. It passed, finally and unanimously, as an unequivocal demand for Free Trade.

Unable to resist openly, the Administration played for time: the Viceregal reply was evasive. The popular retort was not. Parading a few days later at the customary celebration of William of Orange's birthday (November 4) around his statue on College Green, Captain Napper Tandy's Artillery carried placards depending from the muzzles of their cannon reading: "Free Trade; or else————!"* The House of Commons underlined the point by granting supplies for six months only.

The English Government gave way. In December 1779, and January 1780, Acts were rushed through the English Parliament abolishing nearly all restraints upon Irish trade.

Flushed with their victory, the Opposition, backed by the Volunteers, pressed forward with new demands. In April 1780, Grattan moved a resolution denying the right of the English Parliament to legislate for Ireland. The Administration secured a postponement of the vote. The Opposition then introduced a Mutiny Bill in identical

* Legend tells of an exchange between two great Irish *Ri-mor:* "Pay me my Tribute, or else————!" "I owe you no Tribute, and if————!"

terms with the English Army (Annual) Act which was held, in England, to apply in Ireland. The intention was to put the English Government in a dilemma. If they rejected the Act, they would bring on a direct conflict with the Irish Parliament. If they accepted it they accepted in principle the claim of the Opposition to the Legislative Independence of Ireland. The Privy Council threw the dilemma back upon the Irish Parliament by accepting the Bill with the clause limiting its operation to one year struck out. The Opposition, under protest, accepted the mutilated Act and returned to the attack with a Habeas Corpus Act. This the Privy Council accepted without alteration.

The English Government had, in fact, lost all power of resisting. Its last army of any size had surrendered to Washington; the American War had as good as ended in total defeat. It was merely a question of how long Premier Lord North could delay the inevitable coming to power of the Whigs.

The Patriot Opposition filled in the interval with a Catholic Relief Bill which repealed the Penal prohibitions which debarred Catholics from bequeathing, inheriting, or purchasing estates, and from taking leases of 999 years. The coming to power of the Whigs in England ensured the Bill's acceptance by the Privy Council.

Meanwhile, the Volunteer agitation proceeded. On February 15, 1782, a Convention of 243 delegates from every Volunteer corps in Ulster met in Dungannon, County Tyrone, and carried with virtual unanimity the following resolutions, among others:

"(1) The claim of any body of men other than the King, Lords, and Commons of Ireland to make laws to bind this Kingdom is unconstitutional, illegal, and a grievance.

"(2) The Powers exercised by the Privy Council ... under pretence of the Law of Poynings, are unconstitutional and a grievance.

"(3) As men, as Irishmen, as Christians, and as Protestants, we rejoice in the relaxation of the Penal Laws against our Roman Catholic fellow-subjects, and we conceive the measure to be fraught with the happiest consequences to the union and prosperity of the inhabitants of Ireland."

Similar resolutions were adopted by similar conventions in the other three provinces.

Thus mandated, Grattan in Parliament moved (February 1782) a Declaration of Irish Right. The Administration once again contrived a delay; but it was only momentary. Led by Charles James Fox, a friend of Grattan and his policy, the English Whigs were of one mind with the Irish Opposition. Accordingly the Irish Parliament met on April 19, 1782, specially summoned "to consider Irish grievances".

Grattan made his way to the House through streets lined with Volunteers in parade uniform, who presented arms as he passed, while their cannon roared a salute. For the third time he moved his Declaration; and this time there was no resistance. The Declaration was adopted by acclamation, and the English Government and Parliament at once complied with Acts (May 1782) which conceded all Grattan's demands.

The Irish Parliament celebrated its new-won freedom by limiting the Mutiny Act to two years. As an appreciation of the Revolution he had accomplished, Parliament voted Grattan £50,000 to purchase an estate. He could have had double but was satisfied with this.

Flood: and the Convention of 1783

At this critical stage in the struggle, the Opposition was split and Grattan's leadership was frustrated by a "Leftist" drive headed by Henry Flood.

Grattan had known perfectly well that, if the English Government had resisted his demands, his next step would have been necessarily to overthrow the Irish Administration by the armed force of the Volunteers. This step he was prepared to take, though he knew that it carried with it the risk that the movement would grow beyond his power to control it. The timely surrender of the English Government gave him the chance to shift the struggle to a new plane and begin a purely Parliamentary struggle for instalments of reform which would leave political power in the hands of the smaller landed gentry in alliance with the wealthier traders and merchants. Like all his class Grattan had a horror of democracy; but he was eager to broaden the base of the property interests represented in Parliament by including Catholics as voters, and among those qualified for sitting in Parliament. To achieve reform while keeping the movement within moderate bounds it was necessary to keep the more radical elements in the Volunteers under the leadership of a political alliance of the progressive aristocracy and the moderate bourgeoisie.

Flood upset this plan by affecting to believe that a simple repeal of the Act which had asserted the right of the English Parliament to legislate for Ireland was not enough. He demanded an express Renunciation of that claim.

This line, as Flood knew, was bound to be popular with the Volunteer rank and file because of their ingrained suspicion of English statesmen; and it had the further advantage that it enabled Flood and his aristocratic allies to pose, without risk, as being far more "revolutionary" than Grattan himself, or his bourgeois supporters.

Grattan thought the demand for Renunciation bad in principle and worse in practice. It made Ireland's Right dependent on an English Act of Parliament; and it imperilled the Party Grattan was building up with such care. Soon the rival Harrys were treating the House to a display of Billingsgate, after which they would have gone out to pistol each other if they had not been restrained by force. In the end Grattan was beaten by a rally to Flood of the extreme Right as well as the extreme Left. Within a few months of receiving public thanks for his services Grattan found himself deserted by the Volunteers and by the bulk of the Opposition.

The English Parliament showed what it thought or the dispute by passing the Renunciation Act (1783) with hardly a word of debate.

Flood followed up his victory by manoeuvring to get control of the crucial Volunteer Convention which met in Dublin in November 1783. Like Grattan, Flood was the son of a legal dignitary; unlike Grattan, he was a man of wealth with connections with the upper strata of the aristocracy. He and his friend, Lord Charlemont, the Volunteer Commander-in-Chief, were able to pull sufficient wires to secure the election of a majority of delegates favourable to their point of view.

The Convention was virtually unanimous in favour of a programme of Parliamentary reforms—Ministerial responsibility to the House; the exclusion of placemen and pensioners; and an extension of the suffrage with elimination of "rotten" boroughs. The real crux came with the question whether the Catholics should be admitted to the vote and to Parliament. The genuine Radicals, led by the Belfast delegation, were ardently in favour of Catholic Emancipation. Flood and the "fake" Radicals were as determinedly hostile. In the end Flood gained a majority (with the aid of notorious Castle hacks and placemen who had contrived to get elected as delegates).

Having won his point Flood worked a characteristic stunt. He proposed that while he and the other M.P.s then present should carry the Convention's Reform demands to the House, as they were, in Volunteer uniform, the Convention should continue permanently in session to await an answer.

There was literally no point in the proposal unless

Flood was prepared to reply to a refusal by calling for, and leading, an immediate resort to armed insurrection by the thousands of Volunteers then assembled in Dublin. A large proportion of the delegates were ready for this; but the House knew perfectly well that Flood had no such intention and, accordingly, refused flatly to consider proposals "presented at the point of the bayonet". Flood despite his "revolutionary" posturing could do nothing but return to the Convention and propose an adjournment to "consider the situation". The Convention met several times more, but its spirit had evaporated. After prolonged wrangling it dispersed–disillusioned, disorganised, and demoralised.

The Volunteers and the Radical movement they had fostered declined rapidly from that moment. And with the collapse of the Volunteers Flood lost his momentary significance. He introduced his Reform Bill as a private member's motion; but, while it was given a debate, it was heavily defeated–as everybody had foreseen.

As Flood sank swiftly into obscurity, Grattan patiently set to work to rebuild the Party Flood had shattered. The Reform agitation did not really revive, however, until entirely new men had set on foot an entirely new movement.

CHAPTER VII

THE RISE OF THE UNITED IRISHMEN

What the American Revolution was to Grattan and the Volunteers, the French Revolution was to the Society of United Irishmen (1791-1798) led by Theobald Wolfe Tone (1763-1798). The great achievement of the United Irishmen was that of combining Catholics and Protestants. Thus they secured the largest single instalment of Catholic Emancipation ever known. How they did it, and what followed thencefrom is told in this chapter.

Ireland in 1790-1

Though balked in their main desires the Grattanite Whigs secured some reforms of advantage to the economic development of Ireland. They secured Protection for Irish manufactures and a Corn Law which—by checking imports and encouraging exports by a bounty when the price was low, and reversing the procedure when the price was high—secured a stable market for Irish-grown wheat at a satisfactory price.

This made grain-growing profitable on all but the smallest holdings, and made for the general prosperity of the farming community; which prosperity in turn provided a brisk market for home manufactures. The prosperity was, of course, unequal. The trend towards grain-growing and away from grass-farming was a gain for the labourers and cottagers, but the intensified competition for good arable land caused a general rise in rents. The repeal of the restrictions on Catholic landowning caused some increase of Catholic proprietors on the land; at the same time the new prosperity of manufacturers caused an influx of the Protestant "gentry" into that field. In town and in country the intermingling of Catholics and Protestants was promoted.

In the south of Ireland, in 1760, it was asserted that the bulk of the business of money-lending was in Catholic hands. In the North, the craftsmen and manufacturers were predominantly Dissenters; but Catholics also were well represented. In short, economic development had destroyed a great deal of the segregation which the Penal Code had been designed to create. This was seen in the frequent combination of Catholics with Protestants in agitations for reform. Even the Munster Whiteboys, it was rumoured, were beginning to find Protestants to lead them.

Such was the general background for the rise of the Society of United Irishmen in 1791 under the leadership of Theobald Wolfe Tone.

Theobald Wolfe Tone

Tone was born in Dublin, on June 20, 1763, the son of a coachbuilder whose father had been a substantial freeholder in Co. Kildare. The family came of Cromwellian planter stock. Tone, the eldest son, had been educated for a barrister. The law had few attractions for him; but, having contracted an early marriage, he was drudging at his profession when the thunderclap of the French Revolution aroused him as it did everybody else: "Two years before," he writes in his Autobiography, "the nation was in lethargy... As the revolution advanced, and as events expanded themselves, the public spirit of Ireland rose with a rapid acceleration. The fears and animosities of the aristocracy rose in the same or in a higher proportion. In a little time the French Revolution became the test of every man's political creed, and the nation was fairly divided into two great parties, the Aristocrats and the Democrats... It is needless, I believe, to say I was a Democrat from the beginning."

His friend, Thomas Russell, an Army officer then stationed in Belfast, wrote, early in 1791, telling Tone of a proposal to celebrate the second anniversary of the taking of the Bastille, and asking him to draft resolutions suited to the occasion. Tone responded with a resolution embodying three propositions: (1) That English influence in Ireland is the great grievance of the country. (2) That the most effective way to oppose it is by a reform in Parliament. (3) That no reform would be just or efficacious which did not include the Catholics.

Learning that his third proposition had met with opposition, Tone at once set to work upon a pamphlet, entitled *An Argument on Behalf of the Catholics of Ireland by a Northern Whig*. He aimed, he tells us, at convincing the Dissenters: "That they and the Catholics had but one common interest and one common enemy; that the depression and slavery of Ireland was produced and perpetuated by the divisions existing between them; and that consequently to assert the independence of their country, and their own individual liberties it was necessary to forget all former feuds, to consolidate the entire strength of the whole nation, and form for the first time but one people."

Tone confesses that he was "not a little proud" of his work which, in a few weeks, produced remarkable results. He was called to Belfast to assist in forming (October 1791) the Society of United Irishmen, for which he wrote an invitation from the Catholic Committee in its statement of objects. Then, more unexpectedly, he received Dublin to take up the post of salaried agent for that body.

Both these events were to prove momentous.

The Society of United Irishmen declared itself as "constituted for the purpose of forwarding a Brotherhood of Affection, a Communion of Rights, and a Union of Power among Irishmen of every religious persuasion, and thereby to obtain a complete Reform in the Legislature, founded on the Principles of civil, political and religious liberty." Thus the Society took as its point of departure what had been the high-water mark of the Volunteers' agitation defeated in 1783. But, although the founders had contacts with the few Volunteer regiments then surviving, it is noteworthy that they went beyond the Volunteers and aimed at a political party organisation recruited directly among the people at large. It pre-dated by a year the formation of its nearest English counterpart, the London Corresponding Society, which, by general consent, was the starting-point of all organised working-class radical-democratic and revolutionary political struggle in England.

While the immediate object of the Society was Parliamentary Reform, it was well understood, by those nearest to Tone, that he desired that reform as a means to a wider end: "To subvert the tyranny of our execrable Government; to break the connection with England, the never-failing source of all our political evils; and to assert the independence of my country—these were my objects. To unite the whole people of Ireland, to abolish the memory of past dissensions, and to substitute the common name of *Irishman* in place of the denominations of Protestant, Catholic, and Dissenter—these were my means."

For that reason the invitation from the Catholic Committee—the recognised mouthpiece of all the Catholics in Ireland—was doubly welcome. It was welcome, in itself, as offering Tone lucrative employment at a congenial task. It was still more welcome as evidencing a profound change in the political temperature of the Catholic Committee.

Till then the Committee had pursued the policy of currying favour with the Crown through the Viceroy, hoping in that way to secure protection against the bigoted animosity of the ruling oligarchy, in Parliament and out of it. Their invitation to Tone proved a complete change of attitude. Previously they had begged for favours as a sect. Now they were preparing to demand their rights as citizens. That, in itself, was a revolutionary change which delighted Tone beyond words. He had expressed his opinion of Grattan's "Revolution" in his *Argument* in words which the Catholic Committee had read and noted: "The Revolution of '82 was a revolution which enabled Irishmen to sell at a much higher price their honour, their integrity, and the interests of their country; it was a revolution which while at one stroke it doubled the value of every boroughmonger in the Kingdom, left three-fourths of our countrymen [the Catholics] slaves as it found them, and the Government of Ireland in the base, wicked and contemptible hands who had spent their lives plundering and degrading her ... Who of the veteran enemies of the country lost his place, or his pension? Not one. The power remained in the hands of our enemies, again to be exerted for our ruin, with this difference, that, formerly, we had our distresses *gratis* at the hands of England, but now we pay very dearly to receive the same with aggravations at the hands of Irishmen—yet this we boast of and call a Revolution."

To have seen this fact so clearly showed penetration; to have stated it so boldly showed courage; but to have got Belfast Protestants and Dissenters to applaud the statement, and to take action upon it, and simultaneously to have produced an equivalent response from the leaders of the Catholic community showed that Tone possessed political genius of a very high order.

The Rights of Man in Ireland

Tone himself, as modest as he was fearless, attributed the result wholly to the French Revolution; and, indeed, it is difficult to over-estimate the delivering power of that Titanic event. To it must be attributed the immediate and rapid spread of the Society of United Irishmen. Within a month (November 1791) Tone, Russell, and Napper Tandy were assisting other notables to found a Dublin Society; and thereafter the two Societies of Belfast and Dublin were the twin parent-societies of a rapidly proliferating organisation. Belfast made contacts most readily with Protestants; Dublin most readily with the Catholics. Between them they began to spread a network of affiliated individuals and local societies throughout the country.

They propagated their views, 18th century fashion, in after-dinner discussions among an invited company, or in meetings specially summoned to discuss addresses and resolutions on topics of the day. Their primary contacts were among professionals, merchants, and manufacturers, with a sprinkling of the more progressive gentry; but from the first they had a profound effect upon the substantial working-farmers, the independent artisan-craftsmen, and the work-people employed by the leading members of the Society.

At its foundation the Society stood broadly on the principles of Paine's *Rights of Man* (first published, 1792) which work, Tone notes with glee, at once became the "Koran" of Belfast. Its programme soon grew specific; and eventually included the points (also approved by the English and Scottish "Jacobin" Societies) of: (1) Manhood suffrage; (2) Equal electoral districts; (3) No property qualification; (4) Annual Parliaments; and (5) Payment of Members. That is to say the United Irishmen anticipated the programme of the English Chartists by half a century and secured for this programme a mass support which far exceeded the support obtained, until much later, by the English Radicals.

The United Irishmen did not confine themselves to purely political demands. They declared for the abolition of church establishments, and of tithes; for resistance to rack-rents; and, ultimately, for sweeping measures of agrarian reform. Through their organ, the *Northern Star* (founded by Samuel Neilson in Belfast early in 1792) they gave a cordial welcome on their first appearance to Mary Wollstonecraft's *Vindication of the Rights of Woman* and to Paine's *Age of Reason*.

Their internationalism was not less pronounced than their nationalism. They corresponded cordially with the Jacobin Society in Paris, and reported its proceedings regularly in their journal. They sent a delegation to the British National Convention (1792) and when Thomas Muir, the Scottish Jacobin, was sentenced to fourteen years' transportation the Belfast Society made him an honorary member. The progress of the revolution in France—the overthrow of the monarchy, the foundation of a Republic, the victories of the conscript armies—all received enthusiastic applause from the United Irishmen.

Tone (a good barometer) notes in his diary on August 19, 1792: "The King of France dethroned; very glad of it, for now the people have fair play. What will the Army do? God send they stand by the Nation. Everything depends on the line they will take."

He records the execution of Louis XVI almost with indifference: "The King of France was beheaded (January 21, 1793). I am sorry it was necessary."

Taken altogether it is clear that the object aimed at by the Society of United Irishmen was well summed up by Tone in his phrase: "the establishment of the Rights of Man in Ireland."

Tone and the Catholic Committee

Before Tone took up his work with the Catholic Committee it had undergone an internal revolution. Tired of the timid, cringing policy of the Catholic lords and ecclesiastics who, till then, had dominated its counsels and dictated its policy, a wealthy Dublin merchant, John Keogh, advocated a bolder course. He proposed an Address to Parliament direct, calling attention to Catholic grievances, and demanding redress as a right.

The peers were horrified; the bishops were scandalised; timid laymen predicted every calamity. Tone compares the struggle to the victorious uprising of the Third Estate in France: "Their peers, their gentry (as they affect to call themselves), and their prelates, either seduced by the Government or intimidated, gave the measure all possible opposition. At length, after a long conflict ... the question was decided on a division by a majority of at least six to one in favour of the intended application."

The defeated Catholic aristocrats and prelates withdrew. Timid as hares in the face of English authority, they were raging lions against the "mutinous" Catholic laymen. When the Committee's petition was presented to Parliament (with a supporting petition from the United Irishmen of Belfast) it was confronted with a counter-petition from the seceders denying the right of the Committee to speak for the Catholic community. Reactionaries in Parliament were delighted to have so plausible an excuse for rejecting the plea with studied insult.

On Tone's advice the Committee adopted a plan to secure a properly representative Committee. Delegates elected by parishes would meet to elect county and town representatives who when assembled in Dublin would be in effect a "Parliament" of the Catholics of Ireland.

The Reactionaries fell into a panic. Led by Lord Chancellor John Fitzgibbon, Earl of Clare (a rancorous bigot and anti-democrat), all the Judges on Circuit laboured mightily to induce all the Grand Juries to adopt resolutions denouncing the scheme. The Catholic bishops, alarmed, added their condemnation; parish priests followed suit.

Again acting on Tone's advice, the Committee sent its most influential members to tour the provinces, to win over bishops, priests, and laymen to the project. Tone himself, who had toured Ulster to gain support for the United Irishmen, now toured Leinster, Connacht, and parts of Ulster to secure support for the Catholic Convention; generally with John Keogh. So well did they work that the bishops withdrew their ban, the priests came over, and the elections proceeded with enthusiasm.

To us, delegate conventions are commonplace things; in the autumn of 1792 they were "portents dire". In fact the very name "Convention", which popular usage fastened upon the assembly, underlines the fact that, while the delegates were being elected in Ireland, the National Convention was being elected in France. For world-background the Catholic Convention had the upsurge of the Jacobin Republic in France, the storming of the Tuileries, the purging of the prisons, the rush of the conscript levies to clear the frontiers, the cannonade at Valmy; and all to the crashing rhythms of the *Carmagnole* and the *Marseillaise*.

A passage in Tone's diary, though expressed in terms of jest, gives a revealing glimpse of the public excitement engendered by the discussions, public and private, incidental to the elections of delegates to the Convention: "November 9 '92. At court [i.e. the Four Courts, Dublin]. Wonderful to see the rapid change in the minds of the Bar on the Catholic question. Some for an immediate abolition of all penal laws. Certainly the most magnanimous mode and the wisest. All sorts of men, and especially lawyer Plunkett [afterwards Irish Lord Chancellor] take a pleasure in girding at Mr. Hutton [Tone] 'who takes at once all their seven points in his buckler, thus.' Exceeding good laughing. Mr. Hutton called Marat. Sundry barristers apply to him for protection in the approaching rebellion. Lawyer Plunkett applies for Carton [the Duke of Leinster's country seat, near Maynooth]. Mr. Hutton refuses inasmuch as the Duke of Leinster* is his friend, but offers him Curraghmore [the Marquis of Waterford's seat]. This he does to have a rise out of Marcus Beresford [brother of the Marquess] who is at his elbow listening. Great laughter thereat. The Committee charged with causing the non-consumption agree-

* Duke of Leinster: elder brother of Lord Edward Fitzgerald, and cousin to Charles James Fox.

ment against Bellingham beer. Mr. Hutton at the risk of his life asserts the said charge to be a falsehood! Valiant! All declare their satisfaction thereat! Everything looks as well as possible. Huzza!"*

And again the next day, without jesting: "Hear that Government is very much embarrassed what to do ... The Chancellor talks big. If he attempts to use violent measures I believe a war will be the inevitable consequence. My own conviction is that the Government must concede."

The Catholic Convention

On the day appointed (December 3, '92) 244 delegates assembled: representing every county in Ireland, forty large provincial towns, and the City of Dublin. No assembly even nearly so representative had met in Ireland since the "Patriot" Parliament of 1689.

The spirit of the assembly was in proportion. The first resolution declared the Convention "the sole body competent to voice the opinions of Catholic Ireland". After this repudiation of the aristocratic and ecclesiastical seceders, the Convention settled down to debate the kind of petition to be adopted. It was decided to have done with all half-measures and demand, boldly, that Catholics should be restored to a "position of equality with Protestants".

The next question was: to whom should the petition be presented? Amid thunderous applause, a delegate proposed to pass over all the middlemen and present the petition to the King himself. A query was raised whether this course might not be deemed "disrespectful to the Administration". Amid redoubled enthusiasm the mover

* Tone's diary was written for the information and amusement of his family circle—his wife, his sister, and his friend Russell. The name "John Hutton" was a family joke; the real owner of that name being a coachbuilder, a trade rival of Tone's father.

answered: "It is intended to be so." The proposal was adopted unanimously.

A delegation was appointed to carry the petition to the King; and then, before adjourning, the Convention first adopted and approved a Vindication of the Catholic Committee drafted by Tone, and then carried a unanimous vote of thanks to the citizens of Belfast, "To whom," said a delegate, "we owe it that we meet here in safety."

This was no figure of speech; and it was more than a formal compliment to the contingent of Belfast Volunteers who had mounted guard over the Convention. It was a recognition that it was the resolute attitude of Belfast, led by the United Irishmen, which alone had prevented the Chancellor from attempting violent measures.

The Catholic Relief Act (1793)

Tone accompanied the delegation to the King. The state of the winds and tides induced the delegates to travel *via* Donaghadee and Stranraer. This entailed passing through Belfast, and there they met a royal reception. Met at the City boundary, they were entertained at the leading hotel, and then escorted on their way amid enthusiastic plaudits from all the democrats in Belfast. The horses were removed, and wealthy merchants vied with artisans in competition for places at the drag-ropes. At the boundary they were sped on their way with cheers and loud wishes for their success.

Belfast is often enjoined to "Remember 1690". When it again recovers a pride in remembering 1792, Ireland's day of final deliverance will be at hand.

Arrived in London the delegates would not allow themselves to be swayed from their purpose. They saw the King, were "received graciously", and returned convinced they had not had their work for nothing. They were right. They had barely reached Dublin again when the Viceroy informed Parliament that the King "recommended a consideration of the situation of the Roman Catholics". The English Government, foreseeing war with France, had decided to force the hands of the Irish Administration.

Grudgingly the Administration gave way; but even then they wriggled out of conceding the complete emancipation which would have been "both magnanimous and wise". By backstairs methods they induced Keogh and a majority of the Committee to accept less than "equality with Protestants".

Tone was so furious that he nearly broke with Keogh. He gave in at last—there was no help for it—and contented himself with noting in his diary: "Merchants, I see, make bad revolutionaries."

With all its faults the Catholic Relief Act (1793) remains the largest single instalment of emancipation ever gained for the Catholics of Ireland. It virtually swept away all that was left of the Penal Code, except that, while it conceded the vote, it denied Catholics the right to sit in Parliament and to enter the higher grades of the law, the Civil Service, the Army and Navy. Incidentally it also removed the Sacramental test which had banned Dissenters as well as Catholics from public service. It coupled every concession, it is true, with petty restrictions; but on the whole it gave so much relief that Keogh and the Committee felt satisfied they had got as much as it was reasonable to expect at one blow.

Before it finally adjourned the Committee voted £1,500 and a gold medal to Tone as a mark of esteem and gratitude for his invaluable help.

Tone was greatly pleased. But he would have been more pleased still if they had stood out to the last and made a fight of it.

CHAPTER VIII

THE WAR UPON THE UNITED IRISHMEN

In February 1793, before the Catholic Relief Act became law, war was declared with the French Republic. The Government took this as a chance to wage war also with the United Irishmen. As a result, the Society was proclaimed illegal (May 1794) and driven underground. Tone was driven into exile. Open counter-revolution made its appearance with the Orange Society (September 1795).

This chapter describes the stages of this struggle.

The Programme of Reaction

The chance to declare war upon France (created by the execution of Louis XVI, January 21, 1793) was also a chance for the counter-revolutionary bigots in the Administration, with their hangers-on, to obtain revenge for the concessions they had been forced to make to the Catholics. The English Prime Minister William Pitt (1759-1806) favoured a policy of winning the well-to-do Catholics by concessions; but wartime exigencies compelled him to allow the "Protestant Ascendancy" bigots at the head of the Irish Administration a much freer hand than he would otherwise have done. This faction saw their chance to achieve their old end by a different road. By treating the United Irishmen and their allies as a "desperate Jacobin conspiracy" to be repressed at all costs, they hoped to win from the fears of the Catholic property-owners all that Pitt hoped to gain from their gratitude and expectations.

The risk involved in this policy was that the United Irishmen, till then a constitutional party, would become in fact what the Government alleged they were—a Jacobin Conspiracy—and this is what resulted. In the end, as we shall see, Pitt had to come to the rescue of the Irish Administration.

The Administration foreshadowed its programme in three Bills introduced concurrently with the debates on the Catholic Relief Act: (1) a Convention Act, (2) an Arms Act and (3) a Militia Act.

The first, which made all assemblies of delegates illegal, was designed to prevent the United Irishmen and the progressive Catholics from developing a political party by organising the newly emancipated Catholic voters. The second, by prohibiting the importation, manufacture, and sale of arms and gunpowder, was designed to cripple in advance any attempt at insurrection. The third was designed to provide a counter-revolutionary force with which to suppress any movement by the Volunteers or similar bodies. In this way all further advance by the United Irishmen was to be barred.

The Convention Act and the Volunteers

The Convention Act was prompted in part by the great success of the Catholic Convention; but it was also prompted by a fear of a repetition of the historic Dungannon (Volunteer) Convention of '82.

While the elections for the Catholic Convention were proceeding there had been notable signs of a Volunteer revival and of a movement towards re-creating '82 on a more radical plane.

As we have noted, there was, after the abortive Convention of 1783, a rapid decline in the numbers and significance of the Volunteers. The aristocrats and gentry who had commanded, and, in some cases, maintained corps of Volunteers, their end having been attained in '82, grew conservative thereafter; and, as far as possible, put an end to Volunteering and parading. The more popular corps which survived underwent a social change, as the more aristocratic officers and the more moderate members withdrew, and their places were taken by more democratic-bourgeois officers and a more plebeian rank and file. Grattan expressed the change forcibly: the Volunteers, he said, had been the "armed property" of Ireland: they were fast becoming its "armed beggary".

There were, it is true, still a Lawyers' corps in Dublin and Merchants' Corps in both Dublin and Belfast. But Grattan's point was made by the fact that these "respectable" corps held together expressly to provide a counterpoise against such non-respectable corps as Tandy's famous Dublin Artillery.

The outbreak of the French Revolution and the rise of the United Irishmen prompted somewhat of a revival in Volunteering in Belfast and Dublin. Many corps in other parts which had been in a state of suspended animation showed signs of reviving when, in September 1792, Napper Tandy supported by Tone and others recruited a new corps in Dublin, frankly modelled on the French National Guard. The uniform adopted was similar, except that dark green was used instead of blue, and a National cockade of green replaced the French tricolour. The buttons bore a cap of Liberty on a pike.

The new corps set an example the other Dublin corps followed. It refused to parade, decorated with orange ribbons, at William III's statue on November 4. Instead, all corps held an ordinary parade at their customary meeting-places, where, after discussion, it was agreed to hold a ceremonial parade a week later in honour of the French victories of Valmy and Jemappes. Citizens were also asked to illuminate their windows in honour of the occasion. The United Irishmen, for the same night, called a meeting to adopt an address of congratulation to the French Republic, and an address of exhortation to the Volunteers.

By a proclamation (in which penalties were threatened to all "seditious" associations) the parade and the meeting were both prohibited. The Authorities could not prevent the citizens from illuminating their windows—which most of them did—and the United Irishmen held a "private" meeting in a Volunteer drill hall at which the Address to the Volunteers was read.

The central point of this Address (which to the scandal of all reactionaries opened with the words "Citizen Soldiers") was a reminder to the Volunteers of the momentous consequences which had followed the Dungannon Convention of February 15, 1782: "The 15th of February approaches, a day ever memorable in the annals of the country as the birthday of a New Ireland. Let parochial meetings be held as soon as possible. Let each parish return delegates. Let the sense of Ulster be again declared from Dungannon, on a day auspicious to Union, Peace, and Freedom, and the Spirit of the North will again become the Spirit of the Nation... Fourteen long years have elapsed since the rise of your Associations [1778] and in 1782 did you imagine that in 1792 this Nation would still remain unrepresented? How many Nations in this interval have gotten the start of Ireland?"

For the publication of this Address the Chairman, William Drennan, and the Secretary, Archibald Hamilton Rowan, were both prosecuted on a charge of "sedition". Their trials were, however, postponed; they did not take place until more than a year later.

Meanwhile the anxiety of the Authorities was deepened by this call to revive the Volunteer agitation of 1782. A Convention, not confined to Volunteers, but elected by parishes, did, in fact, assemble at Dungannon on the historic date. Being a Sunday all the delegates—Catholics, Dissenters, and Episcopalians—attended the parish church and heard a sermon of cordial welcome and spirited exhortation from the rector of Dungannon. Next day the Convention assembled, and, after deliberating, issued a call for an All-Ireland Convention.

It was then that the Authorities introduced the Convention Act and rushed it into law.

When the Government had secured, along with the Arms Act, an augmentation of its Army from England, it proceeded to the next step–the suppression of the Volunteers.

Here the United Irishmen were patently caught napping. They had called the Volunteers, rhetorically, "to arms!" But they had made no preparations for doing so, in fact. Hence their position fell to a Governmental assault without a blow.

The Dublin Volunteer Corps all received (without warning) a peremptory order to deliver their cannon and stores of powder and ball to the Government "for safe keeping". The result was described by Henry Grattan, junior, in a single, sufficient sentence: "The Government seized by surprise the Artillery of the Liberty Corps, made a private arrangement by which it got possession of that of the Merchants' Corps; and induced the Lawyers' Corps to give up theirs–first making a public procession before they were surrendered."

Dublin being thus disposed of, it was the turn of Belfast. On the afternoon of Saturday, March 9, 1793, parties of the English dragoon regiments stationed in nearby camps swarmed into Belfast. Being ostensibly off-duty they made, first of all, for the taverns. Then, refreshed, they dispersed through the town in small parties and began to attack everything they thought offensive. Shop signs with the heads of Benjamin Franklin and George Washington, and anything green in any window, each and all provoked a furious assault. It was apparent that the dragoons were provided with lists of the addresses of leading United Irishmen. Their homes, and the printing office of the *Northern Star*, were attacked without scruple. Eventually the military rioters retired to the taverns for the night.

A town's meeting, hastily summoned, assembled at daybreak with the local Volunteers under arms as a guard. A collision between the dragoons and the Volunteers was averted by the arrival of the officer commanding the dragoon regiment. He agreed to march off the dragoons if the Volunteers were similarly withdrawn.

The Mayor sent protests to the Government and to the military authorities; but he got no sort of satisfaction. In succeeding weeks several renewals of the rioting occurred, including another attack on the *Northern Star*. The Mayor, protesting again, told the Government that the homes of leading citizens would have suffered "serious outrage" if they had not been guarded by Volunteers. The Government replied by suggesting, with brazen impudence, that the Volunteers had caused all the trouble. It removed all troops from the vicinity of Belfast; but it also ordered the Volunteers to surrender their arms and disband. One "respectable" corps protested that this was hard usage after their zeal in protecting a noble lord's eviction party which regular troops had refused to guard. But, as they were not prepared for an armed struggle with the authorities, all the Belfast corps submitted. They were disarmed and disbanded. So ended the Volunteers.

The Resistance to Militia Conscription

The Militia Act empowered the Government to raise a force of 15,000 men by the method then practised in England—the method of drawing lots, called balloting.

Even if the war had been popular, this highly haphazard method of selection would have excited protests. Great hardship was inflicted when breadwinners were taken away without compensation to their helpless dependants. As it was, with the peasants' sympathy wholly on the side of the French, resentment, protest, and resistance were almost universal.

The officers, too, were all drawn from the local Protestant landlords, squireens, and rack-renting middlemen.

Nothing would persuade the peasants otherwise than that the balloting was faked to make the lots fall upon those who had been boldest in defying these local tyrants; particularly in respect of electing delegates to the Catholic Committee, which these tyrants had tried to prevent. Once in the militia, it was believed, these victims would be spirited away to Botany Bay.

The very fact that they were to be called upon to fight the French was a grievance. Like themselves, the French were Catholics and a peasant people. That these French Catholic peasants had stormed, looted, and burned their landlords' chateaux, and chased the landlords from the country, might horrify London or Dublin Castle. It was glorious news for the Irish peasant, in whom each fresh French revolutionary "outrage" excited mounting admiration and envy.

Resistance to conscription became general. Regular military operations were required to break up the bands of peasants who took to the hills and defended themselves with desperate courage.

In Sligo, large companies forced their way into the homes of the gentry, took all the arms they could find, and drank "success to the French" in the gentry's own wine. Pitched battles were fought at Ballinafad, Sligo; at Enniskillen, Fermanagh; and at Athboy, Meath; in which latter place the troops were beaten up. In Wexford, conscripts were rescued by force, and the rescuers themselves were attacked and dispersed with many killed.

Near Baltinglass, Wicklow, the assembled peasants sent notice to the military-magistrate that his quota of conscripts was waiting for him to collect them—if he cared to take the risks entailed. He "prudently declined to obey the requisition".

The resistance was overcome after months of struggle, partly by terrorism, partly by concessions. The commander of the troops, Lord Carhampton, the head of the

Luttrell family—whose surname was a synonym for treachery among the Irish—led the way in trying the captured peasants by "courts martial" composed of the local gentry and squireens at which scores were sentenced, in defiance of all law, to terms of penal service in the King's Navy. The victims had no chance of legal assistance; they were flung in irons, into wagons, carted to the seaports, and put on board a man-of-war before they, or anybody, knew where they were going. Once entered upon the ship's books there was, in practice, no remedy. At a later date Parliament obliged with an Act of Indemnity absolving Lord Carhampton from the consequences of his barbarous illegalities.

Combined with coercion went concessions. Men with dependants were excused service; a fund was subscribed by the gentry to provide a bonus for every volunteer; the pay, and the dependants' allowance, were both increased. Gradually the resistance subsided, and the militia became embodied.

The United Irishmen and the Defenders

During this minor civil war in the West and parts of the South, it seemed evident to the Administration that the peasants' resistance was such as presupposed an organised leadership and direction. An understanding of the peasantry and their point of view would have forced the obvious inference that this was ready to hand in the Whiteboy quasi-freemasonry of the country-side and the survival of clan traditions. But an understanding of the peasants' point of view was as alien to the mentality and conventions of Dublin Castle as an understanding of the point of view of the Australian blackfellows was, at that date, to a Police Commissioner newly-arrived in Botany Bay. Authority jumped to the conclusion that the peasants' resistance was directed either by "the French" or by the United Irishmen. A House of Lords Committee was set up to fish for evidence, and several fierce legal tussles with the United Irishmen resulted.

Actually there was, at this date, very little connection between the United Irishmen—whose organisation was primarily located in the towns—and the self-contained, historically-evolved, peasants' secret societies. Such contacts as there were had arisen quite casually as incidental byproducts of the organisation of the elections of delegates to the Catholic Committee; and where they had arisen they had been of a totally different character from what the Authorities wished to suppose.

There had been, for example, bickering between Catholic and Protestant peasants in Co. Armagh, which had evolved into a feud between rival sectarian agrarian organisations in Armagh and Down, before the Society of United Irishmen was founded. It had arisen, in Armagh, through an influx of Catholic tenant-farmers seeking an escape from land-hungry Connacht. The newcomers, acting in ignorance, had rented farms which Protestants had abandoned rather than pay the increased rents and the exorbitant "fines" demanded for the renewals of leases. The action of the Catholic newcomers was resented as "black-legging"—as a breach of the traditional code of honour of the peasantry.

This dispute had been adjusted with satisfaction all round; but it had lasted long enough to give local bigots an excuse for attacking Catholic farmers not implicated in the original dispute, and raiding their farms under a pretext of searching for concealed arms. This practice spread from Co. Armagh into Co. Down; and from their habit of making their raids at break of day, the Protestant terrorists came to be known as Peep-of-Day Boys. Soon the Catholics responded with a counter organisation, the Defenders, who, being unable, legally, to buy arms, took a leaf out of their enemies' book and raided the homes of the gentry to procure arms.

So far we have a notable example of how, in special

circumstances, a spontaneously-arising defence-organisation of the peasantry—which, normally, would make for solidarity and mutual aid throughout the whole countryside—becomes differentiated into a bitter antagonism of rival organisations. To understand its further development there must be borne in mind the generally disturbing and antagonising effect produced by the middlemen who, intervening between the landlord at the top and the actual tiller at the bottom, imposed upon the latter conditions of increasing insecurity and fierce competition for good farming land. Needless to say, the more embittered the strife between Catholic and Protestant peasants—the more ready each side became to disregard the old Whiteboy code and bid against each other for farms—the better pleased these middlemen squireens became. The more often the farms changed hands the more they profited. Analysed to the bottom, the root cause of the feud between Peep-of-Day Boys and Defenders is found in the middlemen, and in the spread of their disintegrating rapacity from 1778 onwards. There can be no possible doubt that these squireens more than once revived the feud deliberately when it had lapsed and when, if left to itself, it would have died out. We shall have a classic example of this to deal with shortly. Here we note an instance of the opposite kind produced by the intervention of the United Irishmen and the Catholic leaders.

While engaged in organising the elections for the Catholic Committee, Tone and Keogh came upon a local feud between Defenders and Peep-of-Day Boys in County Down into which the local gentry had been drawn on both sides. They were able to induce both sides to agree to join in forming a Volunteer Corps which would act impartially to repress every would-be disturber of the peace. Urged forward by the United Irishmen and the Catholic leaders acting in conjunction, the policy had a striking success. In one place Peep-of-

Day Boys supplied a drill sergeant to teach the Defenders how to handle their weapons. In another place the situation was reversed—the Catholics lent their weapons to the Protestants and stood by applauding while a Catholic drill sergeant put them through their exercises.

The success of the policy was so great in Ulster that the irreconcilables had to go outside of Ulster into County Louth to keep the feud alive. And when Defender organisations sprang up in Louth, the Authorities took a hand in the game by prosecuting their leaders under the Whiteboy Acts.

At this point only did the Authorities find any evidence connecting the United Irishmen with the illegal side of the Defenders' activity. Napper Tandy, himself a Co. Louth man, was called upon for consultation by the Louth Defenders. But before they would divulge any details they made him take their customary oath of secrecy. This, under the Whiteboy Act, made him liable to the penalty of hanging. And in May 1793, Tandy learned, in the nick of time, that a Government informer had sworn information against him on this ground, and that a warrant for his arrest had been issued. Tandy had only just time to get on board a ship and escape to the Continent.

The Society of United Irishmen Suppressed

By the beginning of 1794 the Authorities were ready—and eager—to suppress the United Irishmen by force. The Society up to this point had confined itself to the advocacy of Parliamentary reform; and, although it was a fairly open secret that some of the leaders of the Society hoped to use a reformed Parliament, when gained, as a base from which to struggle for separation from England, this was not, in itself, a ground for legal proceedings.

Nor was the fact that the members of the Society were

all sympathisers with the French and hostile to the conduct and continuance of the war. To a milder degree the Whigs, led in England by Fox and in Ireland by Grattan, were also French sympathisers hostile to the Government's foreign policy, and they also advocated Parliamentary Reform, though not favouring the radical-democratic reform advocated by the United Irishmen.

Tone regarded the Whigs as rather more to be despised than "the common prostitutes of the Treasury Bench" and their supporters. They limited the Government's freedom of action somewhat, but they hampered much more the United Irishmen's freedom of opposition. The Government had secured the Convention Act with Whig aid; and this prevented the Society from developing from the stage of an aggregation of local societies into a unified national political organisation. And the Government had secured, also with Whig aid, the Arms Act and the Militia with which to thwart anything in the nature of an insurrection. The Government thought it safe, therefore, to proceed to a legal persecution of the leaders of the United Irishmen.

In January 1794, they at last proceeded to put Hamilton Rowan upon his trial for the "Citizen Soldiers" Address to the Volunteers—the trial of William Drennan being still further postponed.

Rowan was defended by the greatest popular advocate then living, John Philpot Curran. Born in Munster, a descendant of a planted Cromwellian soldier, Curran from the poverty of his family circumstances had associated on familiar terms with the Catholic peasants, farmers, and shop-keepers since childhood. Though, for the reason indicated, Curran would be classed by "racialists" as of English descent, his physique, features, eloquence, wit, and the general cast of his mind made him stand out as a Gael among the Gaels. Through the whole of the terrors of the time upon which we are entering, no man's name stands out with a greater lustre, for fearless steadfastness in the teeth of every terror, than that of Curran—unless it be the name of Tone himself.

Curran's defence of Hamilton Rowan was a magnificent effort; and, though it availed nothing with a carefully hand-picked jury, it ensured that, thereafter, no State trial was complete without Curran leading for the defence.

Found guilty of sedition, Rowan was sentenced to a heavy fine and to two years' imprisonment.

Rowan had been convicted of "publishing" the Address by reading it to an assembly of Volunteers (among whom it had been circulated as a leaflet). The desire of the Government to shackle the press was shown when they elected to proceed against Drennan on a charge of "procuring its publication" in a Dublin newspaper. The proprietors and printers of the *Northern Star* were also prosecuted, at the same time, for publishing the same address. A conviction was secured (May 1794) against the printer of the *Northern Star*, but the jury refused to find a verdict against Drennan.

It was on the eve of these press prosecutions that the Government passed to the direct suppression of the United Irishmen. On May 4, 1794, a party of soldiers, headed by one of Dublin's military magistrates, forced their way into the Tailors' Hall, in Back Lane, the regular meeting-place of the Dublin United Irishmen, and ordered the meeting then proceeding to disperse. All papers were seized, and the building was retained in military occupation. A proclamation was issued suppressing the Dublin Society, and the Attorney General announced in Parliament that any similar association anywhere in Ireland would be dealt with in the same way. He charged the United Irishmen categorically with "treasonable association with the King's enemies".

The evidence on which this charge was based had been secured a week earlier by the arrest of the Rev. William Jackson and his valet-associate Cockayne.

Jackson, a clergyman of the Church of Ireland, had been domiciled in Paris from before the Revolution. He had been present at a meeting in Paris attended by all the well-to-do Englishmen, Scots, and Irishmen then resident in Paris—which meeting applauded the setting up of a Republic in France, and applauded also the offer of the National Convention to move to the aid of any people struggling to attain their freedom. Jackson had come from this meeting all agog to discover how far the peoples of England and of Ireland respectively would welcome a French Army coming to their aid.

Whether he had or had not a commission from the French Foreign Office is not known. What is known is that Pitt's secret service was so good that he knew of Jackson's trip from before his landing in England, and had planted Cockayne, one of his agents, in Jackson's path. Jackson fell completely for Cockayne's hard-luck story, and took him with him to Ireland as his secretary-valet.

In Ireland Jackson sought out the leading United Irishmen and asked their opinions. Tone, at first, would have nothing to do with him; but, finding him trusted by others, including Hamilton Rowan (who was allowed to have all the visitors he pleased in prison) Tone agreed to draft a memorial on the state of Ireland. In it Tone emphasised the complete contrast between England and Ireland: "Any invasion of England would unite all ranks in opposition to the invader.... The Government of Ireland is only to be looked upon as a government of force; the moment a superior force appears it would tumble at once as founded neither in the interests nor the affections of the people."

A copy of this memorial was despatched by Jackson (through Cockayne) to an address in London, with instructions to forward it to a banker in Hamburg—whom Pitt knew to be in touch with agents of the French Republic. It was this intercepted despatch which was the basis of the charge against Jackson personally and also against the United Irishmen generally.

A week after the raid on the Dublin United Irishmen, the English Government swooped down upon Thomas Hardy, Horne Tooke, and the other leaders of the English "Jacobin" Societies.

The news of the "discovery" of treasonable communications between the United Irishmen and the French Jacobins created a state of public excitement bordering upon panic-hysteria. Reactionaries howled for blood; faint-hearts began to fall away from the United ranks. Hamilton Rowan bribed his gaoler and escaped to France. John Reynolds, a leader of the Ulster Freemasons and a member of the United Irishmen—who had, incautiously, entertained Jackson and introduced him to others—also fled the country. The leading Whigs—Grattan it is sad to say among them—begged Keogh and the Catholic Committee to sever their connection with their deeply-compromised agent, Tone.

Greatly to their credit Keogh and the Catholic Committee refused: Tone, in his memoirs, records his undying gratitude. There can be no question that if the Catholic Committee had cast him off, Tone's life would not have been worth a twelve months' purchase. While he remained the salaried agent of the Catholic Committee (whom the Government desired to placate) he was safe at any rate from arrest on suspicion.

Here the Irish Administration was influenced by a political change in England. Faced with continued failure abroad—the continued military success of the French at the expense of the Allies—and with dangerous opposition at home, William Pitt had decided to broaden the base of his administration by making an alliance with the moderate Whigs who followed the lead of the Duke of Portland. This left Fox and the anti-war Whigs reduced to a small faction, unable seriously to resist the Government.

As the price of their support, the Portland Whigs demanded the direction of Irish affairs; and a new Viceroy, Earl Fitzwilliam, an ardent reformer, was sent across to initiate a new policy of moderate reform, based on conciliating the Catholics, and admitting them to Parliament. In this way it was hoped to make a breach between the Catholics and the Jacobin United Irishmen, and to establish with Catholic support a new, moderate, Whig Administration with Grattan as the head.

This scheme included, however, an important detail which proved its undoing. To make room for the new Administration, the "old gang"–the clique of Fitzgibbons and Beresfords who made patronage under the Administration a family preserve for years–had to be cleared out, not only to create vacancies, and to effect the transfer of authority, but because this clique was the directing centre of the most virulent Protestant–Ascendancy bigotry in Ireland.

Infuriated at the threat to his Party's places and power, Fitzgibbon, the Earl of Clare, slipped secretly to England, where he so worked upon the King and the inner Court-clique that George III's Protestant religious mania was inflamed; and, using this as a convenient tool, the clique forced Pitt and Portland to retreat.

The Catholic Relief Bill (which would have completed the work accomplished in 1793) was withdrawn; Fitzwilliam was recalled; Clare and the Beresfords were re-established; and Grattan was permanently excluded from all hope of office. Ireland was handed back, without reserve, to the rabid counter-revolutionary faction; while Pitt, for his part, began, from that moment, to concert plans for the Union he saw to be the only alternative to the overthrow of the "old gang" by a democratic-republican upheaval from below.

Fitzwilliam's regime had never actually been instituted. It had lasted nominally from the beginning of July 1794, to the middle of March 1795; but while it had lasted, the drive of repression against the United Irishmen had been virtually suspended. As Fitzwilliam departed, so the drive began again.

Jackson was put on trial on April 24. In part, the delay in bringing him to trial had been due to the Government's hope that he would turn informer and directly incriminate Tone, against whom they had only hearsay evidence. When this hope failed Jackson's conviction followed as a matter of course from the evidence of the English informer, Cockayne. He made a dramatic exit by dropping dead in the dock (having taken poison) before the Judge could sentence him.

With Jackson convicted, Tone's position became untenable; and, accordingly, he accepted as a compromise (negotiated, it would seem, by Grattan) the proposal to go voluntarily into exile. Six weeks after Jackson's conviction, Tone and his family sailed from Ireland for the United States.

The Orange Society Founded

The Fitzwilliam episode taught the more corrupt and reactionary strata of the Governing caste that it was faced with a double danger. It was threatened in front by the rising wave of democratic-republican enthusiasm stirred up by the United Irishmen and the Catholic Committee in alliance—an enthusiasm which imperilled this caste along with the whole body of the landed oligarchy and gentry. But it was no less threatened by the proposals of the English Moderate-Whigs to stave off this frontal attack by concessions to the upper stratum of the Catholic Community, since it was with their political privileges, and with the places of profit they had hitherto monopolised, that the English "Liberals" proposed to buy over the wealthier and more moderate Catholics.

English Whigs proposed to break up the popular unity by buying over the wealthier Catholics; the threatened

Castle clique retorted by stirring up the more ignorant, debased, corrupt, and reactionary stratum of the Protestants to create disunity and disturbance under a pretence of zeal for the Protestant religion.

Under the influence of the United Irishmen, sectarian divisions were fast being replaced in Ulster by political unity; and, inspired by this, the more Catholic provinces were responding with public-spirited zeal. The last weapon left to the reaction was the traditional fear of the Papacy and hostility to the Catholic religion, which was strongest in the social strata, and the location where zeal for republican-democracy was greatest, namely, among the Dissenters. In Ulster, therefore, and among the most ignorantly prejudiced, the most corrupt, and the most debased of all classes of the Protestant population, the Castle clique sought and found a weapon against the United Irishmen.

As we have seen, County Armagh, where the population was fairly evenly divided between the sects, had been for years the scene of sporadic faction fighting between Peep-of-Day Boys and Catholic Defenders. This had died down to nothing under the influence of United Irish agitation. When the pro-Catholic Fitzwilliam was appointed Viceroy, the Peep-of-Day Boys suddenly resumed activity after nearly two years of quiescence. It is impossible to miss the connection between this fact and the lie deliberately circulated by the Clare-Beresford faction—that Fitzwilliam was coming to replace Protestant ascendancy with Catholic ascendancy. And if this point could have been missed it would have been made clear when the most reactionary Protestant magistrates in County Armagh took advantage of these renewed disturbances to search Catholic homes for "seditious literature". The Peep-of-Day Boys took the hint and began again to "search" Catholic homes for "concealed arms". That it was now legal for Catholics to possess arms did not trouble the Peep-of-Day Boys.

Soon the Defenders' organisation was again in action, beating off Protestant attacks; and every successful defence, trumpeted abroad as a "Catholic outrage", brought a fresh magistrates' search for evidences of "sedition" followed by a spread of anti-Catholic violence to areas previously peaceful. In a few weeks a regular pogrom was in full swing in Armagh and the counties adjoining. The victims, fleeing from their burning homes, spread panic all through Catholic Ireland.

The motive actuating this "Protestant" villainy became unmistakable when it was seen that it was the most improved farms, on the best land, which were first attacked, and whose occupants were first offered the alternative of "Hell or Connacht". Poor and struggling Catholic farmers scratching a living from a stony hill-top farm rarely, if ever, excited Protestant zeal even in the heart of Antrim. To this day the richer soil in the valley-bottoms in Eastern Ulster is Protestant to the last half-acre while Catholics survive on every barren hill-top.

This artificially worked-up pogrom culminated, on September 21, 1795, in an incident—the "Battle of the Diamond"—which has taken a front place in Orange mythology ever since.

The myth-version is that a body of "peaceful" Protestants was set upon by a multitude of "cowardly" Catholics whom the brave Protestants routed with great slaughter. The truth, vouched for by contemporary Protestant testimony, is that a semi-secret assembly of Catholics in the hills was sniped persistently by Protestant sharpshooters; that this brought on desultory fighting, which continued off and on for several days, but was ended on the joint intervention of a Protestant magistrate and a Catholic priest.

The Catholics, it should be noted, were almost entirely unarmed, while the Protestants were an organised and armed force.

Just as peace had been concluded, and the Protestants

were formed up ready to march away, a new body of Catholics arrived, hastening to the aid of their fellow-Catholics. These newcomers, misunderstanding the situation, attacked the Protestants and had suffered some loss before the situation could be explained to them and the incident brought to an end.

Peace was restored. But that same night a body of magistrates, squires, squireens, and parsons in County Armagh met together and formed the Mother Lodge of the Orange Society. Under a pretext of zeal for law, order, and the Protestant religion an oath-bound secret society on the Masonic model was organised, which, in practice, proved a fomenting centre, as well as a cloak of protection, for the organised knavery into which the Peep-of-Day Boys had degenerated. The Orange Order became an organised conspiracy of all the most degenerate reactionaries of every social strata—an instrument whereby the *lumpen* strata were used as tools to break up the solidarity engendered by the United Irishmen, and to replace the struggle for democratic advance by disintegrating it into an embittered war of sect against sect, from which the only ones to profit were the Clare-Beresford clique in Dublin Castle and their hangers-on of every social grade.

In evaluting the Orange Society it must not be forgotten that the bodies it was founded to disrupt and destroy—the United Irishmen and the Defenders—functioned, the one as a great liberating force, and the other as a tenants' protection league and an agrarian trade union. The Orange lodges functioned as a "union-smashing" force, operating in the interest of an oligarchical clique threatened with overthrow by a revolutionary-democratic advance. They constituted the first Fascist body known in history.

CHAPTER IX

"THE FRENCH ARE IN THE BAY"

The key moves in the Anglo-Irish struggle from the end of 1795 to the end of 1797 all centred around the endeavour of Wolfe Tone to secure a successful French landing in Ireland. The countermoves of the Irish Administration were aimed primarily at smashing up the underground organisation of the United Irishmen, and making it impossible for them to co-operate effectively with a French invasion. This chapter deals in detail with Tone's mission in France and with the Administration's dragooning of Ulster.

Wolfe Tone in France

Before he sailed for America, Tone's mind was made up: he was determined to get from France the arms, officers, and military support necessary to ensure success for an Irish insurrection. His friends (Russell, T. A. Emmet, and others) were warmly in agreement. On Cave Hill, Belfast, he and they "took a solemn obligation ... never to desist from our efforts until we had subverted the authority of England over our country and asserted our independence."

In Philadelphia he met a check. The French Minister received him so coolly that his hopes fell to zero. He was lifted from his gloom a few months later by letters from Russell, Keogh, and others, all urging him "in the strongest manner" to carry out his pledge and to "move heaven and earth to force my way to the French Government in order to supplicate their assistance."

Next day the French Minister met him with cordiality and arranged the business at once. On January 1, 1796, Tone sailed from Sandy Hook. Fellow-exiles, John Reynolds, Hamilton Rowan, and Napper Tandy, made special trips to wish him good luck. He reached France without mishap or delay and at once set to work. How he set about his enormous task we can only indicate baldly, using as far as possible Tone's own description, given in his diary—the most movingly human of all autobiographies.

His honest commonsense shines out from the first. Asked by a French statesman if the Irish could do anything unaided, Tone told him: "Most certainly not. If a landing were once effected everything would follow instantly, but that was indispensable. I begged him to state that as my opinion . . . if 20,000 French were in Ireland we should in a month have an army of 100,000, 200,999, or, if necessary, 300,000 men; but the *point d'appui* was indispensable." Personally, he explained, he would go with "a Corporal's guard"; but to do the thing properly 20,000 trained men were the minimum that was required.

His good sense, his frankness, firmness and disinterestedness compelled respect. He won over Carnot (the "organiser of victory") and he had an instantaneous success with the intrepid Jacobin general Lazar Hoche. As the prospect brightens, Tone grows whimsical: "I am a pretty fellow to negotiate with the Directory of France, pull down a monarchy, and establish a Republic; to break a connection of 600 years' standing and contract a fresh alliance . . . What would my old friend Fitzgibbon [the Chancellor] say if he could read these memorandums? 'He called me a dog before he had cause!' I remember he used to say I was a viper in the bosom of Ireland. Now that I am in Paris I will venture to say he lies, and that I am a better Irishman than he and his whole gang of rascals—as well as the gang that are opposing them— as it were."

French fears that a liberated Ireland might prove monarchist, aristocratic, or clericalist, took a lot of dissipating: "We then for the hundredth time beat over the old ground about the priests without starting any new ideas; and I summed up all by telling him that as to religion we would content ourselves with pulling down the Establishment, without setting up another; that we would have no State religion, but let each sect pay its own clergy voluntarily.

"As to royalty and aristocracy they were both odious in Ireland to such a degree that I apprehended much more a general massacre of the gentry and a distribution of the entire of their property than the establishment of any sort of government that would perpetuate their influence; that I hoped this massacre would not happen and that I for one would do all in my power to prevent it ... At the same time the pride, cruelty and oppression of the Irish aristocracy was so great that I apprehended every excess from the just resentment of the people."

Tone's contempt for the aristocracy and gentry is equalled by his faith in the common people: "Our independence must be had at all hazards. If the men of property will not support us they must fall. We can support ourselves by the aid of that numerous and respectable class of the community the men of no property."

His scorn for the Whigs is profound: "The Whig Club, I see, are taking up the condition of the labouring poor. They are getting frightened and their guilty consciences will not let them sleep. I suppose they will act like the gentry of Meath, who from fear of the Defenders raised their workmen's wages from eightpence to a shilling a day, but took care at the same time to raise the rent of the hovels and the grass for their cows in the same proportion so that at the end of the year the wretched peasant was not a penny the richer. Such is the honesty of the squirearchy of Ireland. No! No! it is we who will better the condition of the labouring poor if ever we get into that country; it is we that will humble the pride of that execrable and contemptible corps, the country gentlemen of Ireland. I know not whether I most hate or despise them, the tyrants of the people and the slaves of the Government."

The point comes up again later when he and a friend (Lewines) are negotiating with the Dutch Government. A statesman who had travelled in Ireland observes that "from the luxury of the rich and the extreme misery of the poor, no country in Europe had so crying a need for a revolution. To which Lewines and I replied, as is most religiously the truth, that one great motive of our conduct in this business was our conviction of the wretched state of our peasantry and our determination if possible to amend it."

The European Situation

To appreciate fully the conditions in which Tone laboured from 1795 to the end of 1798 one must possess a detailed grasp of the vast complex of historical reactions set in train all over Europe by the immense upheaval of the French Revolution. It is impossible, here, to do more than note that from July 1789, to July 1796, the Revolution rose through a succession of spectacular successes which destroyed the absolute Monarchy and the powers of the semi-feudal aristocracy and the ecclesiastical Hierarchy. That of itself was sufficient to scare the feudalistic Absolutists in all the great monarchies and principalities of Europe; who accordingly banded together to destroy the Revolutionary French Republic.

In self-defence the Revolution was forced to wage war in all the states adjacent to its frontiers. The victories of the armies of the Republic gave the Revolution freedom to complete itself in France; but from July 1794, it entered upon a conservative phase in which, through a succession of political defeats inflicted upon the lower classes, power came to rest in the hands of the upper stratum of the bourgeoisie—the money-lords, land-speculators, and Army contractors—supported by the main body of the peasantry who had gained greatly from the liquidation of their feudal burdens.

The Republic however still needed armies to protect itself from the vengeance of the princes, kings, and Emperors whose political systems had been thrown into confusion by the upheaval. Hence Napoleon Buonaparte, his armies, his conquests, and his quasi Republican Empire—which was revolutionary to the kings and emperors while it was conservative and even counter-revolutionary in France itself—were all historically necessitated so long as France was faced with the need to fight for its life against a feudalistic-monarchist European coalition.

That is where England and the policy of its ruling class, as expressed by William Pitt, comes into the picture. But for Pitt, and the financial and naval aid he put at its disposal, the Coalition of Kings and Princes could never have survived the victories of the Republic. However plausibly it may be argued that it was a political necessity for England to make a stand against the Napoleonic Empire, it remains a fact that but for Pitt's policy—which was that of the King, the Court, and the ruling-oligarchy of England—there would have been no Napoleonic Empire.

So far as the French Revolution involved the overthrow of the Bourbon Monarchy—with which England had been repeatedly at war since 1690—and the overthrow of the Bourbon Empire—which was England's greatest rival—the English bourgeoisie and ruling-class could view the French Revolution with complacency; and so far they put no obstacles in the way of the spontaneous expression of sympathy by the progressive bourgeoisie and petty-bourgeoisie of England with the victory of their class counterparts in France.

When, however, the lower orders looked like triumphing permanently in France, the ruling oligarchy in England saw the justice of the alarms expressed by the Emperors,

Kings, etc. The war upon France, in alliance with the Coalition of Kings, etc., was also a disguised form of war upon the lower orders in England, and still more (and without disguise) upon the people in Ireland.

When the continental victories of the French Armies created a fear that the Republican Empire might grow to be an even greater menace to England's Empire than the Bourbon Empire had been—and particularly a fear that England's trade and manufactures might be shut out completely from the valuable European market—the English bourgeoisie found their abstract sympathy for the French Revolution dwindle and disappear in face of the realities of economic rivalry. Thus, in the end, Pitt was able to rally behind him all the property-owning interests of England in his war to the death with revolutionary France.

This in England, and still more in Ireland, involved an intensification of the domestic war against the lower orders, whose aspirations had been quickened by the triumph of Revolution in France.

Here emerges the radical difference between England and Ireland. Tone was never so right as when he saw that while a French invasion of Ireland could count with confidence on the mass support of virtually all classes below the level of the Ascendancy-oligarchy, in England an exactly opposite result would be produced.

The lower orders in England were exploited, and resented it, as the Irish people also resented the exploitation they suffered. But the English lower orders were exploited as classes; and a successful invasion, instead of easing their position, would worsen it by imposing a national subjection which would hamper at every point their class-struggles for emancipation.

That which the English lower orders feared as a possible calamity was something which had already happened in Ireland. The Irish people were already enslaved as a nation. An invader would come to them as a welcome ally against the enslavers from whom they yearned to be freed. Thus, what was a nightmare bogey to the English masses was the thing of things to be desired by the Irish masses.

It is against this background that we must envisage Tone drudging away doggedly at persuading first this Minister and then another until at last he extorts a definite promise of an Army of Liberation for Ireland—drudging on until the expedition is actually being assembled; until preparations are complete; until, at last, he and the expedition are actually at sea, bound for Ireland!

It is against the same background that we must envisage the United Irish Leaders labouring in Ireland to perfect their organisation; to obtain stores of arms and powder; to see that, failing muskets, every man had at least a pike. And, above all, labouring to keep their followers patient under every provocation until the day when the French should actually have landed in force.

It is against the same background that we must view Dublin Castle as a centre in which a company of aristocratic conspirators plot, scheme, and plan to anticipate every move of the United Irishmen; to break their connections, raid their stores, arrest their leaders, and in every way to try to provoke enough resistance to provide a pretext for the barbarous repression they desire in their hearts to see and will soon accomplish in deeds.

And it is against the same background that we must envisage William Pitt and his Cabinet in London, sending out subsidies to keep this King or that Emperor steadfast in the struggle against the French; sending out proclamation after proclamation to the fox-hunting Tory squires, and their bottle-companions the parsons, keeping them all up to their job of holding the countryside in order; suspending the Habeas Corpus Act; facing mutinies in the Militia, mutinies in the Fleet, food-riots and other manifestations of a will, half-formed in the lower orders, to start a revolution and fight the French at the same time!

French Attempts to Invade Ireland, 1796-97

It was with hopes keyed up to the highest pitch that Tone sailed from Brest with the French Fleet towards the end of December 1796. It was in a condition bordering upon absolute despair that he returned on the ship he had sailed on, a fortnight later, with nothing done. It was, he noted, a year to the day since he had landed in France, fresh from America, with a hundred guineas in his pocket and a determination to move the earth, if need be, to free Ireland.

The expedition had carried 15,000 trained men, and arms for 20,000 more. Lazar Hoche was in command. The rendezvous was Bantry Bay. They passed the English blockade squadron in a fog; and all seemed set fair for success. Then misfortunes began. A gale scattered the Fleet; those who first arrived off the Irish coast had to wait for the rest to struggle up in ones and twos. Then, when the Fleet was nearly complete again, one of the few ships still missing was the ship which carried Lazar Hoche. As they waited the stipulated three days the wind freshened into a terrific gale from just the one quarter which made a landing impossible. And so they continued while the gale blew with unabating fury for eight days. One by one the ships were blown from their anchorage; until, at last, facing the fact that success was now impossible, the Admiral ordered the few ships that remained to slip their cables and make their way back to France.

Tone had gone through the heart-rending experience of being for ten days within clear sight of the Irish shore —at times near enough to toss a biscuit on to the rocks— and yet as far from setting foot on Irish soil as if he were still in Paris. Any man less of a hero than Tone would have been nerve-shattered and will-broken for life after such a strain. It testifies, as with trumpets, to his unconquerable spirit that he was hardly on shore again before he was again at work preparing a new expedition.

Hoche, whose ship had been chased by English cruisers –and then, half-wrecked in the gale, blown leagues out of its course–had contrived to struggle back to Paris via Bordeaux. He was all agog for another try; and Spain being France's ally, the Spanish Fleet was called upon to slip out of Cadiz, make its way to Brest, and there help to cover the French Fleet with Lazar Hoche on board as it made another dash for Ireland. It was a pretty scheme and, but for "the devil", it might have come off. The devil, however, intervened–in the form of the English Fleet led by Sir John Jervis and including Commodore Horatio Nelson among its captains. On February 14, 1797, off Cape St. Vincent, the Spanish Fleet got such a mauling that it went back to Cadiz and stopped there.

Failing the Spaniards, there were the Dutch; and, to them, Hoche and the indefatigable Tone made their way to prepare another expedition. Preparations went forward without hàste–as things were wont to go with the Dutch. Tone had to face the appalling exasperation of being totally unable to profit by the unique chance presented by a succession of mutinies in the Home Fleet of England. Plymouth, Spithead, the Nore, Yarmouth, all were involved. For the better part of two months the English Home Fleet was immobilised. But what was the good of that when the fleets blockading Brest and Cadiz kept holding on like bulldogs? And while, in the Texel, one administrative delay after another, French as well as Dutch, made it impossible for the expedition to sail? Then, when all things were ready once again, the wind deserted to the English.

It was, it seems, only possible to get out of the Texel roads when there occurred in conjunction a high tide, and a wind from a certain direction. Normally ships seldom had to wait more than five days for this conjunction to occur. This time the wind remained foul for seven weeks straight off, and by then the season was too far advanced for the attempt to be made.

The expedition was put off until the following spring; but before then all hope of it vanished when the Dutch Fleet was destroyed by the British Fleet under Duncan at Camperdown on October 11, 1797.

Nearly desperate now, Tone returned to Paris, and there secured a promise that another expedition would be prepared which would definitely sail in the following spring—that of 1798.

The Dragooning of Ulster

When the French Fleet lay tossing in Bantry Bay, the Castle "gang" were in an agony of suspense. There were not 3,000 troops that could be relied upon in the South of Ireland; and those in the North could not be moved for fear of what the United Irishmen would do in their absence. If the wind had dropped for so little as three hours, Ireland would have been lost to the British Empire.

The saying that a "reign of terror" is usually the "reign of the terrified" is not wholly true; but it truly describes the reign of terror which was instituted in Ireland as Dublin Castle's response to the portent of a French Fleet in Bantry Bay. The Irish Parliament met and, in a session which lasted only from January 21 to April 15, occupied itself with only two measures: an Act of Indemnity for "all such persons as had, in the previous half-year, exceeded their legal powers in the preservation of the public peace", and with it an Insurrection Act—"one of the most severe and comprehensive in Irish history".

The first of these covered with legal oblivion the state of things which had supervened in Ulster as soon as the Orange Society had settled down to work. It began with a campaign of terrorism in Armagh which devastated the county and extended through the border counties into Connacht: it culminated with the Orange magistrates refusing to convict Orangemen even when plainly guilty of murder; with the same magistrates (quite beyond their legal powers) awarding sentences of transportation for life to Catholics who procured arms to defend themselves against the Orange gangs. Even friends of the Ascendancy were forced to protest. Lord Gosforth, the Lord Lieutenant of County Armagh, in an address to the county magistrates, spoke with indignation of the "persecution" and the "ferocious cruelty" which was driving thousands from their homes. "Of late no night passes that houses are not destroyed and scarce a week that dreadful murders are not committed." The Catholics, aided by United Irishmen, fought back wherever they could; but this only brought in a Government Terror to supplement the Orange Terror. The Indemnity Act was designed to cover the villainy of the magistrates who had abetted the Orange Terror, and to put difficulties in the way of the victims who claimed compensation. The Insurrection Act was designed to complete the work; and, in addition, to cope with the awkward fact that Orange persecution had driven the Defenders in the North and the Whiteboys in the South over to the United Irishmen in a body.

The state of the North may be inferred from a single circumstance: the Indemnity Act was popularly believed, by the victims as well as by the terrorists, to guarantee immunity for everything done, or to be done, in the name of the Orange order. On top of that the Insurrection Act gave the Government powers to suspend the Habeas Corpus Act and impose martial law upon any area proclaimed as "disturbed". It imposed death as the penalty for administering a "seditious" oath, and transportation as the penalty for taking one. It ordered the registration of all arms, which the magistrates could confiscate at will, and imposed transportation, or imprisonment, as the penalty for possessing or concealing unregistered arms; for "tumultuous assembly"; or for possessing, distributing, or selling "seditious" papers. Magistrates were given large powers of arrest on suspicion.

Almost before the Act was passed the Administration had appointed General Lake Military Commander for Ulster, and he had issued a proclamation imposing martial law over the greater part of the province. The proclamation ordered the surrender of all arms by a certain date.

Being none too certain of the troops—especially in view of the mutinies which began to be reported from England—and more than doubtful about the militia regiments, Dublin Castle had given permission to the country magistrates and gentry to form corps of "Yeomanry" on the English model. Like some of the earliest Volunteer corps these were, at first, corps formed by the gentry and the squireens from their family connections, their dependants, and such tenants as they thought they could rely upon. Later, infantry companies were added. In practice these Yeomanry corps were little else than Orange Lodges and Peep-of-Day Boy gangs put into uniform and given an official licence to work their will upon the countryside in the name of law and order. To secure a parallel end Orange Lodges were established in each militia battalion, and a systematic purge was instituted, beginning with the officers, to weed out every man suspected of unwillingness to go to any length in Orange terrorism. Yeomanry and militia regiments were brought over from England which were, as in the case of the evilly-notorious "Ancient Britons", commanded by Sir Watkin Williams-Wynn, little else than Church-and-King mobs supplied with weapons, pay, and rations, for displaying the ignorant brutality which in England they displayed from a love of savagery, stimulated by bribes of guineas and beer.

When the date fixed in General Lake's proclamation had expired, a general house-to-house search for arms was ordered through all the proclaimed area in Ulster. For tactical reasons it was deemed expedient to keep the troops (and most of the militia) concentrated in the towns. The actual raiding for arms was conducted, therefore, by the Orange Yeomanry. Soon the whole country was ringing with tales of their barbarity and outrage.

In the first surprise impact of the raids a considerable quantity of arms was discovered. Five thousand muskets were found in Co. Armagh alone. Thereafter few were found. Convinced that arms were being concealed, the Orange Yeomanry proceeded to show what they could do. From simple assault and robbery they proceeded to arson, rape, and murder. A competition developed between the "Ancient Britons" and the Orange Yeomanry as to which could inflict the greatest barbarity in the name of "the Law" and "loyalism". To extort confessions of concealed arms, they resorted to flogging; but this, even when the victims died under the lash, soon jaded the palates of these upholders of the law. Picketing—a variety of crucifixion in which the victim was fastened, back to the ground, his wrists and ankles drawn to full stretch by cords tied to picket pegs—half-hanging and pitch-capping—crowning the victim with a linen cap filled with hot pitch—these, with roasting the soles of the victim's feet at a turf fire, were the methods fashionable with the Yeomanry engaged in dragooning Ulster. When the terrified inhabitants fled at their approach, they could do nothing worse than burn the house down.

To this Orange terror the magistrates added an accompaniment of arrests on suspicion. When the gaols could hold no more, they were cleared, on a simple magistrate's order, by the expedient of "impressing" all the prisoners for service in the Fleet.

The rumour circulated by Pitt's Government, that the Naval Mutinies of '97 at Spithead and the Nore were the work of "Jacobin agents" working through the United Irishmen and the London Corresponding Society, has been proved to have been a plain lie, invented to excuse the savagery of the Yeomanry in Ireland, and the suppression of all democratic societies and trade-unions in England. But in face of what was happening in Ireland it was the sort of thing that could be only too easily believed.

Waiting for the French to come

To justify their dragooning of Ulster, the Irish Government recited a long list of "outrages". Arms had been collected and concealed in large quantities. Ash trees had been cut down (without leave) on gentlemen's estates to make pike-handles; magistrates had been fired at; informers had been murdered in broad daylight in the middle of Belfast; a quantity of gunpowder had been looted from a Government store; seditious literature was in every home; detached parties of Yeomanry had been attacked by armed bands; and so on.

Nor was this all. Anyone who joined the Yeomanry was met with insult and ostracism by "disaffected" employers as well as by work-people. People gathered in "great masses" to stack the hay, cut the corn, and lift the potatoes of men detained in gaol. If the military dispersed these "seditious assemblies" by day, they came back and did the work by moonlight. There were, of course, secret drillings. The "wish that the French would come" was expressed openly and everywhere. And, to cap all, an honourable member assured the House that there existed a "generally-expressed determination to abolish all taxes and all tithes, and reduce rents to a standard of 10s. an acre for the best land, and so downwards in proportion". Another honourable member added the last word: "They were facing a war of the poor against the rich."

The dragooning of Ulster was, in fact, only a very qualified success for the Administration. It secured some arms, and in various ways threw the United Irishmen's organisation into confusion. It created an excuse for the final suppression of the *Northern Star*, and the wrecking of its machinery. It had the effect, too, of scaring out of the United ranks a number of well-to-do waverers who, in some cases, turned informers to save their necks. But as a set-off against these gains there were losses.

The places of the deserters from the United ranks were taken by more resolute spirits roused to furious indignation by the Government's methods. The panic spread by the victims of the Orange pogroms, and those of the official terror in Ulster, drove the most sluggish of the peasantry in all the other provinces to take measures for self-defence. The partial disarming of Ulster was set off by a zealous, secret arming of the rest of Ireland. By the Government's own policy the United Irish system was helped to spread into the remotest points.

The troops, too, began to be affected. The militia, mostly composed of Catholics, had to be purged and re-purged. Even the establishment of Orange Lodges did not always accomplish anything beyond inflaming the national and Catholic zeal of the rank and file; often the new recruits were more "disaffected" than the discharged ones had been. One English regiment was found to be definitely "corrupted" and had to be bundled back to England; another was "very doubtful". In May 1797, at the time when mutiny had immobilised the Fleet at the Nore, courts-martial were sitting on cases of "disaffected" soldiers in Cork, Limerick, and Belfast. When a number of Cork militiamen were found to have taken the United Irish oath, and were sentenced to death, a Scottish regiment refused in a body to take any part in the execution. Only with difficulty could a "reliable" regiment be found.

Brawls which grew to the dimensions of pitched battles broke out between parties of Yeomanry and militia over the wearing of partisan badges of Orange and of Green.

All Ireland was one great question—When, and where, will the French land?

CHAPTER X

THE RISING OF 'NINETY-EIGHT

The struggle between the forces of Revolution and Counter-Revolution passed into the phase of actual war and bloody repression in May 1798. In this chapter we examine the stages whereby this culmination was reached and what followed as its immediate consequences.

The Case of William Orr

The policy pursued by the Administration as a sequel to the dragooning of Ulster was illustrated in an event to which enormous importance was attached at the time, though to us it seems of minor significance.

Among the Ulster leaders arrested in 1796 (along with Thomas Russell) was a young Antrim farmer William Orr. Detained with the rest without specific charge, he was, without warning, put on trial in October 1797, on a charge of administering an illegal oath.

The offence was graver legally from the fact that it was a serving soldier whom Orr was alleged to have sworn in as a United Irishman. The soldier himself and a comrade of the same regiment were the witnesses.

The prosecution made the most they could of this "proof" of the "Jacobinical" and "treasonable" designs of the United Irishmen to "seduce from their allegiance" the "men who are the Kingdom's only safeguard against the foreign foe".

The people at large took more notice of these things: (1) The offence, even if proved, was more than twelve months old. If the evidence had only just been unearthed, of what value was it after so long an interval? If the evidence had been known to the authorities all the time, what excuse had they for their delay? If they had ignored the charge for twelve months, why act upon it now? (2)

The penalty imposed under the Insurrection Act was death. This penalty had been denounced as barbarous when the Act was passed; as nearly two years had elapsed without its being enforced men had come to regard it as a dead letter. Did the bringing to trial of William Orr mean that the Government intended to enforce the penalty in every case? Did that mean that the hundreds of prisoners then in the Government's hands (all uncharged) were each and all threatened with the fate of William Orr? The fear was general, and was not wholly without justification.

The actual trial did not differ greatly in its incidentals from any normal State trial of the period. The United Irishmen knew in point of fact that Orr had not administered the oath on the occasion sworn to. We have the evidence of an eye-witness (Jamie Hope) for that. The soldier witness perjured himself; he was proved to be a bad character; he retracted his evidence in a sworn affidavit, and then retracted his retraction. But that does not differ greatly from the usual course of the informers of the period.

The jurymen swore that a whiskey jar was illegally passed into the jury room, and that those who for hours stood out for a verdict of acquittal gave in finally under the influence of drink. Even that was not wholly unprecedented.

The real crux of the case was something which did not appear on the pleadings, but of which everyone "in the know" was fully aware. The United Irishmen's oath had been administered to a soldier—whether it was Orr or another who administered the oath was merely incidental. Strict law might boggle over trifles of that kind. What the Authorities were after was a verdict that would strike terror into every United Irishman who had ever administered that oath or was ever likely to administer it.

Accordingly, though his execution was three times postponed, William Orr was hanged at Carrickfergus in January 1798, surrounded by an extra strong military guard. The inhabitants of Carrickfergus, to show their horror, deserted the town at daybreak on the day of the execution and did not return until all its traces had been cleared away.

Curran's Indictment of the Government

One reason for remembering the case of William Orr is that it led to a speech by John Philpot Curran which is among the most remarkable of his many remarkable speeches.

Its occasion was a charge of libel against the *Press* newspaper, the journal founded by Arthur O'Connor to replace the *Northern Star*. The *Press* had published an open letter to the Viceroy commenting scathingly on his refusal to show clemency to Orr. Curran's line of defence was a counter-attack—an indictment of the Government, root and branch.

"You [the jury] are called upon to say, on your oaths, that the Government is wise and merciful—the people prosperous and happy; that military law ought to be continued; that the constitution could not with safety be restored to Ireland; and that the statements of a contrary import by your advocates, in either country, are libellous and false.

"I tell you that these are the questions. And I ask you if you can have the front to give the expected answer in face of a community which knows the country as well as you do.

"Let me ask you how you could reconcile with such a verdict the gaols, the gibbets, the tenders, the conflagrations, the murders, the proclamations we hear of every day in the streets and see every day in the country? What are the prosecutions of the learned counsel himself [the Attorney General] circuit after circuit? Merciful God! What is the state of Ireland, and where shall you find the wretched inhabitant of this land?

"You may find him perhaps in a gaol; the only place of security–I had almost said, of ordinary habitation! If you do not find him there you may find him flying with his family from the flames of his own dwelling–lighted to his dungeon by the conflagration of his own hovel! Or you may find his bones bleaching on the green fields of his country! Or you may find him tossing on the surface of the ocean, mingling his groans with the tempests, less savage than his persecutors, that drive him to a return-less distance from his family and his home–without charge, or trial, or sentence!

"Is this a foul misrepresentation? Or can you, with these facts ringing in your ears and staring in your faces, say upon your oaths they do not exist? You are called upon in defiance of shame, of honour, of truth, to deny the sufferings under which you groan, and to flatter the persecution which tramples you under foot."

It was in these circumstances that the struggle between the Irish Nation, as represented by the United Irishmen, and its enemies, as represented by the Irish Administration and its supporters, entered upon its final phase.

Moving to a Crisis

In the light of after-events it is easy to see that the turning-point in the fortunes of the United Irishmen's movement came when the French failed to grasp the golden opportunity presented to them by the Naval Mutinies of 1797.

Till a French Fleet was actually tossing on the waves of Bantry Bay the real possibility of a French landing had been believed in only by a few "Jacobin" enthusiasts in the United Irish ranks and those ardent peasants scattered through the countryside who still dreamed dreams of the coming again of the "wild geese" that had "flown to France".

All this was changed after the end of 1796. That a landing had not been achieved was, of course, bad luck. But all doubts as to the willingness of the French to invade, and of their ability to make a landing, were dissipated when once the attempt had been made, and had missed success only by the narrowest of margins. Expectation became tensed to its highest pitch, and as the year 1797 slipped away, month by month, the strain grew unendurable. Weaklings began to despair again. The fiery spirits began to chafe and ask each other: Why wait for the French before starting? Won't they come anyway when they know we're up? The quicker we start, the quicker they'll be here!

In this way the further the year 1797 advanced, the more critical became the silent struggle between the leaders on each side, the one to provoke, the other to prevent a premature insurrection—"premature" in each case meaning before the French had effected a landing in force.

There was, of course, plenty to do to keep the ardent spirits from fretting too much. There was recruiting, organising, and drilling. Arms had to be got, and distributed; trees to be cut down and sawn up for pike-staves; pike-heads to be forged. And all the time a look-out kept against surprise by the Yeomanry or the military. Now and then there were collisions—a detected informer, tied heels to neck, thrown over a bridge with weights in his pockets, to take his information to the devil who begot him; a party of Yeomanry to beat off; arms to be concealed in the bog. Or a party to organise to give help, mowing, reaping, stacking, carting, or potato-lifting for the friends fallen into the hands of the enemy. All the same, men began to weary—losing hope or growing angrily impatient.

Under the impact of martial law, primitive instincts—greeds, jealousies, and fears—rose nearer the surface. The Catholic gentry, equally with their Protestant neighbours, saw every day a rift widening between them and their tenantry. One by one these gentry drifted over to the Government camp. The Catholic Hierarchy, genuinely fearful of the worst, exhausted itself in appeals for "submission" to the "powers that be, ordained of God". The parish priests, as in duty bound, passed the injunction on. But their words were frozen on their lips as the tales spread of the Catholic chapels burnt and of other infamies perpetrated by the Yeomanry on the Catholics of the North.

The Government, too, did not neglect the arts of propaganda. To the Catholic gentry and well-to-do they told tales of the horrors and the confiscations of the "atheistic" Jacobins of France. To the Protestant gentry they told tales of the Catholic "massacres" in the rising of 1641 and of the grave danger that a repetition was being planned. To the comfortable middle-class they told both tales—adding, for Catholics, reminders of what the "Republican" Cromwellians had done in 1649-50. To all they told the tale that maps had been prepared and were circulating which indicated where each historic clan had once been located, and suggested what lands should be confiscated and by whom. They spared no effort to ensure that the rising, when it did come, would find all the men of property, regardless of sect, in one camp, and ready to inflict condign punishment upon the mutinous *Jacquerie*.

For their part the United Irish chiefs diligently circulated the information among the "faithful" that an expedition was being prepared which would definitely be despatched to Ireland not later than at the beginning of May 1798. It would consist of only 10,000 men but there would be arms for plenty more. The United men were enjoined to be ready to strike immediately the landing had been made. The weary ones were reinvigorated; the impatient ones were calmed down. Every prospect seemed bright when two blows fell in quick succession.

The sudden death, at the end of 1797, of Lazar Hoche had helped to clear the road for the rise to power of Napoleon Buonaparte. All Ireland (in common with all England) had heard of the army, designated as "of England", which had been assembling in the North of France since the end of 1797. Tone was attached to this army; and this, with other confidential information, had led the United Irish chiefs to count confidently on this Army's being despatched to Ireland. Suddenly a rumour began to spread, which daily grew more circumstantial—that this camp was being broken up, and the army marched elsewhere.

Was Buonaparte going to break his pledged word?

The United chiefs did not credit the slander: it must be one of those brilliant manoeuvres for which this young general was already world-famous. They went on with their work. An ominous calm "broken only by constant accounts of attempts to murder magistrates and informers, of attacks upon sentries, and of nightly raids for arms" fell upon the country. It was felt to be specially suspicious that the peasantry had suddenly changed their habits. Drunkenness and faction-fighting at fairs and markets disappeared entirely.

Then definite news came that Buonaparte had—all pledges to the contrary notwithstanding—decided to use the "army of England" elsewhere! Tone got to know of the bare fact and nearly died of chagrin and indignation. We know, now, what he did not till later, that what Tone (who never wholly trusted Buonaparte) had said in jest had turned out to be only too true. Buonaparte was "trying to reach London by way of Calcutta starting from Egypt!" Years later, an exile at St. Helena, Buonaparte had leisure in which to realise how little he had gained—and how much he had lost—when he decided to double-cross the Irish.

This blow had barely had time to land before the second blow fell. The inner conflict in the United ranks between the "wait-for-the-French" and the "strike-by-ourselves" schools had been suspended by the definite promise of French aid by a particular date. With that promise rendered null and void, the disruptive conflict was bound to break out again in greater violence than ever. A special meeting of the Leinster Directory of the society—which included the members of the National Directory—was summoned on March 12 to devise means of coping with the crisis. This entire Directory—with the exceptions only of Arthur O'Connor imprisoned in England and Lord Edward Fitzgerald who was on his way to the meeting but had not reached it—was captured in a surprise raid by a military magistrate with a strong force.

In the nick of time the Government had found just the informer they needed.

Enemies to Ireland, and to the popular cause in all lands, have sought to spread the story that the Government knew all the secrets of the United Irishmen all along. It is an obvious falsehood, which expresses not the truth but what sycophants and reactionaries always wish to be true. The Government in 1798 knew of course that something was brewing. So much was self-evident without the use of a single spy. That there were professional informers in plenty in Ireland was also true. The Penal Code had been designed to turn the whole nation into informers—it was bound to have succeeded to some extent. And, for the matter of that, there were swarms of informers in England at that date—professionals, in the pay of Pitt, and amateurs who did it out of pure malevolence. But the fact remains that, when the Government wished to convict the prisoners captured in this raid of March 12, the only witness they had was this one informer, Thomas Reynolds, a landed proprietor and retired silk merchant. His price was £5,000 down and a pension. His excuse was that he feared the confiscation of his property whichever side won. Whatever his motive, his information gave the counter-revolution its victory. In regard to informers we note here that the most useful secret information Pitt obtained about Ireland was got from ex-aristocrats employed in the French Government service. And, we may say here, categorically, that the only Irish informers who did serious damage to the United Irishmen's cause were all of them drawn from the well-to-do and educated classes—as was Thomas Reynolds.

Counter-Revolutionary Terror

From the moment of the swoop of March 12 the civil war of 1798 began, for all practical purposes. The Government, for its part, announced to an appropriately "horrified" House of Commons that a "diabolical conspiracy" to bring in the French and "plunge the country into the horrors of civil war" had been unearthed. But, in cold fact, when the Attorney General had done with expressing astonishment, horror, indignation, and his loyal resolution to die, heroically, with his back to the last wall, all that needed to be done, really, was to send to England for more troops and to extend to all Ireland the Insurrection Act passed early in 1796.

This, however, was quite enough to reconcile the two schools of thought which had contended in the Government councils. Those who thought an insurrection ought to be prevented by firm measures, and those who thought it ought to be provoked in order that it might be crushed with force and arms, were equally satisfied with a measure which treated all Ireland as if it were in actual insurrection though no rising had been formally declared.

The proclamation of March 17, 1798, says Lecky, one of the most cautious and have-it-both-ways of historians, "opened a scene of horrors hardly surpassed in modern Europe". And, we may add, even the Hitlerite thugs were able to go beyond its horrors only in the greater extent of their operations.

Pending the arrival of troops from England—which, when they arrived, included, as well as dragoons and infantrymen, a number of conscript-serfs of the Grand Dukes of Hesse and of Brunswick, hired to the English Government at so much per head—the troops in Ireland were ordered to "repress disturbances" especially in Kildare, Tipperary, Limerick, Cork, Kilkenny, King's County, and Queen's County. They were authorised to "crush rebellion" in every shape and form, and forcibly to disarm all rebels. Officers were ordered to quarter their troops without payment upon anybody they thought fit; to requisition horses, carriages, and carts; to demand forage and provisions; to hold courts-martial; and to issue proclamations.

All that had happened in Ulster was now repeated all through the Midlands and the South, but on a more wholesale scale and with even greater ferocity. As was to be expected, the Yeomanry and their rivals, the Ancient Britons, were well to the fore in every barbarity, and they were soon joined by worthy rivals in the Hompesch Dragoons, some of the Hessian troops before-mentioned, who were, as it chanced, actually on board a troopship bound for the West Indies when the need arose for diverting them to Ireland.

The consequences to the people may be imagined. Homes were burned wholesale; stores of provisions were looted; hundreds were murdered; thousands were arrested. Tortures of incredible barbarity—flogging especially, carried to the point of actual death under the lash—were inflicted systematically upon a scale that would seem incredible if the evidence permitted any doubt. Even the relatively good-humoured horse-play of the military, militia, and Yeomanry—their snatching, tearing, or cutting from women any green garments they wore ("searching" them for green petticoats or green garters was deemed a great joke)—even when this did not prelude fouler outrage, all indicated to the Irish common people that they were to be regarded, at best, as conquered slaves, and at worst as wild beasts to be hunted without mercy.

Even when military discipline somewhat abated the grosser forms of physical outrage, the economic inflictions imposed by military decree all worked to the same end. The imposition of "free quarters" was in itself sufficient to ensure ruin and starvation to any region in which it was imposed. And to cap all, and reveal the class motive behind the whole system of barbarity, military proclamations warned the victims that the troops would remain at free quarters, not only until all arms had been surrendered, but also until "all rents, taxes, and tithes had been completely paid up".

And, be it noted, all these things were done before the rising of 1798 formally began.

Lord Edward Fitzgerald and the Rising

At the time of the swoop of March 12, the Secret Directory of the United Irish conspiracy—its military command—consisted of three men, Thomas Addis Emmet, Arthur O'Connor, and Lord Edward Fitzgerald.

Emmet was, as we have noted, a friend of Tone, who held him in higher esteem than almost any man he knew. Like Tone, Emmet came of Protestant Cromwellian stock. He was a barrister, famous for his dramatic act of subscribing the United Irishmen's oath in open court in the course of a speech in defence of a prisoner charged with the "crime" of administering that oath.

Arthur O'Connor, a nephew of Lord Longueville, was a landed proprietor in County Cork. He had been a member of Parliament, and had distinguished himself by his championship of the Catholic claims—losing his seat in consequence through the withdrawal of his uncle's patronage. He was an ardent champion of agrarian reform, and rather prided himself upon the possession of military capacity. He did, in fact, in after years, serve with distinction under Napoleon and retired with the rank of General. He has a special interest for English readers as the uncle of Feargus O'Connor the Chartist leader, whom he actually outlived by a few months, being 97 when he died.

Lord Edward Fitzgerald occupied a commanding position in Irish eyes as a younger brother of the Duke of Leinster, and therefore one of the senior line of the Geraldine family, the premier family in the Norman-Irish aristocracy. He had served with distinction as an officer in the English army; but his political sympathy with republican France went beyond that of his cousin Charles James Fox.* He had repudiated his courtesy title, and preferred to be addressed as Citizen Fitzgerald. But to the Irish, and especially the peasantry, he was always known affectionately as "Lord Edward". There is evidence of an indirect kind that he had more than once devoted his time to teaching the Defenders to drill, and how to handle their weapons.

On the eve of the swoop of March 12, this Secret Directory—who between them, it is interesting to note, combined the three main "racial" strands in the Irish nation: the old Gaelic, the Norman-Irish, and the planted English-Irish—realising that action could not for long be delayed, had sent Arthur O'Connor to make contact with the French and represent the imperative necessity of keeping to the promise of an expedition at the earliest possible moment. Arthur O'Connor with others was arrested while attempting to get a boat for France at Margate. Acquitted on an English charge by an English jury, O'Connor was detained at the instance of the Irish Administration. He was on his way back to Ireland in custody when, in the swoop of March 12, his fellow-director, Tom Emmet, also fell into the hands of the enemy.

* The mothers of Fox and Fitzgerald were sisters—grandchildren of King Charles II.

This left the Directorate solely in the hands of Citizen Fitzgerald who, realising that no further delay was possible, at once set to work to arrange a rising. He gathered a new Directory consisting of himself, two gentlemen-barristers from Co. Cork, the brothers John and Henry Sheares, and William Lawless, a kinsman of the newly-ennobled merchant-peer, Lord Cloncurry. Together they fixed upon the night of May 22-23 as zero-hour, and issued a call accordingly.

Lord Edward himself and the others—with Samuel Neilson acting as Lord Edward's shadow—spread the word as well as they could, with the military and the Yeomanry smashing connections in all directions. A proclamation had been issued offering £1,000 reward for Lord Edward's arrest, but he contrived to evade capture. All seemed reasonably hopeful until, on May 19, Lord Edward was surprised in a house in Dublin, and arrested. He resisted arrest so strenuously that he killed one of his would-be captors and wounded three others; but was himself in a dying condition when he was carried to gaol.

The brothers John and Henry Sheares were arrested on May 22, a few hours only before the zero-hour. The remaining director, William Lawless, warned in the very nick of time, just contrived to slip on board a ship as it sailed from the North Wall quay, Dublin. To complete the destruction, Samuel Neilson, the ablest of the United chiefs left at liberty, was captured while rounding up a party to storm the prison and liberate the captives.

Thus zero-hour arrived, with the whole central direction of the rising destroyed by "enemy action".

The result was what it was bound to be. Dublin was too well-watched for a move to be made; and anyway there was no one left there to give the signal. In more than a score of places in the Midlands the peasants rallied to the appointed rendezvous, and scored local successes of greater or less moment. But, all central direction and plan being lacking, each local rising was as isolated as if it had been the only rising in the country. The rebels in every case fought bravely, in some cases conspicuously so and with temporary success. But one by one each party was overpowered and forced either to surrender, to disperse, or to take refuge in the hills and bogs.

The temper with which the rising was met could have been inferred from the terror which had preceded it. In nearly every case the troops gave no quarter. They pursued the flying rebels into the houses in which they took shelter; and after they had despatched them, burned down the cottages. A general who allowed the rebels to disperse, unmolested, after they had given up their arms, was denounced in the Irish Parliament as a "traitor" for his "criminal clemency". By the end of a week, the rebellion had all but burned itself out in the Midlands; but, to the general surprise, it was just then that it flamed out, where it was least expected, in Wicklow and in Wexford.

The Boys of Wexford

Much speculation has been wasted over the alleged fact that Wexford, "the County least organised into the United Irish system", was the one in which the nearest approach to success was attained. The speculation is wasted because the "fact" is mythical. The Government did not capture details of the Wexford organisation at the swoop of March 12—not because there was no organisation, but solely because the Wexford delegates had not arrived when the swoop was made.

Wexford was, in fact, well organised; but mostly by the Whiteboy-Defender branch of the organisation; and it is of special interest as manifesting the response which the malignants in the Government camp had tried earlier to provoke from Ulster.

Since the March 17 proclamation Wexford and the adjoining counties had been dragooned by militia and

Yeomanry, led by local magistrates, with a savagery that stood out all the more sharply because of the complete absence of disturbances in the area since the excitements attending the militia-conscription of 1793.

The whole East-Munster and South-Leinster area was ravaged by the North Cork militia, of evil notoriety—a corps whose officers and sergeants were all rabid Orangemen, who instituted new Orange Lodges in every place where they were quartered, and whose rank and file was composed mostly of debased "Castle Catholics". The magistrates of County Wexford were conspicuous for their Orange arrogance; and for the alacrity with which they instituted systematic flogging to extort confessions of concealed arms, and also the practice of burning down every cabin from which the inhabitants had fled in terror on hearing of their approach.

One of these magistrates paraded his district at the head of a corps of Yeomanry escorting a cart on which a flogging-triangle, a cat-o'-nine-tails, and a hangman's halter all decorated with orange ribbons were prominently displayed.

So great was the terror excited by the nightly visitations of the magisterial parties, that whole villages were habitually deserted every nightfall. The villagers took refuge in the woods; preferring to risk the destruction of their homes rather than face torture by flogging and other barbarities. At least one case is known of an elderly man who dropped dead from fear on hearing that a magistrates' party was near at hand.

Even the Protestant gentry were not safe, unless they had purchased immunity by joining an Orange Lodge. Several landowners, including Beauchamp Bagenal Harvey—who owned a considerable estate in the barony of Bargy in the extreme south of the county—were imprisoned as suspects because of their United Irish leanings. Anthony Perry, a son of a Co. Wicklow proprietor, was submitted by the North Cork to a refinement upon the pitch-cap torture. Gunpowder was rubbed into his scalp and the hair set on fire to "give him a real rebelly crop!"*

From the official point of view the rising in Wexford began when the magistrates of its Northern Baronies met in Gorey on April 25 and, declaring the county in a state of insurrection, ordered all arms to be given up on pain of severe reprisals. There had been arrests and domiciliary raids even before that; but it was then that repression began in earnest.

The rebellion, as such, began on the night of May 25, when signal fires were lit on the hills of Corrigua and Boulavogue in answer to similar fires lit on the Wicklow Hills. The Wicklow men had risen on the night of May 22-23; but had found, as they approached Dublin, that something had gone wrong with the plans. They had, accordingly, retreated to the hills, where they defied every effort to dislodge them. Now they signalled to let the surrounding counties know they were still holding out. The men of Boulavogue, infuriated by the militia-persecution, had resolved to respond to the call. They waited in a body on their parish priest, Father John Murphy, and called upon him to lead them. He had agreed, and it was at his command that the fire had been lit on Boulavogue. The morning following, acting under his command, they successfully ambushed a party of Yeomanry; and then marched to capture the seat of Lord Mount Norris at Camolin Park. Here they found a great prize—all the pikes and muskets that had been surrendered since March 17 were stored here; and with them were some sixty carbines, and as many sabres, intended for the use of the Camolin Yeomanry.

* Crop, Croppy: As had been the case in England in 1640, a visible distinction between the idle rich and the working population was preserved by the fashion of the gentry for wearing their hair *en queue*, while workers and peasants wore theirs close-cropped. A "Croppy" became the cant name for a rebel peasant and by extension for any United Irishman; as "Roundhead" had been a similar cant name in 1640-60.

The news of this success spread far and wide, and brought recruits swarming to every hill-top in the county. Any hesitation was dispelled when, the day following, Father John's men routed and nearly exterminated a party of the North Cork militia; and it was in this fight that it was discovered what a terrible weapon the ten-foot pike can be when used with energy, under the direction of a resolute commander.

The North Cork, despising the ill-armed peasantry, had pursued some outlying parties whom they met on the skirts of the hill, and followed them up to the hill-top without troubling about formation. The fleeing peasants were, however, acting under orders—retreating to where, concealed behind a ridge, the main body of the rebels lay in waiting. At the proper moment this main body leapt from concealment and charged. The straggling line of infantrymen, most of whom had no time to load, could do nothing against the shock-assault of the pikemen. Only five of the North Cork, out of 110, managed to escape alive.

After this success the rising became virtually universal throughout Wexford; and parties from all the nearby counties made their way to join in the fight. An approximate estimate of the rebel strength puts their number at 130,000 men. Their great handicap was lack of firearms, and still more lack of the powder required for even such firearms as they had. Their only cannon were such as they contrived to capture; yet for a week or two they held virtually the whole of County Wexford and made desperate efforts to advance beyond its borders.

The feature which most distinguishes the Wexford rising—one which has provided a pretext for gross misrepresentation—is the number of priests and curates who figured as leaders in the fighting. In the case of Father John Murphy the excuse has been advanced that he only joined the rising because his chapel had been burned down by the Yeomanry. This fails as an excuse, since the chapel and priest's house were burned (with 140 other houses in Boulavogue) after the rising had begun. Moreover, all excuse is needless. To explain the "Croppy" priests of Wexford it is only necessary to know that they all came from the same kindred, the same birthplaces, and the same class as the peasants whom they went out to lead. John Murphy, Michael Murphy, Francis Kavanagh, Moses Kearns, Michael Redmond, and Philip Roche—all these priests had been educated originally by hedge-schoolmasters, and all had been, in the only way such a thing was possible under the Penal Code, scholarship pupils in the seminaries in which they qualified for holy orders. That is to say, the expenses of their journeys abroad, and of their maintenance in their seminaries had been made up, wholly or in part, by voluntary contributions from the peasantry in the parishes of their origin. That they were priests was incidental—and made only the difference that if they had survived, they would have incurred the severe ecclesiastical censure they risked when they took up arms. They went out and fought not because they were priests but because they were themselves Irishmen in revolt along with their kinsmen and their life-long neighbours.

That the touts of the Ascendancy faction should represent the Wexford rising as a Catholic war waged to exterminate Protestants, was to be expected. They had been predicting something of the kind as a staple of their scare-propaganda. But that Catholic Nationalists should fall into the trap and apologise for the Wexford rising as they have done is less easy to understand. When it is remembered that the Wexford peasantry were faced with what amounted to a Protestant war of extermination waged, primarily, against men ninety percent of whom were Catholic, it should be self-evident that any rising in self-defence was bound to take the form it did. The peasantry did, it is true, burn most of the houses of Protestants in Co. Wexford. But as ten times as many homes of Catholics had been burned previously either by these very "Protestants" acting as magistrates, or by their political associates, the theory that Catholic "religious fanaticism" caused the rising is not merely gratuitous but dishonest. A much more reliable clue is provided by the fact that while the Yeomanry and militia burned every thatched cottage they came across, being confident that its occupant was bound to be a Catholic, and a rebel or a sympathiser with the rebellion, the rebels, in retaliation, burned all the slated houses on the corresponding theory that their occupants were either "Orangemen" or sympathisers with their deeds. It was in short a class war—in fact just what Tone feared would follow from the "pride, arrogance, and cruelty" of the "gentry" of Ireland.

Another and more fatal weakness of the rebellion arose from its very universality and spontaneousness. They sadly lacked competent leaders, and their effort to obtain Protestant leaders, if they could, was pathetic in its very naïvety.

Bagenal Harvey, who had figured with distinction in the Dublin Society of United Irishmen before it was driven "underground" was, when Wexford Town was captured, and the prisoners were released, morally forced to agree to take the post of leader of the rebel army. His plans for the attack upon New Ross were quite well designed; and, with a better-disciplined army, success would have been assured.

But the rebel army was not an organised force: it was an agglomeration of groups, each of which fought under its own standard, usually that of its parish or barony.*

* One of these flags occasioned an item of Protestant mythology worth preserving for its crass stupidity. The flags were of any colour that came handy (except orange). One black flag bore the letters M.W.S. signifying "Marksmen: Wexford and Shelmaliere". "No Popery" mythology interpreted this as meaning "Murder Without Sin". The murder of this mythologist would probably fall under this category.

It resembled very closely an army of clans of the pre-historic period, in that its one conception of strategy was to hurl itself upon the enemy in a mass and decide the issue by personal valour in a series of personal combats.

At New Ross all Harvey's plans for a converging series of attacks from different points—feints followed by real assaults—came to naught when the enemy, in a dastardly manner, shot down the bearer of a flag of truce who was carrying Harvey's ultimatum to the opposing commander. Seeing their comrade shot down, the rebels rose up as one man and hurled themselves upon the enemy. Exhaustion, failure of supplies of ammunition, over-indulgence in looted whiskey and, more than all, the skilled dispositions of the opposing officers, compelled the rebels to retreat; but not until the battle had raged for a full ten hours.

Similar displays of reckless personal bravery, combined with a total lack of collective discipline, characterised each of the fights in the Wexford rising. Against the Yeomanry cavalry they were invariably successful. The daring fox-hunter squires, who would take any hedge, dyke, or stone wall at full gallop when nothing more lethal than a running fox was to be met with on the far side, found it another sort of proposition when in the field beyond a bristle of pikes in determined hands waited to hurl them back. The rebels were successful, too, in reviving an ancient war device in the shape of a drove of bullocks goaded into a maddened rush upon the enemy ranks and followed smartly by a charge of pikemen. But they could do little against disciplined infantry, well-supplied with ammunition, and operating under skilled commanders. And against artillery even the most fabulous courage merely multiplied the extent of the slaughter.

At one point, if they could have known it, they had as good as won the campaign. From dawn until dark they attacked Arklow, on the coast road through Wicklow to

Dublin. The enemy, his own ammunition exhausted, and his troops wearied out, and cowed, by the reckless persistence of the Irish attacks, had begun the evacuation of the town. Only a covering party was left which would have been withdrawn in the night. If the rebel army had merely camped for the night on the battlefield, they would have found in the morning the way clear before them; and no serious obstacle between them and Dublin itself. As it was, they did not know; instead of camping they retreated, and the chance never came again.

They won at least half a dozen distinct successes against yeomanry, militia, and English infantry; they fought heroically in at least as many hard-fought defeats; but they were overpowered in the end by the combined operations of a dozen English generals, including the famous Sir John Moore himself.

Apart from a party holding out in the Bog of Allen, the rising was over when the rebel headquarters at Vinegar Hill, near Enniscorthy, were stormed on June 21.

The Rising in Antrim and Down

While the Wexford rising was in progress, a rising broke out in Antrim and Down. On June 7—a fortnight after the zero-hour fixed by Lord Edward Fitzgerald—the Antrim Republicans took the field under the command of Henry Joy MacCracken. The numbers who rallied were fewer than Tone would have hoped for; but more than might have been expected after the dragooning of Ulster. The Defenders in Antrim turned out almost to a man; in fact, in general, the lower orders responded to the call, while the well-to-do, who should have occupied the posts of colonels and generals, were nearly all missing. At Ballymena, Kells, and other places the rebels were able to take possession of the town; but, as no one came to lead them, they dispersed to their homes.

MacCracken led his forces gallantly to the capture of

Antrim town, and had secured possession of the town-centre when a false alarm caused the rebels to retreat. The Government forces rallied, and were reinforced. At their second attempt the rebels were beaten off. Thereafter the rebel force disintegrated; and after a day or two MacCracken dismissed the few that remained. Captured while trying to make his way into Down, MacCracken was court-martialled and hanged.

In Down 7,000 men assembled. Ably led by a Lisburn linen-draper, Henry Munro, the rebels scored inconclusive successes in two hard-fought engagements. But despite their courage and determination they were defeated and scattered on June 14 at Ballynahinch. All the leaders were hanged; Munro before his own shop door.

Vengeance on the Vanquished

When it was clear that the rebellion had missed its mark, Ascendancy circles, whom its outbreak had thrown into a literal panic, took vengeance for their fright in a frenzy of blood-lust. As a rule no prisoners were taken; or were spared on the field of battle only to be executed later. All the Wexford leaders were hanged, Bagenal Harvey one of the first, as were the leaders in Antrim and Down.

Any commander in the field suspected of giving quarter was denounced for "treasonable clemency". Horribly as the Yeomanry and militia had behaved before the rising, they were incited by Ascendancy clamours to out-do all their previous efforts and pursue to extermination everyone who had taken to arms and everyone who gave them help or harbourage.

"The minds of people," said Lord Cornwallis, Viceroy and Commander-in-Chief, speaking of the Viceregal circle, "are in such a state that nothing but blood will satisfy them ... Their conversation and conduct point to no other mode of concluding this unhappy business but that of extirpation." It was more than suspected that the poorer quarters of Dublin harboured thousands of sworn United men and quantities of concealed arms. To extort confessions, suspects were rounded up and systematically flogged without mercy one after the other. This went on for days under the personal supervision of the chief sine-curist and corruption-fund-manager to the Government, John Claudius Beresford.

The hunting for rebels, the courts-martial, hangings, floggings, and house-burnings went on for weeks.

In their blood-frenzy the Ascendancy gang made determined efforts, with the aid of transparently vile in-formers, to secure the conviction and hanging of both Grattan and Curran. To such a length did this frenzy go that the Viceroy himself and even the savage Earl of Clare and the merciless Viscount Castlereagh (then Chief Secretary) were accused of showing "criminal sympathy with traitors" when they insisted that officers of militia and Yeomanry must keep their men under disciplined restraint.

The English Generals, each as he arrived and saw the state of things, were horrified. They insisted flatly that clemency must be conceded to the men who surrendered. And it was their clemency, and the good behaviour of the English and Scottish regular troops towards the civilian population and the prisoners, which did most to restore quiet in the countryside. The contrast between the pri-vate soldiers who insisted upon paying for everything they obtained (the Scottish troops having an especially good repute for this) and that of the gentleman-officers of the Yeomanry and militia was so great that it was pre-served in fireside legend for years afterwards.

And Sir John Moore himself, writing a fierce protest at the conduct of the Yeomanry, and of some of the Eng-lish militia regiments whom they had corrupted, declared emphatically that "if I were an Irishman I would be a rebel".

The English Government, stirred up by its generals, joined them in pressing the Irish Administration for an Amnesty Act, under which all not proved guilty of murder should be allowed to depart unmolested. This Amnesty Act was passed by the Irish Parliament on July 20.

It excluded from pardon two categories: (1) the State prisoners arrested before May 23 and (2) those guilty of murder. This second category gave the Yeomanry and Orange magistracy a pretext for maintaining their terror for years. The pretence of searching for suspected "murderers" was nearly as satisfactory to them as had been that of searching for arms. Men were still being hanged in 1802 for crimes they were alleged to have committed in 1798.

Barbarities had been committed by the rebels in the course of the rising in Wexford. A slave-revolt is, for obvious reasons, always likely to reflect in barbarous deeds the barbarities which have provoked it. But the horrors of the Wexford rising have been so much the stock-in-trade of reactionaries that we are absolved from the necessity of saying more than that—they were inexcusable; but they were, in every case, matched with equal and greater barbarities inflicted before, during, and after the rising by the other side.

As soon as the Wexford rising had been crushed, the Government turned its attention to the State Prisoners. Lord Edward had died of his wounds, so the first to be disposed of were John and Henry Sheares. Both were hanged. Then the Government turned its attention to the prisoners captured on March 12. They soon made it clear that, with the aid of the informer Reynolds, they proposed to work through the whole list one by one. The prisoners through their representatives—Thomas Addis Emmet, Arthur O'Connor, and William James Mac-Nevin—asked for a parley; and offered, in return for permission to go voluntarily into exile, to give the Government all the information in their power—except such as would incriminate individuals. The offer was, in the end, accepted; but two of the leading United Irishmen had been hanged before the negotiations concluded—a barbarity which Emmet and his fellow-negotiators thought a plain breach of an honourable undertaking, but which they were powerless to resist. (Another breach was that the prisoners, though released from gaol, were detained in internment at Fort George in Scotland where they were kept until the peace with France of 1802.)

But then, just as this negotiation was concluded, the French came after all.

The French Expeditions of 1798

When the news of the rising of May 23 reached Paris, Tone and his fellow-exiles besieged the French Government with frantic demands that aid should be sent to Ireland, at once. The Government eventually agreed to try a plan Tone had suggested in 1796—that of a staggered expedition.

Incompetence and the absence of the French Fleet in Egypt combined with downright sabotage to cause heartbreaking delays. The first expedition did not leave until August 7, and then it left without proper authorisation. This expedition, led by General Humbert, made a landing at Ballina, Co. Mayo, and inflicted a defeat upon a force of militia led by General Lake.

But Humbert's force was too small, and it came too late. It was forced to surrender to a superior force of English regular soldiers at Ballynamuck, Co. Longford. The French were given the treatment proper for prisoners of war; the Irish peasants who had joined them were pursued and exterminated without mercy. Two Irish refugees who were officers in the French service—Luke Teeling's son, Bartholomew, and Tone's younger brother Matthew—were taken to Dublin and hanged.

A few days after Humbert's surrender a single French ship, with a few refugees on board, headed by Napper Tandy, and carrying a large cargo of arms and ammunition, reached Rutland Island, off the Coast of Donegal. Learning that Humbert had surrendered, these invaders departed.

Three weeks later, a larger French force making for Lough Swilly was intercepted near Tory Island by a greatly superior English force. After fighting against four English vessels for four hours, the French flagship, the *Hoche*, of 74 guns, was reduced to a wreck and forced to surrender in a sinking condition. Among the prisoners taken off her was Theobald Wolfe Tone, who, during the action, had fought like a demon.

Sent, chained, to Dublin, he was tried by court-martial and sentenced to be hanged. He claimed, as a soldier, and an officer in the French service, the right to be executed in the military manner. His claim being denied, he took an opportunity, on the night before the day fixed for his execution, to cut his own throat. So, defiant to the last, died the first man to dream of a United Irish Republic.

He died on November 19, 1798, and was buried by his father in the churchyard in Bodenstown, Co. Kildare.

CHAPTER XI

THE UNION: ROBERT EMMET: SUMMARY

As soon as it was clear that the Rebellion was crushed, and that the French, in consequence of the crippling of their Fleet by Nelson at the Nile (August 2, 1798), had ceased to be immediately dangerous, Pitt and the English Government proceeded to exact their price for saving the Ascendancy Administration from the mess into which it had landed itself. That price was the Act which, from January 1, 1801, United the Parliaments of Great Britain and Ireland.

The attempt at insurrection by Robert Emmet, in Dublin, July 23, 1803, was, in part, a response to the Union; more basically it was the last flare-up of the fire lit by the United Irishmen, and a transition to new conditions of struggle.

The Act of Union

Pitt had always regarded the independent Irish Parliament as (from his imperialist point of view) an anomaly and a danger. The rising gave him his chance to get rid of it.

There was no denying the fact that with every initial advantage in their hands the Ascendancy Oligarchy had only been saved from annihilation by the prompt intervention of British troops in large numbers and by the constant vigilance of the British Navy.

Everything the corrupt, bigoted, oligarchical, and tyrannical Ascendancy Administration and its "managed" Parliament had done counted in the indictment against it. The aborting of Grattan's Revolution—the arrest of its progress at the half-way stage which enhanced the power of the oligarchy while adding little to the power of the people; its refusal to unite the Irish Nation by making the Parliament truly representative; its proved inability to keep a divided nation under control; its resort to the counter-revolutionary barbarities of Orangeism and the Orange Yeomanry; all these things proved the dangerous incapacity of the oligarchical Irish Administration.

The insurrection had, therefore, barely been crushed before Pitt was pressing proposals for a Union of the two Parliaments and, thereby, of the two Kingdoms of Ireland and Great Britain.

Passed independently by each Parliament, the Act of Union came into force on January 1, 1801. Thereafter Ireland became, politically, part of Great Britain, and the Irish people in theory became "British". The history of Ireland since that date is a demonstration of the absurdity of the theory and the growing contradiction between its assumption and concrete actuality.

In the Repeal and Home Rule agitations of the 19th century Irish Parliamentarians made much and overmuch of the methods whereby "Bloody" Castlereagh smoothed the path of the Act of Union through the Irish Parliament; and too little of the respects in which the Union under a pretence of making two nations into one greatly intensified the actuality of their separation—by adding considerably to the power of the English Government and ruling class to hold the Irish people in permanent subjection and to divert Ireland's economic development into channels profitable to the English ruling class.

So far as the Union was real, it was a union of two branches of one and the same oligarchy—of land-owning aristocrats with their financier allies. The "Irish" branch parted with a precarious semi-independence, and gained, in return, the security of fusion with its English counterpart. That the Irish aristocracy and gentry only consented to the change on receipt of a handsome compensation in cash, or titles, or both, speaks highly for their ability to drive a bargain. They allowed themselves to be "bribed" into doing what, after all, was directly in line with their class interests—something which, if Pitt had not been in a hurry, he would have found nearly every man of them willing to do for no bribe at all. The ability of the Irish gentry to "grab a guinea so tight that King George squealed for mercy" was never better demonstrated.

The Anglo-Irish landed aristocracy was, in 1798-1801, what it had been since 1690—England's garrison in Ireland. Even where they were "Old Irish" by descent they held lands and titles by tenures which English conquest had created and imposed, and which were secured against encroachment and destruction at the hands of an insurgent Irish Nation by English political and military might. A connection with England was, therefore, indispensable in one form or another to the landed oligarchy which monopolised Parliamentary power in Ireland. While England preferred to rule Ireland, indirectly, through this "garrison", there were, of course, incidental emoluments, jobs, and pickings to be gained by the instruments. The much-talked-of "bribery" which secured the passage of the Act of Union was from this angle no more than the customary compensation paid to a hireling whose services were no longer required.

"Would you sell your country?" asked an indignant patriot of a noble lord. "I would that," was the reply, "and thankful I'll be that I've got a country to sell!"

The point will be seen most clearly if we look at it through the eyes of the English branch of the ruling oligarchy.

By the Act of Union the English ruling class got rid of three great menaces: (1) of Revolutionary Republicanism, militant in Ireland, but also potential in England; (2) of a French invasion and occupation of Ireland; and (3) of Ireland's potential economic rivalry with England. In exchange it accepted a new danger—whose dimensions at that early date were, however, negligible—namely, that whereas till then the first impact of Irish discontent had fallen upon the Irish Administration, in the form of struggles by this or that class for relief of one kind and another, from the Union onwards these impacts fell directly upon the English Government and increasingly assumed the form of Nationalist struggles to recover Freedom for the Irish Nation as such.

This risk, however, had a set-off which at the time more than out-weighed its force. The 102 members added to the English Parliament—nearly to a man nominees of the landed interest—were an invaluable reinforcement to the oligarchy in its political resistance to the rising clamours of the English trading and manufacturing bourgeoisie for Parliamentary Reform. Growing out of this was yet another gain. Ireland supplied an unanswerable pretext for maintaining the standing army at a far higher level than Whig theory regarded, normally, as either desirable or safe. Thus, once again, Ireland filled the role of a reservoir from which the counter-revolutionary rulers could draw the force necessary to crush revolution in England.

In these various ways the Union revealed the agreement and solidarity of the landed oligarchs, English and Irish, and their radical opposition to the classes they exploited. Also, under a pretence of "uniting" the two countries, it revealed their national differences; and made these differences acute by perpetuating the "colonial" subordination of Ireland's economy to that of England. In that negative sense the Union proved a powerful factor in the development of Irish nationality and Nationalism.

The Catholics and the Union

The Orange Order was, at first, hostile to the proposed Union. Its special interest being bound up with the existence of an Irish Administration, which it could blackmail in the name of "Protestant Ascendancy", the Orange Order saw in the relegation of that Administration to a very minor role a direct attack upon its own immediate interest. It took strong political pressure, and a promise of favours to come—with assurances that "Ascendancy" was safe—to induce the Orange Order to relapse into a sulky acquiescence with the Union.

The Catholic Hierarchy, on the other hand, favoured the proposal and brought over to its support a majority of the well-to-do Catholics. From its relation to the Papacy as a temporal power the Hierarchy is invariably biased in general in favour of the Established Order in every country. The Irish Hierarchy, with its eyes on a possible reconversion to Catholicism of wealthy England, has always tended to regard Ireland, primarily, as a jumping-off point for that desirable end. It has always been eager, wherever possible, to oblige the rulers of England.

During the Rising of '98, the Hierarchy led the way in expressing its "detestation" of the rebellion, and its "unswerving loyalty" to the Crown. It ordered the parish priests to check the spread of rebellion, and to secure the surrender of arms. There were many instances where rebels were refused the sacraments until they had proved their "repentance" by turning informers.

As the Rebellion developed into a "war of the poor against the rich" the Hierarchy, members of the most wealthy land-owning corporation in the world, sided (as it always does in such emergencies) with the owners of property against their enemies. They, too, desired the Union as a safeguard against revolution. The same motive made Catholic property-owners range themselves on the Government's side against the rebels. Catholic peers raised Yeomanry corps which were active in suppressing the rising. Catholic merchants and lawyers, especially, were zealous recruits to the Yeomanry, showing as much bitterness against the poor "Croppies" as did any Orangeman. There was thus a powerful Catholic support ready-made for the Union.

The influence of the work of the Catholic Committee

was not, however, wholly lost; and it needed a tempting bribe offered—through Castlereagh—by Pitt to win the majority of Catholics over to an uneasy acquiescence in the Union. Pitt, through Castlereagh, let it be believed that, in return for the Act of Union, he would secure the admission of Catholics to Parliament, and to the higher grades of the Law and the Services. He also mooted the suggestion that the Catholic clergy might be subsidised by the State.

The proposal was particularly tempting to the Catholic merchants, manufacturers, and town-dwellers generally, in that the admission of Catholics to Parliament would have broken the monopoly of the Irish Protestant landed-aristocracy, and would have allowed the Catholic urban bourgeoisie to wrest the representation of the rural areas from the territorial lords. Fear of the consequences of such a happening caused the more reactionary section of the territorial oligarchy in England to intrigue against Pitt's proposal through the Court cliques. Once again George III's religious mania proved a trump card, and the Irish Catholic bourgeoisie found itself double-crossed.

Emmet's Conspiracy

Another aftermath of the Rising of '98 was the conspiracy organised in 1803 by Robert, the youngest brother of Thomas Addis Emmet—who, released with the other State Prisoners after the Peace of Amiens in 1802, had made his way to Paris and entered the French State service.

Robert Emmet—who had visited his brother in Paris, and been given an interview by Buonaparte, then First Consul of the French Republic—had returned to Ireland convinced that the French would soon invade England. This, he thought, would give Ireland her opportunity; and he planned accordingly. His calculations were based broadly upon two main considerations: (1) that the mass of the people in Ireland were disgusted and humiliated by the Act of Union which had reduced to a nullity such small power as they had possessed of influencing the decisions of Parliament; and (2) that the United Irishmen of Dublin, with those of Wicklow and parts of Kildare, had suffered least from the savage repressions following the Rising.

His plan was essentially Blanquist—just such a plan as Auguste Blanqui himself would have loved. It built wholly upon a belief that the people would respond instantly, and in mass, if only the signal for revolt was given by a well-planned *coup*. He planned therefore to capture Dublin Castle, and thereafter Dublin city, by a surprise assault. And, on paper, his plan was excellent. He secured the co-operation of all the really trustworthy old United men he could find; and he had the support of the Wicklow men led by Miles Byrne and Michael Dwyer and a body from Co. Kildare.

The plan broke down, as Blanquist *coups* are bound to do—since the secrecy which conceals the design from the authorities also conceals it from the masses. Consequently, the more completely the Government is surprised, the more the masses are bewildered and made suspicious. The more a Blanquist *coup* succeeds, at the outset, the more certain it is to fail in the end.

Robert Emmet's plans worked satisfactorily right up to the point where, in the dusk of Saturday, July 23, 1803, he sallied out from his headquarters with a small company and advanced to the capture of Dublin Castle. The Wicklow men were all hidden safely in working-class homes, stables, and warehouses along the lower quays, awaiting the prearranged rocket signal. The Kildare men were on the look-out for the second rocket which would be their summons. But the condition precedent for both signals—the capture of Dublin Castle—was never attained.

Emmet's followers, wild with excitement, went chasing

after the first red-coats they saw. The Saturday night crowds in the streets only joined in so far as they thought it was a common riot against the soldiers and the police. In a few minutes Emmet found himself a leader without a following: a fine Saturday night street-row was in progress, but the insurrection as such had completely evaporated. Worse still, one party of his followers, chasing red-coats, had come upon a judge, riding in his coach, whom they mistook for the "hanging-judge", Lord Norbury.* Him they piked to death on the spot. He was, in fact, Lord Kilwarden, one of the few honourable and humane judges left on the Bench. Thoroughly horrified, Emmet abandoned the enterprise. The signals to the Wicklow and Kildare men were never given.

The rioters held possession of a street or two for a couple of hours; but the rising as such was all over in a few minutes.

Emmet might have got away to France as easily as Miles Byrne did. As is well known, he lingered in the neighbourhood through inability to tear himself away from his sweetheart, Curran's daughter, Sarah.

He was sold by an informer, and hanged, as were a score of his followers. The romantic circumstances of his end–his passion for Sarah Curran; the fact that Curran, normally generous and always dauntless, for the first and last time in his life refused to defend a United Irishman, he being infuriated at his daughter's clandestine affair and not a little angry at being himself put again in personal peril thereby; the fact that the counsel who did defend Emmet, Leonard MacNally, was proved, years later, to have been the informer who had sold him–these things, with his youth and his gallantry, have thrown an imperishable halo of romance over the name and memory of Robert Emmet.

* His character is indicated by an anecdote told of him and Curran at a Bar dinner. "Is that *hung* beef you have before you, Mr. Curran?" "Not until your Lordship *tries* it, Lord Norbury."

Deepening the tragedy was the fact that it brought death also to Tone's friend, Thomas Russell. With the other State prisoners he had been released in 1802; but, meeting Robert Emmet in Paris, he had been fired by his hopes, and had returned with him to try to rouse the North simultaneously with Dublin. To their dismay and sorrow he and Jamie Hope (the Antrim weaver who had fought under MacCracken and now joined Robert Emmet as his first recruit after Miles Byrne) found that not a man in the North would move. Russell, sheltered in the homes of Dublin labourers, despite three rewards of £500 each offered for his capture, was spotted in the street by a military magistrate who knew him personally. He was overpowered, carried to trial, convicted, and hanged.

Emmet died on September 20, 1803; Russell died on October 21 in the same year. With them the Society of United Irishmen passed from the world of fact and practice into the realm of immortal memory.

What the United Irishmen Accomplished

To write-off the United Irishmen's movement as a complete failure simply because they did not attain the object they set themselves would be a complete error. After the movement was all over and done with, the fact that it had been remained operative in the transformed Irish national consciousness with which the English conquerors thenceforward had to deal.

How greatly the United Irishmen affected their period can best be estimated from the systematic deception which has conspired with romantic misconception to throw a sevenfold veil of falsification over the whole struggle from 1791 to 1798–a process in which Irish romantics have done, if anything, more mischief than English imperialists.

The favourite contention of reactionaries has been that, in attempting to draw Catholics, Dissenters, and Protestants into a common, united, national movement, they were attempting the unattainable—since the insurrection proved the absolute impossibility of uniting Catholics and Protestants.

We have set out in broad outline the proof of the falsity of this assertion. We have shown how practical, economic, political, and social forces had been at work which had evolved historically an Irish nation as a fact, and one which found its expression in the Society of United Irishmen. Far from the United men attempting the impossible, they fought primarily to bring to life a general awareness of something which history had in fact already established. And the frenzied malice of the Orange Order—founded expressly for the purpose of dissipating the success the United Irishmen had attained—is proof that the reaction was at its wits' end how to stave off that general recognition. But for their frenzied intervention, Irish National unity would have been inevitable—as indeed it has proved and will prove to be in the long run.

The utter falsity of the charge that the Rising of '98 proved, in practice, to be nothing but a war of extermination waged by the Catholics against the Protestants, we have already demonstrated. The form of the rising, in Wexford in particular, was dictated as we have shown by the counter-revolutionaries, who had been at work in the Government's interest for years before '98, and who, in all their activity, manifested a savage readiness to exterminate Catholics in general and rebel Catholics in particular. So far as the Rising of '98 did take the form of a war of sect against sect, this must be attributed, firstly, to the historical process which had made the line of division between the sects coincide broadly with the line dividing the rich and the poor; secondly, to the sectarian savagery of the Government itself and its Orange

196

agents; and, thirdly, to the unbridled falsifications the Government agents put out on purpose to inflame anti-Catholic prejudices in England.

The often-repeated allegation that it was the Rising's turning out to be nothing but a "great Catholic conspiracy" which caused the falling away from the United Irishmen of the Protestant North shows, as to the first part, a total ignorance of the actual state of the Catholic question between 1782 and 1798; and, as to the second part, shows a total ignorance of the historical determinants of the rise and decline of the United Irishmen's movement in the North.

The central fact this allegation ignores is that (except in one respect) there was less need, in 1791-8, for the Catholics to conspire as Catholics than there had been for a century previously. The worst and most insulting provisions of the Penal Code had been repealed, especially those which imposed restraints on the clergy and the Hierarchy. And, by the subsidies paid by the Administration for the building and maintenance of the Catholic seminary of Maynooth, the Catholic religion was actually more favoured then than it had been at any time since the Reformation. To make the "conspiracy" theory good its propounders are forced back upon the desperate expedient of contending that Grattan and the Volunteers, and Tone and the United Irishmen, were all (along with the Whiteboys and the Defenders) the purchased tools of "Popish" intrigue—something difficult to believe, even in Portadown; but easy to credit, it would seem, in English newspaper offices.

The exception we have noted proved the rule: the only reason Catholics as such had for conspiring in 1798 was to protect themselves against the sectarian barbarity of the Orange Yeomanry and militia. This, as we have sufficiently indicated, was a frantic endeavour by the worst and most degenerate reactionaries in the Protestant camp, to destroy the unity the revolutionary Protestants had achieved, and to re-establish in practice the social and political subjection of the Catholics which had been abolished in law.

To the evidence we have already cited may be added here the testimony of a Quakeress, Mary Leadbeater, who lived throughout the rising in Co. Carlow. She testifies categorically (according to Lecky) that, while the rebels had the upper hand, "nothing in the least resembling a desire to massacre the Protestant population came within her observations. 'Women and children,' she says, 'were spared and Quakers in general escaped; but woe betide the oppressor of the poor, the hard landlord, the severe master, or him who was looked upon as an enemy'."

This direct testimony of the class character of the Rising gives a clue to the ferocious character of the repression which, more than once, evidenced a desire to exterminate the rebels wholesale as slaves who had mutinied and broken their chains. The extent of the slaughter and the cold-blooded deliberation with which the "Croppies" were butchered while unarmed and helpless—and often when entirely innocent of participation in the rising—are glossed over in the official and "loyalist" records but cannot wholly be concealed even there. Mary Leadbeater notes a grim fact: "For several months there was no sale for bacon cured in Ireland from a well-founded fear of the hogs having fed on the flesh of men."

The special savagery of the Yeomanry and the militia officers is more than accounted for by the fact that they were mostly drawn from the ranks of the most arrogant and brutal class that ever existed in Ireland—the rack-renting, middlemen, squireen class. The circumstances in which this class had evolved made it regard the peasantry, in general, as at best a cheap variety of beasts of burden, and at worst as vermin to be hunted to complete extermination. Arthur Young, who toured Ireland on the
f Grattan's revolution, recorded his disgust and de-
on of this class and of the abject servility they de-

manded from their tenantry and labourers. Edward Wakefield, who made a minute study of Ireland just after the Union, concurs with Young's opinion at every point.

Even without their testimony we would be forced to the same conclusion by the opinion this class entertained of its own character. This opinion has been embalmed in a couple of songs which have survived in consequence of the spirited Irish airs to which they were set—namely, the *Rakes of Mallow* and *Garryowen* respectively. A few lines from each are all we need to quote:

> Beauing, belleing, dancing, drinking,
> Breaking windows, damning, sinking,
> Ever raking, never thinking,
> >   Live the rakes of Mallow.
> Racking tenants, stewards teasing,
> Swiftly spending, slowly raising,
> Wishing to spend all their days in
> >   Raking as at Mallow!

Mallow, it may be explained, was at this period in Ireland what Bath was in England. Garryowen was then a fashionable quarter of Limerick City. Its anthem echoes the Mallow theme:

> We are the boys that take delight in
> Smashing the Limerick lamps when lighting,
> Through the streets like sporters fighting,
> >   Tearing all before us.
> We'll beat the bailiffs out of fun,
> We'll make the Mayor and Sheriffs run,
> We are the boys no man dares dun,
> >   If he regards a whole skin.

It needs little imagination to picture how such a class would react to a general revolt of their tenantry. Nor is it hard to understand that yeomanry corps raised, purged, and commanded by such men would become, as the Commander-in-Chief, Lord Abercromby, said: "A licentious and brutal banditti, terrible to everybody except the enemy." To cover up their deeds and the retaliation they provoked under the pretence that it was all a regrettable display of "religious bigotry" is a feat of hypocrisy so colossal that one stands in awe before its matchless impudence.

The Falling-away of the North

But why was it that the North, once the stronghold of the United movement, fell away so sadly?

In part, of course, this is accounted for by the dragooning of Ulster; but historical causes were operating to produce a decline in the revolutionary tempo of the North even before this dragooning began.

The North was roused in the first place by the enthusiasm engendered by the French Revolution. While that revolution was passing through its ascendant phases, rising from triumph to triumph, the revolutionary democratic and humanitarian enthusiasm of Belfast and the North knew no bounds. When, in due course, the Revolution passed its zenith and entered upon its phase of increasing conservatism and decline, the revolutionary enthusiasm of Ulster underwent a corresponding change.

In 1792 it was the newly-born French Republic which was isolated and forced to fight in desperation against a coalition of aristocratic enemy states. In 1798–and still more in 1803–it was Britain which was isolated; while France, at the head of a European coalition, was developing rapidly into an imperialist rival of Britain.

If Tone and the United Irishmen could have seen into the future they would have perceived that the possibility of a revolutionary war of universal liberation began to fade from the moment when in July 1794, Robespierre was overthrown and he and all the members of the Commune Council of Paris were executed in a single batch. While Carnot remained the Commissar for War, and

Jacobin Generals such as Hoche remained to head the armies, a measure of the Jacobin impulse survived. But when Hoche died of consumption in 1797 and, in the same year, Carnot was driven into exile, the hope of Ireland's liberation by a revolutionary French army shrank rapidly towards extinction.

The more sharp-sighted and sensitive Ulster Jacobins perceived this process intuitively. As the revolutionary tempo slackened in France, and the revolution entered ever more plainly into its conservative phase, these Ulster Jacobins felt their willingness to run risks in the cause of world-revolution suffer a killing frost. In addition their own circumstances had undergone a change. Many merchants and manufacturers in Antrim and Down participated in the new enterprises begotten by the industrial revolution and grew rich correspondingly. When the testing hour came their riches determined their choice between preserving the status quo and risking all in a general overturn.

That is how it came to be that, in the end, it was, as Patrick Pearse said, "the great, faithful, splendid common people" who rose in '98.

PART THREE

FROM O'CONNELL TO
YOUNG IRELAND

CHAPTER XII

AFTER THE UNION

The theory that the Union made one country of England and Ireland is contradicted by the fact that, between 1820 and 1850, Ireland was the field for two great constitutional agitations, one agrarian "war" and one attempted insurrection; from all of which England was free.

The economic causation from which these movements arose is examined in this chapter.

Ireland's Place in England's Economy

In England, between 1801 and 1850, the Industrial Revolution rose to its peak and on its basis England attained a hegemony of the world-market. Ireland's manufacturers were prevented from sharing in this advance (1) by the loss of Parliamentary power to protect their home market; (2) by the lack of adequate coal and iron deposits; (3) from lack of capital: all the revenue extracted from Ireland by the landlords being drained away for consumption and investment in England. Thus Ireland's manufacturers were, with few exceptions, left further and further behind while England became, conversely, a better and better market for Irish agricultural products.

What the Commercial Restraints and Navigation Acts were needed to bring about in the seventeenth and eighteenth centuries, economic competition did unaided in the Age of Steam.

Inexorably Ireland was forced back upon the role of feeder to England's economic superiority; supplying it with cheap foodstuffs, with raw materials, and cheap labour as well as investment capital wrung from the Irish people in the form of rent and tithes.

These causes produced a progressive increase in the numbers and proportion of the population engaged upon the land. At the same time this increase brought no improvement of methods or conditions in agricultural production. In each case the poverty of the people and the indifference of their exploiters was an absolute bar to advance.

Edward Wakefield, a careful observer, notes one fact as universally observable in the period immediately after the Union. The Irish landlord was not a partner in production, investing capital in fencing, draining, farmbuildings, and cottages, and bound thereby to the cultivator by social and economic ties. He was simply the receiver of a rent charge. When the labour of the cultivator multiplied the produce of the soil the rent-charge was raised ruthlessly until the whole increase was swept into the landlord's maw. Irish landlords, says Wakefield, were not to be compared to English squires so much as to the "feudal" lords who owned the land upon which London stands.

The absence of any alternative to land-work (short of emigration) gave rise to an intensified demand for land, especially in small plots; and this, as in the earlier period, gave scope for the operations of the middleman. On good land competition led to excessive division and subdivision–or, alternatively, to the replacement of tillage by pasture farming. On poor land the landlord saved himself trouble by letting land to whole villages collectively. In these "rundale" villages relics of the clan system survived in the custom of allocating strips or portions of the common fields by lot, annually. A rundale village usually indicated an easy-going landlord who renewed leases as a matter of course.

Thus, whether landlords were "easy" or "hard", agricultural technique had no chance to progress. A "good" landlord was merely one who did not use to the full his power to crush the tenants utterly.

Labour paid by an allocation of potato patch and cow's grass continued in this period. Wakefield records that labour was valued at from 4d. to 8d. per day; 220 working-days in the year were fairly often the price of a cottage, potato-patch, and cow's grass.

An observer giving evidence in 1825 cited examples of rent which exceeded the total yield of the land. The cottager had to supplement the gains from his holding by earnings from domestic industry or from harvest work in England or Scotland before he could pay his rent.

> "There are parts of Connacht where a man plants his potatoes at the proper season and shuts up his cabin and goes to England and labours; and perhaps his wife and children beg on the roads; and when he comes back to dig his potatoes, with the wages of his English labour in his pocket, he is able to pay a larger sum in rent than he could have extracted from the soil."
>
> Lewis: *H. of L. Select Committee* (1825).

Despite the general poverty, house-rents in towns were often high in consequence of landlord monopoly. "Houses are dearer in some of the remote corners of Ireland," says Wakefield, "than in the best parts of London.... The whole town of Belfast belongs to one proprietor who has it in his power to exact whatever rents he thinks proper."

Poverty in Ireland: its extent

Some indication of the numbers included in the various categories of the population may be gained from the returns for the hearth-tax. The figures for 1791 show 701,102 dwellings in Ireland. Of these 112,556 were exempt from the 2s. tax as "inhabited by paupers". One-hearth dwellings numbered 483,990. Add these two together and 85 percent of the total houses are shown as of the poorest class.

This category was increased after the Catholic Relief Act of 1793 which gave the vote to "freeholds" of an annual value of 40s. Landlords, agents, and middlemen multiplied these tenancies without stint to enhance their political importance (and the bribes they could command). The vote was expected to be paid as part of the rent.

Excessive subdivision, and the poverty of the tenants, ensured a progressive deterioration of the soil which intensified the poverty. The tenant either could not manure or feared to do so lest his rent be raised. It was common practice as a lease drew to its termination for the tenant to destroy his improvements (fences, drains, outbuildings, even chimneys) as otherwise their value would be included in the "fine" exacted for a renewal of the lease. Alternatively, if left intact they might induce greedy land grabbers to overbid the occupier ruinously when the lease was put up for public "cant" (auction).

In Ulster a custom had become established which gave the tenant a property in his improvements. The absence of such a custom elsewhere in Ireland had a fearful effect in depressing the condition of the cultivators. In 1791 quite a number of the dwellers in one-hearth habitations held 40 acres or more. It was positively dangerous for them to indulge in the luxury of an improved dwelling. The census of 1841 revealed nearly 500,000 families as still living in one-room mud-cabins.

An additional infliction would be unbelievable if it were not well attested.

> "I have frequently seen the cattle of the occupying tenant driven to the pound and ... sold, when he had paid his rent to the middleman who had failed to pay it to the head landlord. The numerous instances of such distress, which everyone who has resided some time in Ireland must have witnessed,

are truly deplorable, and I believe them to be one of the causes of the frequent risings of the people which ... have been attended with atrocities shocking to humanity and disgraceful to the Empire."
Wakefield: *Survey of Ireland*, vol. 1.

There was acute distress in England all through this period. The handicraft workers and the peasant cultivators were being crushed, ruthlessly, out of existence. They, with their wives and children, were being drawn into the vortex of the new "factory hells", and cheap food was required to keep their labour "cheap".

The Irish manufacturer or handicraft worker, unless he was willing to emigrate, was flung back upon the land—and the mercies of the middleman, agent, landlord, and tithe-proctor. The cheap food wrung from the Irish peasant ruined the English peasant and drew him into the factory, where the product of his sweated labour ruined more Irish handicraftsmen and drove them to the land—to put up the rents and increase the cheap food supply that kept the vicious circle spinning.

There was famine in Ireland in the late forties; they were the "Hungry Forties" in England, too. The difference was that in England the toilers were exploited as a class; the Irish producers were, in addition, exploited as a subject nation. That is why, when agitation in England took the form of working-men's Chartism, in Ireland it took the form of a National agitation for a Repeal of the Union and even for the setting-up of an Irish Republic.

CHAPTER XIII

O'CONNELL AND CATHOLIC EMANCIPATION

From such a crushing defeat as that experienced by the Irish masses in 1798, recovery was necessarily slow. It was made through tentative approaches, much more limited in their aims than the earlier demand for an outright national independence.

The first recovery was made under the leadership of Daniel O'Connell (1785-1847), a master-agitator, who dominates his period as few agitators have ever been able to do. His victorious struggle for Catholic Emancipation (1829) is the theme of this chapter.

Daniel O'Connell

Born in Kerry, in humble circumstances, but the nephew of a landed proprietor who made him his heir, Daniel O'Connell, whose ancestry was Gaelic-Irish without admixture, was educated originally for the priesthood. The Jacobin revolution (1792-4) broke up the French seminary in which he was a student; and he returned to Ireland and studied for the law. The foundation for his great national popularity was laid by his outstanding success as an advocate.

A big man physically, full of abounding vitality, he showed distinctively Gaelic qualities at a score of points. Innumerable tales are told of his wit, his dexterity as a cross-examiner, his athletic feats, his amours, his eloquence, and above all his wonderful voice which could attain an astonishing range without losing any of its extreme beauty of tone.

He made his way to the front in the debates of the Catholic Committee, from whose leadership he eventually ousted old John Keogh. In 1823 the Catholic Committee having dissolved, O'Connell made a new departure by founding the Catholic Association.

Its key idea was a "rent" paid voluntarily by every Catholic. This "rent" was collected at the Chapel doors, and was forwarded through the priests who were made *ex officio* members of the Committee of the Association. The "rent" was fixed at a minimum of a shilling a year; or, as O'Connell was fond of saying, "a penny a month, a farthing a week—and four weeks thrown in for nothing". In this way O'Connell (1) secured the finances of the Association; (2) gained the support of the priests; (3) stilled the doubts of the Hierarchy; and (4) ensured his own leadership, since it was his personal popularity which made the scheme workable.

Orangeism, the Tories, and the Whigs

O'Connell chose his time for launching the Association very astutely.

The social transformation and unsettlement produced by the Industrial Revolution in England and by the reverberations of the French Revolution, which still echoed on the Continent and in America, were making it evident that the aristocratic oligarchy which had ruled England since 1688 would have to concede reform at some point or become itself reformed out of existence.

Growing conflict between such commercial and industrial interests as were represented indirectly in the House of Commons, and the landlord interest represented largely in the Commons but to the exclusion of all rivals in the House of Lords, was leading to constant quarrels between the Houses.

A coalition of moderate Whigs and progressive Tories held office, precariously; steering its way tortuously between Reformers and Radicals to the Left and reactionary Tories to the Right.

To such a Government an Association acceptable to the mass of the Irish, whose leadership and control was in responsible and moderate hands, was doubly welcome as a stabilising force which would canalise explosive discontents into safe channels; and, at the same time, act as a counterpoise against the reactionary Orange Order which was giving considerable trouble.

Extended to the Army and Navy by the officers, English and Irish, who had served in Ireland in '98, the Orange Order, with the Duke of Cumberland (brother of George IV and William IV) as its nominal head, had fused with extreme anti-Jacobin Toryism to become an all but open conspiracy aiming at a counter-revolutionary *coup* which would repress with violence the "Jacobin democracy" and discontent with which the lower orders were seething; or ferments which the factory owners were encouraging by their clamour for Parliamentary Reform.

At a later date the Orange Order actually reached the point of conspiracy to exclude the Princess Victoria, the heir-apparent, from succession to the throne—on the ground that a young girl, notoriously under Whig influence, would be unable to cope with the rising tide of Radicalism. This danger was averted; and the succession of the Duke of Cumberland to the Throne of Hanover* took the leaders of the conspiracy out of the country. But it is cardinal to remember that in the period from 1820 to 1837 the Government of England was more than once in greater peril of a counter-revolutionary *coup* from the Right than of any armed insurrection from the Left.

An indication of the Orange danger was evoked when a Whig Viceroy, Lord Wellesley, wishing to placate the Catholics, forbade the customary parade and decoration of William III's statue on College Green on November 4, 1822. The Viceroy was assailed with insults in the theatre, and porter-bottles were thrown from the gallery at his head. An Orange jury refused to convict those

* Owing to the operation in Hanover of the Salic Law, Victoria, while succeeding her uncle Wm. IV on the throne of Britain, was debarred from succeeding him on the throne of Hanover. This left Cumberland as the next heir.

notoriously guilty. And while the Irish public in general condemned the outrage without stint, the English House of Lords found it a good excuse for rejecting a Catholic Relief Bill which had passed the Commons by a majority of one.

It was at this point that O'Connell launched the Catholic Association which met with an immediate success—and, at first, with cordial approval from the Whigs.

The Association established a series of reading rooms and discussion societies which were immensely popular. And under O'Connell's inspiration the Association set up, with the voluntary aid of sympathetic lawyers and magistrates, a machinery for arbitrating disputes between neighbours and between landlords and tenants. This went a long way towards preventing any recurrence of "outrages" by those Whiteboy secret societies which O'Connell held in profound abhorrence.

His very success was turned into a weapon against him. Alarmed Reactionaries in the English Parliament, egged on by Orange intriguers, asked what would become of property and of the Constitution if the lower orders in England were to copy O'Connell's example and set up a similar Association to serve their "predatory" class ends.

Under pressure the Government introduced a Bill suppressing both the Catholic Association and the Brunswick Club, the open association set up by the Orange Society as a cover for its secret organisation. The Bill passed; but proved a nullity. The Tory magistrates would not act against the Brunswick Clubs; and O'Connell merely changed the name of his Association. For the next year or two comic-relief was introduced into Irish public life by a diverting catch-as-catch-can game played between O'Connell and the Attorney-General for Ireland—O'Connell inventing new names and rules for his Association, and the Attorney-General thinking-up legal pretexts for suppressing anew what he had already "suppressed", in theory, a score of times before.

During the General Election of 1826 an incident occurred which changed the situation radically.

The Beresford family, which had monopolised the representation of Co. Waterford for seventy years, found themselves, to their astonishment, opposed, in the Whig interest, by another county landowner, Villiers-Stuart. To make matters worse, Villiers-Stuart appointed as his election agent Daniel O'Connell; and there descended upon the county a swarm of canvassers from the Catholic Association. Even then the Beresfords were not seriously alarmed. They had the goodwill of the other county landlords; they had created a number of new 40s. freehold* votes; and they had spent a considerable sum in direct and indirect bribery.

At the nomination, O'Connell himself was proposed (by collusion). He spoke for two hours in declining nomination, devoting most of the time to giving a history of the Beresford family before, during, and since '98. At the poll itself, to the horror of the Beresfords and the delighted amazement of Catholic Ireland, the 40s. Freeholders—once so docile—revolted almost to a man. After the first day the issue was never in doubt; on the fifth day the Beresfords abandoned the struggle.

The perfect order and discipline shown by the peasantry amazed beholders. They marched to the hustings in military formation, each man behind the banner of his barony, and returned in the same order. A vow to touch no whiskey, while the poll was open, was universally taken and scrupulously kept.

Similar revolts on a less spectacular scale took place at the elections for Westmeath, Monaghan, Armagh, and Louth.

In revenge the landlords distrained upon or evicted

* 40s. Freeholders: These were really leaseholders for life, or the lives of three people named in the lease.

every freeholder with his rent in arrears—which meant not less than 90 percent.

O'Connell replied by announcing a Campaign for Catholic Emancipation.

The Clare Election and Emancipation

O'Connell's chance came with the advent of a new Ministry in 1829. He arranged meetings to petition for Emancipation in every Catholic parish in Ireland—all of them timed for the same hour on a single day. At least a million and a half attended, and voted for the petition. Both Houses of Parliament began to show signs of giving way.

A by-election was due for Co. Clare. The Government candidate was a man with a good record, personally, but the Government was not pledged to emancipation. It was decided to oppose him, and O'Connell himself was nominated against him.

A certain liveliness was introduced into the contest by two of O'Connell's agents, both famous duellists, who offered to give "satisfaction" to any gentleman aggrieved at having his tenants canvassed against his wishes. There were no takers. In fact, the election was an exact replica of the Waterford election. On the sixth day, his opponent having retired, O'Connell was declared elected.

Catholic Ireland went delirious with joy; and even the English soldiers sent to keep order in Ennis joined in the cheering.

The Orange faction threatened to "kick the Crown into the Boyne" if there was any "weakening" of resistance to the Catholic claims, but the Government recognised that further resistance would only produce serious trouble.

Accordingly, the Government, in 1829, introduced and carried three Acts: (1) An Act admitting Catholics to Parliament, to Commissions in the Services, and to the Inner Bar; (2) An Act disfranchising the 40s. Freeholders; and (3) An Act suppressing the Catholic Association positively for the last time.

It was proposed that, in imitation of the grant to Henry Grattan, a similar sum should be raised and presented to Daniel O'Connell. On consideration, this was changed to an annual "tribute", collected at the Chapel doors, on an appointed Sunday in each year. Until the Famine it was collected without fail every year.

CHAPTER XIV

THE TITHE WAR

With O'Connell at Westminster absorbed in the struggle for the Reform Bill (1832), it was expected that Ireland would remain tranquil.

Instead, it flamed into a fury of agitation against Tithes. In this chapter the story of the Tithe War is told.

The Tithe System in Ireland

When there was only one church in England, and its priest or parson was a public official whose services all made use of, to pay him every tenth sheaf, and so on, constituted no special grievance for the tillers. In Ireland the tithe was claimed for a church which nineteen-twentieths of the rural population did not use, and never had used.* Moreover, the tithe had been racked up by lay impropriators, and in other ways, until it often reached nearer to a quarter of the produce than one-tenth. Cases were known where the tithe actually exceeded the rent.

In theory an appeal could be made to the courts; and in Ulster, where half the tillers were Protestants or Dissenters, the owner of the crop could count on a sympathetic hearing. The Church complained that, in Ulster, assessors' courts were all conspiracies to rob the Church. In the rest of Ireland it was a proverb that appealing against a tithe-assessment was "going to law with the devil, and the court in hell!"

There were special exasperations. Landlords had secured exemption from tithe for all grazing farms. The poverty of the peasantry made it hard for them to support even their own Catholic clergy. To have to bear the

* One parish in Armagh, with only 4 resident Protestants, yielded the rector £216 a year in 1832.

whole support of the Protestant parsons as well was felt by the Catholic peasantry as a first-class grievance.

In addition, Catholics had to pay a rate for the upkeep of the Church building; and, as a final stroke, the proctor who assessed the amount due for tithe charged a commission for doing it.

The Tithe War: First Phase

Emancipation made no practical difference to the mass of the tillers; but the fact that it had been won stimulated the peasantry into a readiness for mass resistance. This was made manifest in March 1831, when the curate in charge of the parish of Graigue, Co. Carlow—with less than 70 Protestant parishioners to over 5,000 Catholics—broke a customary law and claimed tithes from the Catholic priest.

This would have been resented anyway; but this particular parson united in himself every possible cause of unpopularity. He was young, conceited, and quarrelsome. He was English. He knew nothing whatever about Ireland or its people; and he thought there was nothing to know. He was a fervent Evangelical, rancorously anti-Catholic, zealous for a "new Reformation", and had already caused trouble by his proselytising efforts. To cap all, he insisted upon acting as his own tithe-proctor; and, to show he was not to be trifled with, he impounded the priest's horse.

There was an instant response from the Catholics of the parish; to a man they refused to pay tithes at all.

The parson, nonplussed for once, appealed to the resident magistrate, who appealed to the parish priest. He replied that "things had got quite beyond his control". They had. The Whiteboys had come to life again, and had passed the word for a fight to a finish. "All Ireland was watching Graigue."

Called upon to enforce the law, the R.M.,* with 600 soldiers and police, spent a couple of months dodging and chasing cattle round the county. He gave up in despair with less than a third of the tithe collected.

The strike against tithes spread from county to county. Collisions between police and people grew into serious affrays. One occurred at Newtownbarry, between Wexford and Carlow, in June 1831. Cattle rescued by the peasants were recaptured by the police. The yeomanry opened fire; the peasants, armed only with farm implements, charged the yeomanry repeatedly, in the face of sustained fire and a free use of the bayonet. The peasants dispersed with the loss of 12 killed and many wounded, 12 of them mortally. Similar conflicts, attended with bloodshed, occurred at Thurles, at Castlepollard, and in Kilkenny Town.

The most serious conflict occurred at Carrickshock, Co. Kilkenny. A notable fact here was that the peasants had offered to pay if granted an abatement—the previous rector had claimed only £350, the present one demanded £1,700. Refused redress, the peasants organised under the leadership of a hedge-schoolmaster, an old United man. Attempts to serve writs wholesale led to fights between the peasants and the police escort. Trapped in a sunken lane between high stone walls, the police, attacked front and rear, were nearly exterminated. Eleven were killed and seventeen wounded. The peasants also suffered severely.

After this a truce was granted. O'Connell had asked for one, in vain, after the fight at Newtownbarry.

* Resident Magistrate R. M.: Stipendiaries appointed by the Government to keep the squireen Justices of the Peace within some sort of legal constraint.

In general, the clergy ceased to press for tithes. Pending legislation, they were granted a Government loan of £60,000; and in June and August 1832, Acts were passed converting the Tithe into a fixed annual payment. The arrears due, however, had to be paid up in full. Meanwhile, the truce had been broken.

In April 1832, the parish of Doon, Co. Limerick, witnessed a spectacle. A cow, seized from the parish priest, was brought to the auction ground by an escort composed of: (1) a strong body of police; (2) one troop of Lancers; (3) five companies, Gordon Highlanders; and (4) two pieces of artillery. Amid deafening uproar, the cow was sold to the priest's brother—a constable, acting under orders—for £12. The military then retired. The soldiers were barely out of sight when the crowd attacked the police and drove them, some out of the town, the rest into their barracks. The Lancers, brought back at the gallop, charged the crowd in the teeth of volleys of stones. But not until the Highlanders returned and opened fire did the crowd disperse.

A similar sale under military protection was attempted in May at Rathcormack, Co. Cork; but here the throng and the uproar were so great that the sale was abandoned. An impromptu mass meeting of the peasants adopted three resolutions: (1) It is requested that no auctioneer will lend himself to the sale of cows distrained for tithe. (2) It is requested that no person will purchase cows distrained for tithes. (3) It is Resolved that the citizens will have no intercourse or dealings with any person who aids in the sale of cows either as auctioneer or as purchaser.

This was the start of a nation-wide movement of "exclusive dealing" directed against all who paid tithes, or aided the sale of distrained cattle. Anti-tithe meetings were held everywhere; a directing committee sat in

Dublin; and when Parliament gave its sanction to the forcible collection of arrears the resistance became universal.

Wealthy landowners—Protestants as well as Catholics—were forced into line by the refusal of farm-workers and domestic servants to work for anybody who did not take the Anti-Tithe Pledge. The movement culminated in a huge assembly near the battlefield of Carrickshock. One hundred thousand farmers and cottagers marched to the meeting—5,000 on horseback—all in military order, behind the banners of their baronies, and obeying promptly the orders of their chosen leaders. A Protestant magistrate presided, and resolutions calling for the abolition of tithes were carried unanimously. The meeting dispersed in perfect order, as it had assembled.

For presiding at this meeting, its chairman was dismissed from the magistracy, and Dublin Castle ordered magistrates to "prevent any meeting likely to lead to a breach of the peace".

This in effect forbade all meetings and, expecting disobedience, the Castle rushed troops over from England.

The peasantry defeated the Castle by attempting no meetings at all. None were needed. The "underground" organisation was sufficient. The peasants were solid against tithes.

The Tithe War: Third Phase

War was renewed in September 1832, when government agents, protected by police and soldiers, set about valuing farms for the purpose of the Tithe Composition Act.

At Wallscourt, Co. Tipperary—a parish of over 3,000 inhabitants, only one of whom was a Protestant—the valuers, headed by the rector, and protected by police and Highlanders, were held up at a farm, in which the tenant insisted there were growing crops, which trespass would damage. He was backed by a strong party of peasants.

The police fired; the peasants charged, scattered the police, and were only halted by the Highlanders drawn up in square. A battle developed in which four peasants were killed and many were wounded. The valuation was carried out; and the Ascendancy Press was jubilant.

Dublin Castle, despite O'Connell's protest that the trespass was illegal, announced that it had 12,000 attachments for arrears of tithe (now due to the Crown) ready for service; and it intended to collect every penny, if necessary, at the point of the bayonet.

In October 1832, the police engaged in posting notices about tithe arrears in Co. Cork came into conflict with the peasants. The police officer said a young girl, Catherine Foley, headed a rush upon the police. The peasants alleged that the police fired without warning, and then charged with the bayonet. The arrival of soldiers stopped the fight; the peasants had 12 killed (including the girl named) and a considerable number wounded. A coroner's jury of responsible citizens brought in a verdict of wilful murder against the police officer. He was arrested, but released soon after without being charged. The Protestant rector was forced to quit the parish permanently.

This incident roused the whole countryside. The secret societies became active; the land-war reopened. Landlords, agents, and tithe-proctors were shot at; several were killed. Raids for arms on the houses of the gentry recommenced. Parties of police were attacked in open day. The General Election of 1832 was held in the midst of turmoil, and 82 members were returned from Ireland, all pledged to Abolish Tithes; 45 of them were also pledged to the Repeal of the Union. The Government's answer was a Coercion Act.

In May 1833, a party of military entered the village of Kilmurray, Co. Waterford, broke into the houses, seized cattle, and carried men off as debtors to the Crown. In June a fight at Carrigtwohill, Co. Cork, was broken off when one of the soldiers was shot, accidentally, by the police. In June also 70 soldiers and police were routed at Mullinahone, Tipperary, by an "immense" body of peasants. A few days later the *Gazette* announced that the collection of tithe arrears would be suspended.

The valuation, however, went on. In August 1833, the valuing party beat off an attack near Tipperary. In September, at Thomastown, Tipperary, the valuers were routed and their tapes, instruments, etc., were destroyed. Meanwhile, in various parts cattle were hocked, landlords shot at, and tithe-proctors horse-whipped. Exclusive dealing was universal. Police were prevented from posting notices at Pallaskenry, Co. Limerick, in February 1834. The peasants were defeated, with 3 killed and 20 wounded, at Newcastle West, in April 1834.

The last blood was shed at Rathcormack, in Co. Cork, in May 1834. The collection of 40s. arrears of tithe from a widow was only effected after 12 peasants had been killed, 7 mortally wounded, and 35 wounded less seriously. A considerable number of the soldiers engaged were wounded.

The Rathcormack "Massacre" raised such a storm that the Tories were forced to abandon resistance to the Tithe Commutation Act, in principle. They still obstructed, however, in detail, and thereby delayed its passage until 1837.

This Act reduced the amount due for tithe under the valuation then in progress by 25 percent and converted the remainder into a rent-charge payable directly by the landlord, but recoverable by him in the rent.

On the surface, the gain to the peasantry was small. Actually it was greater than it seemed. Intimidated by the peasants' solidarity, the landlords in many cases did not attempt to pass on the tithe-charge; others passed on only a portion. The evil of extortionate assessment was done away with, and particularly the evil resulting from the tithe-proctor's unseasonable demand for ready cash from people who only handled money in any quantity at special times of the year. The proctor had, in fact, acted as pace-maker for his jackal, the gombeen-man—the small-loan money-lender who was the curse of the countryside.

Thus, despite its shortcomings, the Act registered a real victory for the peasantry and their solidarity.

Thomas Drummond

A chapter on the Tithe War would not be complete without a mention of the man who really brought the war to an end. This was Thomas Drummond, Chief Secretary to the Viceroy, 1835-9. He brought the war to an end by refusing to use the troops or police for the collection of tithe arrears, except where a breach of the peace had actually occurred.

To circumvent him, the landlords, an Orange peer at their head, revived the medieval procedure of obtaining "writs of rebellion" which empowered the person named in the writ to call upon magistrates to supply a force for the "arrest of the rebel". Drummond ordered all magistrates to refuse to obey. Tested in Court, Drummond's action was upheld. The Orange Order memorialised both Houses for Drummond's removal; but Melbourne, the Prime Minister, stood by him and the attack failed.

Drummond counter-attacked by issuing strict instructions to the police to put a stop to all faction-fighting between Orangemen and Catholics. When a magistrate, high in the Orange Order, presided at a banquet to commemorate the Battle of the Diamond, Drummond dismissed him from the magistracy with a scathing public rebuke.

He followed this by dismissing from the police force

everyone, officer or constable, proved to belong to the Orange Order. When, in April 1838, the Tipperary magistrates asked the Viceroy for "the strongest force the laws permit" to put down agrarian crime, Drummond retorted that evictions in Tipperary had been double in 1837 what they were in 1833. He suggested that the landlords themselves were the cause of their own troubles: "Property has its duties as well as its rights. To the neglect of these duties in times past is mainly to be ascribed that diseased state of society in which crimes take their rise." The fury with which these home-truths were received gives a measure of the mind of the landlord-class and of their political tools, the Orange-Tory party.

Drummond's early death in 1839 was a great loss to the Irish peasantry. He is the only English administrator ever honoured by a statue in the Dublin City Hall.

CHAPTER XV

THE TRANSITION TO REPEAL AGITATION

O'Connell is best known in England from his leadership of the agitation for the Repeal of the Act of Union. This, however, did not begin in earnest until 1843. The causes of the delay between 1829 and 1843, when examined, help to fix O'Connell's real position as a National leader.

O'Connell's Political Standpoint

First and last, Daniel O'Connell has been the object of so much extravagant abuse, and so much equally extravagant laudation, that it is difficult to recover an objective view of the real man.

That he was sincerely set upon Catholic Emancipation, even his worst detractors would not attempt to deny. They question, at most, his sincerity in his agitation for Repeal—arguing, as they do, that he merely agitated the question, demagogically, as a means of maintaining his popularity and preserving his political ascendancy among the Irish people. The contemporary jibe, "The Big Beggar-Man", has no other meaning.

An examination of O'Connell's career gives the lie direct to this foolish theory. It proves two things: (1) That O'Connell spent more years and more energy in keeping Ireland quiet than he did in stirring it into agitation; (2) that in the years between 1829 and 1843 he was all the time seeking to gain a Repeal of the Union by a dexterous succession of political combinations—first with one English party, then with another.

Repeal, the logical consequence of Catholic Emancipation, was the goal O'Connell set himself to achieve. His limitations were that he desired to preserve, along with Repeal, the connection with England, and further, that he was inveterately opposed to anything in the nature of insurrection or revolution.

O'Connell, in fact, emerges as a tragic figure of colossal proportions—a man born with every qualification for a revolutionary leader of the very first rank, save only the essential qualification of the will to revolution. Instead, his horror of these things, acquired in his youthful experience in France in 1792-3, and in Ireland in 1798, constantly made him stultify himself just when the road seemed clear before him. He, more than any man who ever lived, could have called all Ireland to arms with a single word. Yet he was the one Irishman who ever lived who would never, in any circumstances, utter that word.

In 1829 he caught the rulers of England napping. They thought then that he was ready for revolution; and they knew that in England at that time, he would find a large mass of powerful allies. In later years they knew him better; but there was always the fear that the agitation he conducted might grow beyond even his magisterial control. His attitude towards the Tithe War—which he not only refused to lead, but did everything he could to divert into safe constitutional channels—and his attitude towards Chartism—which he patronised while it was weak, and fought unsparingly when it grew strong—gives an accurate measure of O'Connell's place as a National leader.

O'Connell and the Chartists

O'Connell's attitude to the Chartists is especially decisive because he was in general sympathy with all of the points of the People's Charter, and because the Chartists for their part were always staunch supporters of Ireland's claims, even to making Repeal of the Union one of the demands in their Second National Petition, in 1842. O'Connell, from his first entry into the House of Commons, had helped the Reformers in their fight for the Reform Bill; in fact, it was by the votes of O'Connell and his supporters that the Bill was carried in 1832. He classed then as a Radical, and the Chartists counted

227

upon his aid. His later lukewarmness and his eventual opposition seemed to them a base desertion.

It is, however, explicable quite otherwise. O'Connell's attitude to the Chartists was embittered by personal hostility between him and the Chartist leaders James Bronterre O'Brien and Feargus O'Connor; but this hostility itself arose from a fundamental political antagonism. Both O'Brien and O'Connor were agrarian revolutionaries who wished to make an end of landlordism altogether. O'Connell, himself a landlord, who envisaged Utopia as a place where landlords did their duty indulgently, hated on instinct everything that O'Brien and O'Connor fought for. O'Brien applauded every stage of the Tithe War, and blamed O'Connell for spoiling it by his interference. O'Connor applauded the "glorious deeds of the Whiteboys"—whom O'Connell thought "miscreants" who ought to be exterminated. And O'Connor, inordinately proud to be the nephew of a leading United Irishman (Arthur O'Connor) always thought and spoke in terms of just such a revolution as the United Irishmen had envisaged. O'Connell's fanatical hatred of revolution in general and the French Revolution in particular extended without abatement to the "Jacobin" United Irishmen. Thus, at every point O'Connell's outlook was radically incompatible with those of all the Chartist leaders—except, possibly, the "moral force" Chartists. For these reasons he used his every endeavour to keep the Chartist movement out of Ireland, and he was careful on principle never to embarrass the Government with Irish agitation when they had anything to fear from the Chartists.

It was with genuine pride that he boasted in Parliament (July 1840) that, when England had been faced with a Chartist rising, in November 1839, Ireland remained perfectly tranquil:

"He was Counsel for Ireland and he was there to plead her cause. England was discontented and disaffected—Ireland was tranquil. England was distracted by lawless bands of physical force Chartists. Ireland did not seek to attain her ends by violence, by resistence to the law, by destruction of property. In England rebel bands were led against the armed soldiery; but these soldiers knew their duty and performed it. What were they? *Irishmen!* In England the lives of the gentry were threatened... Had the Irish in England joined the Chartists? Had they evinced a desire to link themselves with these assassins? With a few insignificant exceptions they had not. Had the Irish in Ireland taken any part with the Chartists?... No! Ireland had become tranquil... Her military force was diminished. And why? Because the troops which were necessary to struggle against rebellion, sedition, and treason in England were not required to maintain the good order which prevailed in Ireland."

M. F. Cusack: *Speeches and Public Letters of the Liberator*, Vol. 2.

This would seem strange reading—so soon after the Tithe War—if we did not know that it expressed what O'Connell wished for, rather than what he believed to be the literal truth.

A fresh flare-up of Chartism in 1842 found O'Connell busy in office as Lord Mayor of Dublin. But he found time to use all his influence to keep Ireland quiet even though the Chartists had declared for the Repeal of the Union.

Before his term of office as Lord Mayor expired, an event occurred destined to be of far-reaching importance. A weekly journal, the *Nation*, appeared for the first time in October, 1842.

"What is the tone of the new journal?" asked one High Court Judge of another.

"Wolfe Tone!" was the sufficient answer.

Three young men, the oldest under thirty—Charles Gavan Duffy born in Monaghan, John Blake Dillon born in Mayo, and Thomas Osborne Davis born in Mallow, Co. Cork—were the founders of the *Nation*. Duffy and Dillon were Catholics; Davis, a Protestant, and the son of an Englishman, an army surgeon. Davis and Dillon were barristers, Duffy a journalist. All had literary talent, and all three were ardent members of the Repeal Association which O'Connell had founded in 1841.

They declared the object of the *Nation* to be "to foster a public opinion in Ireland and make it racy of the soil"; and they sought to reach this end by making the journal informative without being dull, and inspiring without being hysterical. They were staunchly loyal to O'Connell, and ardent for Repeal, but they sought always to give a reasoned case in support of their objects; and, therefore, paid particular attention to cultivating that pride in self-reliant nationhood which they conceived would be the best means of re-creating a United Ireland. From the first they took their stand upon the claim that the Irish people was, in fact, a Nation, and should insist upon being treated as such.

A feature of the *Nation*, which was immensely popular from the start, was its original ballad-poetry; usually upon historical themes in which Davis and Duffy both excelled. They became a source of inspiration to a host of other young writers, whose work bore comparison with that of their inspirers. Written to be sung to well-known airs, these ballads were martial and inspirating. In their leading articles, and their prose generally, the writers of the *Nation* kept loyally within the programme marked out by O'Connell; but in their poetry they transcended these limits, and sang of the Rising of the Clans, of Owen Roe O'Neill, of the Irish Brigade at Fontenoy, of Clare's

Dragoons, of the Volunteers of '82, of the Men of '98, and of Wolfe Tone.

The *Nation* writers were in the main a group of middle-class intellectuals; but some very fine verse, and some sound prose, was contributed by plain wage-workers and working-farmers. Acute observers detected the resemblance between the work the *Nation* group was trying to do in Ireland and the work Heine and others had done in the Young Germany movement of the 'thirties and the work Mazzini was doing with the Young Italy movement. Not inaptly they dubbed the *Nation* group Young Ireland. It has been well said that whereas O'Connell's demand was, in effect, "Good Government or else–Repeal!" Young Ireland's demand, implicit at first, but becoming explicit later, was "Repeal or else–Separation!"

Thomas Davis

Of the many writers in the *Nation*, the one whose influence was most vital, was Davis. His teaching was the clearest and most searching, and he summed up its total significance himself in the phrase "Ireland's aspiration is for Unbounded Nationality". O'Connell, in banking everything upon persuading an English party that it would be safe, as well as expedient, to grant Repeal, was apt at times to whine, and, at others, to bluster. Davis did neither. His teaching was always manly, and always charged with the self-respect which is a necessary condition for developing a respect for others. Says Patrick Pearse: "There was a deep humanism in Tone; and there was deep humanism in Davis. The sorrows of the people affected Davis like a personal sorrow... he was a democrat in this truest sense that he loved the people, and his love of the people was an essential part of the man and of his Nationalism."

Davis showed his sound democratic instinct when he persisted quietly in spite of O'Connell in urging a change of attitude towards the English Chartists. Duffy reports that: "Davis, who recognised in the English democracy a growing power, with no interest hostile to ours, and which might become our ally, recommended the Repealers to come to a good understanding with them, making no more account of O'Connell's personal quarrel where a national object was in view than he would have made in such a case of any personal feeling or interest of his own." And, although Davis's advice was not taken soon enough, it was this spirit which caused the influence of the *Nation* to spread from the first with the speed of a flame running through dry grass.

An immediate increase resulted in the membership of the Repeal Association. The movement came suddenly to life. O'Connell, prompt to scent every change in public sentiment, especially among his followers, realised at once that unless he acted promptly, and on a big scale, the young men of the *Nation*, without intending it, would take the leadership of the movement quite out of his hands.

Accordingly at the beginning of 1843 O'Connell announced that a new agitation would be launched; and that "this year" would be, definitely, the Repeal Year.

CHAPTER XVI

THE CRISIS OF THE REPEAL AGITATION

Throughout 1843 O'Connell developed an agitation such as, till then, the world had never known. How the agitation ran its course; how it was met by the English Government; and what followed in consequence, is told in this chapter.

The Monster Meetings

In his Repeal Agitation O'Connell stirred Ireland to its roots; and aroused the excited interest of the whole world. His method was simple. Local meetings in every parish led up to meetings in large towns and counties. These again led up to Monster Meetings in which the people of areas equal to provinces were assembled in immense masses. The whole was designed to culminate in a mighty meeting which would declare the Nation's will.

As in the Waterford and Clare elections, and in the Anti-Tithe demonstrations, the order, sobriety, and method of the meetings were as remarkable as were their phenomenal proportions. In the preparations for these meetings—the appointment of wardens and marshals, the planning of routes, and stations, and for the provisioning of the people on their way to and from (as well as in the discussions before and after) and the reading in the Repeal Reading-rooms of press-reports, and of the correspondence the meetings evoked—the whole people became organised and nation-conscious.

No man ever did so much to rouse a people from abjectness as O'Connell did by his Repeal agitation of 1843. But it is only fair to add that his work was made much easier by the propaganda of the *Nation*. Needless to say, all the meetings of any size were addressed by O'Connell, who was indefatigable in supervising, planning, and inspiring the whole effort.

How big, exactly, these Monster Meetings were will never be known. Duffy, a stickler for accuracy, puts that at Mallow at half a million. He will not allow more for the meetings at Mullaghmast and at Tara, though he concedes that others put the one at three-quarters of a million and the other at a whole million. He notes that at Tara not one of the objects of antiquarian interest excited so much notice as the "grave of the men who fell at Tara in '98". He notes how the grave was decorated by the people spontaneously; how they waited patiently for their turn to kneel and say a prayer for the dead at the graveside.

Even a voice as marvellous as O'Connell's could reach only a fraction of a throng so immense. Duffy notes that from no point was it possible to see the whole meeting in one view. "People covered the plain as far as the eye could reach."

While O'Connell, in all his speeches, was careful to say that the Repealers would never rely upon physical force to gain their ends, the immensity and fervour of the gatherings imparted a note of militancy to his oratory which somewhat overstepped his politic bounds. Replying to an Orange demand that his Agitation should be put down by force, he delivered at Mallow a famous "Defiance": "Are we to be trampled underfoot? Oh, they shall never trample *me*, at least! [Shouts of 'No! No!'] I say, they *may* trample me; but it will be my dead body they will trample on and not the living man!" Loud cheering prolonged for several minutes.

In spite of himself, O'Connell was driven by his own success to the very brink of insurrection.

Reactions to the agitation

Every democratic, republican, and revolutionary movement in the world was excited by O'Connell's agitation. Radicals on the Continent joined Irish exiles in

234

sending encouragement and offers of help. American politicians hinted that "if England made war upon Ireland, she would lose Canada". English Chartists, despite O'Connell's disparagements of them and their leaders, declared that, if Ireland were attacked, "the English aristocracy would have two nations to crush instead of one".

Even Orangemen began to be infected and to join the Repeal Association—on the understanding that they were free to advocate a Federal connection with England as a substitute for the Union. A Committee of Whigs was set up to devise a Federal plan.

The Ascendancy faction, almost beside themselves with fright, warned the landlords that O'Connell was talking now of "fixity of tenure" for the peasants. Those who had refused tithes could equally well refuse rents. Where was it all to end?

English manufacturers took the alarm. If Repeal were conceded to agitation, what an example that would be to the Chartists!—to the factory hands clamouring for the Ten Hour Bill!—to the Trade Unions! Even the Liberal Whigs, who favoured Repeal, feared the consequences of conceding it to agitation.

Early in the agitation Dublin Castle, under Orange influence, had struck its first blow by removing from the lists of magistrates those who supported the Repeal Association. This had brought an ominous reply. Scores of distinguished Protestant magistrates resigned, in protest, and joined the Association. Soon they were presiding over arbitration courts all over the country, which left the official courts nothing to try but casual drunks and common thieves.

As the agitation grew, this defection from the magistracy grew more alarming. The Government, thoroughly scared, began to move troops into Ireland; and re-enacted the Arms Act of 1793.

The Crisis at Clontarf*

It had been planned that the series of Monster Meetings should culminate in a final, stupendous, All-Ireland rally on the historic battlefield of Clontarf. As the day fixed (Sunday, October 5) drew near, every resource was employed to ensure that the gathering would be the greatest ever.

The Authorities prepared no less strenuously. More and more troops arrived. Police barracks were loopholed for musketry, and prepared to stand a siege. Forts and martello towers were prepared for defence. But how far this was show, and how far an indication of real resolution, nobody knew.

The Tory Government was in a dilemma. Half, at least, of the Protestant Community in Ireland had either gone wholly over to Repeal or were working feverishly with the Whigs to discover some means of conciliation. The Chartists had been crushed in 1842, but they were reviving. The Whigs and Radicals were agitating against the Corn Laws and looked more than half inclined to use the Irish as a stick to beat the Tory dog with. It was a moot point; but, on a balance, Wellington and Peel decided that to concede anything to agitation, then, meant conceding everything. They decided, therefore, that O'Connell's bluff must be called.

On the afternoon of Saturday, October 4, Dublin Castle issued a proclamation forbidding the Clontarf meeting.

Boatloads of excursionists had arrived from Belfast, Glasgow, Liverpool, and Holyhead; and more were arriving with every tide. Contingents were on their way from all parts of Ireland. More would set out through the afternoon and night. Only a tiny fraction of this multitude could ever learn of this proclamation before reach-

---

* Clontarf: Here Brian Boru inflicted a decisive and final defeat on the "Danish" invaders in 1014.

ing the meeting-ground which they would find occupied by the military. What would happen?

O'Connell, for his part, had no doubts. Whether the people submitted or resisted, the result would be equally disastrous for his leadership. If they gave way to the proclamation, the Government would know they commanded more authority than he. If the people did not give way, whether they were massacred–as he thought, or said, they would be–or whether they overpowered the troops by sheer weight of numbers, it would be equally impossible for him to keep them any longer under control. It was possible, even, that, while the troops were all occupied at Clontarf, a determined band might seize Dublin Castle, proclaim a Republic, and distribute arms to the people. The reaction to a massacre would be as it had been in the Tithe War; but on an immensely higher scale. To go on was to be committed to insurrection and revolution–the final disaster for his "moral force" policy and his leadership.

O'Connell therefore met the situation promptly. A counter-proclamation was issued by the Repeal Council cancelling the meeting. Messengers, on fast horses, galloped down all the roads leading out of Dublin to meet and turn back the marching myriads. Workmen removed the gigantic platform erected at Clontarf. Crowds arrived, of course, but only as sight-seers to view the soldiers in possession of the ground.

For O'Connell the situation was saved. But a veteran of '98 passed a different judgment: "Ireland was won at Clontarf; and at Clontarf it was lost again."

The Trial of "O'Connell and others"

Swift on the heels of the surrender came the pursuit. A State prosecution was launched against O'Connell and eight others–including the editor of the *Nation*, Gavan Duffy.

The indictment as presented when the trial opened on January 16, 1844, was a scroll, one hundred yards long:

"In this huge document forty-seven overt acts were set out, sixteen of which consisted merely of attending monster meetings. It was charged against the editors [of the *Nation*, the *Pilot*, and the *Freeman's Journal*] that they had reported speeches at these meetings. Fifteen other overt acts consisted in attending meetings of the Repeal Association where speeches by O'Connell, alleged to be seditious, were delivered, the plan of the Arbitration Courts was adopted, and (as respects the journalists) in 'unlawfully, maliciously, and seditiously' reporting these transactions in their newspapers. Another overt act was the 'endeavour to collect a meeting' at Clontarf. Ten of the eleven remaining overt acts were charged against the newspapers. Six were publications in the *Nation*. Of these, four were leading articles, one a poem ['Who fears to speak of Ninety-Eight?'] and one a letter proposing that modern names of places in Ireland should be abandoned and the old Gaelic names revived."

Duffy: *Young Ireland.*

There was never much doubt about the verdict—the jury list had been too well cooked for that—or about the judgment—though one of the judges dissented. The trial, in fact, after its opening excitements, grew unutterably wearisome from lack of any doubt about the result. It was a relief from boredom when the jury returned their expected verdict and the judges sentenced all the prisoners (save one who had died) to six months' imprisonment and a fine apiece.

Brought before the House of Lords, on a Writ of Error, the verdict and sentence were quashed—three months later—on the grounds that the jury list was defective, the indictment bad, and the judge's direction faulty.

The prisoners (who had been incarcerated in the private apartments of the prison Governor, with access to his grounds) received an immense ovation on their release.

O'Connell changes his front

O'Connell, who was a past-master in political finesse, tried to pretend that at Clontarf the people had defeated the Government (by obeying his cancellation order); and that the House of Lords verdict had restored the position to what it had been before Clontarf. Actually he, like everybody else, knew that Clontarf had been a nodal point at which the whole quality of the agitation became transformed.

That part of the movement which had been merely drawn into it by the impetus of its success became detached again, and began to disintegrate from the moment when it was no longer possible to believe that O'Connell had only to command and the Government must obey. That part of the movement which was more Catholic than Nationalist—which venerated O'Connell as virtually a lay Primate of all Ireland—remained docile to his leadership as before. But, as O'Connell knew, passive docility counts only negatively in a political struggle. The part of the movement which was most virile, most to be relied upon in action, and most intensely Nationalist—the part which had followed O'Connell as a National leader primarily because he was going their way—began, from the moment of the Clontarf surrender, to look for ways and means of going on without him. This break-away tendency was subconscious; but it was none the less real. Davis, though he remained loyal to O'Connell's leadership to the end, expressed this tendency instinctively in a poem written immediately after Clontarf:

> Earth is not deep enough to hide
> The coward slave who shrinks aside;

Hell is not hot enough to scathe
The ruffian wretch who breaks his faith.
But–calm, my soul!–we promised true
Her destined work our land shall do;
Thought, courage, patience will prevail!
We shall not fail!–we shall not fail!

On the eve of his trial O'Connell was perturbed about
the leadership of the Association during his (expected)
imprisonment. The machine had been run, under his
direction, by his son John and his friend Rae, both of
whom were included in the indictment, along with the
two editors (of the *Pilot* and the *Freeman's Journal*)
whom he controlled. The man he most feared–Davis,
whom he appraised more justly than Davis, in his
modesty, appraised himself–would be left free to take the
place of command that was his by natural right.

O'Connell was, therefore, more delighted than anybody when the State Prosecution brought the Repeal Association a new recruit in the person of William Smith
O'Brien, son of Lord Inchiquin and lineal descendant of
Brian Boroimhe. O'Brien, as M.P. for Limerick, had always
taken a boldly Nationalist line; but he had, till then, held
aloof from O'Connell and his "demagogue" methods.
With O'Connell's delighted approval, Smith O'Brien was
popularly acclaimed *Tanist* of the Repeal Association.

To his intense chagrin he found that Davis and Young
Ireland took to O'Brien and he to them, by instinct. If
O'Brien had been anything of a soldier they would have
constituted a Lord Edward-Tone combination all over
again. As it was, Davis and O'Brien set to work upon the
patient, ideological, and educational consolidation they
saw to be imperative; and in this work the *Nation* was
invaluable. It and it alone saved the Repeal movement
from collapse in the moral revulsion after Clontarf.

Once released, O'Connell soon showed signs of a complete change of front. There was no renewal of agitation;

but neither was there any encouragement for that policy of systematic education of the rank and file which Davis had initiated, with O'Brien's support, through the Repeal Reading-rooms. There were displays of impatience with the "young oracles" of the *Nation*; and a hint of real anger when Young Ireland displayed scornful merriment at the suggestion that the decision of the House of Lords was the result of a direct intervention of Providence in answer to the prayers of the faithful. Along with this went a steady drift towards O'Connell's old policy of co-operation with the Whigs.

In later years Young Ireland writers attributed this to O'Connell's jealousy, to the break-down of his morale in "prison", to the onset of the mental break-down of his last days. A truer and more obvious explanation is that the Young Ireland group and the *Nation* were, by revivifying the Repeal Movement, welding it into a real force, and so were re-creating for O'Connell the dilemma from which the Government had rescued him by banning the Clontarf meeting.

It was significant that his first open quarrel with Davis and the *Nation* was contrived in a way which made him appear as the champion of Catholic faith against insidious "godlessness". Davis had welcomed the proposal to establish undenominational University Colleges in Belfast, Galway, and Cork. He welcomed the co-education of Catholics and Protestants as a means towards breaking down sectarianism; and till then O'Connell had advocated that line, too. Now, without warning, he repudiated the line taken by Davis and the *Nation* as "not a Catholic view". Davis defended himself, and for his pains was grossly insulted by a notorious blackguard—the O'Connells, father and son, applauding the insulter loudly. A disgraceful scene was ended by the personal intervention of Henry Grattan, junior, and Smith O'Brien, who extorted a grudging apology from O'Connell.

The deed, however, had been done. O'Connell had

contraposed "Old" Ireland to "Young" Ireland and made the division identical with that between Catholic zeal and "godlessness". It was tragically significant that it was O'Connell who thus contraposed Catholicism to Separatist Nationalism as mutually exclusive opposites; and the incident derives additional force from the fact that the Orange-Tory zealots also denounced the colleges as "godless".

The immediate effect of the incident was to undo at a stroke all the work the *Nation* had accomplished in binding Orange and Green together in a United National Movement. Davis in particular had been especially successful in convincing liberal Protestants that Repeal would not mean Catholic Ascendancy. In effect O'Connell had now declared, *ex cathedra*, that it would.

Before the mischief could be repaired the *Nation* suffered a fearful blow. On September 15, 1845, Thomas Davis died after only a few days' illness. "It seemed," says Duffy, "as if the sun had gone out of the heavens." "The loss of this rare and noble Irishman," said Mitchel, "has never been repaired, neither to his country, nor to his friends."

CHAPTER XVII

FAMINE: AND 'FORTY-EIGHT

A new endeavour to revive the United Irishmen's movement culminated in an abortive attempt at revolution in July 1848–viz, Smith O'Brien's Rebellion.

The events which led up to this–especially the Great Famine of '46-7–are examined in this chapter.

The Great Starvation

Underlying and conditioning the political events of 1845-50 was the great calamity which the English called the Irish Famine but which the Irish called The Great Starvation.

The bedrock facts are these: (1) Failure of the potato crop (a consequence of the concurrence of several sorts of epidemic disease) was partial in Ireland in 1845, general in 1846, and absolute in 1847. (2) In consequence, in each of the years next following the ones indicated there were deaths from hunger, hunger-typhus, and cholera, upon such a scale that the numbers have never been ascertained. Deaths and emigration reduced the population of Ireland by one-third in ten years; which means that the rural population was reduced to little more than one-half. (3) The failure of the potato crop, from the causes named, was general throughout Europe; but only in Ireland was there famine, because–(4) only in Ireland was the peasant population totally or mainly dependent upon the potato crop.

A second set of facts must be set in comparison with the foregoing: (1) In the "famine" years Ireland produced foodstuffs (grain, cattle, dairy-produce, etc.) in abundance; (2) No disease (except that of the tillers) afflicted either the corn harvest, which was superabundant, or the cattle; (3) The landlord and the tax collector not merely took their tribute as usual but also took the occasion to squeeze out arrears due; (4) The amount of corn, cattle, etc., exported from Ireland in these years would have fed all those who hungered twice over. (5) Therefore, the Irish are quite right when they say: "God sent the blight; but the English landlords sent the Famine!"

Further facts reinforce this deduction. English philanthropists, as well as American and Continental, were much moved at the distress, and raised large sums for famine relief. Parliament voted as much as would have kept the late war going for half a day. But "political economy" prescribed that these sums must not be given to the Irish lest they become "demoralised". (If any Irishman objected to "demoralising" landlords by giving them corn and cattle he was liable to transportation as a felon.) The Irish were made to earn their relief by labour—building bridges over dry brooks, making roads to nowhere, etc.—work which qualified for a ration of maize meal, etc. But before they were qualified for relief they had to part with all the land they held in excess of one quarter-acre. In conditions in which families holding as much as twenty acres died of starvation—or of cold when all the blankets and sheets had been sold from their beds and the clothes from their backs to buy food—the value of this quarter-acre clause to landlords desiring to "consolidate" their estates, and to statesmen anxious to get rid of the "discontented Irish" cannot be over-estimated.

An English remedy, applied in 1846, was to Repeal the Corn Laws and so make grain cheap enough for the Irish peasants to buy. But making grain cheap meant that it took more Irish-grown grain to make up the landlord's rent. The man who had contrived till then to save a little grain for his family, had now to part with it all and starve. Or, alternatively, to be evicted! Thus the English remedy brought thousands more beneath the famine line; and made evictions easier than ever. Moreover, cheap food is as much beyond the reach of a man with nothing as dear food is. What the blight spared, the landlord took. What the landlord spared, "political economy" and "legitimate enterprise" gobbled up between them. Irish grain bought in England was shipped by relief committees to Ireland and resold there at half its cost. The starving peasants had no money; so it was bought up by speculators, who reshipped it to England, where the relief committee bought it a second time, to send it round the circle again and again.

Before the peasants were too exhausted by hunger, there were (one is glad to note) outbreaks of agrarian "crime". Barns were looted; flour mills stormed; landlords and their agents were shot; and their houses were plundered and set fire to. These things were, however, comparatively rare. Meanwhile, a Royal Duke in England was saying: "I understand that rotten potatoes and seaweed–or even grass–properly mixed, afford a very wholesome and nutritious food. We all know that Irishmen can live upon anything, and there is plenty of grass in the fields even if the potatoes should fail."

A sovereign English remedy was Emigration. Philanthropic agencies subsidised emigrant ships to carry away gratis the victims of famine and the eviction bailiff. The ships were over-crowded, sanitation was bad, the emigrants were insufficiently supplied with money, food or clothing. They were rich only in the germs of typhus and cholera they carried. Soon the worst horrors of the famine were being reproduced in the emigrant ships on the high seas.

The End of O'Connell

The full dimensions of the Famine disaster were not apparent until the autumn of 1846. Between the death of Davis and this date O'Connell achieved his last political victory–that of driving Young Ireland out of the Repeal Association.

His pretext (a transparent hypocrisy) was that the

Young Ireland group "believed in physical force". So they did, in principle; but for immediate practice he might as well have accused them of designing to steal the Dome of St. Paul's. It was a trap into which Young Ireland fell—Meagher worst of all, since in his ardour he was tricked into delivering an oration in praise of The Sword, which earned him his by-name of "Meagher of the Sword" but none the less gave John O'Connell his chance to make the breach absolute.

O'Connell's position was that he saw as clearly as any man that the only alternatives before Ireland—and the victims of the threatening famine—were, either (1) an insurrection which would retain the harvest in Ireland (which in the circumstances would have to be a social revolution as well as a political one). Or, (2) a complete dependence upon the grace and favour of the ruling-class in England. From his standpoint this gave no choice at all. A social revolution, to him, was unthinkable. He was forced to come to an agreement with the Whigs; and to make sure of driving the best possible political bargain with them he had first to get absolute control of the Repeal Association, so that he could turn it into a machine for the repression of agitation and the suppression of "sedition".

So well had O'Connell done his work in the "Repeal Year" that the new policy of coalition with the Whigs had to be broken to the rank and file very gently. He knew that the *Nation*—and especially John Mitchel, who had taken Davis's place as its leading writer—would oppose his coalition policy root and branch. He knew that the *Nation* had so strong a hold on the rank-and-file Repealers that the *Nation's* opposition might swing them against him and defeat his plans. Therefore it was, politically, a life-and-death necessity for him to drive Young Ireland out of the Association and the *Nation* out of the Repeal Reading-rooms.

Once this had been done, as it was, O'Connell prepared

to leave Ireland for the last time–being completely broken down in mind and body. He was struggling vainly to reach Rome, and a Papal benediction, when he died at Genoa on May 15, 1847–of brain-softening and senile decay.

His inept, ill-natured, and dishonest son John promulgated the lie that the Young Irelanders had "broken the Liberator's heart". The truth was that the O'Connells, between them, had broken the hopes of Ireland.

The Irish Confederation

Until O'Connell retired (December 1846) from the leadership of the Repeal Association the Young Irelanders made no attempt to set up a rival organisation. His retirement released the bonds of personal affection and habit, which had kept thousands loyal to O'Connell, while dissenting sharply from his policy. Left to stand or fall on his own merits, John O'Connell found himself deserted by hundreds daily. The formation of a new organisation was forced upon Young Irelanders by the visible disintegration of the Association and its degeneration into nonentity.

The Irish Confederation was founded at a meeting in Dublin (January 13, 1847), attended by 1,500 people. Its object was defined as: "protecting our national interests and obtaining the Legislative Independence of Ireland by the force of opinion, by the combination of all classes of Irishmen, and by the exercise of all the political, social, and moral influences within our reach."

It was decided also that the Confederation was to remain absolutely independent of all English parties, and that any member accepting office from an English government would be automatically excluded from membership. Discussions upon religious questions were forbidden.

So far the Confederation was little other than an at-

247

tempt to re-establish the Repeal Association as it had been before Clontarf. But there were forces at work which were bound to drive them much further. The work done by the *Nation*–particularly the vigour with which it had stressed the danger of delay in coping with the famine situation–had created an outlook which far transcended that of simple Repeal; and this was shown especially in the writings of the man, John Mitchel, whom Duffy had brought on to the *Nation* to help fill the gap created by the death of Davis.

John Mitchel: Duffy: The Chartists

John Mitchel (1815-1875 was born at Dungiven, Co. Derry, the son of a Unitarian Minister–who had been himself a United Irishman. He was a more powerful prose writer than Davis and a much better speaker. He lacked both the breadth and depth of Davis; but he made up for this by the greater directness and intensity of his personal hatred of English rule, and of everybody connected therewith.

He is a difficult man to classify since, although he was ready to co-operate with anybody–including Chartists, Jacobins, Red Republicans, and Socialists–who would help him fight the British Empire, and, moreover, hated the landlord class, and despised the tinsel trumpery of Royalism, he was not, basically, a democrat in the sense that Davis was. He astonished and saddened his admirers in later years by siding with the Southern Confederacy in the Civil War in the U.S.A.–partly because their claim of a Right to Secede seemed on all fours with Ireland's claim for separation (wherein he was profoundly in error), but chiefly because the "Yankees", as manufacturers and traders, seemed to him too like the English to be right about anything.

Probably the truest classification of Mitchel would place him as an oligarchical-republican in the true revolutionary-Presbyterian tradition. He showed the outstanding qualities of the Ulsterman—the qualities which the Orange Order has perverted to base, anti-national ends; but qualities which are, none the less, invaluable, and indispensable ingredients in the sum total of Irish Nationality.

All through 1846 and 1847 Mitchel developed those talents—which Davis discovered in him before he was aware of possessing them himself. By the middle of 1847 he had reached the conviction that something more swift and forcible was required than the patient brick-by-brick building-up of an all-class Association which was Davis's first thought after the surrender at Clontarf.

Charles Gavan Duffy, proprietor and editor of the *Nation*, had none of Mitchel's ingrained impulse towards physical-force insurrection. He had a talent for practical politics, and his Nationalism—which only momentarily became downright separatism—found expression in the conception of an independent Nationalist Party which would force Repeal by a Parliamentary policy which would make the English parties see in Repeal a welcome way out of an intolerable situation. Parnell, years later, credited Duffy with the invention of what came to be known as "Parnellism". Davis, no doubt, could have induced Mitchel and Duffy to work as a team under his leadership. Left to themselves they were bound to drift apart.

On its organisational side, the Confederation developed by the formation of a series of political clubs in all the towns and larger villages of Ireland. Their names—Sarsfield Club, Emmet Club, Wolfe Tone Club, etc.—testified to the inevitable trend of the teaching of the *Nation*.

On the ideological side the Confederation was stimulated by the letters and articles of James Fintan Lalor, one of a family of farmers in Laoighis (Queen's County) who had figured prominently in the Tithe war.

Lalor's idea was that of Moral Insurrection; that the farmers should be taught and encouraged to refuse all rents and taxes until the needs of their families had been satisfied. This insurrection—in which we see clearly the influence of the Tithe war—should be organised, he proposed, by a Tenant League for the country, a Trades Council for each town, and a General Council set up by both to co-ordinate the struggle and prepare for a National Convention.

Lalor's standpoint is openly separatist; and it is clear from the reception his work received that the Young Irelanders (Mitchel at their head) had already reached virtually the same conclusion.

If Lalor had not been physically disqualified from rallying the farmers to his plan—he was a consumptive cripple, and nearly blind—much more might have been heard of him and his plan of moral insurrection. As it was, the debates on Lalor's plan brought out the growing divergence between the tendencies of Duffy and O'Brien on one side, and of Mitchel and his friends on the other.

This divergence led Mitchel, eventually, to sever his connection with the *Nation* (December 1847). The occasion was the introduction of a new coercion Act introduced by the Whig Government. Mitchel explains his position thus:

"I had watched the progress of the Famine-policy of the Government and . . . had come to the conclusion that the whole system ought to be met with resistance at every point, and the means for this would be extremely simple: namely, a combination among the people to obstruct and render impossible the transport and shipment of Irish provisions; to refuse all aid in its removal; to destroy the highways; to prevent everyone by intimidation from daring to bid for grain or cattle if brought to auction under distress . . . in short, to offer a passive resistance universally, but occasionally when opportunity served, to try the steel."*

John Mitchel: *Last Conquest*, Chap. XVII.

Neither Duffy nor O'Brien was prepared for desperate courses at that stage. They were acutely conscious of the negative aspects of Mitchel's plan—its excessive reliance upon spontaneity; its alienation of the landlords; its exposure of the *Nation* to attack and suppression—and on the other hand they lacked Mitchel's faith in the readiness of the farming community for a revolutionary struggle. They still had hopes of achieving results constitutionally; or alternatively, they feared to alienate the middle class by an "unprovoked" resort to violent courses. A majority of the Confederation sided with O'Brien and Duffy.

There is this much excuse for Duffy's and O'Brien's desire to wait before rushing headlong into insurrection, that a strong agitation had arisen in England against the Coercion Bill, and a strong demand was arising, led by the Chartists—whose agitation was booming again—for Justice to Ireland. Confederate Clubs formed in England by Irish exiles were joining in the Chartist movement; and the prospect of a joint agitation seemed to be, and was, very bright.

In Parliament, Feargus O'Connor (elected for Nottingham in 1847) had taken the leadership of the Repeal Party out of the hands of John O'Connell, had moved for a Committee of Inquiry into the condition of Ireland, and had resisted the Coercion Act so effectively that it was only carried by a majority of fourteen. These were facts which, rightly, weighed heavily with Duffy and O'Brien.

Mitchel, meanwhile, was, with Thomas Devin Reilly,

* Mitchel and Lalor: The dispute whether Mitchel did or did not borrow his plan from Lalor without acknowledgment is idle. Both owed the basis of their conception to the experiences of the Tithe war. Lalor's plan, as first formulated, was Utopian in the sense of trying to achieve a revolutionary result by pacifist methods. Mitchel on the other hand wished to get an insurrection started; trusting to improvisation for the outcome.

visiting the Confederate Clubs and urging them to refuse to surrender their arms; or if they had none to surrender, to get armed as quickly as they could even if only with pikes. Fearing the consequences of this course O'Brien introduced a motion on the Council to stop Mitchel and Reilly from advocating their unauthorised policy. This being carried, Mitchel and Reilly, with others, left the Confederation (February 5, 1848).

A week later Mitchel brought out the first number of the *United Irishman* which took as its motto Tone's tribute to the "men of no property". From the first issue onwards Mitchel gave each week lessons in the art of street-fighting.

The Rising of 'Forty-Eight

Mitchel's *United Irishman* created a sensation in England as well as in Ireland. He frankly appealed for Chartist aid—which, according to their ability, the Chartists readily gave—and his friends in the Confederate Clubs began to set up Charter Associations in the chief towns in Ireland. In England the Chartists sold Mitchel's Journal as one of their own. Chartism in England became a "danger" again, while the Confederate Chiefs in Ireland discovered that the mass of their supporters were becoming Mitchel-ites almost to a man.

The British Government, the Catholic Hierarchy, and the rump of the Repeal Association all took alarm together—the latter being tearfully indignant at Mitchel's scornful references to Daniel O'Connell. Their alarm was intensified, before the third issue of the *United Irishman* had appeared, by the overthrow of the Monarchy in France, and the setting up of a Republic, and by the enthusiasm with which this was greeted by Irish Confederates, English Chartists, and Radicals in both countries. Rumblings of revolution began to be heard from every country on the Continent: in fact the Year of Revolutions had begun.

The French Revolution transformed the situation in Ireland in a flash. Mitchel and Reilly walked back into the Confederation without ceremony, to be welcomed there with open arms. The *Nation* began to vie with the *United Irishman* in its incitements to prepare for revolt. The Clubs began to drill and to arm. A deputation–composed of O'Brien, Meagher, and a Dublin craftsman, Hollywood–was sent with fraternal greetings to the French Republic. It got a flowery speech from Acting-President Alphonse De Lamartine; but nothing tangible beyond an Irish Tricolour of Green, White, and Orange (modelled on the French Flag), made to Meagher's design by the daughters of '98 exiles and women descendants of the Wild Geese. It was exhibited first at Waterford, and at a public meeting in Dublin, where it was received with terrific enthusiasm.

Alarmed at the fraternisation of Confederates and Chartists–and by the inflammatory condition of Europe at large–the English Government designed a new Act and rushed it through all its stages in a single day. This Act facilitated the procedure in cases of "sedition" and "treason", and made the offence of "treason" a "felony" instead of a "misdemeanour". In the case of Sedition the Act did away with the distinction between "political" and "ordinary" criminals. In the case of treason-felony it substituted a term of transportation for the customary death penalty. The idea was to rob possible Emmets of their glory by giving them broad arrows instead of a martyr's crown.

Before the Act had passed, prosecutions had been launched against William O'Brien and Thomas Meagher for their speeches; and (two) against John Mitchel for his articles in the *United Irishman.* Juries refused to convict O'Brien and Meagher, so the prosecutions against Mitchel were abandoned–new ones, under the new Act, being substituted.

Meanwhile the Government had contrived to discredit the Chartist movement. A demonstration had been called for Kennington Common on April 10, at which the Chartist Petition was to be formally handed over to O'Connor for presentation to the House of Commons. It had been proposed, originally, to carry it in procession to the House; but, learning of the law (a relic of the Gordon Riots) which forbids any assembly within a mile of the House when in session, the proposal had been abandoned. The Government affected to believe however that an attempt would be made in defiance of the law; and it made preparations that would have been ample if London had been faced with a Napoleonic invasion. When the Petition was sent off in a cab, and the meeting dispersed without disorder, the Press, taking their cue from the Government, pretended to believe that the Chartist movement had been cowed. The anti-Chartist derision of the London middle-class was in proportion to their panic terrors before April 10 was safely got over. Many of the less well-informed Chartists were carried away by this propaganda of derision.

The official press discreetly omitted all mention of the large body of London-Irish Confederates who marched to Kennington Common under a green flag and, in defiance of police regulations, marched back again as they had come. The police, who insisted that no Chartist body should repass the bridges in military formation, allowed the Confederates to pass.

Propaganda was also used in Ireland to scare the middle-class. Dublin was placarded with warnings against Irish "Jacobins" and "Communists whose only object was plunder".

As a final precaution, quantities of arms were sent from Dublin Castle to reliable Orange Lodges.

The real test came on May 25, 1848, when Mitchel was tried for "treason-felony". The verdict was never in doubt, once the Sheriff had contrived, as he did, to "pack" the jury. The veteran Robert Holmes, a '98 man and a brother-in-law of Robert Emmet, made a dauntless speech; and the judge inflicted a savage sentence—fourteen years' transportation. Mitchel, surrounded by mounted police with drawn sabres, was galloped away at full speed to a tender, waiting at the North Wall Quay, which carried him at once to a warship, lying in Dublin Bay, with its anchor "up and down" ready to set sail as soon as the prisoner was on board.

The crucial fact was that the authorities feared a rescue; and Mitchel's whole strategy had been based upon the conviction that a rescue should be, and would be, attempted.* Actually, the men of the Dublin Clubs—particularly the working-men—were eager to make the attempt, and Meagher had promised to lead them. O'Brien, Duffy, and others, however, thought such an attempt would be suicidal. They contrived to persuade Meagher and Reilly to go round the Clubs, and countermand all preparations.

There is little doubt that an attempt to rescue Mitchel would have been a bloody affair; but there is a good deal of reason to believe that it might have proved by far the wisest course. There is quite a possibility that it would have succeeded; not only in effecting the rescue, but also in precipitating a general rising. Earlier, when Meagher had been arrested in Waterford, the Confederates there had barricaded the long bridge over the river which the police had to pass to carry him to prison. Meagher himself ordered the Confederates to demolish the barricade and let the police pass. He was carrying out the policy of the Confederate Council which had decided (1) upon an insurrection in the Autumn when the crops had been gathered in; (2) upon simultaneous revolts in the rural districts; and (3) upon a strict preservation of the peace until the Government struck the first blow. A pedanti-

* Mitchel and Rescue: Mitchel nowhere admits that this had been his strategy; but it is a fair inference from his conduct in general, and from his observations on the fact that nothing of the kind was attempted.

cally-formal adherence to the strict letter of this plan ruined the Rising before it could start.

The Government showed no such stickling over formalities. It suspended the Habeas Corpus Act and began arrests right and left.

Within a fortnight of the suppression of the *United Irishman*, Dalton Williams had founded the *Irish Tribune*. It was suppressed a fortnight later, just as its successor appeared—the *Irish Felon*, edited by Mitchel's lifelong friend John Martin, with whom was associated James Fintan Lalor. It contrived to reach its fourth number before it was suppressed.

Seeing that it was only a choice between letting themselves be arrested one by one, or taking the field at once, the Confederate Council decided to issue the call for a Rising immediately. Before Duffy could get the call circulated the police raided the *Nation*. They broke the formes before a copy had been printed—before the official note-taker could see what it was that Duffy was about to print. Because of this ill-directed (or possibly collusive?) excess of zeal, the prosecution against Duffy failed, as did that against Williams. John Martin got fourteen years' transportation like his friend. Lalor was in such a state of health that the authorities thought he could not live long enough to be tried. He was released, without being charged, to linger for more than twelve months before he died.

Meanwhile the leaders of the Confederation had dispersed to various parts to find out what readiness existed for revolt. In the country-districts in general they found none. The famine had broken men's spirits. Now that it was abating, the tiller's one thought was of his crop. In the towns there was readiness, here and there, but there were no arms, and O'Brien (who had gone to Tipperary) would not sanction any confiscation of arms until the enemy had struck the first blow.

Some hundreds gathered in Tipperary at O'Brien's call.

They had few arms, and no provisions. There was no commissariat. O'Brien gave them what money he could; but he would sanction no looting of the houses of the gentry. He would not allow a barricade to be erected until the owner's permission had been obtained for his trees to be cut down for the purpose. In the end the insurrection fizzled out ingloriously in an attempt to persuade the police imprisoned in a farm house to surrender their arms. When two of his men had been killed, O'Brien ordered the rest to disperse.

O'Brien had many fine qualities, but those of a leader of revolt were not included among them. Like the majority of the Council he feared the consequence of a revolt of the working-men of the towns nearly as much as the Government did.

For their share in this Rising—in which hardly a blow was struck on the rebel side—O'Brien, Meagher, and others (as well as those already named) all received long terms of Transportation.

PART FOUR

THE TENANTS' RIGHT LEAGUE TO THE
FENIAN BROTHERHOOD

CHAPTER XVIII

ECONOMIC CONSEQUENCES OF THE FAMINE

In this Part Four we trace the process of Nationalist revival in Ireland from the disastrous calamities of the
Famine and 'Forty-Eight, through (1) the Constitutional
agitation led by Gavan Duffy and the Tenants' Right
League, and (2) the classic revolutionary conspiracy of
the Fenians; culminating in their attempts at insurrection
in 1865 and 1867.

In this first chapter of Part Four we examine the economic impulsions underlying these movements.

Free Trade in Land

Until 1832 the English landed-oligarchy controlled the
English government absolutely. From then until 1846 they
retained preponderance through an alliance with that section of the manufacturers which had a direct interest in
maintaining in Ireland an industrial reserve army which
they could draw upon for supplies of cheap labour. From
1846 onwards the manufacturing capitalists gained increasingly a preponderance, until from the 1870's they
in turn gave way to the imperialist finance-capitalists. The
fall in world prices for agricultural products implied that,
if possible, agricultural productivity should be increased
to cover the fall in monetary returns. Hence arose that
drive towards the "consolidation" of farms which was
facilitated drastically by the calamity of the Famine.

Two things resulted (1) the elimination of the middleman, and (2) the getting rid of large numbers of smallholders. The middlemen disappeared as a category either
by selling out to the more prosperous farmers (which occurred largely between 1822 and 1840), or by themselves
becoming ground-landlords (as a result of the Encumbered Estates Act).

The getting rid of the smallholders was a necessary precondition for the establishment of capitalist farming on any considerable scale, and this was necessary to meet (and supplement) the growing yields from the wheat fields of America. Cheap labour was required for this type of farming, and a supply of cheap labour was created by the "consolidation" which cleared estates of their "superfluous" small tenants.

In 1841 there were 135,314 holdings of less than one acre. In 1851, their numbers had shrunk to 37,728. Holdings between one and five acres numbered 310,436 in 1841; in 1851 there were 88,083. Farms between five and fifteen acres were 252,799 in 1841; in 1851 there were 191,854. There was a corresponding increase of farms from fifteen to thirty acres, and a much greater increase of those above thirty acres.

Evictions from 1845 to 1847 numbered 3,000; from 1847–49 there were 25,700; from 1849–1852 there were 58,423 (affecting 306,120 individuals). The significance of this development was multiplied by the sentimental attachment felt by the Irish peasantry for their localities of origin—itself a fruitful source of calamity in the Famine years:

> "The class of poor and destitute occupiers, who are debarred by law [from poor law relief] unless they give up their land, struggle, notwithstanding their great privations, to retain it; and endeavour by every effort to pass through the season of difficulty by which they see a prospect of their former mode of subsistence returning, provided they continue in the possession of their land. The use for a long time of inferior food has in such cases sometimes induced disease fatal to the occupier himself, or one or more members of his family."

Report, Poor Law Commission, 1847.

The report of the Census of 1851 is more frank. It admits that those who died in this desperate struggle to save their holdings ran into "thousands". The quarter-acre clause was universally regarded as "eviction made easy", and the survivors felt a bitter hatred at the callousness with which it was enforced.

It is, of course, not true to say that either the resident landlords (many of whom ruined themselves in their efforts to aid the suffering) or the English people *en masse* regarded the calamity callously. The point is that Government policy was fettered by theories of "political economy" which had as brutal an effect as the most complete callousness would have produced. That the Government applied these theories equally to the English poor saves their credit for impartiality, but only at the expense of their credit for humanity and good sense.

The Manchester school had one universal panacea—Free Trade—the application to the relations of landlord and tenant of the principle of unrestricted competition. The application of this principle to Irish land tenures underlies the whole of Irish unrest from 1850 to 1870.

The Encumbered Estates Act

The first step was the Encumbered Estates Act (July 1849). Before then entailed estates could be sold only through the slow and expensive procedure of the Court of Chancery. Under this Act owners or creditors could appeal to a special court which disposed of the matter expeditiously—the creditors' claims being liquidated from the proceeds of the judicial sale. The purchaser was compelled to take over leases already granted, and could not vary their terms; but the old lax days when a favoured tenant paid what he thought he could afford, or when a year or two of arrears was thought nothing of were swept away. Particularly there was swept away the personal knowledge possessed by the old landlord of the improvements made by the more diligent and enterprising tenants. These things were now treated as part of the property bought and paid for. The tenants' right was a thing un-dreamed of.

More than 3,000 estates were sold, and of their 80,000 purchasers 90 percent were Irishmen. The purchase price amounted in gross to £25,000,000, nearly all of which went to creditors. Estates sold for a half or a third of their estimated value. The loss of the estate-owners was not less than £15,000,000.

As an endeavour to induce English and Scottish farmers to settle in Ireland the scheme was a failure. The estates passed to speculators who were concerned only to rack the last penny of rent possible out of the soil of which they became absolute owners. All customary and tradi-tional protection for the tenant was swept away. Leases tended constantly to be replaced by yearly tenancies, or simple tenancies-at-will. Virtually the entire agricultural population, who were not occupying owners, became evictable, and liable to increases of rent inflicted as punishments for any improvements they were rash enough to make.

In such conditions Whiteboyism, under its new name of Ribbonism, was bound to reappear. Capitalist land-lordism was a thing till then unknown to the Irish tenant. He paid rent as a tribute which secured him the right to occupy a plot of land in perpetuity. Its acceptance was an acknowledgment of the tenant's right; not his paying it an acknowledgment of the landlord's right. If he erected fences, made drains, cleared, manured and worked up the soil, the tenant felt he had a right to dispose of these im-provements at will; to sell his right in them if he wished to leave; to bequeath them to his children; or, at the least, to occupy his holding without interference so long as he paid the quit-rent custom decreed. The "right" of the owner to raise the rent on him, or to eject him at will, still more to confiscate his improvements—these common-places of "Free Trade in Land" were to the Irish tenants abominations which negated all right.

Against the landlord's robber-claims he set up his claim to the "Three F's"—fixity of tenure, at a fair rent, with freedom of sale for his own improvements—and whether he fought for them by the methods of the Whiteboy, or through parliamentary agitation, these were the central objects of agrarian struggle in this period.

Emigration and its Consequences

Excessive subdivision of holdings was an evil; but its prevention produced the alternative evil of emigration.

Emigration to America from Ireland began early in the 18th century; but a radical difference distinguishes the earlier from the later emigration. The earlier emigrants had been the more successful farmers, or their children, who had amassed sufficient working capital to justify a belief they could prosper on a bigger scale in a freer land. The later emigrants, particularly those of the Famine and post-Famine years, were driven to emigrate not by success but by failure. They went as proletarians seeking wage-labour, and never lost the sense of grievance at having been driven into exile by the rack-renter and the evictor.

The Famine, the evictions, the rack-rents, the worsening of conditions, the enforced emigration—these were the root causes of the upheaval of revolutionary republicanism known to Irish history as Fenianism.

CHAPTER XIX

DUFFY'S TENANTS' RIGHT LEAGUE

Charles Gavan Duffy, the only Young Ireland leader left at liberty in Ireland after the turmoils of '48, attempted to organise a constitutional agitation to secure the "Three F's". His Tenants' Right League met with considerable success in 1852, but was brought to nothing by the sabotage and desertion of a group known derisively as the Pope's Brass Band.

The Persistence of Agrarian Terrorism

A persisting fact in Irish history from 1760 onwards, to 1922, is the fact of agrarian crime—terroristic attacks upon landlords, agents, tithe-proctors, and above all "land-grabbers" (those who bid for farms from which other men had been, or were to be, evicted). At its most brutal level this crime took the form of cattle-maiming and murder, and the notable fact is that this type of outbreak dwindled to nothing when a promising political movement was on foot, only to recur again when that movement ended in failure, or lapsed into quiescence.

Reactionary English writers have inferred from this a guilty connection between the organisers of the political movement and the local organisers of outrage. But the analysis made by Karl Marx of the situation of the French peasantry and its political affiliations suggests a much profounder explanation:

> "The small peasants form a vast mass, the members of which live in similar conditions, but without entering into manifold relations with one another. Their mode of production isolates them ... the isolation is increased by bad means of communication and poverty ... The smallholding admits of no division of labour, no applications of science, and there-

fore no multiplicity of developments... In so far as millions of families live under economic conditions of existence which separate their mode of life, their interests and their culture from those of other classes, and put them in hostile contrast to these others, they form a class. In so far as there is merely a local interconnection among these small peasants and the identity of their interests begets no unity, no national union, and no political organisation, they do not form a class. They are consequently incapable of enforcing their class interests in their own name, whether through a parliament, or through a convention. They cannot represent themselves, they must be represented."

Marx: *Eighteenth Brumaire.*

Applied to Ireland this means that, left helpless, save for such purely local combinations as he could contrive, the peasant's first thought in extremity has been–the despairing resort to terrorism.

If it is remembered how much of the English conquest of Ireland has turned upon confiscating the land, and imposing alien conditions of tenure upon the tillers, it will be clear why the tradition of resistance to the alien–in the person of the landlord or his agent–forms a permanent ground-theme in the history of Irish struggle. It will also become clear why the peasants, although intensely national, never themselves set on foot a nationalist agitation. At the same time they were constantly ready to respond *en masse* to the call of each national agitation as it arose.

An analogous consideration applies to religious conflict. A North of Ireland Protestant clergyman wrote (1870):

"All that is really important in the history [of Ireland] for the last three centuries is the fighting of the two nations for the possession of the soil. The Reformation was in reality nothing but a special form of the land war. The oath of supremacy was simply a lever for evicting the owners of the land. The proc-

267

ess was simple. The king demanded spiritual allegiance; refusal was high treason; the punishment of high treason was forfeiture of estates, with death or banishment to the recusants. Any other law they might have obeyed and retained their inheritance. This law fixed its iron grapples in the conscience and made obedience impossible without a degree of baseness that rendered life intolerable. Hence Protestantism was detested, not as a religion so much as an instrument of spoliation."

Rev. James Godkin: *Land War in Ireland*.

It must also be remembered, as we have had occasion to observe earlier, that in the various localities the Whiteboy or Ribbon lodge functioned as a defence-organisation analogous to a trade union:

"Rockism and Whiteboyism are the determination of a people who have nothing that can be called theirs, but a daily meal of the lowest description of food, not to submit to being deprived of that for other people's convenience."

John Stuart Mill: *Political Economy*.

Or, as an English Radical M.P. wrote to a Prime Minister:

"But for the salutary dread of the Whiteboy Association ejectment would desolate Ireland, and decimate her population, casting forth thousands of families ... to perish in roadside ditches. Yes, the Whiteboy system is the only check on the ejectment system; and weighing one against the other, horror against horror, and crime against crime, it is perhaps the lesser evil of the two."

Charles Poulett Scrope: *Letter to Lord Melbourne* (1834).

The Tenants' Right League

When Gavan Duffy restarted the *Nation* in 1850, he had to record, along with a wide-spread outbreak of Ribbon outrages, the progress of two distinct agitations for legislation to abate the rapacity of that new type of landlord which was emerging daily from the Encumbered Estates Courts. In the North the agitation, led by Protestant and Presbyterian ministers, arose from a well-based fear that the new speculator-landlords would destroy (as under the new Act they could) the "Ulster custom" which gave tenants a property right in their improvements. Concurrently, in the South, a group of public-spirited young priests were agitating for the adoption there of the (imperilled) Ulster custom, as a reform.

Under the influence of the *Nation*, these distinct "Tenants' Protection Associations" came together and formed a Tenants' Right League. It had the support of the surviving "Repealers" in Parliament; of Sharman Crawford the Co. Down "federalist" whose early advocacy of extending the Ulster Custom earned him the title of "the Father of Tenant Right"; and of such English radicals as Poulett Scrope. It was agreed, all round, that a Land Act embodying the "Three F's" would be a real gain. A call was issued urging voters everywhere to support only such candidates as would pledge themselves to give support to Tenants' Right Principles, which were defined thus: "Rent must be *fixed by valuation* of the land; the power of raising rents at will, or of recovering a higher rent than one so established must be taken from the landlord.

"The tenant must have a *fixed tenure*; he must not be liable to disturbance, so long as he paid the rent established by valuation. If he chose to quit, or could not pay he must have the right to the market value of his tenancy.

"Nothing shall be included in the valuation, or be paid under it to the landlord, on account of improvements made by the tenant in possession, or those under whom he claims, unless these have been paid for by the landlord in reduced rent, or in some other way."

A campaign in support of these principles was carried

all through Ireland; and, to the delight of the campaigners, and the astonishment of all, North and South joined hands with enthusiasm. The *Fermanagh Mail*, strictly Protestant in its principles, and circulating in a deep Orange area, acclaimed the movement without reserve. "All! All are uniting," it said, "in harmonious concert to struggle for this dear old land!"

The lyric enthusiasm of the *Mail* was forgivable. A movement in which Catholics, including priests, were welcomed at public meetings in the North, while Protestants, including Orangemen, were similarly welcomed in the South—one which promoted meetings at which resolutions were proposed by Grand Masters of the Orange Order, and seconded by Catholic priests; which brought a delegation of Presbyterian ministers South to receive an enthusiastic welcome in Wexford, and in Kilkenny—such a movement deserved all the enthusiastic approval the *Fermanagh Mail* had to bestow.

As the general election of 1852 approached, the League busied itself successfully in extorting from candidates pledges to support the principles of the League. Few candidates were more emphatic in giving this pledge than William Keogh and his fellow members of the Catholic Defence Association.

The Pope's Brass Band

Keogh, in 1851, was already a member of parliament, and the Catholic Defence Association, of which he was the head, had newly sprung into being in response to a casual circumstance which opportunist politicians of all colours had fastened upon as an excuse for bogus displays of zeal.

The Pope of the period, newly returned from the exile into which he had been driven by the revolution of 1848, celebrated his return by appointing a Catholic Hierarchy for England. The Whig Prime Minister, Lord John Russel, urged on by "No Popery" zealots, at once brought in a Bill to make it an offence for Catholic prelates to adopt territorial designations in the British Islands.

Protestant landlords, and ultra-Orange zealots, saw here a first-class chance to side track the Tenants' Right League and the unity it was promoting. Through the Grand Lodge of the Orange Order they issued a call to Protestants to stand firm by their "menaced institutions". Protestant landlords, meeting in Dublin, beat the No Popery drum until the echoes rang.

As it chanced, the head of the Catholic Hierarchy in Ireland (Dr. Cullen) was both newly-appointed and an ultramontane of the most pronounced type. He reacted semi-automatically to the "No Popery" challenge by forming a Catholic Defence Association at whose head he placed William Keogh (barrister and M.P.) and John Sadleir, the founder of a Tipperary Bank (which in intimate financial circles was suspected of shady practices).

As Russell's Ecclesiastical Titles Bill made its progress through the Commons—in the teeth of opposition from the Tories, led by Gladstone, and from the Radicals led by Cobden—both Keogh and Sadleir outrivalled everybody in the ferocity of their opposition. Hence it became easy for Keogh and Sadleir, with a team of followers, to enter the general election of 1852 as the ecclesiastically-approved Champions of the Catholic Church in Ireland.

Keogh, who (one contemporary said) "could whistle the birds off the bushes" and who (Duffy says) "rarely gave an honest vote, or uttered an honest sentiment", never appeared in public without bishops to back him. So flamboyant were he and Sadleir and their followers in their protestations of zeal for the Faith, and in defence of the Pope that they acquired the nick-name of the Pope's Brass Band.

Duffy and the Tenant's Right League resisted the sectarian diversion initiated by the Band so successfully that its members all pledged themselves ("So help me,

God!" swore Willie Keogh) to fight unswervingly for Tenants' Right and keep the Party pledge.

The general election in the autumn of 1852 resulted in the return of nearly fifty members pledged to Tenants' Right; Duffy himself being elected for New Ross. A conference of these Tenants' Right members (attended by Keogh and Sadleir) agreed unanimously to support no ministry that would not support a Tenants' Right Bill.

When Parliament assembled the Whig Government found itself in a precarious position. Whigs and Tories were nearly equal; the Irish Party held the balance. The Government, accordingly, temporised; and allowed two Tenants' Right Bills, one promoted by Sharman Crawford, the other by the League, to pass their second reading and go to a select committee. Shortly afterwards the Whig Government was replaced by a Coalition Administration.

Success seemed certain for the Tenants' Right League –but, of course, on condition that its party members in Parliament honoured their pledges and maintained their independence, and with it the power of overthrowing the Government.

The Great Betrayal

To the consternation and disgust of the Tenants' Right Party the new ministerial appointments when announced included John Sadleir as a Junior Lord of the Treasury, and William Keogh as Solicitor-General for Ireland. Nineteen of their "Catholic Defence" followers went over with them to the Government benches. All, in due course, received material rewards.

This defection at once placed the new Government in a position to disregard the Irish vote. Both Tenants' Right Bills were allowed to die in Committee.

At the by-elections necessitated by their acceptance of office, Sadleir and Keogh were assailed fiercely by the

Tenants' Right League. They were defended by both the Protestant landlords and the Catholic Hierarchy. The latter body affirmed that Sadleir and Keogh had obtained a pledge that the Ecclesiastical Titles Act would be allowed to fall into disuse. Russell denied this flatly, but that was in fact what happened. Meanwhile the Hierarchy took the view that preserving the right of bishops to their titles was work of far greater importance than preserving the Tenants' Right to their improvements in the soil. Hence they defended Messrs. Sadleir and Keogh with all their strength and authority.

The League succeeded in defeating Sadleir by a margin of six votes only. They failed to defeat Keogh, who, says Duffy, "came on to the platform to return thanks, just like Richard III, hanging on the arms of two bishops".

How far the result was achieved by actual collusion, or how far it was begotten by a fortuitous conjunction of interests cannot be known; the fact remains, however, that the Catholic Cardinal Cullen, the Orange Grand Master, the landlords, the Whigs, and the Tories, were all of one mind. The aims of the Tenants' Right League were, they said, "Communistic", and they had to be thwarted accordingly.

Within a few weeks of the Great Betrayal, the young Catholic curates who had done the donkey-work of agitating and organising were each and all ordered by their respective bishops—set on by Cardinal Cullen—not to set foot outside their parishes, and to confine themselves, strictly, to their spiritual functions.

In desperation, the Catholic laymen in the League sent a delegation to Rome to beg for a Papal reversal of the Cardinal's inhibition. The delegates were received politely, and were assured that the matter would "receive consideration". For all anyone knows it is receiving it still.

Duffy, completely disheartened, gave up the struggle. There was, he said, "no more hope for Ireland than for a corpse on a dissecting table". He resigned his seat; and, in 1855, emigrated to Australia, where he had a distinguished career.

It capped the story of the Great Betrayal when, a few years later, the Tipperary Bank failed, ruining thousands of small depositors. Sadleir, to escape the penalty for a truly colossal series of forgeries and frauds, poisoned himself at midnight on Hampstead Heath. Two other prominent members of the "Band" fled the country to escape prosecution for complicity in fraud.

William Keogh, though suspected, was never charged. Instead he became Lord Chief Justice of Ireland, and in that capacity, as we shall see, inflicted savage sentences on most of the leading Fenians.

CHAPTER XX

THE FENIAN BROTHERHOOD

Duffy's emigration left the field of (constitutional) political action in Ireland free for political adventurers and crooks, of whom Keogh and Sadleir were classic examples. Apart from sporadic outbreaks of Ribbonism, there was no alternative—until there arose the Fenian Brotherhood, which revealed its existence in the period of the Civil War in the U.S.A. (1861–65).

Fenianism—or the Irish Republican Brotherhood—was, frankly, an endeavour to resume the work done by the United Irishmen. It constituted one of the most remarkable and enduring revolutionary secret societies in history. In this chapter we recount the story of its rise and progress to the crisis of 1865.

The "Phoenix" Conspiracy

Left over from the Irish Confederation and the Repeal Association—which collapsed in 1848—were a number of isolated clubs and local debating-societies. These were most numerous in West Cork and Kerry; and, under the influence of Jeremiah O'Donovan of Skibbereen, the clubs of that region federated in 1856 into a secret society, known as the Phoenix—so called because, like the fabled bird, it intended to rise from the ashes of the burnt-out Young Ireland movement.

O'Donovan was better known then and later by his title "ROSSA", which denoted, alternatively, his flaming red head and his origin in the Ross-Carbery region of South-West Cork. He was famous for his size, and his fiery energy.

In 1857 the Phoenix was visited by James Stephens, a Kilkenny man who had acted as aide to Smith O'Brien in 1848; and who, since then, had lived partly in Paris and partly in the U.S.A. Stephens brought news of a movement about to be launched in the U.S.A., which would be a valuable reservoir of aid to any revolutionary movement in Ireland. At Stephens' prompting, the Phoenix men began drilling, and preparing to collect arms.

Revolutionary Affiliations of Fenianism

The American movement, of which Stephens brought news, was, then, little more than an idea and a name. Three exiles from 1848–Michael Doheny, originally a schoolmaster, who had been connected with the *Nation*, James Stephens himself, and John O'Mahoney, an enthusiastic Gaelic scholar–had conceived the idea of an oath-bound military conspiracy, which in allusion to the legendary following of Finn MacCumhall, they called the Fianna or Fenians.

Their stay in Paris had brought these three into contact with the Red Republican Clubs and Communist secret societies of the period; particularly those led by Auguste Blanqui. And it was from Blanqui's notion of a pledge-bound, hand-picked, disciplined *élite*–which would act at command as the shock-troops of Revolution–that they derived their conception of a revived and improved version of the United Irishmen's conspiracy.

Neither of the original three ever declared himself, openly, a Socialist or a Communist; but all three, at different times, showed close sympathy with Socialist and Communist aspirations. O'Mahoney–so O'Leary tells us–was "an advanced democrat or even a socialist", Stephens, at one time "planned to write a history of socialist theories". Doheny was strongly in sympathy with the agrarian "communism" of Fintan Lalor. All hinted more or less plainly at an agrarian revolution as a necessary consequence of the establishment of an Irish Republic; and there is evidence, of a kind, that both O'Mahoney and Stephens were individual members of the Interna-

276

tional Working Men's Association. It helps considerably to elucidate the obscurities of Stephen's conduct if we suppose him constantly waiting and hoping for a grand-scale resumption of the Continental Red-Republican and "Communist" upheavals of the 1848 period.

In 1856 (or thereabouts) the triumvirate moved to New York. Doheny, the oldest, engaged in journalistic work. O'Mahoney and Stephens, working among the Irish exiles, gathered a nucleus which they thought sufficient to begin with. They called their open organisation the "Fenian Brotherhood"; but this was primarily a cover (as well as a recruiting ground) for the "underground" I.R.B.–which initials, O'Leary says, could be translated as Irish Republican Brotherhood, or Irish Revolutionary Brotherhood according to taste.

O'Mahoney stopped in the U.S.A. to organise the supply of funds, arms, and trained officers. Stephens went to Ireland to recruit the army. He had returned to America to report the progress made with the Phoenix men when, in 1858, the police made a swoop and captured all the Phoenix leaders. In this connection a new aspect of the affair arose.

"Felon Setting"

After Duffy's departure, the *Nation* had been continued by various successors without a break. Its editor and proprietor in 1858 was Alexander M. Sullivan, a Bantry man, whose policy was nearer to that of O'Connell than to that of Davis. He was not only a Catholic but an ardent clericalist, and he had fossilized O'Connell's hostility to insurrection into an absolute dogma. Never, under any circumstances, might Irishmen resort to arms without mortal sin–unless, of course, the Church called them to arms.

Early in 1858 Sullivan was urged by the Catholic Bishop of Kerry to warn the people against "foolish courses" such as dabbling in "privy conspiracy and rebellion". Sullivan consulted Smith O'Brien, then newly returned from exile; and he, honestly enough, wrote for the *Nation* an Open Letter advising against insurrectionary conspiracies on general grounds.

Nobody found fault with O'Brien; everybody knew he would never favour a revolution not led by the gentry and the educated class. What infuriated the revolutionaries was that Sullivan added a leading article, in his own, best, sentimental-picturesque style, pleading with the young men of Kerry and West Cork in particular to take O'Brien's advice, and to heed the injunctions of their clergy. Shortly afterwards the police arrested all the leaders of the Phoenix Society in Kerry and West Cork. There was little the police could urge against them, and, by arrangement, they all pleaded guilty and were bound over.

Stephens never forgave Sullivan, whom he accused of playing the part of a setter-dog who points out the game to the huntsman. "Felon-setter" was his name for Sullivan, and "felon-setting" his description of "moral force" propaganda. This feud between Stephens and Sullivan continued to provide a running commentary of acrimony through the whole course of the Fenian agitation. Indignant at Stephens' "unfairness", Sullivan became every day more hysterically and sentimentally Pacifist, Papalist and clerical.

Garibaldi and the Pope

In 1859–60, for example, when Napoleon III, for opportunist reasons, joined Victor Emmanuel, King of Sardinia, in expelling the Austrians from North Italy, European Radicals and Republicans were disgusted to see the long-desired unification of Italy advanced a stage by the interested manœuvres of a King and an "Emperor". That Napoleon III got Nice and Savoy as his share of the loot, made it a thoroughly bad business from the Radical point of view. The disgust of the Radicals reassured Sullivan, who seized the opportunity to organise a stunt—the presentation of a Sword of Honour to the French Marshal MacMahon on the ground that his name and descent were Irish.

That the traceable ancestors of the Marshal, in Ireland, had always fought on the anti-popular side; that Mac-Mahon himself was an adventurer like Louis Napoleon, and had helped him to bring off the *coup d'état* which destroyed the Second Republic and replaced it with the Second Empire; that MacMahon, earlier, had assisted in butchering the Parisian workmen in the Days of June, 1848—as he was later to butcher the Communards of 1871—these things weighed nothing with Sullivan. Mac-Mahon was an ardent clericalist; therefore he could be boosted as "Irish", and presented with a sword of honour by the very men who were "horrified" to learn that Irish lads were drilling by moonlight.

A few months later a rising occurred at Palermo in Sicily, and the Republican leader, Joseph Garibaldi, made his famous raid with a thousand volunteers, which led the rising which drove the Neapolitan troops out of Sicily. Crossing to the mainland, Garibaldi then drove the King of Naples from his throne.

Even Sullivan could not defend King Bomba—the best-nated king in Europe—but he could, and did, take alarm at the prospect of a Garibaldian-Republican revolution in the Central Italian States, ruled by the Pope as a temporal prince.

Amid the applause of the *Ultramontanes*, headed by Cardinal Cullen, Sullivan raised a whoop about the "Pope in Danger", and the Irish lads who might not drill by moonlight to learn to fight for Ireland were invited to volunteer to form an Irish Brigade for the defence of the Pope.

Here again it was nothing to Sullivan that the administration of the Papal States was a byword for incompetence and corruption—as was proved when at least half of the Irish brigade never so much as got arms in their hands. Nor did it bother Sullivan much that the Pope made a deal with Victor Emmanuel—which squeezed Garibaldi out. Nor that the Pope thought so little of his Irish helpers that Sullivan had to raise more money to save them from starving and bring them home again. These things did not bother Sullivan and his friends. They had pulled off a stunt and found a slogan. When Fenians said "Felon-setter" Sullivanites replied "Garibaldian"—which meant an enemy of the Pope in all things. "Garibaldi or the Pope?" was the opening challenge in many a faction fight for years thereafter.

The MacManus Funeral

An event which considerably aided the Fenian movement was the funeral of Terence Bellew MacManus, a popular Liverpool Confederate who in 1848 crossed to join in the rising and who, after his escape from Tasmania, had lived and, for a time, prospered in San Francisco.

When MacManus died, in the last days of 1860, his friends in the Irish Colony in San Francisco thought so highly of him that they decided to send his body (embalmed) home for burial in Ireland. A refinement upon the original project—one of which the organisers of the Fenian Brotherhood made full use—was to send the body to Boston overland, in those days a perilous adventure in itself. At each resting place upon the journey memorial meetings were held; and each memorial meeting became a recruiting-rally for the Fenian Brotherhood and the *Clan na Gael* (the American equivalent of the I.R.B.). So many towns in America with Irish colonies put in demands that the funeral should be routed to include them, that it was not till September 1861, that the body at last left America for Ireland.

In Ireland arrangements had been made for continuing the work. Cardinal Cullen, however, instructed the Church to refuse its countenance; none the less, virtually the entire population of Cork took part in the ceremony. It was noted that a considerable number of private soldiers and non-commissioned officers in uniform joined in the procession.

The final procession in Dublin on November 10, 1861, saw a number variously estimated at from 50,000 to 100,000 marching in military formation, while an equal number lined the streets. A halt was made at every spot sacred in the revolutionary-republican history of Ireland—the house where Lord Edward was mortally wounded; the house where Wolfe Tone's body lay before burial; the Church before which Emmet was hanged; and so on. Night had fallen before the body was at last laid to rest in Glasnevin.

The Civil War in the U.S.A. and Fenianism

The MacManus funeral had proved the existence of a solid core of intense Nationalist feeling among the Irish, both in the U.S.A. and in Ireland. The outbreak of Civil War in the U.S.A. between the pro-slavery South and the anti-slavery North gave the American-Irish a chance to learn the use of arms under actual war conditions. Both sides raised Irish Brigades; but that on the Northern Side, led by Thomas Francis Meagher, was by far the more popular with the Irish-American masses.

Mitchel's pro-Southern propaganda—based, as it was, mainly on the expectation that the English government would at once support the North—was concretely refuted by the strong pro-Southern sympathies shown by the English ruling-class—who would have recognised the South, and gone to war in its aid, if they had not been stopped by the mass-opposition of the English workers, and a section of the middle-class.

"It was not the wisdom of the rulers but the heroic resistance of the working-classes of England which saved the West of Europe from plunging headlong into an infamous crusade for the perpetuation and propagation of slavery on the other side of the Atlantic."

Marx: *Inaugural Address I.W.M.A.* (1864).

Stephens and O'Mahoney took the much more plausible line of arguing that as hostility between England and the U.S.A. was bound to result in war either before or after the ending of the Civil War—which they thought the North was bound to win—all Irishmen of military age should join either the Federal Army or, if they preferred it, the English Army, in order to become trained in readiness for the crisis.

It is significant that Irish Emigration to America noticeably increased during the Civil War years of 1861-5. When the North began definitely to gain the upper hand by the victories of Vicksburg and Gettysburg (both on July 4, 1863) Stephens decided to open a political offensive in Ireland by publishing a revolutionary journal.

The Irish People

The Fenian journal, the *Irish People*, was first published in Dublin on November 29, 1863. Its editors, Thomas Clarke Luby and John O'Leary, had both been "out" in '48; and both were close friends of Fintan Lalor. Charles Joseph Kickham, who was associated with them, was an older man who had contributed to the *Nation*. All were men of education. Luby came of a scholastic family; O'Leary was a man of independent means who had studied for the medical profession.

The business-manager of the journal, upon whom much of the work of building its circulation fell, was Jeremiah O'Donovan-Rossa.

The founding of the *Irish People* marked a turning point in the history of Fenianism. The work of building a circulation; the contacts gained; the correspondence published; and the struggles against rival constitutionalist journals backed by the priests–all were means of aiding that development of the "underground" organisation at which Stephens and Luby laboured diligently. The open hostility of the priests, and of employers set on by priests–who discharged employees freely for having any connection with the *Irish People*–made the journal itself the best organiser of the Fenian movement.

CHAPTER XXI

THE CRISIS OF FENIANISM

Civil War ended in the U.S.A. in April 1865. This released for action in Ireland something near to 200,000 men who had been sworn in as Fenians in the course of the struggle. It was a natural inference that something would be attempted in Ireland soon. Actually the English Authorities made the first move by raiding the *Irish People* and arresting the leaders. A daring escape effected by Stephens excited hopes (and fears); but the other prisoners were left to be convicted and carried off to penal servitude with nothing done. Fenianism had already suffered a heavy moral set-back when an attempt at insurrection made in 1867 ended in complete failure. The Manchester Rescue and the Clerkenwell Explosion were the closing episodes in the Fenian Movement in its classic period.

The Arrests of 'Sixty-Five

James Stephens, Chief Organiser of the Irish Republic "now virtually established"—so ran the I.R.B. membership pledge—was placed squarely before the need for action by the cessation of the Civil War in the U.S.A. He had boasted of the numbers of Fenians in the American armies, and of those enrolled likewise in the ranks of the English army. Would he give "the word"? Or would he wait?

He chose to wait. Many guesses were made as to the reason. The most probable guess is that he had no real plan at all; but was waiting, opportunistically, upon events. The English Authorities thought it wisdom to get their blow in first; and, accordingly, they raided the *Irish People*, and the homes of the Fenian leaders, on the night of September 15, 1865. Luby, O'Leary, Rossa, and a number of minor chiefs were arrested.

Stephens evaded arrest for a time, and in anticipation of the expected insurrection great military precautions were taken by the Authorities in all the main centres of Ireland. Nothing happened; and a month later (November 15) Stephens and Kickham were arrested at a private house in the suburbs of Dublin. Brought before a magistrate Stephens refused to plead; and, being committed for trial, vanished from his cell in Richmond Prison, Dublin, on the night of November 25. Not until long after did the Authorities learn that his escape had been contrived by two (Fenian) prison warders, acting in concert with John Devoy, who was the chief organiser of Fenian circles in the English Army.

At the time of Stephens' escape everybody expected that insurrection would follow immediately. And, as we know now, John Devoy urged it strongly. Nothing, however, happened. The English Government was left free to fill the press with propaganda worked up from the documents produced at the preliminary hearings of the cases against the prisoners. By an unscrupulous use of the correspondence files of the *Irish People*–especially of letters deemed unsuitable for publication which had not been destroyed–the Ascendancy and Constitutionalist press were able to represent the Fenians as contemplating every conceivable barbarity, including (of course) the "extermination" of landlords.

There is weighty reason for believing that if John Devoy's advice had been taken, the result would have been to secure for Ireland as much as was secured by the Treaty of 1921-2, without Partition. On the other hand, it is fair to say that American military experts strongly supported Stephens in insisting upon delay.

The Trials of Luby, O'Leary, Kickham and Rossa

All decent feeling in Ireland was outraged when the Judge appointed to try the Fenian leaders proved to be none other than Chief Justice William Koegh—the "solo-trombone in the Pope's Brass Band". He was set off in some measure by the appearance, as chief counsel for the defence, of Isaac Butt, the leader of the Dublin Conservatives, who in 1843 had defended the Union in debate against O'Connell himself. Butt defended all the prisoners (except Rossa, who insisted upon conducting his own defence) with great courage, persistence, and skill. And, in fact, he was so impressed by the character of the prisoners, and by the logical force of their standpoint, that he began from that moment to move over to the Nationalist camp.

The case against the prisoners was that they had said, repeatedly and plainly, that they desired to see Ireland an independent republic, and that no means were available for attaining this end except an armed uprising. The evidence connecting them with the actual preparations for an armed uprising was, at most, indirect, and consisted entirely of documents found at Stephens' domicile. The verdict however was a foregone conclusion; but the sentences shocked even Englishmen. Luby, O'Leary, and Kickham were sentenced to twenty years' penal servitude. Rossa, who fought Keogh with defiance and insult for over eight hours, was sentenced to penal servitude for life.

The Rising of 'Sixty-Seven

The failure of '65 precipitated a violent internal upheaval in Fenian circles. In America, O'Mahoney was "deposed"; a split ensued; and the majority faction, drifting into questionable hands, wasted its force in futile attempts to invade Canada.

Stephens remained in Ireland, despite the £1,000 reward offered by the Authorities for information leading to his capture, until his protector, John Devoy fell into the hands of the enemy. Stephens then left for America (in March 1866) where he contrived a temporary healing of the split by promising, categorically, that the year 1866 "would not pass without a blow struck in Ireland". When that year ended with nothing done the movement split again. In desperation Stephens ordered preparation for a rising early in 1867. But the movements in Ireland and in America each agreed spontaneously to depose Stephens definitely and finally. Not the least enigma attending an enigmatical character is that Stephens accepted his deposition without protest; and never, thereafter, attempted to emerge from the obscurity of private life.

The Irish-American Colonel Kelley, now Head-Centre of the I.R.B. in Ireland, issued the word for a rising on February 11, 1867. This date was later changed to March 5.

Two places failed to receive notice of the change of date—Kerry and the North of England.

In Kerry the Fenians turned out in considerable numbers, and captured a coast-guard station and a police barracks. They also captured the despatch from Fenian headquarters (which the police had intercepted) fixing a new date for the rising. The Fenian commander, at once, ordered his men to disperse to their homes.

In the North of England, the Fenian leader, John McCafferty—a competent commander, and a most desperate character—had devised an ingenious plan to capture the stock of arms stored in Chester Castle. But for a last-minute warning given to the authorities by an informer the surprise would have been complete. As it was the raid proved abortive, and the authorities were put on the alert against any repetition.

The rising on March 5 was foredoomed to failure. The authorities were well on the alert; and, in addition, a blizzard of exceptional force set in that night which raged without abatement for a full week. Thousands of young men turned out—most of them mechanics and shop assistants—but being unprovided with the means of facing such weather, they could do nothing but return home, to be arrested in many cases as they made their way back.

The Fenian General Massey arrived on time at Limerick Junction; but only to find it in the hands, not of Fenians, but of the military. Realising that the plans had been betrayed, he, too, gave the authorities all the information he had. This made the failure absolute.

The Manchester Rescue

Col. Kelley, the Head-Centre, having occasion to visit Manchester, fell into the hands of the police with a companion, Deasy, on September 11. Identified by detectives from Dublin as Fenian leaders, they were committed for trial on September 18. The Black Maria conveying them to prison was held up by local Fenians, armed with revolvers, who drove off the police escort, broke open the van and got the prisoners away safely. Unfortunately in the blowing open of the locked door of the van, a police sergeant was killed. Some of the rescue party sacrificed themselves to hold back pursuit, four of them being captured. These were, later, charged with the "murder" of the police-sergeant. A panic raid on the Irish quarter produced a number of other prisoners, and one of them was selected to be charged along with the first four. He proved to be a "loyal" private in the Marines, home on furlough, who had no sort of knowledge of the affair.

He and the other four, William Phillip Allen, Michael Larkin, Michael O'Brien, and Edward O'Mara Condon were all, despite the efforts of their counsel, Ernest Jones, the Chartist leader, found guilty and sentenced to death.

The journalists present protested unanimously their conviction of the innocence of the Marine, and he was "pardoned". Condon, as an American citizen, was respited and after a term of imprisonment was released. The other three were hanged on November 23, 1867, despite the fact that not one of them had fired the fatal shot, and that, at worst, the death was accidental.

The executions produced a revulsion of horror all over Ireland. Great funeral processions were organised to follow coffins piled high with wreaths and marked with the names of the "Manchester Martyrs". Men who had been bitterly hostile to Fenianism were prosecuted for their share in these demonstrations, John Martin, the '48 man, and A. M. Sullivan among them.

Timothy D. Sullivan, brother of A. M., took the cry of the prisoners in the dock—"God Save Ireland!"—and wrote a poem which was at once adopted as the "National Anthem" of Ireland—an esteem which it retained until it was superseded, after Easter Week, 1916, by the *Soldier's Song.*

The Clerkenwell Explosion

An incident of a different order marked the close of the year. An important Fenian organiser being detained in the House of Detention, Clerkenwell, a group of Fenian sympathisers, acting on their own responsibility, sought to rescue him on the afternoon of December 13, 1867, by exploding a barrel of gunpowder against the wall surrounding the prison yard.

The force of the explosion drove forty tons of masonry out of the wall clean across the prison yard. In the opposite direction it completely wrecked the row of tall, tenement houses which was separated from the prison wall only by the width of a narrow lane. Four people were killed outright, three died of their injuries, and 120 others were injured more or less permanently.

This was not the work of the Fenian organisation, whose leaders all condemned it as a barbarous folly. But it indicated that a degeneration had set in, in which Fenian discipline had evaporated, to leave only irrational hate and an irresponsible readiness for violent deeds.

CHAPTER XXII

THE OUTCOME OF THE FENIAN MOVEMENT

As a military conspiracy the Fenian movement failed completely; none the less it produced permanent results. For one thing it reincarnated for Irishmen the ideal of Wolfe Tone and the United Irishmen, and re-established it as the norm of Irish National struggle. It revealed to Englishmen, and the world, the actuality and extent of the Irish aspiration for unfettered Nationality. At the least it proved that as a means of welding two nations into one, the Act of Union was the completest failure ever. Largely under the inspiration of Karl Marx and the International Working Men's Association the English Radical and working-class movement returned to the Chartist standpoint and demanded Justice for Ireland. Gladstone's reply was to Disestablish the (Protestant) Church of Ireland (1869).

The International and the Fenians

The period of Fenian agitation in Ireland was also a period of Radical and working-class revival in England.

The International Working Men's Association was founded in 1864; the National Reform League, largely inspired by the International, commenced its agitation for an extension of the Franchise in 1865. In 1866, the Reform League demonstration being debarred access to Hyde Park tore up half-a-mile of railings and forced an entry. When the events of 1867 forced the Fenians and the Irish Question to the front, the International led the way in demanding consideration for Ireland's claims, and mooted a possibility of agitating for the Repeal of the Union.

Karl Marx, the theoretical and political leader of the International, was foremost in guiding it along this line. He and his friend Engels had been interested in Ireland since the days when, as supporters of the Chartists, they had supported the demand for Repeal. One of Marx's earliest contributions to the New York *Tribune* had been (June '53) a closely reasoned argument in favour of Tenants' Right. In November 1867–just after the Manchester executions–Marx wrote to Engels describing the debates on the General Council of the I.W.M.A. in which the trial and execution were roundly condemned. He suggested to Engels that while he (Marx) and the I.W.M.A. could not agitate legally for more than Repeal, Engels, who was in close touch with leading Fenians, should urge them to adopt a programme embodying these points: (1) Self-government and Independence; (2) Agrarian Revolution; (3) Protective Tariffs against English competition.

This letter crossed one, no less notable from Engels to Marx, written on the morning after the executions: "All the Fenians lacked was martyrs. These they have been presented with ... Through the execution of these men, the liberation of Kelley and Deasy has been made an act of heroism which will now be sung over the cradle of every Irish child ... The Irish women will take care of that. The only instance of an execution for any similar act is ... that of John Brown after Harper's Ferry. The Fenians could not wish for a better precedent ... Louis Napoleon ... at the head of his band of adventurers at Boulogne (1840) shot the officer on duty ... For this the English government have hanged Allen; but the English queen kissed Louis Napoleon's face, while the English aristocracy and bourgeoisie kissed his backside."

Marx did not succeed in getting the I.W.M.A. to launch an agitation for Repeal–his efforts were cut across by Gladstone's accession to power, and his decision to at once introduce the Disestablishment Bill (1869). But Marx and Engels worked strenuously through the I.W.M.A. in support of the Amnesty Movement which secured the release of most of the leading Fenian prisoners on January 1, 1871.

The Protestant Church in Ireland was undoubtedly an anomaly. Set up on a scale amply sufficient to serve the entire population, it was the Church of a fractional minority only. Of five millions and three-quarters, four and a half were Catholics, three-quarters of a million were Dissenters, and only half-a-million at most were even nominally Episcopalians. Out of 1,478 parishes, only 181 possessed a resident "church" population of over 1,000. In 201 parishes, they numbered less than 40 all told. Ninety-one parishes had less than a score apiece; and among these were a number with not a single Church adherent. The Church had been for centuries merely a device to supply salaries to non-resident parsons nominated by aristocratic patrons.

The best of the resident clergy in the Established Church welcomed Disestablishment; and even the Orange Order could find little to complain of except Gladstone's admission that it was the activity of the Fenians which had brought the Irish Church question "within the range of practical politics". Once the infliction of tithes was removed the resident Protestant Clergy had usually been popular, and were commonly on the best of terms with the parish priests. The best feature of the Act was that by abolishing redundant bishoprics and other ecclesiastical offices it created a fund from which a number of underpaid curates and rectors received welcome additions of salary.

As it removed only superficial grievances, Church Disestablishment made no real difference to the situation in Ireland, except that it destroyed the basis for the easiest form of "Catholic" demagogy.

The Fenian Tradition

The most abiding result of the Fenian agitation was that it established firmly in the minds of Irishmen, in Ireland and in exile, a tradition of fidelity and steadfastness in the cause of National Freedom which has never since been wholly overlaid. While it was in being Fenianism absorbed into itself and its discipline the whole membership of the Ribbon conspiracy. After its failure, the recrudescence of agrarian outrage which followed was condemned, even in the countryside, as a falling away from the disciplined manliness of the Fenian ideal. The concept of an Irish Republic now virtually established might be treated as folly and romanticism by self-seeking worldlings; it remained operative, none the less, as an abiding element in the Irish tradition of Nationality.

The political content of the Fenian doctrine was, consciously and purposefully, in line with the teaching of Tone, and Davis, with an infusion of Mitchel and of Lalor. It was categorically democratic, as well as republican, and it was socialistic, or even communistic, in its agrarian-revolutionary outlook (at any rate in the negative sense of advocating the expropriation of the landlords as a class).

Still more was Fenianism categorically hostile to sectarianism and clericalism. A few passages (mainly from the extracts from the *Irish People* included in the indictments of the Fenian leaders in '65) will illustrate these points.

Their democratic faith is thus attested: "Twenty years ago Thomas Davis appealed to the aristocracy to save the people with their own hands. We make no appeal to the aristocracy ... They are the willing tools of the alien government whose policy it is to slay the people, or drive them like noxious vermin from the soil. The people must save themselves."

"The overthrow of tyranny has always been the work of the people. It is by their combined and determined efforts that rulers are made and unmade. America and France have furnished us glorious examples of this."

"By force of arms Ireland was wrested from her rightful owners, the Irish people. By no other means will she ever be restored."

Their agrarian ideal was not less specific: "Something more even than a successful insurrection is demanded. And what is that? An entire revolution which will restore the country to its rightful owners. And who are these? The People."

"Every man has one simple object to accomplish. It is to rid the land of robbers, and render every cultivator of the soil his own landlord, the proprietor in fee-simple of the house and land of his fathers, which will be an inheritance worth a free man's while to bequeath to his children, and worth the children's while to enjoy in a nation which bows to no power under heaven."

In regard to clericalism, Charles J. Kickham, himself an ardent Catholic, wrote: "Nothing would please us better than to keep clear of the vexed question of priests in politics . . . But the question was forced upon us. We saw that the people must be taught to distinguish between the priest as a minister of religion and the priest as a politician before they could advance one step on the road to emancipation . . . Our only hope is in revolution, but most bishops and many of the clergy are opposed to revolution . . . When priests turn the altar into a platform: when it is pronounced a 'mortal sin' to read the *Irish People*, a 'mortal sin' to even wish that Ireland should be free; when priests call upon the people to turn informers . . . When, in a word, bishops and priests are doing the work of the enemy, we believe it is our duty to tell the people that bishops and priests may be bad politicians and worse Irishmen."*

Luby wrote to similar effect: "Emancipation was a

* Kickham suspected the theological orthodoxy of O'Leary and Devoy. Learning that they, on their release from penal servitude, were spending a holiday in France, studying architectural monuments, he remarked "If that one [O'Leary] goes on looking at Cathedrals much longer, the Grace of God may strike him yet!'

294

measure calculated almost exclusively to benefit the upper and middle-classes of the Catholics ... Emancipation separated from the cause of Independence has turned out to be simply a means ... of bribing or corrupting wealthy or educated Catholics—of seducing them from the National ranks."

O'Leary summed up the first year of the *Irish People* thus: "In one part of the old *Nation's* policy ... we could do no more than follow in its footsteps, and by so doing we have incurred the same reward—the hatred of bigots. And here it may not be out of place to use the words of Davis on a similar occasion: 'We look upon the Protestants' fear of the Catholics, and the Catholics' fear of the Protestants as rank nonsense. Their mutual dislike is something worse. And yet this trash and this crime have ruined the country.' Alas that it should be almost as necessary to write this today as when Davis wrote, and our pseudo-national papers are the main cause that this is the case."

That all these passages (save the last one) should have been included in the Government's indictment against the Fenian chiefs testifies to the effectiveness of the Fenian teaching.

Finally it is worth noting, as James Connolly does, that Fenianism, though unquestionably a national movement and not a class movement, appealed most successfully to the wage-worker class especially among the exile communities in England, Scotland, the U.S.A. and Australia. In Ireland the *Irish People* barely held its own in competition with the constitutionalist journals backed by the power of the Church. Where the field was more free, and the power of clerical intimidation was correspondingly, less, as it was among the exiles, the *Irish People* swept its rivals completely out of the field.

That is to say: The I.R.B. represented the peasantry and received their general support; but its main strength and source of inspiration was in the towns and among the proletarian exiles. Working men, very often of the labourer-class, formed overwhelmingly the backbone of the army of those who sang:

"Side by side for the Cause, have our forefathers
   battled,
When our hills never echoed the tread of a slave;
On many green fields where the leaden hail rattled,
Through the red gap of glory they marched to their
   grave.
And we who inherit their name and their spirit
Will march 'neath the banners of Liberty, then—
All who love Saxon law, native or Sassenach,
Must out and make way for the Fenian Men."

J. Boyle O'Reilly.

PART FIVE

FROM PARNELL TO EASTER WEEK
(AND AFTER)

CHAPTER XXIII

ECONOMIC DEVELOPMENTS, 1870-1916

In Part Five we treat of the process of revival after the failure of the Fenians. It is an epoch which had as its peak phenomena Parnell and his Parliamentary Struggle: the concurrent Land Struggle; and, then, the Revolutionary Struggle, opened by Connolly and Pearse in Easter Week 1916, which issued in the Treaty of 1921 and the Partition of 1925.

In this chapter we deal with the economic roots from which the struggle was fed and grew.

Agricultural Development in Ireland

Before the Famine of '46-8, political economists attributed Ireland's difficulties to its "surplus population". This was removed with a vengence in those years of calamity; consequently progress, thereafter, was able to take a course normal to the conditions then existing. The nature of the conditions can be inferred from the figures set out in the following comparison of the area under crops in the years 1849 and 1914 respectively:

Crop	1849	1914
Wheat	697,646 acres	26,916 acres
Oats	2,061,185 acres	1,028,645 acres
Barley	290,690 acres	179,824 acres
Potatoes	718,608 acres	583,609 acres
Turnips	260,069 acres	276,872 acres
Hay	1,141,371 acres	2,487,513* acres

Every item in this list bears witness to the steady shift over from arable to pasture-farming; and, therefore, to

* For 1914 these were the figures for Meadow and Hay.

a constant economic squeeze of the classes dependent directly upon tillage. Potatoes, for example, declined by one-fifth approximately—a decline which corresponds to the decline of population. The decline of wheat to one-eighteenth of the 1849 acreage is decisive, since this followed a previous decline from the level of 1800. The decline in oats—the staple crop—by one-half, and of barley by over one-third—declines in each case much greater than the fall in the population but much less than the decline in wheat—testify the one to the influence of cattle-rearing, the other to that of brewing and distilling as partial checks upon the general abandonment of tillage farming. This steady lessening of the demand for labour constantly threw the lowest strata of the agrarian population back upon the alternatives of subsistence-cultivation on small-holdings, or—emigration. A census of livestock for the corresponding years gives a conforming picture:

	1849	1914
Horses	525,924	619,028
Cattle	2,771,139	5,051,645
Sheep	1,777,111	3,600,581
Pigs	795,463	1,305,638
Poultry	6,328,001	26,918,749

These figures also tell their own tale. Ireland in these years concentrated increasingly upon producing and exporting livestock and poultry for the English market. Comparative statistics are not available, but we can infer likewise an increase in the export, but in a different proportion, of eggs, butter and bacon.

This development, to be appreciated, must be envisaged as one pole in a relation. As Ireland's farm production developed, while its manufactures declined, so correspondingly England's manufacture developed out of all proportion to its agriculture. And—since England's demand for bread-stuffs must have grown with its population–the decline in Irish (as well as English) tillage-farming implies the growth of an alternative, and cheaper, source of supply. Similarly the importance of live-stock exports must be viewed against England's demand for (1) prime "home-killed" meat and poultry for luxury consumption; and (2) cheap frozen or chilled carcasses, and tinned meats, for mass-consumption. The result emerges that, in fact and practice, Ireland was in this period relegated to the position of a feeder for the English market almost exclusively; and was, in that market, subjected to an ever-intensifying competition from overseas wheat and grain production–especially that of North America–the meat production of Australia, New Zealand and South America, etc., and the State-fostered dairy-farming and bacon-manufacture of Denmark, etc.

Ireland, in short, had to face the full impact of expanding and intensifying world-competition, with, as its consequence, the progressive fall in prices for agricultural produce. At the same time Ireland was denied all possibility of gaining any countervailing advantage from the growing demand for manufactured articles; and had no power of protecting even its own agriculture. Ireland's power of accumulating capital was reduced to a minimum by the rigorous exaction of the landlord's tribute–much of which went to swell the capital accumulation of England. Necessarily, the intensifying pressure of world-competition ensured a progressive worsening of living-standards for rural Ireland, taken as a whole.

This worsening is denied by those who look only to the very lowest sub-stratum of the population, and judge this stratum from its worst periods. It should be remembered that from 1845 onwards Famine and emigration constantly drained away a proportion of the population equivalent to the number who would have been otherwise submerged and relegated to pauperism. The persisting poverty of the agricultural classes in Ireland is not a static phenomenon;

it is a poverty which was as constantly recreated as it was "cured" by emigration.

That, in essence, is the fact that finds expression in constant agitation, on the one hand, and perpetual Coercion on the other.

The Case of Belfast

Belfast, with its surrounding region, provides, in this period, an outstanding contrast to the state of rural Ireland. And it has been a favourite device of anti-Nationalist politicians to point to Belfast and ask the Nationalists: "If Belfast can prosper, why cannot you prosper also?"

The facts, correctly related, expose the hypocrisy—as well as the ignorance—shown in this question.

In rural Ireland, in the period under examination, the English rulers insisted upon applying the principle of *laissez faire*, of Free Trade in Land. Belfast rose to prosperity because, in its own case, at every critical period, the principle of *laissez faire* was abandoned, and special protective measures were applied.

In 1856 the Belfast Harbour Board were granted special powers by Parliament and a money-donation by the government to enable them to convert a harbour, accessible only at high-tide, into one usable at any time. This was done, deliberately, to supplement the ship-repairing (and, later, ship-building) resources of the Mersey and the Clyde. And it was done, too, to provide the capitalists concerned with an escape from the "rapacity" of the Trade Unions in those areas. The "prosperity" of the region around Belfast is primarily the product of its shipbuilding and repairing industry, which in turn owes its existence (1) to the English Parliament, (2) the English Government, and (3) to the English capitalist class which fostered the rise of Belfast (with capital largely drained from the rest of Ireland) because it suited their economic and their class interests—as it had suited their interest in the 17th and 18th centuries to protect and foster Belfast's second stand-by, the Linen industry.

In rural Ulster generally, the establishment of the Ulster custom (explained earlier) was another negation of the principle of *laissez faire*.

In short, Belfast and Ulster supply a crushing condemnation of the English economic policy enforced in the rest of Ireland.

The Struggle for the Land, 1870-1909

The point just made was exemplified in the condemnation by the Tories of Gladstone's Land Act of 1870—the first of a long series of such Acts—as a "gross interference with the rights of property"—with the right of the landlord to "do what he likes with his own".

Gladstone's Act was, in fact, an attempt to extend the Ulster custom to the rest of Ireland. It failed; partly because it contained restrictions which prevented tenants taking advantage of it; but chiefly because its operation was sabotaged by the landlords.

The growth of a world market for agricultural products, and the progressive fall of prices in that market, made the tenants increasingly unable to pay their rents. The landlords sought a remedy by "consolidating" their estates—clearing them of the holders of small-scale farms, to make room for farming on a large scale. Concurrently, the landlords increased their rents; partly to facilitate clearance, partly as its consequence. When the land-hungry, driven from one place, competed all the more intensely for those small plots which were still available elsewhere, rents, in general, rose. Simultaneously, prices for agricultural products fell—one consequence of this policy of freezing out the "little man".

This policy produced its results; first the Land League organised by Michael Davitt, and supported by Parnell and the Parliamentary Party; then the Land Act of 1881, which introduced the principle of "dual ownership". This proved satisfactory only in so far as it facilitated, though not to any great extent, the purchase of their holdings by the tenants.

Unrest and agitation, continuing, led to (1) Gladstone's first Home Rule Bill (1885) which was defeated, and (2) to the Land Act of 1885 which increased the facilities for tenant-purchase. This Act was amended in 1887, 1888, (twice), 1889, and 1891 without giving satisfaction either to tenant or to landlord.

Gladstone's Second Home Rule Bill (1893) was designed, primarily, to shift the responsibility for settling the Land Question on to the shoulders of an Irish local "parliament". Passed by the Commons, it was thrown out by the Lords.

The Land Acts were further amended in 1894, 1896, and 1901. Then in 1903, the Tory Chief Secretary, George Wyndham, introduced a measure providing a Government subsidy to induce the landlords to sell holdings to their occupiers on hire-purchase terms. The Act was modified by the Liberals in 1909, and so, in its turn, was a prelude to the Third Home Rule Bill (1910). After a protracted and embittered Parliamentary struggle, this became law in 1914. Its operation was held up by the Carsonite "revolt", and by the outbreak of European War.

The Rising of Easter Week transformed the situation completely.

It will be seen from this summary that the period from 1870 to 1916 was one in which an agrarian struggle gave impetus to a parliamentary struggle, which after reinforcing the agrarian struggle was itself in turn superseded by an armed uprising. That the national struggle as a whole arose from the economic consequences of the English conquest is self-evident.

Ireland was, in practice, forced to restrict itself in the main to agriculture, for whose products no market but that of England was available. In the English market Irish producers had to sell at prices fixed by world competition, while Irish agriculture, in general, could not advance because it was crippled by the burden of a parasitic landlordism.

Lalor: and the Theory of Agrarian Struggle

The theory of agrarian struggle as leading up to a political policy was first formulated by James Fintan Lalor in the Young Ireland period. At that time, however, his work was noted only for its immediate significance, as one among many modes of effecting an insurrection. He acted as a stimulant to the Young Ireland movement generally, and he exercised a personal influence upon Luby and O'Leary, the Fenian leaders. But it was through the influence of Michael Davitt, leader of the Land League, that Lalor first became recognised in Ireland as the propounder of a distinct political philosophy.

Lalor wrote little, and only for a short time; but his importance warrants a few quotations from his writings: "To any plain understanding the right of private property is very simple. It is the right of man to possess, enjoy, and transfer the substance and use of whatever he has himself created. This title is good against the world; and it is the sole and only title by which a valid right of absolute private property can possibly rest. But no man can plead any such title to a right of property in the substance of the soil."

"I hold and maintain that the entire soil of a country belongs of right to the entire people of that country and is the rightful property, not of any one class, but of the nation at large, in full effective possession, to let to whom they will on whatever tenures, etc. they will; one condition, however, being unavoidable and essential ... full, true, and undivided allegiance to the nation, and the laws of the nation whose land he holds."

"I hold further that the enjoyment by the people of this right of first ownership is essential to the vigour and vitality of all other rights; to their validity, efficacy and value; to their secure possession and safe exercise."

"I trouble myself as little as anyone does about the 'conquest,' taken abstractly—as an affair that took place ages ago. But that 'conquest' is still in existence, with all its rights, claims, laws, relations and results. The landlord holds his lands by right and title of conquest, and uses his powers as only a conqueror may."

"Mark the words of this prophecy—the principle I propose goes to the foundations of Europe, and sooner or later will cause Europe to uprise. Mankind will yet be masters of the earth. The right of the people to make the laws—this produced the first great modern earthquake whose latest shocks even now are heaving in the heart of the world. The right of the people to own the land—this will produce the next. Train your hands, and your sons' hands, gentlemen of the earth, for you and they will yet have to use them."

These are sufficient to show the essence of Lalor's doctrine. That it should have fermented in the mind of Michael Davitt, brooding in his cell in Portland Gaol, until after his release it bore fruit in the Land League, is not surprising. Nor is it surprising that one of the first pamphlets produced by James Connolly was a reprint of Lalor's *Faith of a Felon*; or that in the proclamation of the Republic in Easter Week, 1916, we should find these words: "We declare the right of the people of Ireland to the ownership of Ireland, and to the unfettered control of Irish destinies to be sovereign and indefeasible."

Whether drawn directly or indirectly from Lalor, or discovered afresh by each successive leader for himself, this principle finds perennial expression in the Irish National struggle; and that the more clearly the further we proceed.

CHAPTER XXIV

HOME RULE: THE RISE OF PARNELL

The agitation for Home Rule for Ireland, and the Parliamentary nationalist Party it threw up–which Party came to dominate English politics to the exclusion of everything else–was launched in 1870; largely as a result of the agitation for an Amnesty for the Fenian prisoners of '65 and '67.

In this chapter we trace the movement from its start until the rise of Charles Stewart Parnell in 1877.

The Home Rule Movement Begins

The Home Rule Party differed from its predecessors in so far as it was thrown up by a popular movement whose inspiration was very largely Fenian. Any renewal of armed struggle between 1870 and 1877 was impossible to think of. But to secure any following in Ireland at all the Home Rule Party, which arose in those years, had to be, or seemed to be, an attempt to reach the Fenian end by other means.

The passionate sympathy the Fenian struggle had engendered found expression, first of all, in the demand for Amnesty. Gladstone had admitted that the grievances of Ireland were real. It was obviously barbarous to submit men who, however unwisely, had sought to remedy those grievances to treatment worse than that inflicted on the most sub-human of malefactors.

That the Dublin-Castle-inspired police attacked the first Amnesty meetings savagely only multiplied the passion of indignation.

Led by Karl Marx and the International Working Men's Association, the English workers were roused in support of the Amnesty demand; and a union in struggle of the English workers and the Irish National movement was what every English statesman, from William Pitt onwards, had feared as the final calamity. Timing his "duck-and-get-away" perfectly, Gladstone averted this, in 1870, by concessions to Ireland which included amnesty for a hundred or thereabouts of the Fenians first convicted. The release of the rest followed at intervals.

Gladstone's decision was prompted by the election of O'Donovan Rossa for Tipperary in 1869. Rossa was declared ineligible as a "convicted felon" still in gaol; and this checked a move to nominate Luby for Co. Longford. The "advanced" men accepted John Martin (of the *Irish Felon* of '48) as a compromise; but the local clergy were committed to support the son of the local landlord (Greville-Nugent)—whose elevation to the peerage had caused the vacancy.

The election battle was fought with extreme bitterness—the pious, papalist, anti-Fenian A. M. Sullivan, for example, found himself assailed, much to his surprise, as a "Garibaldian", a "priest-killer" and a "Fenian" for supporting Martin. The priests won, but at the cost of rousing a demand for a mass political movement which would break the power of the landlord-clerical alliance. Only a national movement could do this—one infused with a strong measure of the Fenian spirit tempered with Fenian discipline.

Some brutal clearances underlined the need. In Tipperary, a landlord who attempted to serve notices to quit was three times beaten off—with his police escort—by a rally of neighbours led by a Fenian. An attempt to take another tenant by surprise was defeated by "Fenians" with revolvers and shot-guns. A bailiff and one constable were killed on the spot. The landlord and several of his party were severely wounded; two died of their wounds.

This incident is credited with having "passed the Land Act of 1870". It did more than that. It induced a party of notables of all shades of Nationalism to meet in Dublin in May, 1870, and constitute the "Home Government

Association for Ireland". The leader of the movement was Isaac Butt, Q.C., once the leader of Dublin Conservatives, later counsel for the Fenian chiefs; and his lieutenant was A. M. Sullivan.

The new movement scored an immediate success when John Martin won Co. Meath against strong clericalist opposition. But its great test came in the Kerry election of 1872.

Kerry was regarded as the property of the local landlord, Lord Kenmare; and a vacancy being created by the succession of the sitting-member (Viscount Castlerosse) to the peerage, on the death of his father, the new Lord Kenmare thought he could nominate his successor as a matter of course. To his dismay his nominee was opposed by a Home Rule candidate, who was elected with a comfortable majority. It was the "Clare election" of Home Rule. It was also the last open-voting election in Ireland. Believing the result had been secured by "intimidation", Parliament at once passed the Ballot Act of 1872.

A few weeks later a conference formally established the Irish Home Rule League and pledged its members, if elected, to act and vote together as an independent party.

In the surprise general election of 1874, the League met with success far beyond its hopes. Only two of its candidates were defeated; one by only three votes. Sixty Home Rulers were elected, a gain of fifty seats. All but seven were won from the Liberals. Gladstone's education on the Irish question was advanced by a long stride.

The Home Rule Party in Parliament

By founding a Party pledged to permanent opposition to every Government which would not make Home Rule a Cabinet issue, and to disciplined independence even of a Government that would, the Home Rule League opened a new page in Parliamentary History. To have realised the concept of a Third Party; and to have built it out of Catholics and Protestants, Liberals, Conservatives, '48 men, and Fenians, was in itself a notable feat. The English parties, Liberals and Tories, showed its worth by uniting to vote down every Irish proposal made by the new party. This in itself was a gain. It helped materially to enhance the solidarity, and the National consciousness, of the Party; and it had a still more profound effect upon the mass of the electors in Ireland. Before 1874 they had either been indifferent to Parliament and its concerns, or actively hostile to it—as diverting men's minds from "direct action" and insurrection. Now they began to see that there were possibilities in Parliamentary action after all.

As an instrument for achieving concrete results directly, the Parliamentary Party was a poor enough tool, then as later. But as a means of rousing, mobilising, educating and intensifying the mass-consciousness of Nationality in Ireland, the Party was—or at any rate could become—of a very high value indeed; of much higher value, in fact, than any but a few of its members realised.

One of the few, and the one to realise it most fully, was a young Wicklow man, a Protestant and a landlord—who came from a family which had earned distinction in Grattan's Parliament. This was Charles Stewart Parnell (1846–1891) who was elected, for Co. Meath, in the spring of 1875, to fill a vacancy caused by the death of John Martin.

Scientific Obstruction: Biggar and Parnell

Obstruction—the art of parliamentary procrastination—had always been recognised as a legitimate weapon for the opposition to use in emergencies. Parnell arrived in the House in time to witness some of the earlier efforts of a group of Home Rule members who had come to adopt the practice, not consistently, but as an occasional irritation tactic.

Its real initiator was a Belfast man, Joseph Gillis Biggar, a wholesale pork merchant, Member for Cavan. Unknown to most of his colleagues, Biggar was a member of the Supreme Council of the I.R.B. when he first scandalised the House by "espying strangers" just as the Prince of Wales had taken his seat in the gallery to listen to a debate on improving the breed of horses. "Espying strangers" involved clearing everybody–the Prince of Wales along with the reporters–out of the galleries. As the rules of the House then stood, Mr. Speaker had no option but to order "strangers" to withdraw.

Members of all parties, including his own, joined in denouncing the Member for Cavan for his "ungentlemanly" conduct. As "Joe" Biggar never pretended to be a gentleman, these eloquent denunciations were entirely wasted. So were such press comments as this, from the *World* of March 5, 1875: "Mr. Biggar brings the manner of his store into this illustrious assembly, and his manner, even for a Belfast store, is very bad. When he rises to address the House ... a whiff of salt-pork seems to float upon the gale, and the air is heavy with the odour of the kippered herring. One unacquainted with the condition of affairs might be forgiven if he thought the House of Commons was a meeting of creditors and the right hon. gentlemen sitting on the Treasury Bench were members of the defaulting firm, who having confessed to their inability to pay ninepence in the pound, were suitable and safe subjects for the abuse of an ungenerous creditor."

The gentlemanly correspondent of the gentlemanly *World* was quite oblivious to the fact that it was precisely in the light of fraudulent debtors, who, having shown no mercy themselves, were entitled to expect none, that Joe Biggar–who saw nothing discreditable in salt-pork or kippers–regarded the Treasury Bench.

On the evening upon which Parnell took his seat, Biggar "entertained" the House by speaking for four hours on the subject of swine fever. Butt had asked him to spin out the time, to prevent the next item on the agenda from being reached—a common obstructive device. Biggar came equipped with a pile of blue books; all of which he insisted upon reading to the House, with a running commentary of assent, dissent, or illustrative anecdote. He gave in at last, because his voice had deserted him. As a parliamentary performance it was so extremely scandalous that it went beyond condemnation to reach the audaciously sublime.

Parnell watched the performance with undisturbed gravity. It had given him an idea, which he and Biggar thereafter worked out between them. It was very simple after all. There was nowhere near time enough for the work Parliament had to get through. If every member insisted upon inquiring into and "taking the sense of the House upon" every detail of the routine business the Government had to get through, sessions would have to be four times as long and there would be no time at all for private members—or for measures of reform. Parnell and Biggar, with the followers they gathered round them, began therefore to take their duties conscientiously. They were helped by the archaic and complex procedure the House had evolved through centuries—a procedure which left a wealth of openings to any man who would trouble to master its rules. Certain business could not be taken after a certain hour if it were opposed. Other business could not be taken after a given hour at all. It was a simple matter to say "I object" in the one case, and in the other to develop critical doubts requiring elaborate explanations on the subject preceding it on the order paper.

No contrast could possibly be greater in the externals of speech, physique, and manner than that between Biggar and Parnell. The one squat, deformed, and homely, with a voice and accent as harsh as a corncrake; the other tall, slender, aristocratic, and speaking with an accent that, except for a slight trace of America, marked him as a Cambridge man.

The House could have forgiven them if they had merely wasted time. What it could not forgive was their unconcealed contempt for the "illustrious assembly"; and the pains they took to prevent, if possible, any business being done at all.

Neither was, at first, a fluent speaker. Each was a master of plain statement. Biggar derived a never-ending joy from addressing Mr. Speaker in the manner and vocabulary of one Belfast crony addressing another. Parnell, one of an extremely rare type, not only meant what he said, but said what he meant to say and not a word more or less.

Parnell's complete freedom from rhetoric caused him to be regarded as "frigid". Men were to learn that his conventional correctness of bearing, and his abhorrence of decorated speech, were expressions of a ruthlessly imposed self-discipline, which masked an intensity of political passion which, when it did show itself, made the stage "thunders" of the professional rhetoricians dwindle into insignificance. Orators like Charles James Fox have scorched the Government benches with the fire of their eloquence. Parnell froze them solid with the intensity of his contempt.

It must be recorded to the credit of Parnell and Biggar that, when a chance arose to force a reform upon the Government, they seized it instantly, and made the most of it. In the session of 1877–in which a crisis was precipitated–they worked over in detail two Prison Bills, a Navy and an Army Mutiny Bill, and a South African Government Bill, and even their enemies admitted that they secured valuable amendments–some their own, others those of Radicals–which would never even have been considered but for their efforts. Most notable was the (partial) abolition of flogging in the Army and Navy. Radicals had advocated this for years without forcing a discussion. The tenacity and skill of Parnell and Biggar forced it to the stage of debate for the first time. As soon as the true facts were made public the Government had to give way.

It is surprising, but true, that it took the House quite a time to realise that Parnell and Biggar were something different from the mere cranks and bores which they were at first supposed to be. When it was realised at last that they were trying, deliberately, to make it impossible for the Government of England to be carried on, so long as the House insisted upon legislating for Ireland, Tory fury knew no bounds.

A characteristic episode arose when Parnell, opposing the South Africa Bill, explained that, as an Irishman, who knew at first hand what England's treatment of subject races was like, he would have great satisfaction "in preventing and thwarting the intentions of Government in regard to the Bill". When the storm had abated sufficiently for Parnell's suspension to be moved, it dawned upon the saner section of the House that "thwarting the intentions of the Government" is the normal function of an opposition. The suspension motion was accordingly withdrawn. The incident is typical as showing the state of hysteria into which Parnell and Biggar contrived to throw the House merely by rising to speak–a condition which Biggar took an unholy delight in exacerbating to the limit.

On the South Africa Bill they proceeded to frank obstruction. They had been accused of it when they moved amendments admittedly "framed with considerable skill", and which seldom found fewer than fifty English supporters in the division lobby. Now that it was an issue on which the Irish stood alone they obstructed without scruple.

When members tried to drown Parnell's voice by coughing, groaning, whistling and loud conversation, Biggar suggested, in a voice which rasped through the uproar like a rusty saw, that, if the hon. gentlemen were not prepared to listen, the debate had better be adjourned; and he moved accordingly. This reprisal of moving the adjournment whenever the House refused to listen to an Irish speaker grew into a regular game. After the House had been kept sitting until four in the morning for a number of nights in succession, an English member thought of appealing to Isaac Butt the (nominal) leader of the Irish Party.

Before Parnell and Biggar began their campaign it had been deemed improper for Irish members to intervene on English questions. Butt's generation had accepted that view as a matter of course. Couldn't he do something about these fellows who were turning "the best club in the world" into a bear-garden?

Butt, a kindly soul—as well as, in his prime, a man of great courage and capacity—was always susceptible on this side. He was a gentleman—an Irish gentleman of the old school—one who would either pay his cabman a sovereign for a shilling ride or borrow half-a-crown from him!—Yes! Butt could do something, and would. He went into the House and treated Parnell and Biggar to a lecture on "How to Behave in an August Assembly".

He delighted the Liberals and Tories immensely, and the old man retired hugely satisfied. But the only difference he made was that from that night he ceased in fact to be leader of the Irish Party. He retained the position nominally until his death in 1879, but from that night the real leader of the Party was Parnell.

The Parting of the Ways

The issue at stake lay far deeper than Butt or any of his school could perceive. It was a fight between Parliamentarians who merely happened to be Irish, and Irish revolutionaries who merely happened to be in Parliament—who were in Parliament only because there the revolutionary work of the moment was to be done.

From Butt's point of view, obtaining the good opinion of the House was essential. From Parnell's, it was a matter of indifference—except in so far as it was a positive disadvantage. Butt was genuinely eager for Home Rule, but only as a reform in the controlling machinery of the British Empire.

For Parnell the British Empire was something his ancestors had fought with all their strength. On his mother's side he was descended from men who had broken off the major part of the British Empire to found the U.S.A. His mother's father had been the "Nelson" of the American Navy in the War of 1812. His paternal great-grandfather had been the colonel of a regiment of Volunteers in '82—the colours of the regiment hung over the great mantel-piece in the hall of the Parnell family mansion. That great-grandfather, with his son, had been among the incorruptibles who stood by Grattan in his last struggle to stave off the Union. Parnell was not—as his detractors took care to let the world know—deeply read in Irish history. But from his earliest years he had seen those flags and been familiar with their story. And familiar, too, with the tale of Grattan's dramatic reappearance in the House—like a corpse rearisen from the grave—to pour scorn and denunciation upon Castlereagh and the rest of those—

> "Slaves who sold their land for gold
> As Judas sold his God."

He had heard, too, from the lips of the peasant-grey-beards on his father's estate first-hand tales of '98—of Michael Dwyer and his men, of the yeomanry and their deeds. He could, when he pleased, repeat stories of the barbarous floggings inflicted by the yeomanry, word for word as he had heard them from the lips of the sons of victims and survivors.

Parnell, in short, had no need to ransack libraries to discover reasons for "thwarting the intentions of the Government". They were born in him as an ancestral heritage.

There was another consideration to which Butt was oblivious, but which was self-evident to Parnell. The consideration given to an Irish member by the House did not depend upon his eloquence, or upon his social or personal qualities, at all. It depended bluntly upon the amount of trouble he could cause if he really put himself to it. Parnell was concerned to rouse the Irish people. For that end the hatred and reviling of the House was a hundred times more to be desired than its affection and its flattery. He knew that the more the English members united against him the more the Irish People would unite on his side. He soon had proof. In August 1877, a crowded assembly in the Rotunda, Dublin, gave him and Biggar an ovation. In November 1877, the Home Rule Confederation in England—an exiles' organisation—elected him President in place of Butt.

When old-man Isaac Butt died quietly of heart disease in May 1879, he cleared the last barrier from the road ahead for Parnell. Otherwise the event was—sad to say—of negligible significance.

CHAPTER XXV

DAVITT; THE LAND LEAGUE; AND PARNELL

The Irish situation was altered beyond recognition between 1879 and 1882 by the Land war, waged by Michael Davitt and the Land League (with Parnell's powerful co-operation) and by the concurrent rise of Parnell to the leadership of the Parliamentary Party.

In this chapter the development is traced from the founding of the Land League (1879) to the Kilmainham Compact (1882).

The Famine of 1879

Between the end of 1877 and the general election in 1880, Parnell's position was anomalous. In the Parliamentary Party itself he ranked as an ordinary member only—one whose line the majority did not like but did not dare to reprove too openly because of its immense popularity with the mass of Irishmen, in Ireland as well as in England. Parnell added greatly to his personal popularity by taking his stand, at Davitt's invitation, at the head of the newly-formed Land League.

The rising tide of militancy the Land League expressed can be traced to the rapid general deterioration of the economic position of rural Ireland; a deterioration intensified into a positive famine in the West of Ireland by a combination of causes, chief among which was the failure of the potato crop. This deterioration threw light on the working of the Land Act of 1870; and led in turn to the Land Act of 1881.

Basically the deterioration was due to a fall in world prices for agricultural produce; and this again was due to large-scale agricultural developments, especially in the U.S.A. It was aided also by the great expansion and speeding-up of Marine transport.

Between 1870 and 1875 harvests and prices had both been good in Ireland. From 1875 to 1879 prices fell rapidly and harvests were bad.

This revealed the fatal weakness in the Land Act of 1870 which was designed to give the tenant a qualified property-right in his improvements. While prices remained high, the tenant could borrow on the security of these improvements; when prices fell he was caught in a squeeze between the landlord and the usurer.

While prospects had been bright, and borrowing brisk, the banks had done good business. Favourable rates had induced such farmers as had no need to borrow to invest their savings in these local loan-banks. Banks and depositors alike were caught in the squeeze; and along with them were caught the tradespeople who, being allowed long-term credits by the banks, had thought it safe to allow their customers credit likewise.

Under the Act of 1870, security of tenure was wholly dependent upon the punctual payment of rent. "Any arrears; no security" was the rule. In addition, the tenant could sell his improvements for cash only after he had given notice to quit; and had applied to a landcourt for a valuation. This valuation, when made, the landlord could appeal against. Thus, in practice, the tenant could only realise his improvements in cash after he had been ejected, and after a legal procedure which took a wearisome time, and swallowed up most of the value in costs. Thus, in practice, the banks found they had made advances which could not be recovered. They failed, and ruined their depositors; but not before these had ruined the tradespeople by calling in their credits, and forcing them in turn to ruin their customers or be ruined themselves.

The only ones who escaped were the landlords, and the gombeen-men—the small-loan money-lenders whose usual rate was a shilling per pound per month.

In the West suffering was intensified by the failure of

the potato crop. The all-Ireland value of this crop in 1876 was £12,500,000; in 1877, £5,300,000; in 1878, £3,300,000. Other crops failed too; in the three years after 1878 the value of the total crop of all kinds fell by more than £26,000,000. In addition, in 1879, incessant rains prevented the drying of peat so that in many parts a fuel famine was added to the total of miseries. And, to cap all, a failure of the harvest in England cut off entirely the harvest wages upon which thousands depended for their rent-money.

Ejectment notices began to fall "like snow-flakes". In 1877, 980 families were evicted (a total well above the average). In 1880, there were 2,110.

This was the soil from which sprang the Land League led by Davitt and Parnell.

Davitt, Devoy and the New Departure

Before launching the Land League, Michael Davitt was from 1870 to 1877 imprisoned as a Fenian convict in Portland Gaol. Released in the latter year—in response to an Amnesty Agitation which Parnell and his Party in Parliament supported vigorously—Davitt had paid a visit to America to test the feeling of the Fenian leaders.

Born (in 1846) in Mayo—from which his parents were driven by the Famine to seek work in Lancashire—Davitt while quite a child, working in a cotton-mill, had his right arm caught in the machinery and mangled so badly that it had to be amputated. Despite this, he joined the Fenians in 1865—"if he couldn't shoulder a rifle he could use a revolver, or at least could carry ammunition"—and as the leader of his "circle", took part in the "raid" on Chester Castle. He became the chief "Arms Organiser" for the Fenians in England, and held that post when he was captured and imprisoned in 1870. His standing in the movement was exceptionally high; and his first act on being released on ticket-of-leave was to make contact with the Fenian organisation. He was at once included in the Supreme Council.

While in prison he had occupied himself with reflections on the writings of Fintan Lalor and had come to definite conclusions as to the feasibility, as well as the desirability, of trying Lalor's methods in a modified form. Davitt's theory was, in general, that an organised resistance to eviction, and an organised demand for a reduction of rents, might lead, in time, to a situation from which a transition to armed struggle could be made with a maximum chance of success.

In America, Davitt found that the most reliable and respected of the Fenian leaders, John Devoy and John Boyle O'Reilly, were more than ready to agree with him; but on condition that the land-agitation was linked with, and operated through the machinery of, the Nationalist political agitation which had arisen in support of Parnell and Biggar. It was a ticklish business broaching to the Fenian Old Guard a policy which involved not only "peddling with reforms" but "compromise" with the hated parliamentarianism which it had been a cardinal Fenian principle to repudiate. John Devoy, however, was not easily frightened; and to his great satisfaction, and Davitt's, the "New Departure" of working through an open agitation (while keeping the "underground" organisation in being, ready for eventualities) met with a wide measure of acceptance. The non-Fenian Irish-Americans also rose readily to the slogan "Irish land for the Irish people".

Some of the Old Guard were more than dubious. John O'Leary, and Charles J. Kickham in Ireland would have nothing to do with this "New Departure"; but they agreed not to do anything that would prejudice its chance of a fair try-out in practice. O'Donovan Rossa, the implacable, in America, would not only have nothing to do with it; he denounced it in fury, and quarrelled so fiercely with Devoy that they remained enemies till Rossa lay on his deathbed in 1915.

321

In the overwhelming majority of cases the Fenian rank and file welcomed the New Departure cordially; and an obstacle which might have proved fatal to Davitt's plan was thus surmounted.

Parnell, for his part, also welcomed the land agitation. There is no reason to doubt his knowledge of what the Fenians hoped would come from this policy, and, from his point of view, that was all to the good. He could not rouse all Ireland in support of his political policy if the Fenians remained hostile; and their active help was far better than a frigid-neutrality.

When therefore he was asked by Davitt to speak at a meeting at Westport, Co. Mayo, on June 7, 1879, Parnell assented cordially.

The Westport meeting followed a successful meeting at Irishtown, Mayo, and it was intended to inaugurate a Land League for Mayo. It was successful beyond Davitt's highest expectation. On the eve of the meeting, it and its objects were denounced fiercely by the Catholic Archbishop of Tuam. Parnell refused to be intimidated; and, in his speech to a gathering of over 10,000, gave the movement a slogan: "A fair rent is a rent the tenant can reasonably pay according to the times; but in bad times a tenant cannot be expected to pay as much as he did in good times three or four years ago. If such rents are insisted upon a repetition of the scenes of 1847 and 1848 will be witnessed. Now what must we do in order to induce the landlords to see the position? You must show them that you intend to hold a firm grip of your homesteads and lands. You must not allow yourselves to be dispossessed as your fathers were dispossessed in 1847. You must not allow your small-holdings to be consolidated ... You must help yourselves, and the public opinion of the world will stand by you and support you in your struggle to defend your homesteads."

Parnell's presence at the meeting had ensured the presence of press-reporters; hence his slogan was carried into every home in Ireland. From that moment the movement spread rapidly.

In September an Irish National Land League was founded—with Parnell for President. He was requested by the inaugural conference to proceed to America to obtain assistance, but his journey was delayed by an act of reprisal by the Government. Egged on by the infuriated landlords the Government cancelled Davitt's ticket-of-leave.

Parnell replied with a huge protest meeting in the Rotunda, Dublin, at which he announced that a meeting Davitt had arranged in Balla, Co. Mayo—to stop a threatened eviction—would be held as arranged; and that he, with other leaders, would take Davitt's place.

The meeting was held. It was attended by 10,000 men who, as instructed, came "provided with means of self-defence against police attack". Faced with this assembly, the police abandoned the eviction. The Government changed front; it restored Davitt's ticket-of-leave, but included him in the list of those to be prosecuted for their speeches at a meeting in Sligo. When this case came up for its preliminary hearing, the League contrived to turn the occasion into a week of nightly demonstrations, all addressed by Parnell and other leading speakers. The Press rounded upon the Government, and denounced it for "advertising" the League. In the end the trial was abandoned.

Parliament and the Land War

The famine of 1879 did not reproduce all the horrors of '47. It was not so universal; but the resident-landlords as a class were much less sympathetic than in '47, when scores of them had ruined themselves in their efforts to alleviate distress. That the Land League averted the worst horrors by preventing, at source, the creation of distress, cannot be doubted. It raised a large relief fund.

too, in America, at meetings addressed by Parnell in the early months of 1880.

Davitt finds no praise too high for Parnell's work at this period:

> "It was essential to encourage the country in the policy laid down at the Western meetings—no rent without abatements, no tame submission to evictions, and no land-grabbing to be permitted ... No revolutionist in the movement surpassed Parnell in the fearless assertion of this policy ... [He] openly challenged the law to proceed against him."
>
> Davitt: *Fall of Feudalism.*

Recalled from America by a surprise dissolution of Parliament, Parnell had to face the forlorn hope of conducting an election campaign, without a Party machine, with hardly any available candidates, and with no funds. If Davitt had not been willing (against the rules of the League, and at the risk of trouble with the American ultras) to lend a considerable sum from the League funds, Parnell's efforts would have been crippled. As it turned out the Irish vote, in England and Scotland, was cast solidly against Disraeli and the Tory ("landlords") Party. In Ireland, Parnell fought the "moderate" Home Rulers, as well as both Liberals and Tories.

He was helped by the anxiety of his enemies to defeat him. The landlords denounced him as a "Communist" and a renegade from their ranks. The Catholic Archbishop of Dublin added his voice to the clamour of the landlords. The "moderate" Home Rulers echoed "Archbishop Mac-Cabe's anxious concern for Faith and Morals based on rack-rents and evictions" (Davitt) and thereby promoted notably the process of their own elimination. On the other side, several bishops, and nearly all the priests in the disturbed areas, supported the League, and, so far, Parnell.

Parnell was so short of the candidates he wanted that he had to accept what support he could get. He himself stood for three places—Cork City, Co. Meath and Co. Mayo—in each of which he was elected. In the upshot sixty-eight Home Rule candidates were returned; but of these less than forty could be relied upon by Parnell for disciplined support, and of those again a number were hostile to the Land League. The set of the tide was shown, however, by the election of Parnell as "sessional Chairman" of the Party.

When the House assembled, with Gladstone commanding an absolute majority, Parnell introduced a Bill to give compensation to all tenants disturbed by eviction. Gladstone countered with a Bill of his own. In a fierce struggle the Parnellites forced a number of amendments. Sent to the House of Lords on July 26, 1880, the Bill was ignominiously thrown out.

The news was received in Ireland with anger. There were riots at evictions, assaults upon land-grabbers, rickburnings, and cattle-maiming. The Fenians captured a gun-boat in Cork Harbour and abstracted thence 40 cases of rifles. These things were all shocking enough in the eyes of the Authorities; but Parnell "outraged" the feelings of the ruling-class worse still by his speech at Ennis, on September 19, 1880.

He had reached in his speech the point of what to do with a man who bids for a farm from which another had been evicted. There were loud cries of "Shoot him!" which in turn were loudly applauded. Parnell, in his usual quiet manner, proceeded with his argument: "I think I heard somebody say 'shoot him'—loud cries of 'quite right too' with renewed applause—but I wish to point out to you a very much better way—a more Christian, and a more charitable, way—which will give the lost sinner an opportunity of repenting."

After a pause which secured a rapt silence, Parnell continued quietly and distinctly: "When a man takes a farm from which another has been evicted, you must show him on the roadside when you meet him, you must show him in the streets of the town, you must show him at the shop-counter, you must show him in the fair and the market place, and even in the place of worship, by leaving him severely alone—putting him into a kind of moral coventry—isolating him from his kind like the leper of old—you must show him your detestation of the crime he has committed. And, you may depend upon it, that there is no man so full of avarice, so lost to shame, as to dare the public opinion of all right-thinking men, and to transgress your unwritten code of laws."

It was characteristic of Parnell's precise care in the choice of his words that when an excited auditor translated his "you must *show* him" into an interjected "*shun him!*", Parnell quietly but emphatically repeated "you must *show* him". On reflection it will be preceived that "shun" was not (while "show" was) precisely the word Parnell needed.

The words did more than electrify the audience at Ennis. They fired all the land-tillers in Ireland; and they roused, too, all the trade-unionists in England, who knew what it was to have to deal with blacklegs.

Correspondingly they were received with screams of rage from the whole landlord class, who realised, as Parnell did, that this policy, if it were persisted in, would destroy entirely the effectiveness of their chief weapon—eviction.

Three days later their worst fears were realised in an event which gave this modern application of the old Greek ostracism a "local habitation and a name".

The Case of Captain Boycott

Captain Boycott, an estate-agent for Lord Erne, refused the "fair" rent offered by his tenants; and issued ejectment notices. Mass-resistance prevented the service of the notices. The local branch of the League, with the parish priest at its head, proclaimed him under ban. All his domestics and farm-hands left him. Shopkeepers refused to serve him; the laundress and the blacksmith would not accept his orders; his letters and telegrams had to be delivered by the police.

He set out his woes in a letter to *The Times*; and every drawing-room in England was shaken (while every proletarian was tickled) at the thought of Captain Boycott's ladies washing their own linen, cooking their own meals, and carrying their own coals.

To save his crop, the Captain asked for volunteers. Hundreds in Ulster volunteered. Still retaining some of his wits, the Captain said fifty Orangemen would suffice. They arrived after a ten-mile tramp from the nearest railway station—neither love nor money would procure vehicles—amid a terrific downpour, escorted by a large contingent of police and soldiers (with two field guns). His crops were "saved". But what his saviours, and their escort, left of his shrubs, his kitchen garden, his poultry, and his pigs, wasn't worth "saving" further.

When the volunteers and their escort made their return journey, they marched through the village, in which every blind was drawn, and every shop closed and shuttered. Not a soul was in sight, save the parish priest—who marched at their head to "protect" them from affront.

In a few days Captain Boycott resigned his agency and retired with his ladies along the track of his saviours.

Gladstone tries Coercion

Seriously alarmed, the Government indicted Parnell and the leaders of the league for "seditious conspiracy". The trial opened in Dublin on January 5, 1881, and lasted for twenty days. Such chance as there was of a conviction was reduced to a minimum by the device of citing as witnesses for the defence all the inmates of the workhouse at Castlebar, Mayo, who had suffered eviction. Paraded in the court-house yard, they made such an impression that the counts upon which their evidence would have been relevant were abandoned.

As it became clear that a conviction could not be obtained, the Government, though reluctantly, introduced a Coercion Bill. Next day the State Trial ended in a disagreement of the jury.

In opposition to the Coercion Bill, the Parnellite Party put out its full strength. The debate on the Address announcing the Bill lasted eleven sittings. The Bill's first reading was carried only by a *coup de main* after five more sittings.

On Monday, January 31, the Government announced its intention to secure the first reading during that sitting. Parnell and his men settled down to work. Monday night passed into Tuesday, Tuesday night into Wednesday morning, and still the Irish Brigade fought on. Both sides adopted the relay system—some held the front while others slipped away for a wash, a meal, and a couple of hours in bed. Members on duty tried to snatch a few hours (or minutes) of sleep sitting in chairs in the library. Chairs were at a premium when the frugal Biggar grasped an opportunity to put four chairs together to make a bed on which he would have slept peacefully if the infuriated Liberals and Tories had not walloped the heaviest volumes within reach on the floor with a crash as often as he dozed off. Even so it was Biggar who was addressing the House at 9 a.m., on Wednesday when the Speaker entered, relieved the Chairman, and waved Biggar back to his seat.

The Speaker announced his decision (in which the Liberal and Tory leaders concurred) to stop the debate; and put the question of the first reading. This being done, the House adjourned until twelve noon the same day. The Parnellites contrived to waste the rest of Wednesday; but meanwhile the Government had drafted new rules of procedure, which it put down for discussion on Thursday.

Overnight the Parnellites learned to their disgust that Michael Davitt, his ticket-of-leave cancelled, had been arrested and restored to Portland Gaol. Questioned at the opening of the sitting on Thursday (February 3) the Home Secretary baldly announced the fact. John Dillon rose to extort further information, just as the Speaker called upon Gladstone to introduce his procedure resolution. Dillon tried to explain; the Speaker ordered him to sit down. Dillon persisted; was howled at; grew furious; refused to give way; was "named", and duly suspended.

The House settled to listen to Gladstone, who had hardly uttered three words before Parnell rose and moved, coolly, that the right hon. gentleman be no longer heard. Amid howls of rage, the Speaker declined to hear Parnell. He, too, persisted; was named, and suspended. During the division on Parnell's suspension the thirty-two Parnellites then present refused to take part in the division. They were named and suspended in a body. The few Parnellites who had missed the fun hurried into the House, moved that Gladstone "be no longer heard" and were suspended, each in his turn. The suspension only lasted for the sitting; so the Party was in action again next day ready to fight the Coercion Bill to the last.

The Coercion Act empowered the Authorities to arrest any person "reasonably suspected", and detain him for any period, up to September 30, 1881. Hundreds of League officials were arrested; but each place was filled as soon as it was emptied.

The agitation, instead of abating, grew more intense than ever. In the background the Ribbon Lodges—which the League had superseded—took up their old work, and terrorism kept in step with arrests and evictions. The Government, to sweeten the pill of Coercion, introduced meanwhile the Land Act of 1881.

This Act was designed to concede, with reservations, the "Three F's" for which agrarian reformers had fought for years. It succeeded only in part; its most successful provision being one enabling tenants-at-will to obtain leases at "fair" rents fixed by a Government valuer. The value of the tenant's improvements was excluded when determining the "fair" rent.

The Parnellites did what they could to amend the Act; the landlords in the House of Lords did what they could to wreck it. A conflict between the Houses was averted by a compromise, and the Act became law in August 1881.

The tenants viewed the fixing of "judicial" rents by a Government valuer with the deepest suspicion. There was an obvious danger at this point, and the League decided to put the matter to a test before passing a final judgment. A number of cases were selected for this test; meanwhile the tenants were recommended to abstain from applying for valuations.

This, however, the Government interpreted as a flagrant sabotage of their Act. League meetings were "proclaimed". League speakers began to crowd Kilmainham Gaol, where Parnell was sent to join them on October 12. The news of his arrest, divulged to the magnates of the City of London at a Guildhall banquet, roused them to frenzied demonstrations of joy.

The League responded with a Manifesto calling for a general withholding of rent. The Chief Secretary, Forster, retorted with more coercion, and armed support for the eviction squads. Relief for the victims was organised by the Ladies' Land League which Davitt had prepared for such an emergency. Its American branch was especially helpful. Meanwhile, as Parnell had predicted, in the rural areas "Captain Moonlight"* took charge.

* Captain Moonlight: The Pseudonym customarily appended to the terroristic notices issued, at this time, by the Ribbon Lodges.

Realising that things were going from bad to worse, the Government decided to open confidential negotiations with Parnell, for a compromise settlement. Parnell was approached by one of his nominal followers—Captain O'Shea—who acted, so he said, on behalf of the Radical leader, Joseph Chamberlain. Parnell was asked, in effect, to state upon what terms he would agree to an armistice in the Land War, which would give the Government a chance to try the effect of legislation.

Parnell, for his part, knew that without a central organisation to guide it the agrarian struggle would degenerate rapidly into a multitude of local struggles, which would culminate in anarchistic-terrorism, surrender, or both. Most of the tenants who could pay had already paid their rents and secured judicial abatements. Those who could not pay were threatened with inevitable eviction, sooner or later. It was clear that a tactical retreat was necessary, to secure a basis for any new advance.

Parnell therefore accepted the suggestion and (after consulting Justin MacCarthy and other leading Party members) offered the following terms: (1) Cessation of Coercion; release of all State prisoners, especially Davitt. (2) State Aid to wipe off arrears which prevented tenants taking advantage of the Act of 1881. If these were granted, then (3) the authority and machinery of the League would be used to repress agrarian crime; and (4) the Home Rule Party would co-operate in the promotion of legislation in line with "liberal principles".

These terms were accepted; and, under this Kilmainham Compact, Parnell, Davitt, and their followers were released in May, 1882, while the "Coercion" Viceroy, Earl Cowper, and Chief Secretary Forster, resigned in disgust.

Parnell had clearly won a great victory and opened a road to still further gains. But the whole situation was transformed, when, on May 6, 1882, the new Viceroy (Lord Frederick Cavendish) and his permanent under-secretary Burke were set upon and murdered in the Phœnix Park by assassins armed with long, amputating knives.

CHAPTER XXVI

PARNELL, THE "UNCROWNED KING"

From the embitterment resulting from the Phœnix Park murders (May 1882) and the furious political strife in which it found expression, there emerged the succession of notable events we survey in this chapter: The rise of the Home Rule Party to its maximum (1880–1885); Gladstone's first Home Rule Bill (1885), with the Liberal-Unionist Split (1885); the Balfour Perpetual Coercion Act (1887); *The Times'* attack upon Parnell and his Party (1886–9), and the Special Commission thereupon (1888–90) which completely vindicated Parnell and left him virtually the Uncrowned King of Ireland, and, also, immensely popular with the English masses.

Left-Wing Terrorism and the National Struggle

The Phœnix Park assassinations killed the Kilmainham Compact. They made it impossible for Gladstone to carry out his share of the bargain and end Coercion; and this in turn made it impossible for Parnell to operate the compact from his end. Neither Gladstone nor Parnell was able openly to admit that a compact had been made; Gladstone from fear of his Right Wing, Parnell from fear of his "Left". This turned what had been a strategic withdrawal to a new front, into a retreat in disorder to a base from which no advance could be made, until the Party had been rebuilt from the bottom upwards.

Like the Dynamite War proclaimed from America by Rossa and his associates, the murders were the work of a "break-away" from the Fenian body—self-styled the "Invincibles". Each was closely analogous to the terrorist-anarchist manifestations which evidenced the break-up and degeneration of the Bakuninist sections of the First International, after the fall of the Commune in 1871–

which manifestations supplied these quasi-Fenian degenerations with their initial inspiration.

Terrorist phenomena are liable to occur at two periods in a revolutionary struggle—in its immaturity; and in its degeneration. They are to be distinguished carefully from the disciplined employment of mass-terror which a revolutionary struggle may use as legitimately as does the Government which it seeks to overthrow. The point of distinction is that in the one case (as in an insurrection) the resort to violence does, while in the other (as e.g. Clerkenwell Prison) it does not promote the integration and growth of the revolutionary mass-struggle. Rossa's attempt to "beat England to her knees" by dynamiting public buildings, railway stations etc., was folly, and worse, from the start. The men who carried out the operations did, it is true, take great care to avoid the sacrifice of human life. But more than one of them lost his own life and nearly all the rest suffered the indignity and torture of long periods of penal servitude, resulting in more than one case in the loss of reason. The Dynamite War did not terrify the Government; it did anger and alienate the common people. And it created exceptional difficulties for the better-disciplined regular movement, whose efforts at recruiting and organising were, more than once, brought to a nullity by such senseless displays of brutality as the murders in Phœnix Park*—displays which manifest not the strength, but the weakness of the revolutionary movement; and which accelerate the disintegration and demoralisation from which they arise.

"Leftism" was very prevalent among Irish-Americans at this period. The bitterness left over from the Famine,

* Phœnix Park murders: Few people have done so much disservice to the Irish National struggle as the egregious exhibitionist P. J. Tynan, who tried to palm himself off upon the world as the "Number One" of the Invincibles' conspiracy (which he most certainly was not) and who in a huge volume sought to glorify the deed as a masterly and heroic feat of war.

from the Fenian defeat, and from the repression which followed combined with isolation from the practical realities of struggle in Ireland to make temperamental patriots ready to applaud everything which manifested hostility to England sharply and without reserve. This temper laid Irish-Americans open to the wiles of political bosses (of real or assumed Irish descent) who found that Irish antipathy to English rule could be manipulated to the profit of "spread-eagle" American Jingoism. And some of these dupes succumbed in consequence all the more readily to the propaganda of sincere fanatics who preached Dynamite War upon England.

The organised hard-core of American Fenianism was saved from the political racketeers to the Right, and the dynamiters to the Left by the personal influence of Michael Davitt, John Devoy and Boyle O'Reilly. All were more revolutionary (in the sense of being ready to advocate and take part in armed insurrection) than Parnell was; but they all saw the paramount need for a realist procedure in Ireland.

Davitt, in particular, deserves special praise for his loyalty to Parnell at this crisis.

Davitt's loyalty was severely tried when Parnell insisted upon dissolving the Ladies' Land League, and damping down agrarian agitation. But it was becoming clear even to Davitt that the possibility which John O'Leary and other old-timers had feared—that exclusive preoccupation with the struggle, each man for his own separate holding of land, would tend to eclipse the struggle for the National objective—was fast becoming an actual danger. Once the landlords' monopoly had been broken, as it had been by the Act of 1881, the attack upon the Irish landlords ceased to be an attack upon the central citadel of English rule. Agrarian struggle tended to degenerate into Reformism.

Now that the State had intervened to create—and in a measure, to regularise—dual ownership in the land, the direct political struggle against the central government took on a new significance. Therefore a new mass organisation was required, one oriented upon the political struggle; and this was achieved in 1882, in the Irish National League, which was both the Land League revived and the Land League transformed into a mass political party.

Gladstone's Conversion to Home Rule

To the surprise of its promoters and opponents alike the effect of the Land Act of 1881 was to lower the gross revenue of the Irish landlords by a full twenty per cent. In part this was due to an error in drafting the Act; but in the main it was due to the continuing fall in agricultural prices. This carried with it a decline in the political importance of Irish landlords for English capitalism as a whole. Dual-ownership gave the tenant the initiative in developing the productive resources of the land; but only so far as he could borrow the capital with which to operate. This urge towards borrowing helped to shift the political centre of gravity away from the Irish landlords over to the English loan-banks and financiers.

The two amendments to the Land Act passed in 1883 both illustrate this. One made a State grant to assist tenants to pay off their arrears and so qualify for a judicial rent. The other made it compulsory for landlords to provide cottages for agricultural labourers (each with half-an-acre of land) at a nominal rent. The enforcement of the Act was entrusted to elected boards of guardians. Amended and extended in latter years, this Act (which Davitt inspired) proved ultimately a great boon to the labourers; but it was immediately profitable to the money-lending agencies.

These Acts illustrate the way the political game was played. The Irish Party introduced Bills which Liberals and Tories united to denounce as alike predatory and ruinous. Faced with Irish agitation, Liberals and Tories rivalled each other in the strife for power to coerce the agitation with one hand while conceding some of its demands with the other. The Liberal "Codlin" and the Tory "Short" jostled each other in their eagerness to pose as friends of reform in Ireland—and draw the cash rewards of this "virtue".

The Land Acts of 1883, were accompanied with a ferocious Crimes Act which the Parnellites fought to the point of getting suspended in a body. This did not prevent the Liberal Gladstone, the Radical Chamberlain, the Tory-Democrat Randolph Churchill, and the Tory Lord Carnarvon each making an independent (but secret) approach to Parnell with proposals for political collaboration.

Parnell's response to these approaches was masterly. He would reject no concession, however small, so long as it left him free to fight for the legislative independence of Ireland; he would accept no concession, however great, which did not leave him that freedom. He supported Gladstone's Franchise Reform since, in widening the electorate in Ireland, it widened the basis for his own party; and because also (as Davitt urged upon him strongly) it made available for Ireland a valuable ally in the English and Scottish democracy. At the same time he took a much more realistic view of Gladstone than did any of his contemporaries.

Gladstone, he saw, was adjusting his policy to the fact that power was passing from the aristocratic-landlord wing of the landlord-capitalist alliance to rest more securely upon its industrial and finance-capitalist wing. This would, Gladstone saw, unless it was counteracted, make for a re-oriented Tory-imperialist alliance. He therefore sought a counterpoise in the great middle class which was traditionally Liberal, and hostile to Tory protectionism.

Gladstone saw also another potential danger (which might alternatively provide a new ally) in the growing political consciousness of the wage-worker class. The more capitalism developed the more the working class became consolidated and conditioned for offering concerted resistance to capitalist encroachments. To persist in the traditional Whig-Tory attitude towards the working class was to ensure the formation of an independent workers' party which, in alliance with the Irish, could more than nullify any backing he got from the middle class. Ahead of any of his contemporaries, Gladstone saw that an independent working-class party would destroy the Liberal party—by driving its moderate supporters over to the Tories—while, simultaneously, it attracted the genuine Radicals over to the proletarian and socialist standpoint.

To save the situation it was necessary to do two things: (1) to retain the allegiance of the workers to the Great Liberal Party; and (2) either to get rid of the Irish Party altogether, or to sap its independence, and win it also for a permanent alliance to the Liberal Party. The history of the period is the history of how Gladstone, with masterly adroitness, set about achieving this double objective. Franchise Reform, and Municipal and Local Government reforms were his first moves. About the Irish he was doubtful; but long before 1885 he had decided something must be done about Ireland. The need for a pronouncement was delayed by a prolonged struggle with the House of Lords—over the Franchise Act which, at one time, looked like giving him a winning election-slogan in "Down with the House of Lords". The peers, however, gave way, and for the election of 1885—the first fought under the new franchise—Gladstone had to find a new slogan.

Parnell, weighing up the Party leaders, soon saw that no dependence could be based on Joseph Chamberlain. "He will make the running for Gladstone," Parnell said, "but he will stop short of Home Rule." Randolph Churchill had possibilities, but Lord Carnarvon offered the best prospects since he stood high in the Tory party, and was himself almost a Home Ruler. It was, Parnell foresaw, merely a question of time before Gladstone came over to Home Rule; and that meant that there was always a chance that the Tories would jump in first to "dish the Whigs". A Tory Home Rule Bill would have the advantage that it would not be opposed on Party grounds by the House of Lords.

Parnell was therefore "sitting pretty" when, in May, 1885, Gladstone gave him his chance by announcing (under pressure from his Right Wing) that the Government intended to renew the expiring Crimes Act. Parnell retorted by leading the Irish Party into the Opposition lobby in the division on the Budget, and thereby securing the defeat of the Government. A Tory Government took office wholly dependent upon combined Irish and Radical support. In the few months which elapsed before the inevitable general election, Parnell secured the lapsing of the Crimes Act, and the passing of an Act which earmarked £5,000,000 to enable Irish tenants to purchase their holdings.

Gladstone's slogan for the 1885 election was an appeal for a majority big enough to make him independent of a Tory-Irish combination. Parnell retorted with "Vote solid against Gladstone and Coercion". The result was ideal; the Liberals outnumbered the Tories by 86, which was exactly the number of the Irish Party. Parnell possessed, absolutely, the balance of power.

In Ireland, the result was the harvest of years of work; and it proved the efficacy of the Irish National League. In Ulster, a majority of 17 seats to 16 went to the Nationalists; in the rest of Ireland, two Tories returned for Dublin University alone broke the completeness of Nationalist triumph. Whigs, Tories, Liberals and non-party Home Rulers—all had been swept away, to leave Ireland represented by 18 Tories, and 85 Nationalists. One Nationalist (T. P. O'Connor) returned for a division of Liverpool made the total 86.

Within a few days, Gladstone returned to office; and he at once announced his intention of introducing, immediately, a Home Rule Bill For Ireland.

"Judas" Chamberlain

Gladstone's Home Rule Bill (April 1885) approximated to a proposal to restore Grattan's Parliament. It went beyond this norm in proposing a Ministry responsible to the Irish Parliament; it fell below it in that the Irish Parliament was deprived of all power over Customs duties. It had other grave defects from the Irish standpoint. Its one outstanding merit was that it conceded the principle of Ireland's national right to self-government.

The Bill was foredoomed to defeat from the start. Quite apart from the dead-weight of anti-Irish prejudice which Gladstone himself had helped to create, the Whigs in his camp were filled with great fear. They chafed under a Liberal-Irish alliance; but if the Irish were packed off to Dublin there was every reason to fear that Gladstone would continue his policy of "surrender" by making large concessions to the working-men Radicals in his Left Wing. The defection of the Right-Wing Whigs Gladstone had foreseen and might have got over. It could have been set-off by gains from the Liberal-Conservatives. But nothing could compensate for the desertion, along with the Whigs, of Chamberlain and his following, which included many of the Radicals of the Left. The Home Rule Bill failed to pass its Second Reading.

Chamberlain's opposition to Gladstone was quite unprincipled, and opportunist. He shared the Whigs' dislike for Gladstone's "socialistic"* leaning—not realising as

* Gladstone's "socialism": This, of course, was nothing in the least resembling genuine Socialism. In so far as it was not a figment of Tory imagination, it was an anticipation of the Lloyd George tactic of obstructing real Socialist advance by dexterous concessions to the lower middle class and the conservative upper-strata of the proletariat.

clearly as Gladstone did how urgent the need was to delay the formation of an independent working-class party. At the same time, he was himself fond of posing demagogically as the friend of the poor and enemy of the rich. Tory cartoonists of the period loved to depict him as "Jack Cade". His basic motive was derived from a cold-blooded calculation that Gladstone (who was then over 70) was bound to die, or retire, soon. Thinking himself the legitimate heir to the leadership of the Liberal Party, Chamberlain deliberately sabotaged Gladstone's Home Rule Bill to create an opening for a Home Rule Bill of his own. Many of the Radicals whom he led against the Home Rule Bill, opposed it because it did not go far enough.

A second possibility, which Chamberlain banked upon as a "saver", was that the Tories, being very badly off for a leader in the Commons, might accept him (with his following) in that capacity; and so open an alternative route to the coveted Premiership which he desired with a miser's passion.

As things turned out he lost on both gambles. Gladstone did not retire till after Chamberlain had settled down into a Parliamentary maid-of-all-work to the Tories; and, for their part, the Tories never trusted the man who could throw over his leader as shamelessly as Chamberlain had double-crossed Gladstone. There is little doubt that his final decision to sabotage Gladstone's Bill proceeded from a calculated desire to retain the Irish at Westminster—his jackal O'Shea having led him to believe that Parnell with his Party could easily be manipulated for his own opportunist ends.

Gladstone at once appealed to the country on the Home Rule issue and suffered a heavy defeat. Parnell, in Ireland, retained his following intact.

On actual votes Gladstone's defeat in the 1886 election was a narrow one; a turnover of 100,000 out of the 4,000,000 votes would have given him a majority. On seats the Tory-cum-Liberal-Unionist alliance had a majority over both Liberals and Irish combined; and the new premier, Lord Salisbury, soon let the Irish know that they had nothing to hope for from him. He compared them to "Hottentots, and other races incapable of self-government". He said he would sooner spend public money to secure the emigration of a million Irishmen than in buying-out a single landlord; and that all Ireland wanted was "twenty years of resolute Government". He let it be known, in short, that concurrently with Chamberlain's desertion of Gladstone there had gone on a corresponding shift in the balance of class-power on the Tory side. The new "Unionists" were still aristocratic; but they were Financial and Imperialist oligarchs rather than predominantly landowners; and, as such, they intended to consolidate the Empire, and stand no nonsense from the Irish, the Colonial Nationalists, or from the Socialists.

But for the reluctance of English capitalists to venture into such a risky field as Irish agriculture, the Tory policy would have been a return to "Elizabethan" clearance and plantation. Alternatively there was—plain Coercion.

Parnell's health at this date was such that he was compelled to leave the guidance of the Party almost entirely to his subordinates; and they—or one of them, William O'Brien, the editor of the Party journal *United Ireland*—evolved the Plan of Campaign.

This Plan started from the fact that the continued fall of agricultural prices—and the intensified competition from standardised and state-aided dairy-farming in Denmark, America, Australia and New Zealand—automatically converted what had been "fair" rents in 1882 into rack rents in 1886-7. The Plan was that: (1) in each district the land would be revalued by an agent appointed by the local branch of the League; (2) the "fair" rent thus ascertained would be paid by the tenants to the League; which would offer it to the landlords in full settlement of their claims; (3) if the offer was refused the money would be used to pay legal expenses and compensate evicted tenants.

Whatever faults the Plan had, or virtues, the Tories never troubled to enquire. They treated it as a general mutiny; and in March 1887, replied with a Perpetual Coercion Bill.

Under this Act the League was suppressed, its papers were seized, and its meetings prohibited. No charge was too fantastic. A lad of ten was convicted of "intimidating" a constable (by whistling *Harvey Duff*); an Italian organ-grinder who had trained his monkey to draw and fire a toy-pistol was fined under the Arms Act and the pistol was confiscated.

There was, too, more serious work. At Mitchelstown, Co. Cork, 8,000 people packed the market place for a political meeting so tightly that the official notetaker could not get through. The police tried to clear a path with their batons; they were beaten off to their barracks, whence they fired from the windows upon the crowd, and killed three men. The intervention of priests, and a few soldiers off-duty, alone saved the police from extermination. The District Inspector had telegraphed that morning: *Don't Hesitate to Shoot!* That and: *Remember Mitchelstown!* became slogans in the embittered struggle that followed.

It was, the Tories found, impossible to rely solely upon Coercion. Reform was also necessary. Hence arose the Land Act of 1887 which (shamelessly plagiarising the Parnellites) enabled lease-holders, to the number of 150,000, to take advantage of the Act of 1881. It also conceded the basic claim of the Plan by enabling the land-courts to reduce judicially-fixed rents on their own initiative. The reductions thus secured averaged 28 percent.

Concurrently the Tories intrigued with the Pope for aid. English Catholics, wire-pulling at the Vatican, had secured, in 1883, a Papal condemnation of the National Tribute to Parnell. The result was that the Tribute trebled in a few days to reach a total of £38,000. Now they wire-pulled again, and secured a Papal condemnation of boycotting, and the Plan of Campaign. A few bishops took notice; the bulk of the clergy and the whole of the Irish laity ignored the ban.

Tory Anti-Parnellite Propaganda

For English consumption, the Tories relied chiefly upon propaganda, which sought to fasten upon Parnell and his Party direct responsibility for "outrage"—especially for the Phœnix Park murders.

A series of articles in *The Times*, under the general heading of Parnellism and Crime, was commenced in 1886—to influence the elections—and was continued thereafter to justify Coercion. The basic method of the series was to connect a given speech with some "outrage" occurring in, or near, the neighbourhood where it was delivered.

Most of the "outrages" were things—such as boycotting and resistance to eviction—which no reasonable Englishman ever condemned. And much was made of the (never-concealed) fact that Davitt and other leaders had once been Fenians. Naturally, the more rabid utterances of the "Left" Fenians in America were meat-and-drink to the "atrocity" mongers of *The Times*. The crowning point of the series was a letter reproduced in facsimile, condoning the Phœnix Park murders, which ostensibly had been written by Parnell himself. It appeared on the morning of the day (April 1887) fixed for the second reading of Balfour's Perpetual Coercion Act.

The Tory Government at that date rested upon a somewhat precarious alliance of old-fashioned Tories

344

with ex-Gladstonians, who disliked Home Rule, but also disliked Coercion. The pseudo "Parnell" letter was calculated to reassure the waverers and, at the same time, to discredit not only Parnell but his temporary ally, Gladstone, also. In a word it did the sort of things that Joseph Chamberlain, more than anybody, stood to gain from.

Parnell at once denounced the letter as a self-evident forgery; and indeed it was quite incredible that Parnell, or any man in his position, should have written expressing sentiments he was well known not to hold. *The Times*, however, behaved as if no denial had been uttered.

The Parnellite Party demanded a Parliamentary inquiry. The Government refused; and suggested a libel action. This was adding insult to injury, since a judge, in a civil action, has no power to compel the production of evidence, and a jury of City men would have been glad to find a verdict against Parnell, whatever the evidence. The Party was therefore compelled to let the matter rest for the time; confident that "murder will out".

To the general surprise, an ex-member of the Parnellite Party–F. Hugh O'Donnell (who had resigned from the Party in scorn of the "out-of-works of humble professions" whom Parnell was choosing as his lieutenants, and who, at this time, had attached himself to Joseph Chamberlain)–sued *The Times* for libel, on the ground that he was incriminated, as a member of the Party, during some portion of the period covered.

The charge was fantastic. Libel actions were costly; O'Donnell was, at most, a foreign correspondent to a Tory newspaper. Yet the action was proceeded with. When the action was heard, plaintiff's counsel produced no evidence beyond the copies of *The Times* complained of. In any ordinary action, the defending counsel would have asked at once for the judge's direction that no case had been made out. This, in the end, counsel for *The Times* did; but not until he had used three full sittings of the court to recite all the evidence he would have produced, if it had been necessary—including a large bundle of what purported to be original letters (from Parnell and others) never till then made public, and all highly damaging.

The Times of course got its verdict, and made much of it. O'Donnell (born MacDonald, became MacDonnell and then O'Donnell) dropped out of the picture. He had done what was wanted. He had created the situation which made it possible for the Government to offer (and impossible for Parnell to refuse) a Special Commission of inquiry into the allegations against "certain members of Parliament, and others".

The Times *Special Commission*

The point of a Special Commission is that the Judges, to whom the work of inquiry is committed, have power to call for and compel the production of whatever evidence they feel is necessary to the performance of their task. In form the subject of inquiry was the conduct of *The Times*: in fact the Commission was a trial of the whole Parnellite Party. The fact that the Attorney-General and Solicitor-General were (in their "private" capacity) leading counsel for *The Times*, made this apparent to the dullest.

The crux of the inquiry was of course the authenticity of the facsimile letter (with the other "originals" produced at the O'Donnell action); but *The Times* counsel showed a great disinclination to come to the point. Instead, they roamed at large over the whole history of agrarian crime in Ireland, and produced all sorts of unsavoury witnesses to "prove"—what was never in dispute—that "outrages" had been committed. At length, after many days, and several long adjournments, the question was reached; and counsel began to tell a lurid tale of how the agent of *The Times* had bought the letters (for spot cash) in a hotel-room in Paris from one, Richard Pigott, who acted as broker for certain (imperfectly identified) "Fenians"—who, in turn, had found the letters, in a black-bag, in a hotel-room, where they had been left by Somebody Else—who, like the "Fenians", had absconded!

It was hardly necessary to put Pigott through the torture of a two-days' cross-examination by Sir Charles Russell. His Dublin reputation—as proprietor of "fake" Fenian newspapers, trickster, black-mailer, pornographer, begging-letter-writer and stooge—had caused him to be suspected from the start. Good staffwork by Davitt had nailed Pigott down with a subpœna early in the proceedings; and had compelled *The Times* to put him in the witness box. By the end of the second day's cross-examination Pigott was reduced to such a condition that the very judges laughed him to scorn. A Sunday intervened. On the Monday he failed to answer his name: he had absconded, leaving a full confession of his forgery in the hands of the journalists (Labouchere and Sala) who had extorted it. Pursued to Madrid, with an extradition warrant, Pigott blew out his own brains rather than face arrest.

Counsel for *The Times* had, ruefully, to withdraw so much of their case as rested upon the forged letters, which was, in practice, all there was in the business so far as the general public was concerned.

It should not be supposed that Pigott was the only blot upon *The Times* case—and their counsel. They were able to do—what no counsel, ordinarily, can do—draw upon the resources of Scotland Yard, and of the Secret Service at will. They paraded as their witnesses convicts from prison, and professional informers. And among their witnesses was Captain O'Shea, called, apparently, for no other purpose than to express his belief in the authenticity of the forged letters. Under cross examination he admitted to associating with a gang of notorious *agents provocateurs*—several of them implicated in bogus "dynamite outrages". (We know, now, that it was this gang of crooks who concocted the testimonial to O'Shea's sterling patriotism which induced Joseph Chamberlain to give him countenance, and to ask Parnell, as a personal favour, to secure O'Shea a seat in the House.) An offshoot of the same gang, domiciled in Paris, specialised in concocting "secret information" of Fenian doings, for sale to the more credulous newspaper editors in England and abroad. That *The Times* should have fallen for such a gang proves the length to which their anti-Parnell and anti-Irish prejudice had gone.

The Commission lingered on, with adjournments, for seven months more. Then the judges took three months to draw up their findings. But for all practical purposes the trial ended when Pigott absconded. Thereafter it was *The Times*, and the Government, which were on the defensive; struggling to salve what relics of credit they could.

The English Masses and the Irish Party

The English common-people gave their verdict at the close of Pigott's cross examination. Parnell and his colleagues could barely make their way through the throngs which cheered them enthusiastically. For days their appearance, anywhere, was a signal for renewed enthusiasm. When Parnell entered the House, on the night after the news broke of Pigott's confession and flight, he was given an ovation. The entire Liberal party—with Gladstone conspicuous at their head—the Irish party, and many of the Tories, rose to their feet and cheered continuously until Parnell had taken his seat. For months the Parnellites were the most popular men in England.

The truth is that—apart from the things implied in the forged letters—everything charged against the Irish Party exalted them in the eyes of the English masses. That the Land League had been (as the Commission decided it was) virtually a conspiracy to drive the landlords out of

Ireland, was, in the eyes of English working-class Radicals and Socialists, very greatly to its credit. Boycotting, and "intimidating" land-grabbers, were too much in line with English Trade Union tradition for the English masses to do other than applaud them. That Irish peasants, infuriated by ill-treatment, had inflicted fierce physical vengeance on their oppressors was, English working-men thought, only to be expected. In short, the whole endeavour of the Tory-cum-Liberal-Unionist conspiracy to blacken Parnell, and his party, recoiled upon the heads of the conspirators. The English masses, therefore, applauded the Parnellite Party; and felt nothing but contempt for its enemies.

And to show the sincerity of their admiration these English masses began to clamour for a working-man's party designed in imitation of the Irish Party. Talk of a United Land and Labour League began to be heard in all sorts of places. The beginnings of a revival of active, independent, political organisation among the English masses date from the time of these excitements.

The Tory-Liberal Unionist conspirators, however, still had a shot in the locker.

The Commission concluded its sittings in November 1889. It reported in February 1890. In December 1889, a petition for divorce was filed (in the first instance by the solicitors who had acted for *The Times*) in the name of Captain O'Shea, citing Parnell as co-respondent. The conspirators were (in Winston Churchill's words) out "to recover in the Divorce Court the credit they had lost before the Special Commission".

349

CHAPTER XXVII

THE BETRAYAL AND DEATH OF PARNELL

On November 17, 1890, a verdict was given for the petitioner in the case of O'Shea v. O'Shea and Parnell. Mrs. O'Shea was represented, but offered no defence; Parnell was not represented.

From this verdict developed a political crisis which has no parallel in Irish history—either for the swiftness with which it arose, the bitterness with which it was fought, or the completeness of the tragedy resulting.

The O'Shea-Parnell Triangle

Parnell and Katherine O'Shea met first, on her initiative, in 1880. They were soon drawn into relations which resulted in February 1882, in the birth of a child, which lived only a few weeks. Thereafter, from May 1882, Parnell and Katherine O'Shea lived in unregularised marital-relations, which were not concealed from anyone connected with, or visiting, the household. Two more children were born; in 1883, and 1884, respectively.

During the latter part of this period, and afterwards, Parnell's health was seriously impaired. His illnesses, followed by spells of recovery, continued until, in 1890, Parnell's health seemed to be restored completely. Apart from any other consideration, Katherine O'Shea made herself indispensable to Parnell, as a nurse and household manager. There is little doubt, that, but for her care, Parnell would have died years before he did.

Before passing judgment, it is material to remember that Captain and Mrs. O'Shea were living apart—had virtually separated by agreement—some time before Parnell and she first met. It is also material that, although O'Shea had been a nominal Home Ruler, he had never, even formally, submitted to the discipline of Parnell's party.

O'Shea, ex-captain of hussars, was essentially a financially-embarrassed squireen aristocrat. The son of a wealthy solicitor-middleman (who had acquired an estate through the Encumbered Estates Act), he inherited the estate and squandered it in the traditional manner. Bluntly, Captain O'Shea, in 1890, was substantially in the position of Thackeray's "Rawdon Crawley", except that he was not so good at billiards, and looked to political place-hunting rather than to cards as the source of his revenue. Also, Mrs. O'Shea had a rich, and aged, aunt who was sufficiently fond of her, and her companionship, to pay her and the "Captain" each a separate allowance.

The "Rawdon Crawley" analogy holds further to the extent that O'Shea had been, before 1880, quite willing for Katherine–who was well-connected, cultured, not unintellectual, and personally attractive–to play "Becky Sharp" to any man of wealth or position from whom a "dividend" could be extracted, for his (O'Shea's) benefit. With this end in view, he encouraged the growth of friendship between her and Parnell. He was even willing (he said later) that the friendship should go the length of an "amourette"! But, Parnell was no Lord Steyne, and Katherine was only able to play Becky Sharp up to a point.

O'Shea, distinctly chagrined, consoled himself with what was, to all intents and purposes, blackmail. If Parnell had chosen to defend the divorce action, his chequebook alone would have destroyed all O'Shea's pretences. And, for her part, if Katherine O'Shea had decided to persist in her counter-charges, she could have produced proofs supported by "some seventeen" co-respondents in person.

The action was not defended. The essence of the tragedy, on its personal side, was, that Parnell was so set upon regularising his relation with Katherine, that he was willing, temporarily, to incur the stigma thrown upon him in the Divorce Court. The essence of the treachery, with which Parnell was hounded to death, lies in the fact that the hounding was done by men who knew, and had known for years, that the facts of the case were exactly as we have stated them.

Every Irish Nationalist in Parliament knew—and had known, for years, before O'Shea filed his petition—what were the relations between Parnell and Katherine O'Shea. Every member of Gladstone's Cabinet had known it, as early as May 1882. Every Liberal and every Tory M.P., every journalist about the House knew it; and every leading journalist in the provinces. And everyone in the gossip circle fed by each of them knew it—and had known it for so long that it had lost all value as a spicy tit-bit of scandal.

Finally, the evidence, led in court—which represented Parnell as furtively intriguing with the wife of an unsuspecting husband—was, in part, a legal smoke-screen, invented to cover O'Shea's notorious connivance. In part it was wilful perjury, suborned, deliberately, to damage Parnell.

This brings us to the sinister timing of the divorce petition. Before the middle of 1889, O'Shea—having "expectations" under the will of Katherine's aunt—had everything to lose and nothing to gain from a divorce-petition. Even at the end of 1889 his position was not enviable—in view of the reprisals it was in the power of Katherine and Parnell to make. There is definite evidence that he could have been bought off with £20,000 in cash. Unfortunately for Katherine and Parnell, her aunt's will was contested; and this sum was beyond their compass. Even then, there is evidence that O'Shea took proceedings only with extreme reluctance—as one forced by pressure against his will.

Who was there who could, and would, exert such pressure successfully?

O'Shea at this time was calling himself a "Liberal Unionist". There is evidence that when the disputed-will case was settled, and O'Shea was left seriously disappointed (as he had feared)—directly as a result of his divorce action—that he complained bitterly to Joseph Chamberlain "about everybody and everything"; that he tried to persuade Chamberlain to find him a borough seat in Parliament as a Liberal-Unionist. Then, abruptly, Chamberlain severed relations with O'Shea, who, very unusually for him, lapsed uncomplainingly into silence and obscurity. In view of the fact that, after this breach, Chamberlain was left in possession of every document by means of which O'Shea might have proved an association between them, it is not difficult to formulate a theory to account for O'Shea's silence. He had done his "work". One infers that he drew his "wages".

The Nonconformist Conscience

The first reaction of the Nationalist Party and the Irish people to the Divorce Court verdict was a yell of defiance. Popular instinct judged intuitively and correctly that it was a follow-up of the malevolence which, having missed its mark in *The Times* Commission, now sought to reach its end by hitting below the belt.

Mass meetings in Dublin, in England, and in America, proclaimed unabated confidence in Parnell. Meeting at the House of Commons, on November 25, 1890, the Nationalist Party unanimously re-elected Parnell their chairman.

The very next day an "emergency" meeting of the same Party assembled, and Parnell was requested, by a section, to resign. What had happened in the interval? Gladstone had issued an ultimatum, virtually threatening to abandon the struggle for Home Rule unless Parnell retired, or was retired, from the leadership of the Nationalist Party.

He hinted that this was a necessary sacrifice to the clamour of the Nonconformist Conscience; and, indeed, the self-appointed spokesmen of that "conscience" were very vocal. But Gladstone knew that those clamours themselves were not to be taken at their face value; that they expressed, really—what he himself felt—an intense irritation at the continued Parliamentary dependence of the Liberal Party upon the support of Parnell and the Nationalists.

While Parnell occupied the position of Leader of the Irish nation Irish Nationalism, united behind him, constituted a force it was dangerous either to resist, or to give way to. Gladstone had offered Home Rule to quieten the Irish clamour; but Chamberlain had proved that a large body of English politicians and voters feared that conceding Home Rule would only quicken the Irish National demand for separation. Parnell had never declared for separation; but then he had never declared against it either. And it was not to be denied that under his leadership the Irish had become a political force more to be feared than they had been since the time of Daniel O'Connell; if not greater than ever before. With Parnell deposed, the leaderless Irish would sink perforce into a tail of the Great Liberal Party. And, moreover, Chamberlain (himself a Nonconformist) would at once lose his power of undermining Nonconformist-Liberal allegiance by sneers at the "enslavement" of the Liberals to "Papists" and "rebels". In a word, Parnell was dangerous—to the British Empire, to English capitalism, to Gladstone himself, and to Gladstone's political jackals. Therefore Parnell had to go—the Divorce Court and the Nonconformist Conscience merely provided a timely excuse.

Why did members of Parnell's own party fall into this political snare? In part they were hypnotised by the personality of Gladstone, who certainly was a master of the Parliamentary game. Partly they were scared because they did not realise how big a bluff this "Nonconformist Conscience" was. But the chief reason was that many of them were like Gladstone; at bottom they feared Parnell, and feared him because he had the common people united a his back. A majority of the Parnellite Party were as afraid of Separatism as Gladstone was. That is why they made haste to do Gladstone's bidding.

The Party Split

From November 15 to December 6, save for adjournments of varying length, a battle raged in Committee Room 15 in the House of Commons.

Formally the question under discussion was a proposal by one of Parnell's supporters, that the question of the Party leadership should stand over, until the members had consulted their constituents; and should then be decided at a meeting in Dublin.

The Anti-Parnellite faction opposed this violently. From the contemporary reports of the debate it is clear that Parnell's enemies were quite as convinced as his friends were that, if this course was followed, the masses in Ireland, and especially in Dublin, would declare for Parnell unhesitatingly. The hysterical, and abusive, fury with which Timothy Healy opposed the proposal, bears no other interpretation. Both sides kept the telegraph wires and cables throbbing with appeals and counter-appeals. Parnell, with masterly skill, took advantage of every technicality to keep the debate alive. He refused to accept a motion for his deposition. "It was not you who called me to this position," he said "but the Irish people. They alone shall depose me."

On December 3 the balance was swayed heavily against Parnell by a manifesto from the Catholic Hierarchy of Ireland. It condemned Parnell on "moral" grounds; but it gave, also, a political excuse—"the inevitability of a split, if Parnell were retained". Clearly the intrigue initiated by Gladstone had deep roots.

Three days later, the debate reached a point where the shrieking blackguardism of Healy so provoked Parnell (and several of his supporters) that, Healy swears—though

355

his word is not to be trusted—Parnell would have drawn his revolver, if he had not been forcibly restrained. Healy certainly did his best to produce such a result; but, at that point, Justin MacCarthy, for the Anti-Parnellite majority, led his supporters from the room. Forty-five went with MacCarthy. Twenty-six remained with Parnell.

The Parnellites resolved to appeal to the Irish people directly. As Parnell took his place in the Holyhead train, a large crowd of London-Irishmen thronged round to give him an ovation. Timothy Harrington, one of a delegation touring America at the time of the split, tells a moving story. As he departed from his New York Hotel on his way back to support Parnell, all the Irish hotel attendants gathered to see him off; and all begged him, some of them with tears: "You'll not desert him, will you, Mr. Harrington?"

Broadly that was the case in Ireland, in England, and in America. The youth, the wage-workers, the labourers, and the poorer tenants were all for Parnell; the upper and middle classes, in town and country, followed the call of the Hierarchy and the lure of the politicians.

There were several by-elections pending. Parnell fought them all, and lost them one after the other. Healy transferred to Ireland the blackguardism he had developed in the committee room, while press and platform reeked with verbal and pictorial filth emitted in the name of "religion" and "morality".

Parnell never lost heart. He knew it would be an uphill fight; but he was confident that, if he and his followers could only stick it out for five years, he would win the battle.

The Death of Parnell

As the year 1891 drew to its end, and with the fight growing more and more savage as the weather worsened, Parnell began to show signs of strain. He was seriously ill, when, in September, he travelled to Creggs, Co. Galway, where he spoke in the pouring rain. When he reached Dublin on his way back, the doctor told him it was dangerous for him to travel. He insisted he must go home. "But I'll be back next Saturday week." He was true to his word; but it was in his coffin that he came back.

He died at Steyning, near Brighton, on the morning of October 6, 1891. At every point in the journey where the coffin had to be transferred, crowds of Irishmen were there to do the work. In Dublin he lay in state in the City Hall, and then again rested at the base of O'Connell's statue while scores of thousands filed past. Arthur Balfour, then Chief Secretary, said, years later, that the only crowd of which he was ever afraid was the crowd of 150,000 grim-faced Irishmen who marched in formation past the coffin of their dead chief; and then bore him by torchlight to his resting place in Glasnevin.

With him, for a full generation, were buried the Hopes of Ireland.

CHAPTER XXVIII

THE YEARS BETWEEN

From the death of Parnell, and the Second (1893) Home
Rule Bill which followed, a period of comparative calm
prevailed in Ireland. Then from 1910 the Third Home
Rule Bill and its attendant excitements led to the crisis
of 1912-14.

In this period circumstances and parties all underwent
a complete change. Salient points are (1) the Tory policy
of killing Home Rule with kindness; (2) the degeneration
of the Parliamentary Nationalist Party; (3) the rise of a
succession of popular movements in opposition to the
Party (the Gaelic League; *Sinn Fein* and the Connolly-
Larkin Socialist and Trade Union agitations).

Killing Home Rule with Kindness

Returned to power in 1892 by an election which left
the Liberals dependent upon the (divided) Irish Party,
Gladstone announced his intention at once to proceed
with his Second Home Rule Bill. Passed by the Commons, the Bill was (1893) at once thrown out by the
Lords. Gladstone retired; and the Liberals, finding
dependence upon the Irish irksome, sought relief in an
election (1895), from which the Tories returned triumphant, to retain power until the end of 1905.

In their ten-year spell of office the Tories tried their
hardest to break-up the Irish national movement by cutting its roots. The peasants were placated by facilities for
the purchase of their holdings; the landlords were subsidised to make them agreeable. The urban and rural middle class were pacified by extensions of local government,
and also by a judicious distribution of government appointments, and a network of ameliorative institutions
was spread over the country.

This policy the Liberals continued from 1906 to 1910. Then a combination of causes compelled the introduction of the Third Home Rule Bill. The principle of the policy is seen most clearly in the series of Land Acts, which culminated in the Acts of 1903 (Tory), and 1909 (Liberal), whose general effect was to enable the peasantry to buy their holdings on hire-purchase terms.

The Land Acts, 1870-1909

The "Wyndham" Act of 1903 (amended only in detail in 1909) shows the tendency of the whole English land legislation. Its primary presupposition was a permanently falling market for land products, and, therefore, for land itself. It secured the landlord who sold his estate a much higher price than he could have got in a competitive market. It secured immediate relief to the tenant, by lowering the amount of his annual payments (which counted as purchase-instalments), and bridged the gap between the sale-price and the purchase-price of the land with a cash donation from the State to the landlords. The tenant, on the average, paid double its market-value for his holding; but, even so, his burden was less than the rent had been.

Between 1870 and 1910, over 10,000 estates, comprising over 13 million acres, were acquired by under half-a-million tenants, at a gross purchase price of £120 million; of which the tenants paid £2 million cash down, and the rest in instalments. The cost to the State (without counting administration costs) was £25 million.

An incidental effect of the Wyndham Act was that the landlord found he could buy his own demesne land (land not let to tenants) with State aid and in such a way as to get rid of mortgage encumbrances. He sold to the State; and the State paid off the mortgage (on which he paid 8 to 10 percent). He bought back from the State at a premium of three and a half percent on the cost—thus saving the difference. This alone, once it was discovered, killed opposition to the Act.

The gain to the tenant was set off by the extent to which the tenant merely escaped the landlord to fall into the clutches of the money-lender. And the Acts did nothing to check the fall of the world-price for agricultural produce. Their advantage to the smallholder of uneconomic plots was barely perceptible.*

Something was done (from 1891) for the "uneconomic" holders by the Congested Districts Board–a subsidiary of the State Agricultural Department. Its best work–that of buying out landlords whose tenants held plots smaller than the minimum contemplated by the Land Acts–and other landlords whose estates were untenanted–and redistributing the tenants upon farms of economic size–was at first outside the scope of its legal powers: the members of the Board took the risk of being repudiated and surcharged. More was done for the small and middling farmers by the Irish Agricultural Organisation Society, launched (1893) by Sir Horace Plunket, which sought to improve methods of farming and of marketing–especially in dairy-farming–by instruction and co-operative effort. The advance of the I.A.O.S. was made in the teeth of bitter political prejudice, worked up by the Irish "kulak" class–the gombeen-men and the "ranchers"–but its success, and the benefits it secured, were evident in the number of co-operative creameries which dotted the countryside (to be burned in most cases by the Black-and-Tans in 1920-21).

Much of the gain resulting from the work of the C.D.B. and of the I.A.O.S. was lost again to the exploiting transport agencies–the Irish Railways and the Shipping Companies–in each of which English capital predominated. In

* Land Purchase: It should be noted by apologists for English rule in Ireland that enabling the substantial tenant to purchase his holding *perpetuated* the final outcome of centuries of English conquest and exploitation.

fact the net result, after all efforts at reform, public and private, was stated by a continental expert-observer in 1906:

> "Were the Irishman not capable of reducing his standard of living to the lowest possible point, the continued existence of many farmsteads in the country would be inconceivable."
>
> Moritz J. Bonn: *Modern Ireland and her Agrarian Problem.*

A further point arises here. The process of substituting grass-farming for tillage had been fostered by English capitalism to serve its ends—cheap food as a precondition for cheap labour, and cheap wool for English textile manufacture. The development of alternative sources of supply (the U.S.A., Canada, Argentine, Australia) plus the pressure of the shipping interests slackened off considerably the need for English capitalism to continue the process in Ireland. It continued, none the less, since the tenants, when they became proprietors, had to specialise on supplying the English market either with meat for luxury consumption (on the hoof or in carcass) or with dairy-produce. Thus the Acts did little or nothing for the landless labourers, or to abate such land-hunger as resulted from the normal increase of the population.

Such benefits as the Land Acts really conferred were, therefore, all conditioned upon the continued activity of the emigrant ship. Once that ceased to operate the problem reappeared.

The extension to Ireland of the English system of local-government was a similar reform which aided English rule—rather than the Irish people—by creating a vested interest in maintaining the connection with England—to secure a share of Government patronage for the, newly-promoted, dominant class. The dictatorship of the landlords through the County Grand Juries was broken. But to replace the landlord by the gombeen-man, the parson by the priest, and the Protestant lawyer by a Castle-

Catholic place-hunter was an ambiguous gain; especially as the Castle, by assuming what had been the landlord's obligation to provide half the local rate raised, secured thereby a virtually complete veto on all local spending.*

To complete the picture it must be remembered that all Ireland outside of Dublin was policed by a semi-military force, the Royal Irish Constabulary, directly controlled by the Castle; which also controlled the (unarmed) Dublin Metropolitan Police.

By anticipation, Thomas Davis had given, in 1844, a prediction of the inevitable failure of this attempt to check the growth of Irish nationalism by piecemeal instalments of "reform": "And now, Englishmen, listen to us! Though you were to give us, tomorrow, the best tenures on earth; –though you were to equalise Catholic, Pesbyterian and Episcopalian;–though you were to give us the amplest representation in your Senate;–though you were to restore our absentees, disencumber us of your debt, and redress every one of our fiscal wrongs;–and though, in addition to all this, you plundered the treasuries of the world to lay gold at our feet, and exhausted the resources of your genius to do us worship and honour;–still we tell you . . . we would spurn your gifts if Ireland were to remain a province. We tell you, and all whom it may concern, come what may, bribery or deceit, justice, policy or war– we tell you, in the name of Ireland, that Ireland shall be a Nation."

The Degeneration of the Parliamentary Party

The division of the Party into warring Parnellite and Anti-Parnellite factions was ended in 1900 by the establishment of a United Irish Party with John Redmond (Parnellite) as its nominal leader. The numerical strength

* The perpetuation of this system, after the Treaty, explains the otherwise inexplicable indifference of the Irish to local governing bodies.

of the Party in the period of division never fell below an aggregate of eighty. Morally, and politically, however, it never regained the impetus it had squandered. The factional opportunism which inspired the split was duplicated in every locality; and the hysterical blackguardism with which Parnell was hounded to death set the tone for the gombeen-men as they fought, each in his locality, for control of the Party machine. Soon there was, beneath a surface show of size and unity, nothing left of the disciplined army Parnell had led but the machine for whose control rival opportunists squabbled and intrigued incessantly.

The degeneration of the Party was seen in its abandonment of Parnell's endeavour to use constitutional struggle as a mode of approach to a revolutionary end. Parnell's position had been stated, frankly, at Cork, in 1885: "We cannot under the British Constitution ask for more than the restoration of Grattan's Parliament, but no man has a right to fix the boundary of the march of a nation. No man has a right to say 'thus far shalt thou go and no further'. We have never attempted to fix the *ne plus ultra* to the progress of Ireland's nationhood, and we never shall."

After Parnell, the Party drifted rapidly to the point at which Nationhood became a figure of speech used demagogically to enhance the Party's bargaining-power in a Parliamentary racket—whose object was a division of the spoils plundered from the British Empire at large! To the "racketeers-in-chief" in England the Irish vote in Parliament was a valuable asset to be paid for in jobs and offices allocated to the nominees of the Irish members of Parliament.

Another grave cause of degeneration in the Party was its relapse into the religious-sectarianism, which Tone, Davis, the Fenians and Parnell had all laboured to overcome, and which was the primary cause of O'Connell's failure. Parnell had proved more than a counterpoise to the Vatican's political wire-pullers—which was one of the reasons why the Hierarchy was so prompt to oblige Gladstone, and use its authority to destroy Parnell. Once Parnell was gone, the Sullivan faction, led by the "foultongued" Healy, became again "more Catholic than the Pope". Out of this arose, after 1900, the domination of the Party machine by the Board of Erin—a break-away from a *(bona-fide)* Irish-American friendly society, the Ancient Order of Hibernians.

Originally founded in Ulster, ostensibly to protect Catholic traders and work-people from the Orange racket, the Board of Erin (A.O.H.) degenerated into a Catholic "racket", which reproduced, and outdid, the worst sectarianism of the Orange racket. The falling away of mass support from the Party created an opening for the racketeers to gain complete control of the Party machine.

Patrick Pearse said: "The narrowing down of Nationalism to the members of one creed is the most fateful thing that has occurred in Ireland since the days of the Pope's Brass Band."

Connolly called the Board of Erin "the foulest brood that ever came into Ireland". Its domination of the Party was a prelude to the Party's destruction.

Elements of National Revival outside the Party

Shrunk in numbers, and involved in the set-back, general after the fall and death of Parnell, the (Fenian) I.R.B., which drew its recruits from the intellectuals and men in the humbler walks of life, continued, notwithstanding, to exercise an influence out of all proportion to its numerical strength. It did nothing in its own name, preferring to sham dead; but any movement, making in any way for Separatism, could be sure of getting (without suspecting it) Fenian support:

"When money was needed, at a pinch, for any of the organisations it regarded as key organisations, the

I.R.B. found the money [getting it usually from sources controlled by John Devoy]. The Gaelic Athletic Association, the Gaelic League, the *Sinn Fein*, the *Fianna* [Gaelic Boy Scouts], the Irish Volunteers—strange and transient committees and societies were constantly cropping up, doing this and that specific national work. The I.R.B. formed them; the I.R.B. ran them; the I.R.B. provided the money. The I.R.B. dissolved them when their work was done."

P. S. O'Hegarty, *Victory of Sinn Fein.*

There is a measure of exaggeration in O'Hegarty's claim; but, this allowed for, what he says is substantially true. Of the organisations he names, two—the Gaelic League and *Sinn Fein*—call for special comment.

Founded, in 1893, by men who had no interest in partisan politics of any kind, the League set itself the task of reviving the everyday use of the Gaelic language. Only a small fringe of impoverished peasants on the Western Coast and its islands still used Gaelic as their normal speech. The League set itself to bring education imparted in Gaelic within the reach of that fringe; and, at the same time, to foster the teaching of Gaelic in the schools and among the people of the rest of Ireland.

The League had a surprising and a continuous success. Revival of interest in the language led to revival of interest in Gaelic music, dancing, arts and crafts; and it—most surprisingly and gratifyingly—united Protestant parsons and Orangemen with Catholic priests and laymen in a common enthusiasm for the language.

Fearless in their zeal, the pioneers of the language revival repelled every attempt of the Parliamentarians, on the one side, and of the theologians on the other, to impose conditions on its advance. When a parish priest objected to mixed study classes on the—

"specious ground of public morals, it asserted its right to control its own activities, and established once and for all, so far as it was concerned, that the sphere of the clergy's activities is not co-extensive with human life."

Mitchell Henry: *Evolution of Sinn Fein.*

The more recent (and mistaken) efforts to make it compulsory to teach all school subjects in Gaelic to children who normally speak English have obscured the revolutionary and liberating significance of the Gaelic revival. It is not because of any magic property in the language itself that its study, at this time, by just these Irishmen and Irishwomen produced revolutionary results. After all—all Ireland, outside the towns, spoke Gaelic in the penal days without producing a single revolutionary leader.

To rediscover the language was another matter. Having been arrested in its development at a comparatively early stage, Gaelic leads a student acquainted with the more developed modern languages to realise at once the evolutionary fluidity of language as distinct from its static character. The knowledge of Gaelic also made the place names of Ireland take on a rich meaning, and rescued them from the grotesqueness and absurdity of such English corruptions as, in the case of the "Phœnix" Park, confounded the Gaelic name for a clear spring (white-water) with that of a fabulous bird. Then the extant literature in Gaelic was not only of great antiquity, but also of immense intrinsic worth. The study of this literature, along with a surprisingly large body of folk-song and story, helped the youth of Ireland to rediscover concretely the Gaelic culture which the English conquest had destroyed. They were helped thus to the revolutionary truth that, as English capitalism had a beginning, so most certainly it could be brought to an end.

Before the enthusiasm of the youth of Ireland, all the agencies of orthodoxy and conservatism had to bow. The Gaelic revival was such a success that it received the flattery of imitation from demagogic politicians and synthetic

366

Gaels. A more healthy and enduring result was its influence in begetting a Gaelicisation of outlook in Irish
literature and drama in English.

The *Sinn Fein** movement which began to emerge between 1900 and 1903, had Fenian influences for its father
and the Gaelic revival for its mother.

Fenian influences had begotten a series of Literary and
Historical Discussion Clubs which combined to celebrate
the Centenary of '98. Thereafter they formed a Republican
federation which began to constitute an alternative to the
Parliamentary Party. Armed insurrection, as an ideal, was
never far from their thoughts; but they evolved no practical programme capable of immediate application.

Such a programme was provided by Arthur Griffith in
his journal the *United Irishman*, whose foundation, in
1899, was a direct result of the centenary celebrations.

Griffith took an old doctrine (use only Irish manufactures) and elaborated it into a policy and a programme.
His contention was that the adherents to the Gaelic
League should, in addition to using Irish speech, and Irish
recreations, insist upon buying only articles of Irish manufacture. This insistence would create a demand, which
would beget a supply, and so promote the development of
an Irish National economy. Then the Members of Parliament should be withdrawn from Westminster to form an
Irish National Council, which, with the local governing
bodies, would promote Irish industrial development, and
secure openings for Irish trade abroad! This "self-help"
policy would promote the flow of capital to Ireland, arrest emigration, and enable Ireland, ultimately, to enforce
the restoration of Grattan's Parliament.

Griffith's programme had two notable features: (1) It
provided a practical alternative to Parliamentarianism,
without committing anybody to Fenian "romanticism":

* *Sinn Fein* (pronounced approximately "Shin Fayn") literally
"ourselves alone". Its implied meaning is Self-Help in the
collective-national sense.

(2) it shared with the Parliamentary Party the restriction of its objective to Grattan's Parliament; but it left its adherents free to aspire further if they wished. It should be noted however that the Griffith policy proceeded wholly upon bourgeois-capitalist assumptions.

Between 1903 and 1908 the movement was sufficiently powerful to launch a new political organisation, *Sinn Fein*, and to start a short-lived daily paper of the same name.

The Socialist Republicans

To these other agencies must be added the Irish Socialist Republican Party, founded by James Connolly in 1896. Though it never gained a mass influence or much hold at all outside of Dublin and Cork, the personality of Connolly was sufficient to ensure that it left permanent traces. Its particular virtue was that it popularised the frank use of The Republic as the name for Ireland's objective.

This had a powerful effect upon the Young Republicans of the literary societies and led them to follow Connolly's example. His influence was exerted powerfully in support of the '98 Centenary Celebrations.

Connolly's influence was seen also in a reinvigoration of the Trade Union movement in Ireland; from which important results followed. His proposition that it is in a Socialist-Labour-Movement that the masses of Ireland can, and will, transcend sectarian divisions, has yet to be refuted. He himself scored successes on this line; others, following in his footsteps, may yet carry it to triumph.

In England and Scotland Connolly had an influence that, at first, was greater than his influence in Ireland. Born in Edinburgh of Ulster parents, Connolly spent his early youth in Ireland. Back in Edinburgh he acquired prominence in the Marxist Socialist Movement. In 1896 he accepted an invitation to return to Ireland to help found a Socialist movement.

His theoretical proposition, that Nationalism and Socialism, in an oppressed country, were not opposites—as mechanical pseudo "Marxism" supposed—but were complementary, each to the other, was treated as a "dangerous heresy" by the leaders of the I.L.P. and of the S.D.F. It was, however, accepted and applauded by a group of young men on the "left" of English and Scottish Marxism, and was finally vindicated by the teaching of Lenin and Stalin.

Connolly's popularity with the Left secured their backing when, at the International Socialist Conference in Paris, in 1900, he claimed separate voting rights for Ireland as a distinct nation. Referred to the English delegation for their opinion, Connolly's claim was, under Left influence, endorsed. It was therefore conceded by the Conference; and the recognition of Ireland as a separate nation was thereby established as a permanent precedent in the International.

Economic stress drove Connolly to emigrate to the U.S.A. at the latter end of 1903. During his absence the I.S.R.P. went out of existence; but a labour and Socialist revival led by James Larkin recalled him to Ireland in 1910.

By this time *Sinn Fein* had exhausted its impetus, and the Parliamentary Party was enjoying a revival in consequence of the introduction by the Liberals of the Third Home Rule Bill.

CHAPTER XXIX

THE HOME RULE CRISIS, 1912-14

Tory (and Orange) resistance to the Third Home Rule Bill went to such lengths that Civil War seemed inevitable—until it was averted by the outbreak of European War in August, 1914. A contemporary event, unconnected with the crisis—a Labour War in Dublin, 1913—had consequences which materially affected the sequel.

In this chapter we trace the process, and examine the components, of this crisis.

The Parliament Act, 1911

A salient contributory-cause of the Home Rule crisis was the Parliament Act carried in 1911, which destroyed the absolute veto of the House of Lords. How that came to be must first be examined.

In January 1906, the Liberals were returned to power with the greatest majority ever. Their majority was so enormous that they outnumbered by more than a hundred the Tories (133), the Labour Party (29) and the Irish Nationalists (83) all together.

This, however, concealed a danger. The Radical Left, led by Lloyd George, had been returned in such strength that a possibility was created that, in combination with Labour and the Irish, this Left might make the continued existence of the Government impossible. Lloyd George, in short, dominated the situation since he held a balance of power; and he exploited the occasion by forcing the introduction of a succession of reforms all designed (1) to steal the Socialists' "thunder" while gratifying the reformists; and (2) thereby to create obstacles to the introduction of real Socialism.

It is a cardinal clue with which to unravel the tangled events of this period to remember that fear of the working class in general, and, in particular, fear of a combination of the English workers and the Irish Nationalists were primary determinants of the policy of Tories, Liberals and Radicals alike, in every shift of political alignment.

Playing skilfully upon the weakness of the Tories, Lloyd George purposely pretended that his Liberal reforms were all much more "socialistic" than, in fact, they were. He deliberately intensified the alarm of the Tories in order to make them resist with their full strength, in the House of Lords, such Liberal measures as they could not prevent passing the Commons. This re-created the traditional Lords v. Commons situation, which Lloyd George exploited by including in the Budget of 1909 a Land Tax, which, negligible in itself, he palmed off upon the general public as well as the Tories as a first step in a programme of landlord-expropriation. The Lords fell into the trap and rejected the Budget.

This created the opening for the Parliament Act which provided that an Act could become law, without the concurrence of the Lords, if it passed the Commons three times in one Parliament without alteration. Two more elections (January and December 1910) were necessary before the Act could be passed—the accession of a new king (George V), and his scruples, making the second one necessary. However the end was achieved finally in 1911.

So long as the Tory-dominated House of Lords remained, with its powers undiminished, the Liberals could retain Home Rule in their programme without risk of frightening away the moderates and imperialists in their Right Wing. It pleased their Radical Left; it saved the face of their Nationalist allies; and, since the House of Lords could always be trusted to throw it out, it gained support on the Left without losing any on the Right. That is, the Liberals were in favour of advocating Home Rule, so long as it was impossible to carry it into effect.

The elections of 1910–fought by the Tories under slogans of fierce hostility to "Socialism", "Spoliation", and "Irish Disloyalty"–had reduced the Liberals to complete dependence upon the Nationalists (83) and the Labour Party (41). The price they had to pay for the Parliament Act–which their continued political existence depended upon–was a pledge to introduce a Home Rule Bill immediately the Parliament Act became law.

The Tory Opposition to Home Rule

The passage of the Parliament Act brought the ruling clique of Imperialist Finance-Capitalists face to face with the menace of an ascendant and militant proletariat. The combination of Lloyd-Georgian social-democracy, Labour-Socialism, and Irish Nationalism, might, if it were not checked, grow more menacing every hour. The House of Lords had ceased to be an impregnable defence of their privileges and property; therefore they had to cast around for a new weapon. They found it in open conspiracy to thwart the will of the democracy by force and arms.

They were too astute to attempt this by a frontal assault upon the institution of Parliament itself (though there was talk of ending the farce of democracy). They chose the method of a flanking attack; and, under cover of zeal for the "loyalty", "liberty", "religion" and "property" of a "persecuted minority", organised their counter-revolutionary armed force in Ulster, in the disguise of a "volunteer" movement of collective self-protection in hostility to Home Rule.

It is cardinal to remember that what passed for a "spontaneous" resistance of "Ulster" to the "menace" of Home Rule was (1) not spontaneous but deliberately worked up, with not a little moral blackmail and economic coercion; (2) did not originate in Ulster but in the inner-councils of the English Tory-plutocracy; (3) was taken up with greater enthusiasm among the young counter-revolutionaries of the English aristocracy and the services than among the Ulster people; (4) affected only a portion of Ulster and included only a minority of its population; and (5) was aimed at no "menace" (since the Home Rule Bill contained none) but at preserving the privileged position of a minority-caste in Ireland, as part of the process of maintaining a privileged minority-caste as the real rulers of England, and exploiters of its Empire.

The progress of the opposition proves this. The agitation in Ulster was led by Sir Edward Carson, a Dublin man, who had been Solicitor-General in the Tory Government from 1900-1906. In England it took the form of a demagogic "loyalist" and "Protestant" campaign against "unpatriotic" socialists, "Papist" Nationalists, and their "little Englander" Radical allies. Resistance to Home Rule was palmed off as "defence of the Empire", "defence of property and personal rights", and "defence of the Protestant religion". Every drawing-room in good society became a recruiting office enrolling the young officer class in the conspiracy: and the organisers of the campaign did not scruple to allege that they had the sympathy (if not the support) of the "very highest in the land" for their revolt against the "tyranny" of the House of Commons.

The Opposition in Ulster

In Ulster the first move was to secure a mass of signatures to a Covenant, pledging resistance to Home Rule. In the circumstances it was not difficult to obtain 500,000 signatures in a short time; but nothing was left to chance. Employers let it be known that failure to sign the Covenant might have "consequences" for those who failed. Landlords passed the "List" to tenants; customers did the same to tradespeople. Orange factionists saw to it, in the Belfast shipyards, that those who did not sign, promptly, were run off the job as "Papists".

Then, at a critical stage, a body of Volunteers 80,000 strong was raised, in which force were included all the hooligan elements in Belfast, who were chosen deliberately for their ignorant anti-Catholic virulence. This force was officered and drilled almost entirely by officers holding commissions in the English Army and Navy. A proportion of the Volunteers were armed with rifles from the first—the majority being armed with revolvers. Arms were supplied by the "gentry"; and arms were collected and stored in the Tory clubs in England, as well as in the Orange lodges in Ulster.

Finally, when the Act was introduced a third time, after being twice rejected by the Lords, Carson named a Provisional Government for the six counties of N.E. Ulster; and announced that it would begin to function on the day set for the coming-into-force of the Home Rule Act. Steps were taken to procure rifles, machine guns, etc., for the whole Ulster "Volunteer" force.

The moderates in the conspiracy had hoped to bluff the Liberals out of using their powers under the Parliament Act. When this failed they became reconciled, perforce, to the militants' policy of counter-revolutionary revolt.

Classes in the Ulster Resistance

That there existed, ready-made for Tory use, the whole machinery of Orangeism—anti-democratic and counter-revolutionary from its first invention in 1795—goes without saying. That the Orange Order existed solely to preserve the political, social and economic ascendancy of a small oligarchical faction has been abundantly demonstrated already. What calls for comment is the fact that the proletarian masses of Belfast and the industrial North-East were still blinded by sectarianism sufficiently to react as desired to the "No Popery" bogey, set up to terrify them by the Orange agents of the Tory conspiracy.

The reason for this is found in the fact that, while wages

374

in Belfast averaged in general higher than the average for the rest of Ireland, they were lower than for corresponding occupations in England and Scotland. Belfast's "prosperity" (for the employers) and, incidentally, its importance for British capitalism as a whole, arose in its early stages from its freedom from Trade Unionism. This in turn was a result of the sectarian divisions, which the employers took great care to foster. Once Catholic and Protestant workers had been taught to hate each other like poison, it became a rule for employers to engage just so many of each of the hostile sects as would ensure that 100 percent solidarity was all-but-impossible.

In a measure, the Orange Order became, in certain of its lodges, an endeavour to counter this employers' device; and some, at any rate, of the attempts at driving the Catholics out of the shipyards were, at bottom, crude attempts at creating a basis for shop-solidarity. More frequently the Orange Order functioned as a "scab-herding" agency and as a "racket" to keep all appointments to the posts of foreman, charge-hand, etc., within its privileged circle.

The A.O.H., as we have noted, was formed ostensibly as a defence against these practices of Orangeism; but the A.O.H. made matters ten times worse, since under clerical influences it was also predominantly anti-Trade Union. More than one case of deliberate strike-breaking caused the "Mollies" to be regarded with hatred in proletarian quarters, Catholic as well as Protestant; and the net result of its activities was a revival of sectarian animosities in social-strata where they would otherwise have lapsed entirely–along with all interest in dogmatic theology. As James Connolly said, at this period: "Were it not for the existence of the Board of Erin, the Orange Society would long since have ceased to exist. To Brother Devlin [Grand Master A.O.H.], and not Brother Carson is mainly due the progress of the Covenanting Movement in Ulster."

Whether the Carsonite agitation was originally a bluff or not, it became clear that it ought to be checked. Rank-and-file pressure induced the Government, at last, to forbid the importation of arms and ammunition into Ireland (December 4, 1913); and then to cause the officers at the Curragh Camp to be "warned" for duty in Ulster (March 1914) to quell organised resistance to lawful authorities.

Fifty-seven officers at once tendered their resignations; many more let it be known that they would take a similar course.

Faced with this virtual mutiny—which it was given to understand included potentially a majority of the officers in the Army and Navy Lists—the Government surrendered. It announced that it had no intention of "coercing Ulster. The conspirators, now cocksure of victory, grew thereafter more arrogant hourly.

The causes of the Liberal hesitation were complex. Redmond's biographers report that he had personally vetoed a suggestion that Carson should be prosecuted. He feared the consequences of letting loose civil war in Ireland. Carson, for his part, made no concealment of the fact that friends, in Court circles, had assured him of immunity from any penalty for his "treason". And the Liberals, for their part, saw reason to fear a civil war in England, which, if it did not end in a victory for Tory counter-revolution, would risk creating the conditions for a proletarian, socialist revolution.

Two preceding events had induced this frame of mind: (1) The "Larkin" Labour War in Dublin, 1913; and (2) the formation in November 1913, of the Irish Volunteers.

The "Larkin" Labour War

Working on ground which Connolly had ploughed, James Larkin had built up, from 1907 onwards, a militant trade union of a new type—the Irish Transport and

General Workers' Union. It catered primarily for the un-skilled, and the, till then, unorganised workers; and it relied more especially upon the weapon of the lightning strike, backed up by sympathetic action by workers in related jobs.

In 1913, W. M. Murphy—the richest man in Dublin, Chairman of the Employers' Federation, virtual owner of the Dublin Tramways, and owner of the *Independent*—denounced in that journal some workers then on strike. Larkin called for a boycott of the *Independent* and Murphy replied by calling for an employers' boycott of the Union, purged all the members of the Transport Union from the Tramway Service, and locked out its members employed in Jacob's Biscuit Factory, which he controlled.

Transport Union members fought the scabs who ran the Tramways; newsboys fought the scab sellers Murphy sent out with the *Independent*. Other workers joined in; rail-waymen, transport-drivers, dockers, and seamen all re-fused to handle Jacob's Biscuits or the goods of any of the firms who joined in Murphy's war on "Larkinism". Soon, half Dublin was on strike; and all Dublin was in an up-roar. Battles with the police were fought daily.

To follow the struggle in detail would require a volume. What is significant for our purposes is that the working masses of Dublin found themselves faced with an alliance of Dublin Castle (with its police), the Orange-Tory magistrates, the Nationalist employers, and the Catholic Hierarchy. To make the united front of reaction complete, Arthur Griffith denounced Larkin, unsparingly, in the name of *Sinn Fein*.

Pressed for funds with which to wage the struggle, Larkin and Connolly turned to England and Scotland—from which they received a burst of enthusiastic soli-darity such as had not been known since the great dockers' strike of 1888. Funds were granted by virtually every union, by the T.U.C., by the Labour Party, and by the

Co-operative Union. Jacob's Biscuits were universally boycotted, and the Trade Unions and Socialist Societies combined to stock a food-ship which the C.W.S. supplied at cost-price, they chartering the ship as their share. English and Scottish Socialists volunteered by the hundred to find homes for the children of strikers "for the duration". A party of some three hundred children was actually on its way to the ship at the North Wall, when it was turned back by a frenzied band of hymn-singing women, headed by priests, who feared the consequences to the children's souls if they were fed for a month or so in the homes of "godless" English and Scottish Socialists. The middle-class women who had organised the affair, Dora Montefiore and Louise Rand, were actually arrested on a charge of "attempted kidnapping".

In the end the strike wore itself out to an inconclusive finish. But it left behind as its permanent effects a great growth in militant class-consciousness among the Dublin workers, a great enhancement of the reputation of Larkin and Connolly as leaders, and the establishment of close relations between the young neo-Fenian intellectuals and the Labour movement.

Two incidental results were of decisive importance: (1) In England, a great wave of militant ("syndicalist") trade-unionism flared up to threaten the greatest industrial conflict in history; (2) in Ireland, the Transport Union's "Army", formed of men armed with hurley sticks who guarded the platform against police assaults during strike-meetings, gave rise to the Citizen Army, which, in turn, derived added importance from the founding of the Irish Volunteers.

The Irish Volunteers

In November 1913, a group of well-known men, not too prominently connected with the Nationalist Party, and not connected at all, so far as was known with any more militant, or republican body, called a meeting in the Rotunda, Dublin, to consider the formation of a National Volunteer Force to defend Home Rule from Carsonite assault. Over 30,000 people attended in the Rotunda and at the over-flow meetings in the surrounding streets. Four thousand names were handed in that night.

Ten days later (December 4, 1913) a Government proclamation forbade the import of arms or ammunition into Ireland. The Government had watched Carson's drilling and arming, for eleven months, without saying a word. When Nationalist Ireland followed suit they acted at once.

The conclusion is obvious: the Liberals were, on a balance, less afraid of being beaten by the Tories than of beating them, with the aid of militant English proletarians, and armed Irish Nationalists.

For a week or two Volunteer recruiting dragged. Various bodies—branches of the United Irish League, the American Hibernians, *Sinn Fein*, and the Citizen Army—offered to join bodily. The Volunteer executive insisted upon individual recruits, on a strictly territorial basis. The I.R.B. men—who, working under cover, were really in control—insisted upon this precaution, as a means of keeping control in their hands; but, naturally, they could not say so openly. The Citizen Army, affronted at refusal, set to work to equip and arm itself independently. For a few months there was keen hostility between the Citizen Army and the Volunteers.

The Curragh incident, in March 1914, and the Ulster gun-running on the night of April 24-25—when the Ulster Volunteers seized the ports and customs houses at Larne and Donaghadee, and landed a large cargo of German Mauser rifles and ammunition—changed the situation completely; especially when it was seen that nothing whatever was done about this flagrant defiance of the law. It was clear, too, that there had been connivance; since the warships posted off the Ulster coasts, expressly to prevent anything of the kind, could not be conceived to be as in-competent as the gun-running implied.

Accepting the implied threat as a challenge, Irish Nationalists flocked into the Volunteers by thousands every day; and a great demand arose that Redmond should put his foot down, and insist upon the lifting of the ban on the importation of arms, which now operated exclusively to the advantage of Carson.

Redmond did, in the end, put his foot down; but not in the place expected. He demanded (June 1914), that the Volunteer Executive, "to make the organisation representative", should admit to their number twenty-five men to represent the Party chosen by himself as Chairman.

A majority complied, though with reluctance. Pearse and his Fenian colleagues protested, but nevertheless submitted.

After this had been done, Redmond demanded (July) the lifting of the ban. He had privately protested before; now the bellicosity of the Ulster Volunteers was going beyond all bounds. They were talking, now, of a "march from Belfast to Cork". Their commander-in-chief, General Richardson—who held a high rank at the Horse Guards, despite his connection with partisan politics—ordered all ranks (from July 1 onwards) to "carry their arms openly and resist every effort to disarm them". On July 25, 5,000 Ulster Volunteers paraded Belfast, fully armed, with four machine-guns. Still Redmond received no answer to his demand.

On Sunday, July 26, in Dublin, Assistant-Commissioner of Police, Harrell, received shocking news. A private yacht, he learned, had landed eleven hundred rifles, and a supply of ammunition, at Howth. They had been met by a body of Irish Volunteers, who, even then, were marching back to Dublin with their weapons.

Assistant-Commissioner Harrell realised at once that the entire British Empire depended upon him alone. He assembled all the police within reach, requisitioned a company of Scottish Borderers, and sallied forth to do deeds. He met the "enemy" at Clontarf.

Ammunition had not been served out, but some of the men had revolvers, and Harrell's peremptory demand for a surrender of arms was flatly refused. He ordered the police to seize the arms; a scuffle arose; shots were fired; a few injuries were inflicted. The officer commanding the Borderers insisted upon a parley; and the incident fizzled out absurdly.

While the Volunteer officers were protesting—arguing with the Assistant-Commissioner, and threatening to serve out ammunition and make a fight of it—the Volunteers, beginning from the rear ranks, were dodging through the houses at the sides of the road, and disappearing over the garden walls in the fields beyond—carrying their arms and the ammunition with them. Assistant-Commissioner Harrell was still insisting, indignantly, that the Volunteers were breaking the law, when it dawned upon him that there was nobody before him but a group of Volunteer officers and a few of the rank and file—whose rifles had somehow disappeared.

Much injured in his dignity, Harrell gave the word to return to the Castle. Unfortunately the news had spread. The streets were thronged; and as the police and soldiers neared the centre of the City, they were greeted with hoots and hisses, to which later was added stone-throwing.

The officer commanding the Borderers halted his company in Bachelor's Walk; and ordered his men to prepare to fire. Some ranks, mistaking the order, opened fire at once; others, thinking an order had been given, followed suit. In a few seconds three people had been killed, and some thirty wounded.

Anger had barely had time to blaze up in Ireland, when, radiating from Vienna in all directions, a wave of war spread to engulf the world. On August 4, 1914, Britain entered the war; and, for the time being, everything else was forgotten.

CHAPTER XXX

THE ROAD TO EASTER WEEK

At the outbreak of war, in August 1914, the general feeling in Nationalist Ireland was one of cordial sympathy with Britain and France, faced suddenly with the calamity of war. There was a tradition-based sympathy with France; there was a newly-acquired sympathy with Britain, largely based on the belief that Home Rule had been conceded, and would come into force automatically as soon as the war ended.

The question posed in this chapter is: By what process was this cordiality turned into its opposite, so that an attempt to establish an Irish Republic was made in Easter Week, 1916?

Redmond, the Nationalist Party and the War

When the Prime Minister, Asquith, reviewed the situation, in the House of Commons, in the first days of the war, he was able to say that "Ireland is the one bright spot in the landscape". John Redmond, with a burst of spontaneous magnanimity, told the House they could take every English soldier out of Ireland, and trust its defence to the Volunteers, North and South.

Politically, this was a fatal error—one doomed to destroy Redmond and his party, utterly, and for ever. Yet the essence of the tragedy is—it could have been made to come true; but only if the conspirators at the back of the "Ulster" ramp had been actuated by different motives. If the "Ulster" agitation had been *bona fide*, and open to conviction, Redmond's genuine eagerness to satisfy every complaint would have cleared the way for an amicable settlement.

Redmond's error was a strange one. It revealed him in a flash as an intensely reserved and sentimental Irish gen tleman–of a type which survived only in himself–who had lost all touch with political actualities. He lived from choice (when he was not at Westminster) in a lonely dwelling, in an inaccessible part of Co. Wicklow, a part of Ireland more remote, in practice, than even the Western Isles. He loved the house because it had belonged to Parnell; and his chief occupation, there, was to sit and brood–of his dead chief, and of days, still more remote, when his ancestors had been involved, fatally, on both sides, in '98. He was to learn in bitterness and sorrow how completely the world had passed him by.

What actually happened was tragically different from what, in his emotional excitement, Redmond had assumed would occur. The Home Rule Bill was given the Royal Assent; but was then hung up for the "duration" on the understanding that an "amending" Bill would come into force at the same time, excluding six counties (temporarily?) from its operation.

Meanwhile, no English troops were withdrawn from Ireland; and the flood of Irish recruits to the British army was treated, systematically, with supercilious and offensive lack of consideration. The extent to which the officer caste had been indoctrinated with the die-hard Tory ideology–hostility in principle to the Irish alike as democrats, Catholics, and Nationalists–was revealed in scores of ways.

A few examples will suffice. The proportion of recruits per thousand of population to the British Army was much higher in Nationalist Ireland than in "Ulster"; but this fact was systematically concealed. The "Ulster" regiments were brigaded together; had their own Ulster officers; wore a distinctive badge; and were given every kind of publicity.

One Irish "division" was formed for the rest of Ireland; but it was officered, almost exclusively, by English officers, nearly every one of them being a Tory die-hard. It was refused its own distinctive Irish badge; and when a group of highly-connected Irish ladies worked a banner for the Division, permission to use it was peremptorily refused. Irish recruits were, in practice, refused permission to select their units; and were dispersed, as widely as possible, among English and Scottish regiments. When, by this diversion of recruits to fill the wastage of war, the Irish Division fell below its strength it was reorganised and lost its distinctively Irish character.

Everything was done to prevent Irishmen developing any collective-National self-confidence, or any sort of National pride, based upon proved Irish valour on the battle-field.

When an English officer, with Home Rule sympathies, allowed these sympathies to appear in his recruiting speeches, in an exclusively Nationalist area, he was reprimanded; and ordered to send in his papers. When General Richardson invited Orangemen to enlist, as such, so that they could "learn to drive Home Rule to Hell", no sort of notice was taken, other than commendatory.

Scornful Fenians told aggrieved Nationalists, who complained of these things, that it served them right for lending themselves to do England's work. It took time for the official policy to produce its natural effect of alienating the mass of Nationalist Ireland; but in time it was done, and done irreparably.

The Volunteer Split

The rebuffs and insults inflicted upon the Irish Nationalists by the young blood and the old Blimps of the officer-caste—to whom a counter-revolutionary hostility to democracy and democratic-Nationalism was the "correct thing"—provided a practical criticism of the whole line of the Parliamentary Party since the throwing overboard of Parnell.

Parliamentary Nationalism had, in fact and practice operated on these assumptions: (1) That Ireland's "Nation-

384

ality" was a thing purely relative and conditional; while the connection with England was a thing fixed and inescapable. (2) That England's imperial integrity was vital to Ireland's continued existence. (3) That Ireland's nationhood was, at most, a thing comparable to the provincial pride of an East Anglian or a Wessex man, or the county pride of a Yorkshireman. (4) In effect they denied any reality to Irish nationality–save as a relic from a past which they wished to be able to forget.

"Irish history is something which every Englishman should be encouraged to learn, and every Irishman encouraged to forget." So ran the comfortable paradox; to which the die-hard Tories replied by deeds which proved that, to them at any rate, Irishmen were–what they had been to the Whigs of the Penal Code and the Tories of the days of the Union–"aliens in blood, in speech, and in religion".

The Orange point of view was as realistic as was that of the Fenians; and was equally calculated to de-bunk all the sentimentality of the Redmondite recruiters. Said an Ulster journal: "If the Redmondites will not support the war because it is just, they should not support it because they have got Home Rule. They haven't got it."

That was the tragic awakening which was in store for Redmond and his Party.

Meanwhile they were loyal to their word; and began to take note seriously of the anti-war attitude expressed by the three distinct trends of Republicanism, which began to make themselves manifest.

The Republicans of the traditional school, the old Fenians represented by Tom Clarke, saw nothing in the war but "England's difficulty–Ireland's opportunity". As soon as war was declared, the Supreme Council of the I.R.B. met and decided, in principle, that a Rising must be attempted before the war ended. They followed tradition, too, in looking for aid from abroad. As was virtually inevitable they looked to America for money, and perhaps arms, and to Germany for military assistance. They had no illusions about Germany. They saw Germany as the die-hard Orangeman did, who protested at the depletion of the ranks of the Ulster Volunteers "only because of a European disturbance". "After all," he said, "the Kaiser is a good Protestant." The traditionalist Fenians saw that clearly; but thought that the virtue of being at war with England made up for every deficiency. And, anyway, as a business proposition, Germany, at war with England, might be glad to send arms and officers to Ireland.

The Gaelic Republicans, of whom Patrick Pearse was the best representative, were very sceptical of German help. They saw—what the traditionalists failed to see—that Tone appealed for military aid to France, in 1796, not merely, or even mainly, because it was at war with England, but because it stood, then, at the head of the forces of World Liberation. The French Republic to which Tone appealed was the embodiment and representative of the principles of Popular Freedom, and of the International Solidarity of a Liberated World. He appealed as a democratic-republican to his fellow republican-democrats. And nobody in 1914 could envisage the Kaiser or the Kaiser's Reich as anything of the kind. Pearse's doctrine, which, at times, he expressed in mystical terms which obscured its realistic essence, was that Ireland must herself develop the force that achieves her freedom. His doctrine of the magical efficacy of a blood-sacrifice boils down, in practice, to this elementary truth.

Distinct from Pearse were again James Connolly and the Socialist Republicans. Connolly had even less faith in German aid than Pearse had. "We serve neither King nor Kaiser—but Ireland!" This was his slogan from the first; but, with it, he had a passionate concern for the workers and peasants in all lands, who were being driven to slaughter each other in the interest of the predatory imperialism of their respective rulers. He looked every

386

where, longingly, for a sign of what he wished to see—the general uprising of the masses against the rulers who had made the earth a shambles. And every day he grew more inclined to hope, and to believe, that a popular uprising in Ireland would serve as a signal for a popular uprising everywhere. A (false) rumour that the German Socialist leader, Karl Liebknecht, had been shot for his anti-war propaganda, drew from Connolly a statement of his thoughts:

"The war of a subject nation for independence, for its right to live its life, in its own way, may and can be justified as holy and righteous. The war of a subject class to free itself from the debasing conditions of economic and political slavery should at all times choose its own weapons and esteem all as sacred instruments of righteousness. But the war of nation against nation in the interest of royal freebooters, and cosmopolitan thieves, is a thing accursed.

"All hail then to our Continental comrade who, in a world of imperial and financial brigands, and cowardly trimmers and compromisers, showed mankind that men still know how to die for the holiest of all causes—the sanctity of the human soul—the practical brotherhood of the human race."

Organisationally, the Traditional and the Gaelic Republicans were one; they were united in the I.R.B. and in the Volunteers. Connolly and the Citizen Army—every member of which had, if eligible, to be a member of a trade union—were not merely distinct from the Republicans. There was a measure of hostility between them which was only partly bridged by those such as Madame Markievicz, who was a commandant in the Citizen Army and also a leader of the *Cumann na mBan* (the Women's Auxiliary Army of the Irish Volunteers). Pearse also, drawn by his democratic sympathies and his admiration for Connolly, began to function as an influence for unification.

At the same time each felt it was necessary to make a break with Redmondite Nationalism. Accordingly, in September 1914, the Republican elements in the Volunteer Executive repudiated Redmond's pledge of support to the English Government, and expelled his nominees from the Committee. They issued a call for a National Convention, to elect a permanent executive and define the policy of the new organisation.

Redmond replied with a counter-repudiation; and called upon all loyal Nationalist Party men to boycott the Convention and those responsible for calling it.

Thus, at a stroke, the Volunteer Movement was split between the Republicans—who kept the original name Irish Volunteers—and the Redmondites who took the name of National Volunteers. Of the 200,000 Volunteers enrolled at the time of the split, only 12,000 answered the call, and sent delegates to the Convention on November 25, 1914. Redmond, in derision, called them the "*Sinn Fein* Volunteers", and the name stuck—to create endless confusion later.

The (Redmondite) National Volunteers, despite their majority, began to shrink from the moment of the split. By April 1915, they had dwindled to a tenth of their original number. A year later, only a few companies survived. The Irish Volunteers, on the contrary, grew steadily until they reached a maximum of 18,000, a quarter of whom were drawn from Dublin and its vicinity. The Dublin battalions were all fully equipped with arms and ammunition. Outside of Dublin only a few companies were fully equipped.

The Citizen Army had arms for 200 men; if it could have got the arms, it could have paraded ten times that number. Many would-be Citizen Army men joined the Volunteers to get arms. Soon the Citizen Army and the Volunteers were holding joint parades and drills.

James Larkin left Ireland for America in October 1914, with the object of raising funds for the Union which was financially crippled by the lock-out. James Connolly carried on as acting General Secretary of the Transport Union, Commander of the Citizen Army, and Editor of the *Irish Worker*. He wrote freely, also, for English Labour and Socialist journals; urging, always, revolutionary proletarian solidarity in opposition to the "war of the kites and the crows".

In Ireland he combined that general propaganda with specific agitation of Ireland's national claims, and a repudiation in advance of Home Rule as any sort of satisfaction for those claims. He appealed constantly to the workers of Belfast and the Six Counties; urging them not to be misled by the Ulster capitalist bosses, whose only interest in maintaining the connection with England was to secure the armed force with which to keep their workers in subjection.

Connolly's *Socialist-Republicanism*–preached fearlessly, with unremitting fervour, week by week–had a profound effect upon the young "Fenian" leaders–Pearse, MacDonagh and MacDermott–the last-named being the Manager of the I.R.B. journal, *Irish Freedom*.

They were all attacked as "pro-German" by the "loyal" Nationalist Press, and all were, ignorantly or maliciously, confounded with *Sinn Fein* with which none of them had any connection, and which, as a Party, had dwindled to nothing. Arthur Griffith still maintained his *United Irishman* and kept up his criticism of Redmond's war policy; but he had severed his connection with both the I.R.B. and the Volunteers–disagreeing, totally, with the notion of forcing an insurrection hot-house fashion.

The Chief Secretary (Augustine Birrell) handled the situation with a finesse unusual in occupants of his office. As a Radical he disliked suppressing journals. As a party tactician he saw the unwisdom of making martyrs. But the printers of Republican journals were told, quietly, one after the other, that if they continued to print matter objectionable to the Authorities, their plants might be commandeered for war purposes. A point was reached where *Irish Freedom* had to be printed in Belfast, and the *Irish Worker* in Glasgow (on the press of the S.L.P., which Connolly had helped to found).

In Belfast, incidentally, the Irish and the Ulster Volunteers invariably saluted each other, ceremonially, when they passed each other in their marches. They had, at any rate, one point in common: they each hated (and were hated by) the Board of Erin, A.O.H.

As the fog of war descended, and all propaganda other than war propaganda was faced with increasing difficulty and danger, Connolly grew fiercely impatient for a chance to do something—or set something in motion—which would excite, by sympathetic suggestion, the universal revolt of the exploited and oppressed which he longed to see. He fretted impatiently to be up and doing, at the head of his gallant handful of Citizen Army men. He was confident that, once a start was made, the Fenians would not fail to join in.

Connolly, in truth, became somewhat of a trial to the I.R.B. chiefs. They had learned his resolution, early in the war, when he with Tom Clarke and Sean MacDermott had organised a party to seize the Mansion House, Dublin, on the eve of a great recruiting-rally, at which both Asquith and Redmond were booked to speak—intending to hold it, with rifles, against all comers. The plan broke down; soldiers were already billeted in the Mansion House, and a surprise capture was impossible.

By January 1916, Connolly had reached the limit of his patience. His writings in the *Workers' Republic* (which was printed then on his own press in Liberty Hall, under a guard of Citizen Army men, with rifles loaded and bayonets fixed) began to grow reminiscent of John Mitchel in 1848. The I.R.B. chiefs grew scared lest the authorities should take the alarm. They arranged a secret meeting with Connolly; and, in a quiet spot, let him into the secret that their plans were laid for a Rising in Easter Week, 1916. Connolly agreed to come into the plan; and from thence forward was a co-opted member of the Military Committee, I.R.B.

Preparing for Revolt

The Plan of the Rising was known only to a dozen men, one of whom was the veteran of '65, John Devoy. Its general assumption was (1) that the mass of the Volunteers were Irish enough to respond, at call, to an invitation to attempt a revolutionary *coup d'état*; and (2) that if the Rising could hold its own for a week or a fortnight, the mass of Irishmen would be inspired by National instinct and tradition to join the revolt. Defeat might follow; but the repression, with the fact that an attempt had been made, would reawaken and revivify the National aspiration for Republican Independence. On the concrete side, plans had been made to secure: (1) A supply of arms and ammunition from Germany; (2) a body of officers and instructors with more arms, from the Fenians in the U.S.A.; (3) possibly (though none too likely) an Irish Brigade recruited from war-prisoners in Germany.

The last of these points was Roger Casement's pet scheme. He had cast himself for the rôle of Wolfe Tone in this "new '98", and played his part gallantly–though with little of the genius of his great exemplar.

The second point was one in which Clarke, Connolly and Devoy all placed great hopes.* It came to nothing in the end, since the U.S.A. authorities, getting wind of the scheme, shifted the German liners–which it was proposed to seize and use for transporting men and materials to Ire-

* Con Lehane (formerly Con O'Lyhane) wrote to T. A. Jackson asking him to hold himself in readiness to play a part, presumably as a journalist, in this venture – Ed.

land—away from their berths in the Hudson out to an anchorage beyond Sandy Hook. The first point all were agreed upon; and this very nearly materialised.

The actual quantity of arms in their possession was not large. The cargo run at Howth had been supplemented by another landed a few nights later on a quiet beach in Wicklow. Some of these arms had been lost in the Split; but that business had been so contrived as to leave most of the arms in the right hands. Rifles and machine-guns were hard to get in war-time; but with shot-guns, sporting-rifles, and rifles "looted" from the military (as well as revolvers and automatic pistols) they made out as well as they could. They had lost a number of active organisers, arrested by the authorities and deported to England; but their places had been filled by enthusiastic volunteers. The movement at large knew nothing of the plan, as a concrete actuality; but the atmosphere was electric with the spirit of revolt, and the expectation that something would soon be attempted.

The British authorities knew little more than the rank-and-file volunteers did. They learned, of course, of Casement's abortive effort to recruit an Irish Brigade among the war-prisoners; but they learned little more from Germany—as good as their espionage service was.

The German Government had little to tell. It knew only what Casement could tell them; and that was very little. And in truth the Germans were very little interested in Nationalist Ireland. They had banked on Carson's "rebellion" tying the hands of the British sufficiently to keep them out of the war until France had been smashed. As Carson had failed them the Germans had no confidence in the rest of Ireland. They sent the shipload of arms—all paid for at top prices in spot cash—but they did that more to please their American Ambassador (who thought an Irish rebellion would keep America out of the war) than from any hope of military gain.

Unfortunately for the organisers of revolt, a message they sent, asking for the date of arrival of the arms-ship to be postponed for three days, never reached Germany. It was picked up in a raid, by the U.S.A. authorities, on the office the German military attaché used for under cover operations—meticulously filed for reference!—and it was immediately communicated to the British Government. Consequently British destroyers were off the coast nicely in time for the altered date.

As it chanced, that three days' difference might have saved the situation, but, unluckily, the party despatched with signalling apparatus to give the indication where to land the arms, racing full speed for the rendezvous, failed in the darkness to make a right-angle turn at a critical moment. The car, with its occupants, raced straight on— over the edge of a quay into deep water.

The arms-ship arrived on time at the first-fixed date, and waited the stipulated three days for the signal which never came. Instead, British destroyers arrived, and the arms-ship had to be scuttled to avoid capture. Its cargo would have made all the difference.

Casement was landed on the coast of Kerry, from a submarine, with two companions, while the arms-ship was off the coast. He fell into the hands of the police almost immediately. He had returned in order to advise the Volunteers to call off the Rising if it was dependent on German military aid, which he knew was not forthcoming.

Meanwhile, the nominal chief of the Volunteers, Prof. Eoin MacNeill, had received the shock of his life. Acting on the advice of the Secretary of the Volunteers, he had challenged Pearse, who had informed him, politely, that a Rising would take place on Easter Sunday.

Since their formation, route-marches and field-exercises had formed a prominent part of the Volunteers' training. The authorities had thought it best not to interfere; and police and public had grown so accustomed to them, that they took no alarm—not even when the Citizen Army staged a realistic storming of Dublin Castle, which only stopped short of actually crossing the wall, against which their scaling ladders were reared. For the Easter week-end, manœuvres had been planned on a holiday scale. All ranks had been ordered to supply themselves with three-days' rations.

To his horror, MacNeill learned that, instead of a holi-day "camp-out", what was contemplated was—the real thing.

The conspirators thought it was too late for him to do anything about it. He beat them, there. The Sunday morn-ing newspapers all carried an advertisement, signed by MacNeill as Chief of Staff, cancelling all manœuvres for Easter Sunday. Telegrams and messages had already been sent to the same effect.

Dublin Castle—whose heart had leaped into its mouth at the news of Casement's landing in Kerry—breathed a deep sigh of relief. When nothing happened on Easter Sunday, it relaxed to enjoy a welcome Bank Holiday.

Easter Monday, Dublin, 1916

Brilliant sunshine flooded broad O'Connell Street. Bank holiday crowds thronged thick around the tram terminus at the Nelson Pillar.

Out of Abbey Street marched a small contingent of armed men in uniform—most in the dark-green and slouched hats of the Citizen Army; some in the grey-green of the Irish Volunteers. The contingent crossed to the far side and wheeled right to continue towards the Pillar and the G.P.O.

Nobody gave them more than a glance. "Connolly's lot from Liberty Hall," said the holiday-makers. "What a crew!" muttered an English officer, watching through the window of the G.P.O.

Ranging level with the front of the G.P.O., the column

suddenly halted; faced to the front; fixed bayonets; and, at the word of command, charged into the building.

In a few seconds the public were hustled out, as the glass was dashed from the window frames. Then, as the staff crowded from a back-door, a party of officers advanced from the main front door, their leader bearing a sheet of paper.

Over the pediment of the façade broke three flags– Republican tri-colours (Green, White and Orange) on either side, and, in the centre, a large green banner inscribed in golden letters *"Poblacht na hEireann"*.* The officer with the paper, Patrick Pearse, President of the Provisional Government, began to read: "Irishmen and Irishwomen–In the name of God, and of the dead generations through whom she receives her old tradition of nationhood, Ireland, through us, summons her children to her flag, and strikes for her freedom ..."

He read on. Those, near enough to hear, who were not too dazed to comprehend, noted a striking clause: "We declare the right of the people of Ireland to the ownership of Ireland, and to the unfettered control of Irish destinies, to be sovereign and indefeasible ..."

And, after more sentences with a trumpet-like cadence, the conclusion: "Signed, on behalf of the Provisional Government, Thomas J. Clarke, Sean MacDiarmada, Thomas MacDonagh, P. H. Pearse, Eamonn Ceannt, James Connolly, Joseph Plunkett."

As the reading concluded, with a general cry of "God Save Ireland", a crackle of musketry from across the river told that the Irish Republic had been proclaimed in arms as well as in words.

Looking up at the flags gleaming in the sunshine, James Connolly, with tears of joy in his eyes, clasped the hand of the no-less delighted veteran Tom Clarke, saying: "Thanks be to God, Tom, that we have lived to see this day!"

* *Poblacht na hEireann:* Republic of Ireland.

CHAPTER XXXI

THE EASTER-WEEK RISING

The Rising took the authorities completely by surprise; but they were able to crush it after a week's hard fighting. Executions followed, and wholesale deportations. Superficially the Rising was a complete failure; but, in the end, Pearse and Connolly were vindicated. The fact that an Irish Republic had been proclaimed in arms changed completely the whole subsequent history of Ireland.

The Battle for the Republic

All things considered, the Rising, regarded merely as a military operation, quite justified itself. Decided upon impromptu, after MacNeill's countermand order had wrecked the original scheme, the rebels, at first, mustered no more than 750 men. Of these 200 were Citizen Army men—virtually its whole available strength—and 50 were an unexpected addition from the Hibernian Rifles—a corps of members of the (American) A.O.H. During the week the rebels' numbers increased to a maximum of near 2,000. Small parties, from Meath, Kildare, and Kilkenny, made their way to Dublin in time to take part. There were authentic cases of Irish soldiers in the British Army, home on leave from France, who joined in the fighting (in plain clothes) and, after the surrender, resumed their uniforms and returned to France undetected. Seventy women and girls took part as typists, cooks, and nurses—some of them taking a hand in the shooting. Madame Markievicz herself was second in command on St. Stephen's Green. The social composition of the rebel force gave ample evidence of a deep-rooted popular readiness to join an insurrection even at a moment's notice.

The tactical plan—to hold a roughly circular area enclosing Dublin Castle—was sound enough; or would have been, if their numbers had been sufficient. Lack of numbers, and confusion, caused the two major faults of execution–the failure to immobilise the telephone exchange, and the failure to capture Dublin Castle by a surprise rush at the outset. Misjudgment–a belief that the authorities would shrink from using artillery in a crowded city–had caused the headquarters to be fixed in the G.P.O., where they were exposed to shellfire from a gun-boat on the Liffey. (The shells were lobbed with great skill over the railway-bridge and the house-roofs intervening.)

By Friday night, James Connolly, who acted as military commander, was dangerously wounded in two places; and the G.P.O., fired by incendiary shells, was too well-alight to be tenable. Each of the strong-points in the circle had been surrounded. On Saturday afternoon Pearse surrendered. During the Sunday, the Commandants at the other strong posts surrendered also. Isolated parties, and snipers, held out till the Thursday following.

In a few places in the provinces, also, risings took place. Liam Mellows, in Galway, took Athenry; and was preparing an attack on Galway City when priests intervened and persuaded his men to disperse. In Co. Dublin one police party was ambushed, and the victors, led by Thomas Ashe, captured another party at Ashbourne, in Meath. The Wexford men rose out, and were encamped strongly on Vinegar Hill, when the news of the surrender induced them to give up the struggle also.

Casualties were estimated at something over three thousand. Of these, fifty-six were Volunteers killed in action. The casualties on the British side included 130 killed, of whom six were Redmond Volunteers.

The Blood-Fury of the Reactionaries

The ugliest incident was the quite unauthorised "execution" (while the Rising was still in progress) of Francis Sheehy Skeffington, Ireland's leading Socialist-pacifist.

He and two editors (of the *Searchlight* and the *Toiler* respectively) were shot, in the Portobello barracks, at the order of an officer afterwards pronounced insane. That it was "insane" to shoot a pacifist, and two editors whose journals—the one a simple scandal-sheet, the other an anti-Trade-Union rag*—were each upholders of the Castle, is true. But the "insane" Captain's attitude towards Irish rebels and Socialists—the shoot-at-sight attitude—was exactly in line with the customary thinking and talk of the Blimps and Die-hards who had pulled the wires of the Carsonite conspiracy. He was "insane" in the sense of being feeble-minded enough to take this talk at its face-value, and act accordingly.

This was shown as soon as the rebellion was over. English officers, being gentlemen, "wondered how many marks Pearse had in his pocket when he surrendered". The ignorant identification of the rebellion with *Sinn Fein* enabled the authorities to make a great show, and arrest everybody who had ever been prominent in that party. It had the advantage, too, of saving the English authorities from having to confess that the "Fenians"—whom Englishmen had supposed all dead and buried years before—had come to life in sufficient strength to put up the best fight for Ireland since '98.

Redmond, in the House, expressed "horror and detestation" at the Rising. Redmondite County and Town Councils followed suit. Sir John Maxwell, governing Ireland under martial law, ordered a trench to be dug big enough for a hundred bodies; and set his courts-martial to work.

On May 3, three of the Seven signatories to the proclamation were shot: Thomas James Clarke, Patrick Pearse, and Thomas MacDonagh. One signatory—Joseph Plunkett—and three less-known men—Edward Daly, Michael

---

* The *Toiler* was subsidised by the employers to injure Larkin and the Transport Union. One of its specialities was an endeavour to "prove" by faked photos, etc. that Larkin was an illegitimate son of Carey, the "Invincible" leader who turned informer.

O'Hanrahan, and William Pearse—were shot on May 4. Next day only one was shot, Major John MacBride (who had fought for the Boers, and knew nothing of the rising until after it had started, when he joined at once). On May 8, another signatory, Eamonn Ceannt and three others, Michael Mallin, Con Colbert, and Sean Heuston. Then next day, Thomas Kent, a Corkman, who, with his brother, had resisted arrest and killed a policeman, after his brother had been killed, was shot in Cork.

It looked as if the killing in cold blood would go on interminably. It was rumoured that ninety prisoners whose sentences only awaited confirmation had been condemned to death. Irishmen, and others, did not fail to note that the War Cabinet which confirmed the sentences included Edward Carson, and his Tory abettor, Bonar Law.

The *Manchester Guardian* said bluntly: the executions are "becoming an atrocity". Bernard Shaw, prophesying that the men executed would take their place beside Emmet and the Manchester Martyrs, protested: "I am bound to contradict any implication that I can regard as a traitor any Irishman taken in a fight for Irish Independence against the British Government, which was a fair fight in everything except the enormous odds my countrymen had to face."

Laurence Ginnell, M. P. for Westmeath, screamed "Murder" across the House, as Asquith read the list of the executed. John Dillon who had been marooned in his Dublin home by the rising, rose, semi-hysterical, to add his protest. Asquith replied tartly, that the rank and file could be spared, but the instigators could expect no mercy. The words were ominous. Two of the seven remained, Connolly and MacDermott. They were duly executed on May 12. Neither could walk to the execution post. MacDermott was crippled by rheumatoid-arthritis; Connolly had had a foot amputated, and was too weak from loss of blood to stand. He was shot seated in a chair. Reactions in Ireland had, at first, been sharply divided.

The Redmondites, trained in the O'Connell doctrine of the sinfulness of armed insurrection, were, at first, loud in condemnation. Murphy's *Independent* was so bitter that he was accused of using a public occasion to gratify his private spite against Connolly and the Transport Union. He denied this; but another of his journals, the *Irish Catholic*, was even worse. Before any executions (April 29), it said: "The movement... was as criminal as insane."

After Pearse's execution, it said: "Pearse was a man of ill-balanced mind, if not actually insane... selecting him as chief magistrate was enough to create serious doubt of the sanity of those who approved... crazy and insolent schoolmaster... extraordinary combination of rogues and fools..."

And after Connolly had been shot: "What was attempted was an act of brigandage pure and simple... no reason to lament that its perpetrators have met the fate... universally reserved for traitors."

This was not the unanimous opinion among the Hierarchy. Dr. O'Dwyer, Catholic Bishop of Limerick, was reputed to be pro-British. Possibly for this reason, Sir John Maxwell requested him to silence certain priests in his diocese who had shown sympathy for the Rebellion. Dr. O'Dwyer (May 17) refused flatly; and told Maxwell his conduct was "wantonly cruel and oppressive". He went on: "You took care that no plea for mercy should interpose on behalf of the poor young fellows who surrendered to you in Dublin. The first intimation we got of their fate was the announcement that they had been shot in cold blood. Personally I regard your action with horror; and I believe that it has outraged the conscience of the country."

Dr. O'Dwyer was right; the conscience of the country was outraged, and in England as well as Ireland. But nothing could save Casement who was hanged in Pentonville, August 3. It added to the indecency that the

Attorney-General who led for the prosecution was
F. E. Smith, who had been Carson's "Galloper", and was
afterwards to become Lord Chancellor.

Judgments on the Rising

The English Labour Movement had been, and was,
sympathetic to Home Rule. Its orthodox upper-strata
was, then, co-operating cordially in the prosecution of
the war. It easily took the view of the Redmondites–that
the Rebellion had been totally unrepresentative of the
main body of Irish opinion.

The anti-war Socialists, to the Left of the Labour Party,
were, most of them, either bewildered or condemnatory.
Ramsay MacDonald advanced the opinion that the
Rising was as "militaristic" as the Government it thought
to overthrow. The unofficial (Glasgow) Left-wing frankly
could not understand how a Socialist, like Connolly,
could have got mixed up in a Nationalist rising. Unable
to pass the crux that "a man must be either a Nationalist,
or an Internationalist", the editor of the Glasgow *Forward* had to confess–"it remains a mystery".

It was no mystery to the small group of militant Marx-
ists whom Connolly had helped to train. They had accepted Connolly's doctrine that Internationalism is not
the negation of Nationalism; and least of all when the
Nationalism is that of a subject people. And they had–
though none of them knew it–a mighty ally in–Lenin.

To those who sought to belittle the Easter Rising as a
mere "putsch", he replied that this was "monstrously
pedantic":

> "To imagine that a social revolution is conceiv-
> able without revolts of small nations in the Colonies
> and in Europe, without outbursts from a section of
> the petit-bourgeois, with all its prejudices–without
> the movement of the non-class-conscious proletarian
> and semi-proletarian masses against the oppression

of the landlords, the church, the monarchy, the foreign yoke, etc.–to imagine that is tantamount to repudiating social revolution.

"The misfortune of the Irish is that they rose prematurely, when the European revolt of the proletariat had not yet matured. Capitalism is not so harmoniously built that the various springs of rebellion can immediately merge into one, of their own accord, without reverses, and defeats."

Lenin: *Selected Works*, Vol. V., pp. 301-306.

Connolly's vindication came when, nine months after his death, Tsardom fell; and when, nine months after that, the Red Flag flew, triumphant, over the Kremlin.

CHAPTER XXXII

THE TRANSITION TO A NEW CRISIS

At the outbreak of war, in 1914, public opinion in Nationalist Ireland had been—on the surface—overwhelmingly on the side of the Redmondite Nationalist Party, and in sympathy with England in its war difficulty. How greatly that public opinion had been changed was revealed in the election which immediately followed the war, in December 1918. In that election the Nationalist Party was virtually wiped out.

The process of that immense turn-over of public opinion is examined in this chapter.

The British Government and Ireland

It is often said that if the British Government had shown clemency to the leaders of the Easter-Week Rising, subsequent events might (and would) have been radically different. To say this is to miss a great truth and, in addition, to make a false assumption.

The false assumption is that the Government in 1916 was still the Government which had forced the Home Rule Act to the stage of Royal Assent, over the heads of the House of Lords; and had done so despite the threats of the Tory-Orange counter-revolutionary conspiracy. It was nothing of the kind. The counter-revolutionary conspirators had taken advantage of the war emergency to force their way into the Government on their own terms; and, as events proved, Lloyd George and his Radical followers had capitulated to them from (1) fear of socialism; and (2) traditional Nonconformist dislike of "Papistry".

Between them they had evolved the device which would enable them to pretend that they had "conceded" Home Rule, while in reality they were conceding nothing: the device of Partition.

But for the war-begotten need to conciliate the U.S.A., the repression after Easter Week would have been bloodier than it was, and Home Rule would never-more have been heard of. The sense of this radical reorientation of the English Government, coupled with a feeling that the Redmondite Party was either a con-senting-party to the reorientation, or too stupid to notice it, went a long way towards effecting the revulsion of public opinion in Ireland. The treatment of the prison-ers; the war-time censorship; and finally the attempt to impose Conscription in 1918 were all so many confirma-tions of the fact that the English Government had be-come essentially counter-revolutionary, and prepared for a fresh conquest of Ireland.

The Fenian Dead

The "great truth" that is missed in the view we are combating, is that the normal demand of the Irish Na-tion is, and has been since Tone and the United Irish-men, the demand for complete Independence. Irishmen have not always been conscious of this; and they have for long periods been willing to confine their demands within the limits of a constitutional demand for "Re-peal" or "Home Rule". But, instinctively, the mass of Irishmen have valued these things because, and so far as, they saw in them means of approximating nearer to-wards the Independence they felt, intuitively, to be the only normal status for an Irish Nation.

That is why the popular heroes of Ireland—especially among the young—have always been "the men who fought, and died for Ireland". Patrick Pearse expressed this truth in his speech over the grave of O'Donovan Rossa in the middle of 1915: "I hold it a Christian thing, as O'Donovan Rossa held it, to hate evil, to hate un-truth, to hate oppression, and hating them, to strive to overthrow them. Our foes are strong, and wise, and wary; but ... they cannot undo the miracles of God who ripens in the heart of the young men the seeds sown by the young men of a former generation. And the seeds sown by the men of '65 and '67 are coming to their miraculous ripening to-day.

"Rulers and Defenders of the Realm had need to be wary if they would guard against such processes. Life springs from death and from the graves of patriot men and women spring nations.

"The Defenders of the Realm have worked well in secret and in the open. They think they have pacified Ireland. They think they have purchased half of us and intimidated the other half. They think they have foreseen everything, think they have provided against everything; but—the fools! the fools! the fools!

"They have left us our Fenian dead, and while Ireland holds these graves, Ireland, unfree, shall never be at peace!"

And Pearse's true words gained added truth and additional point when his name, also, with that of his colleagues, was added to the list of the Fenian Dead.

The Emergence of a New Party

The English Authorities aided the elimination of the Parliamentary Party by the wholesale character of its arrests and deportations after the Rising. Whether they herded them as "convicted prisoners" in gaols, or as unconvicted prisoners in concentration camps, the result was the same. The inspiration of a bravely-fought battle nerved the prisoners to struggle unflinchingly against every attempt to treat them with humiliation. Struggle begot solidarity, which found expression in organisation. The gaols and the concentration camps were so many training schools for a new party: and when the untried prisoners were released, at Christmas 1916, they dispersed to their homes in every part of Ireland, convinced

Republicans, eager to be at work building local organisations for a new uprising.

Six months later, in compliance with American opinion, which it was now imperative to placate, the convicted prisoners were released also—to be received with demonstrations of frantic enthusiasm by the people, who now realised that it was the Men of Easter Week and not their Parliamentarian enemies who had truly represented the will and interest of Ireland.

The men first released at once set to work to build an organisation. A Prisoners' Aid Society was a good beginning: the Gaelic League branches were good rallying centres for a start. The Volunteers began to re-form, and to parade in uniform—but armed only with hurleys and sticks—in spite of proclamations and arrests. The convicted prisoners were in great demand, after their release, as speakers at meetings and demonstrations. Soon the English authorities were at work arresting speakers for "creating disaffection" and Volunteers for "illegal drilling".

The new mood of the Nation showed itself in the attitude of the arrested men. They refused to recognise the jurisdiction of the court; and, in gaol, demanded the treatment of political prisoners, answering refusal with hunger-strike. The death of one of these prisoners, Thomas Ashe (distinguished in Easter Week) evoked great indignation; and brought an immense concourse to his funeral, which was made a military one.

Three volleys were fired over the grave. Michael Collins (now the leader of the revived and powerful I.R.B.) said shortly: "Those volleys we have just heard are the only speech it is fitting to make above the grave of a dead Fenian."

Bowing to the inevitable, the authorities conceded "political" status to the prisoners. Still the struggle went on. Since the English insisted upon calling the Republicans *"Sinn Feiners"* they accepted the hint and revived the

Sinn Fein party; but with an entirely new constitution and programme. De Valera, the only surviving Commandant of Easter Week, was elected its President at the Annual Convention in October 1917, Arthur Griffith accepting the position of Vice-President. New ground was broken by (1) the decision to maintain the Volunteers; (2) by the tacit adoption of a Republican standpoint, and (3) by the tacit decision that the Volunteers would resist forcibly any attempt to impose conscription. The hegemony of the new *Sinn Fein* Executive, as virtually the Government of the Irish Nation, was recognised by the Gaelic League, and by all the other Irish National organisations.

Lloyd George's Circus

All this time a "Convention", arranged by Lloyd George (then the Premier) and composed of hand-picked politicians and prelates, was meeting in Dublin to attempt to reach an agreed modification of the Home Rule Act which had been hung up "for the duration". It was clear, from the start, that the Convention would never be allowed to reach any conclusion but one–a sharply restricted form of Home Rule, for twenty-six counties only. Redmond himself was repudiated by the Parliamentary Party delegation when he proposed a compromise which might have averted partition.

Worn down by illness, disappointment, and grief at the loss of his son and his brother (both killed in France), Redmond withdrew, cut to the heart–only to die ten days later.

The Convention at last presented a "majority" report qualified by no fewer than seven minority reports. Lloyd George hailed the result with delight–since it "proved" to his satisfaction that "the Irish can't ever agree!"

Lloyd George discovered that the Irish could agree most notably, when, in the middle of 1918, he attempted to impose conscription in Ireland. Beaten in the House on this issue, the Parliamentary Party decided to "go *Sinn Fein*"–and left Westminster in a body.

A conference met at the Mansion House, Dublin, attended by representatives of *Sinn Fein*, Labour, the Nationalist Party, and the (Healy-O'Brien) "All for Ireland" Party, and the delegates adopted unanimously a pledge to join in common action against conscription. The Hierarchy, and the College of Maynooth, concurred with the decision.

Thus Lloyd George's design (which was to smash up the reviving Volunteers) did more than fail: it united all sections of Nationalist Ireland in resistance.

Lloyd George fell back upon the trick of "discovering" a German plot. All the leaders of *Sinn Fein* who could be picked up were hustled into gaol on a charge of "associating with the enemy". The warrant for the arrest of Michael Collins could not be served. He had begun his life on the run which was to last till the Truce of 1921.

Labour showed its determination, and power, by calling a one-day General Strike, which was observed with scrupulous fidelity everywhere in Ireland outside the Unionist areas of the North. Collins set to work to build a General Staff which would direct the resistance of the Volunteers to every attempt to conscript or disarm them. Whatever the reason, the attempt to impose conscription was delayed, on various pretexts, until the ending of the war made it unnecessary.

The General Election of 1918

A number of by-elections, since Easter Week, might have been taken as a warning of what was coming; the were, however, treated as "wartime" elections which "prove nothing". Count Plunkett (a man of inchoate views, but the father of one of the Seven of Easter Week) was elected for North Roscommon in a three-cornered contest. Joe MacGuinness (then in gaol) was elected for Longford. A much sharper test was the election, for Clare, to fill the vacancy created by the death of W. E. Redmond. De Valera (sentenced for life) was elected by a two-to-one majority. W. T. Cosgrave (an Easter-Week man, then in gaol) was elected for Kilkenny. The Parliamentary Party went to the polls in December 1918, tensed for the fight of its life.

Twenty-five seats were surrendered to the Republicans without a struggle: Tim Healy and William O'Brien being among those who surrendered. The rest went down like corn before the sickle. John Dillon, the new Party leader, went down before a two-to-one majority in Mayo, his home county, which he had represented without a break since 1880. In the end, of the 83 seats they had held in 1914, the Party retained 7; and one of these was in England—and four of these seats, located in Ulster, they owed, in part, to an electoral agreement with *Sinn Fein*. In the twenty-six counties they won only Waterford, where John Redmond's son was elected to succeed his father. Two (new seats) were won by the Tories. The rest were unbroken *Sinn Fein* (that is, Republican).

It was noted that amid the yells of "Up the Rebels!" "Up *Sinn Fein!*" and "Up the Republic!" that greeted the results, there were also cries of "Remember Parnell!"

English journalists, when Parliament met, noted with a pang that the benches below the gangway on the opposition side, which had been the "Irish Quarter" since 1885, were now occupied by an overflow of the Tories unable to find room on the Government benches.

It was a Nemesis without equal in the whole history of parliamentary elections.

CHAPTER XXXIII

ANGLO-IRISH WAR AND THE TREATY

The Republicans, elected in 1918, met in Dublin and constituted themselves the Governing Body of "the Republic established in Easter Week". From this gesture arose an Anglo-Irish War—fought with intense savagery from the English side, and stubborn bitterness from the Irish side. A Truce (July 1921), followed by a Treaty (December 1921), ended one war—but opened another between the acceptors and the rejectors of the Treaty.

In this Chapter we trace summarily the salient aspects of this struggle.*

Dáil Eireann

The completeness of the Republican victory at the polls was greater even than it seemed. Every endeavour had been made by the English authorities to prevent it. Election meetings were prohibited; election agents and speakers were arrested; election addresses were censored or suppressed; election literature was confiscated. Warnings against electing *Sinn Fein* candidates were posted, and scattered from aeroplanes. Of the 73 Republicans elected, 36 were in gaol, and a score were either "on the run" or in the U.S.A. evading arrest. In these circumstances, to poll two-thirds of all the voters in Ireland for Republican candidates was doubly decisive.

Those of the elected who were at liberty decided to convoke an Irish National Assembly. Everyone elected in Ireland in 1918 was invited regardless of Party. Only Republicans responded; and the twenty-seven of them

* In this work it is not possible to do more than summarise very broadly. The reader can find all the details, and all the relevant documents, set out clearly in Dorothy MacArdle's excellent work *The Irish Republic*.

who were available met in the Mansion House, Dublin, on January 21, 1919, and constituted themselves *Dáil Eireann* (the Assembly of Ireland). A declaration was adopted affirming: That Ireland is "a sovereign and independent nation"; that a Republic *(Sáorstat Eireann)* had been established in Easter Week, 1916, of which the *Dáil* constituted itself the heir and continuation. The *Dáil* adopted a "Democratic Programme", which showed profoundly the influence of Connolly and Pearse, and which some members, later, found "communistic".

An Acting President was appointed (Cathal Brugha) who had power to appoint ministers—it being understood that the post of President was left open for Eamon de Valera, then in gaol. (His escape was being contrived at that moment by Michael Collins.) On March 5, all prisoners and internees were released.

The situation then was that there were two "Government" Authorities in Ireland: one, *Dáil Eireann*, backed by the moral authority of a majority of the people, the other that of the English Authorities, operating from Dublin Castle, who possessed the physical force (police, constabulary, army and navy) to impose their decrees. The struggle that ensued was, therefore, in essence, an attempt by the English authorities, through their armed forces, to coerce the Irish people into withdrawing the moral authority they had given to *Dáil Eireann*. Subsequent electoral tests marked the result of their efforts.

In municipal elections (January 1920), out of 126 town and city councils, 72 went to Republicans, 26 to a Republican-Nationalist coalition, and 29 only to the "English" (Unionists). In elections (June 1920) for County and Rural District Councils, and Guardians, 28 counties out of 33, 182 Rural Districts out of 206, and 138 Boards of Guardians out of 154 returned Republican majorities.

At a general election in May 1921 (of which mention will be made later), there were elected in the Twenty-Six Counties 124 Republicans and 4 Unionists; in the

Six Counties, in this same election, there were elected 6 Republicans, 6 Nationalists, and 40 Unionists. This gave an All-Ireland total of 130 Republicans, 6 Nationalists, and 44 Unionists.

Tried by the electoral test, the Irish people gave their choice to the Republic persistently, and refused it to the English authorities. This was all the more emphatic because, from the middle of 1919 onwards to July 1921, a ferocious war between the forces of the Crown and those of the Republic reduced all Ireland to a chaos.

The War with the Army

The first phase of this war was an attempt by the British to prevent the *Dáil* from establishing any machinery of Government. The *Dáil* itself, and all its subsidiaries—including a system of arbitration courts it was able to establish in nearly every county in Ireland—were proclaimed "illegal assemblies". The Loan, called for by the *Dáil*, was treated as "seditious". Newspapers which published advertisements of the Loan were suppressed; it was an offence to possess or distribute any literature connected therewith; and every endeavour was made to locate the places (and names) in which the (much-over-subscribed) Loan was banked. Virtually everybody, of any prominence in the Republican movement, lived, in this period, either on the run or in prison.

"Military" operations on the Republican side grew out of this constant harrying and pursuit of Republicans. To achieve their end the English authorities needed an elaborate apparatus of spies, informers, and "intelligence officers". The backbone of this force was supplied by the R.I.C., which, in the rural areas, knew everybody and everything that was going on. In addition the Authorities had their usual fringe of slum elements at the bottom and English officers at the top.

To meet, check, and, finally, to defeat this force was

the work undertaken by Michael Collins as Director of Intelligence, operating with a force of specially-selected Volunteers as a striking arm, and a network of counter-espionage agents which grew to be as numerous and as ramified as that of the English. The "execution" of key men in the English espionage service aroused intense fury among counter-revolutionary English politicians, and their press. It was justified by Collins on the ground that, while the English could replace their soldiers almost interminably, these key men, with their exceptional knowledge, and their ability to identify particular individuals, could not be replaced. In the end Collins succeeded in paralysing the whole English intelligence service in Ireland.

Concurrently with the War of the contending Intelligence Services, the Volunteers developed a series of raids for arms on isolated police-posts, stores, etc., out of which developed a succession of fiercely-fought battles. In this struggle it soon became apparent that the Volunteers—who, from early in 1919, came to be known as the "Army of the Irish Republic"; or, popularly, the I.R.A.—had the support of the people, man, woman and child. The I.R.A., when hard-pressed, could always rely upon assistance; the R.I.C., and the military, could always expect obstruction. This passive, social pressure produced the result of wholesale resignations from the R.I.C.; and this, in turn, produced a corresponding diminution in the effectiveness of the Crown forces. Troops from England, ignorant of the country, and totally unacquainted with the people, were no substitute for men who knew every path and track, and every individual, for twenty miles around. As their sense of impotence grew, the troops degenerated into an undisciplined *banditti* of alien invaders; bent, perpetually, upon loot and reprisals.

This led (January 1920) to the imposition of a Curfew Order in the towns, and the official adoption of a policy of terrorism, operated (from March 1920) by the "Black-and-Tans" and "Auxiliaries".

Those were both officially off-shoots of the R.I.C. The first was a special grade of temporary constables, mostly recruited in England, and chosen for preference from the "tough" class. A criminal record was a recommendation; men imprisoned for crimes of violence had their sentences remitted if they volunteered for service in the "specials". They were paid 10s. a day (with separation allowance) and all found.

The Auxiliaries were "Cadets" recruited from ex-officers in the Army, Navy and Air Force. They operated as a separate force of "shock troops". Individually, they ranked as the equal of senior-sergeants in the R.I.C.; their pay, rations and allowances were double those of the specials—who came to be called "Black-and-Tans" because of the haphazard mixture of English khaki and R.I.C. black in their uniforms and equipment.

The political significance of the institution of this Black-and-Tan force—which term came to include, in practice, the Auxies also, and which, it will be noted, had exactly the same social composition as that of the S.A. and the S.S. force of Nazi-terrorism, and that of Mussolini's *fascisti*—was that, for diplomatic reasons, Lloyd George and his counter-revolutionary backers found it imperative to pretend that nothing was called for in Ireland beyond "police measures". To have agreed with the demand of the military commanders to proclaim Martial Law would have been an admission that Ireland was in general revolt; and that, therefore, the real position of the English authorities was that of an enemy invader in hostile occupation. The Black-and-Tans were, deliberately, a "fascist" device—which Mussolini, Hitler and others copied–to conceal the fact that, morally, the English invaders were back where they had been in 1169.

The struggle that developed shocked the English people profoundly, and revolted the whole world. Murder, arson, torture of prisoners, rape, and the systematic beating-up and looting of whole areas developed into a routine of monotonous horror. The I.R.A. fought back with increasing resolution; and, in the struggle, developed into a force which became able to meet, and defeat, parties of Black-and-Tans and Auxies on equal terms. The primary I.R.A. tactic was that of the ambush; to which the "Tans" replied by beating-up, looting and destroying the habitations in the area where the ambush occurred. This, in course, drove more recruits to the I.R.A.; and so the struggle developed. The work done by Liam Mellows, as Director of Purchases, in supplying the I.R.A. with arms–purchased abroad and smuggled into Ireland–was an invaluable contribution to the Republican war-effort.

As the R.I.C. dwindled, it retreated from the outlying districts. In these areas, Republican Courts were established, whose decisions were accepted by the people. Order was maintained in these areas, and punishments imposed by the Courts were enforced by the Republican police (I.R.A. men detailed for this duty). These proofs of the impotence of the English authorities, and the popular acceptance of the authority of the *Dáil*, reported in the press of the world, roused the counter-revolutionaries to fury. Into those areas advanced flying-squads of Black-and-Tans, in armoured cars, resolved to loot, burn, smash, destroy, arrest and kill. If they were resisted–or, more usually, were ambushed on their way back–more flying squads repeated the performance, with similar results.

The Black-and-Tans had all retreated to barracks in the bigger towns–from which they emerged only at the risk of attack and ambush in open day–and the gaols were crammed with prisoners arrested for conducting Republican Courts, or simply on suspicion, when (on July 11, 1921) a Truce was agreed upon by Lloyd George and Eamon De Valera, as a preliminary to negotiations for a Treaty.

While the Tan-War raged, two events of great political significance occurred: (1) A Government of Ireland Act (December, 1920); and (2) Organised pogroms in Belfast.

The Government of Ireland Act (1920).

Faced with multiplying political difficulties on every side, Lloyd George, in 1920, made a gesture towards settling the Irish Question by introducing the long-deferred amendment of the Home Rule Act (1914). This Government of Ireland Act (1920) represented a compromise which the "Ulster" representatives accepted with reluctance. It conceded a measure of Home Rule to the Twenty-Six Counties (called "Southern Ireland") and imposed another measure of Home Rule on the Six Counties (called "Northern Ireland"). The die-hards who wanted no Home Rule at all accepted the compromise only because they calculated it would make Home Rule unworkable in the Twenty-Six Counties, by restricting their economic and fiscal resources to an almost exclusively agricultural region.

The Act included a provision that the two parliaments might, if they chose, set up an All-Ireland Council to which each might concede powers of common concern. In this way they could achieve a reunited Ireland. This was merely eye-wash for Americans, English Labour Party men, and other political innocents, who did not know (as Lloyd George did) that the faction dominant in the Six Counties would never consent to any such reunion since they had a vested interest in Ireland's unsettlement

416

Dáil Eireann, as such, took no notice of the Act. But the *Sinn Fein* Party resolved to use the elections as a demonstration of national unity. The result was that the only non-Republican candidates elected were the four allotted to Trinity College. No contests took place. No one would accept nomination against a Republican.

The Belfast Pogroms

As a running-commentary upon the Tan-War and Lloyd George's manœuvres with the Government of Ireland Act, Belfast staged a series of pogroms, aimed at driving the Catholics out of the industrial area completely. Their opening (July 21, 1920) coincided with the introduction of the Black-and-Tan Terror; and they had been preceded by inflammatory propaganda meetings, in which it was suggested that the Catholics were "creeping-in", and "were taking away the jobs of Protestants". The beginning of the post-war unemployment crisis gave point to the oratory; and there is no reason to doubt that what followed was organised, as well as deliberately incited.

A corps similar to the Black-and-Tans had been recruited as "occasional special Constables" by the Six-County Government, members of this corps, recruited fom the hooligan element in Belfast, were in the front of the mobs which, carrying Union Jacks, attacked the Catholic quarter—looting and burning down the shops and houses of Catholics. Every Catholic was driven from the shipyards; every Catholic worker from the factories where "Protestants" predominated. Any attempt at self-defence was crushed with stones, bludgeons, and revolver or rifle-fire. Only after four days did the military interfere. Twenty-two civilians were killed, and 188 were known to be severely wounded.

The pogrom extended to Lisburn on August 23-24; forty Catholic houses and shops were destroyed. Then the pogrom was renewed in Belfast, August 28-September 1, and similar barbarities were enacted. Apart from scores of killed, and hundreds of wounded, 9,000 were driven from their employment, 30,000 were rendered destitute, and thousands were rendered homeless into the bargain.

Carson's cynical comment virtually admitted Orange-Tory complicity in the pogrom. He said that the Catholics "had only to take an oath of allegiance to the King, and pledge their loyalty to the Empire, and the trouble would cease instantly". Which means, if it means anything, that the Belfast Catholics were to be used as hostages in the war for the new English conquest of Ireland.

The resignation of 148 Irish magistrates; mutinies in the police force, and of three hundred men of the Connaught Rangers in India–these were eloquent, practical comments on the policy pursued in Ireland.

The pogroms broke out again in Belfast in June 1921, after the elections to the Northern Ireland Parliament; in which, as an Ulster-Tory M.P. said, "too many *Sinn Fein* votes were cast". The riots were almost entirely the work of Special Constables. A score of Catholics were killed, and another 150 families were rendered homeless.

These atrocities, and the steadfast solidarity in the face of every barbarity of the Nationalist population of Ireland, had a profound effect upon democratic opinion in England as well as throughout the world.

The Truce and Negotiations

The Truce of July 1921, and the protracted negotiations which followed, were forced upon both sides by material and moral circumstances. On the Irish side the chief difficulty was the economic chaos into which the country had been thrown by the ravages of the Black-and-Tans, and by the stubborn resistance of the Irish railwaymen and transport workers–who persistently refused to transport troops or war materials. A virtual cessation of railway traffic had resulted; and as, in the course of their defensive operations, the I.R.A. had blown up any number of bridges, and–by trenches and mines–had made the main roads impassable in large areas, the result was a chaos which could not possibly be endured for long.

In addition, the I.R.A. had, virtually, exhausted their supplies of ammunition. They had never been able to put more than 2,000 men in the field at any one time–though they had more than twenty times that number of men to draw upon. Now it was growing difficult to maintain in the field even so few as 2,000.

On the English side a rapidly-intensifying demand for a Truce and a Treaty arose from every democratic quarter, the Communist Party being most active. The Labour Party and Trade Union rank and file joined with the Communist Party and the exiles' organisation–the Irish Self-Determination League–to force the hands of their party chiefs; and they, in turn, brought pressure to bear upon the Government. In addition, a number of General officers, of high rank, had refused to lend themselves any longer to what was being done in Ireland.

General Crozier, appointed to command the Auxies, found to his disgust that his attempt to impose a decent, soldierly behaviour on the force was constantly thwarted from "higher up" (*i.e.* Dublin Castle). Prisoners were tortured and murdered in Dublin Castle itself. A Galway priest–who had been invited to America to give evidence of an attempt by the Auxies to make a raping assault upon a nunnery–was murdered by the Auxies and his body was thrown into a bog. A plot was on foot to murder the Catholic Bishop of Killaloe. And all General Crozier's enquiries into those responsible for those deeds were blocked by the "men higher up". When he found that twenty-five Cadets–whom he had dismissed the force for looting-had all been reinstated, to

419

"keep their mouths shut", General Crozier resigned and could not be persuaded to retract his resignation. Then General Macready, Commander-in-Chief in Ireland, reported, in May 1921, that nothing less than Martial Law over the whole Twenty-Six Counties, with suppression of Civil Courts and all newspapers, and the commandeering of all transport would be effective. To do that would require, he said, a new army and the replacement of nearly the whole of the troops, commanders and staffs.

For the English Government this was an impossible situation. Economic obligation compelled them to bow to public opinion in the U.S.A. and in the Dominions, and in each case this public opinion was largely swayed by the Irish-exile element in the population. Political insecurity compelled them to take notice of public opinion in England, which—under pressure of world chaos and the economic crisis—was rapidly polarising into two great camps of revolution and counter-revolution. An attempt to raise an army openly for a military conquest of Ireland would have immediately precipitated a crisis by ruining England's financial credit in the U.S.A. and the Dominions.

Negotiations were, therefore, opened up with De Valera and *Dáil Eireann*, and, later, with the plenipotentiaries of the Irish Republic, headed by Arthur Griffith and Michael Collins (for whose arrest a reward of £10,000 had been on offer for months). Negotiations were prolonged until December 6, 1921, when a Treaty was signed by the representatives on both sides.

The Treaty of 1921-22

What went on behind the scenes of the Treaty negotiations is not known. There are indications that, at first, Lloyd George and certain leading English Tories were ready to concede all Ireland a "Dominion" status from which the Six Counties, or some portion thereof, might exclude themselves if they wished. There are indications that this attitude was modified, under pressure from the counter-revolutionary faction in the Tory ranks—which represented the more aggressive elements of the Finance-Capitalist oligarchy which had taken alarm from the Bolshevik Revolution; and which was, even then, preparing to crush the forces of the organised workers in England. This faction (which later on brushed aside both Lloyd George, and the "moderate" Bonar Law, to rule through Stanley Baldwin and Neville Chamberlain) saw in open war in Ireland, and the raising of an army for that war, their best chance to pull off the *coup d'état* they were resolved upon. Consequently the Irish representatives were presented with an ultimatum of accepting the Treaty offered or—unlimited war within three days. The delegation reluctantly gave way.

The Treaty conceded virtually complete self-government to the Twenty-Six Counties immediately; with the handing over of Dublin Castle, and the withdrawal of all British troops, police and officials. It gave the Six Counties an option of coming into this arrangement, but did not insist upon their doing so. It did insist upon an Oath of Allegiance (to the King and Empire) to be taken by the Members of Parliament and officials of *Saorstát Eireann** and as a concession included a clause providing for the revision of the "boundary" between "Northern Ireland" and the *Saorstát* (translated literally as Free State "in accordance with the wishes of the population".

There is not the slightest reason to question either the honesty, the patriotism, or the courage of the Irish delegates who signed the Treaty. The utmost that can be said in their condemnation is that, not being professional politicians, they were out-witted by such past-masters in

* *Saorstát Eireann:* This was the translation of the term "Irish Republic" preferred by the best Gaelic scholars. Lloyd George accepted its literal translation but not its original implication. It was suggested sardonically, at the time, that the new state should be called "The Royal Irish Republic".

chicane as Lloyd George, Bonar Law, Birkenhead ("Galloper" Smith), and Austen Chamberlain.

The protraction of the negotiations told all in favour of the English politicians. The whole world was war-weary; and the more men, in Ireland and out of it, grew accustomed to the peace, the less they were inclined for a resumption of war. Whoever was responsible for such a resumption would start with a heavy handicap of public condemnation. Therefore, the English negotiators skilfully tricked the Irish Delegates—and *Dáil Eireann*—into the position of accepting or rejecting the Treaty on the purely formal ground (as it appeared to all Englishmen) of the Oath of Allegiance. The real objection, Partition, was evaded; in part because "Northern Ireland" was already an accomplished fact; and, in part, because it was believed that the Boundary Clause, honestly worked, would reduce the territory of Northern Ireland to dimensions which would be economically and politically incapable of separate existence.

Dáil Eireann after a prolonged debate accepted the Treaty by a narrow majority.

Pro and Anti-Treaty Civil War

Debates on the Treaty generated intense bitterness; and this found expression in a split which eventuated in a Civil War between the forces of the "Free State" and of the "Republic".

Formally, debate centred on the Oath—which casuists and ideologues held to be a violation of the Oath of Fidelity to the Republic already taken by the *Dáil* and the I.R.A. More concretely, it turned on the issue of Partition which, it was contended, the Treaty conceded in principle—leaving its rectification to problematical chances A renewal of the pogrom in Belfast pointed the objection

These grounds of ideological and political division were reinforced and developed into an absolute split by a sharp conflict of economic interests, centering upon the Land Hunger, which was a by-product of the stoppage of emigration to the U.S.A., the Dominions, and England—a result, first, of war-caused prohibitions, then of the post-war unemployment crisis.

As we noted earlier, the Land Purchase Acts presupposed for their ameliorative effect the constant functioning of the emigrant-ship. During the war its place was filled by recruiting. Some 500,000 men from the Twenty-Six Counties served in the British Forces during the war: their demobilisation, in face of the economic situation in England, and in the world generally, precipitated an intense crisis.

In 1919 a land-seizing movement had sprung up in the West of Ireland. The action of the *Dáil Eireann* land courts, and of the Republican police, in suppressing this movement created an intense resentment which helped to swell resistance to the Treaty, which, for its part, was supported strongly by the more bourgeois elements (including especially the much-hated "ranchers"). The line-up was between the actually or potentially Land Hungry, supported by Republican intellectuals and urban revolutionaries, on one side; and the urban bourgeoisie, the State functionaries, the landowners, and the upper strata of the peasantry on the other. The skilled-labour elements—and the Labour Party generally—were paralysed by division.

Involved in the struggle was a conflict which had profound consequences—that between the I.R.B.—which under Devoy's influence was pro-Treaty—and the majority section of the I.R.A. which was anti-Treaty. The resulting dissipation of the moral authority of the "Fenian" body told heavily on the side of disintegration and disillusioned-pessimism in the years that followed.

The formal cause of the Civil War was the refusal of a majority section of the I.R.A., led by Rory O'Connor and Liam Mellows, to submit to the authority of the Free State Government. Its real cause was the fact of Partition; and the response of the Six-County Government to the Treaty.

When the terms of the Treaty were made public, Orange zealots fastened on the terms of the Boundary Clause to raise a scare. The "inner ring" had private assurances, from their die-hard confederates in England, that all would be well; but it was "good politics" to let the zealots of "No Popery" work up as much excitement as they could.

A law was passed by the Northern Ireland Parliament imposing severe penalties for possessing fire-arms without a licence; and upon membership of any "seditious" association. A new category of full-time Special Constables was established and equipped; the number of the "occasional" Specials was increased. Any member of an Orange Lodge, or Unionist Association, could get an arms-licence for the asking; no Catholic could get one in any circumstances. Merely applying for one was a ground for his arrest and detention "on suspicion".

The ground was prepared for a pogrom by a search of the Catholic quarter of Belfast ostensibly for concealed arms. As a result of previous pogroms the quarter was densely overcrowded. Families were living in sheds, and in shacks improvised in back-gardens, and on every spot of waste ground—as well as in halls and church crypts. When the Specials had satisfied themselves that the quarter was destitute of means of defence, the word was given. "Patriotic" Orange mobs marched in with revolvers, rifles and machine-guns and set to work to destroy the entire quarter.

The Catholics fought back as well as they could. A

party of young Protestant-Socialists beat off a murderous attack upon a convent (which had been fired) and helped to extinguish the flames. A few I.R.A. men from surrounding districts fought their way in to take part in the defence. Then the military were called in to fire upon the I.R.A. The military, however, quelled the riot, temporarily; but as often as the soldiers retired riot broke out again–and again! With brazen effrontery Orange apologists blamed the whole trouble upon *"Sinn Fein"* gunmen.

When the riots finally died down, it was estimated that another 9,000 Catholics had been driven from their work, and the number rendered homeless had been increased to 23,000. Altogether between June 21, 1920, and June 21, 1922, 428 had been killed and 1,766 wounded.

A reprisal, which excited much "horror" in the Tory press, was the shooting–on his own doorstep in London, by two Irish ex-servicemen–of Sir Henry Wilson, Chief of the Imperial General Staff, and Chief Military Adviser to the Government of Northern Ireland. Wilson was generally believed to have instigated the pogroms from the first.

The actual occasion of the Civil War between the Free Staters and the Republicans was the resolve of Rory O'Connor to lead the I.R.A. into the Six Counties for a war of reprisals.

O'Connor had taken possession of the Four Courts in Dublin as his headquarters and had begun to commandeer lorries for his raid upon Belfast. The English Government, alarmed at what might happen, urged the Free State Government to dislodge the "anarchists". Finally Griffith and Collins, the latter shortly to become Commander in Chief of the "Free State Army", ordered the attack on the Four Courts, which began at 4 a.m. on June 28, 1922, with the aid of artillery lent by the British Government.

The civil war between the Griffith-Collins Free State Government forces, and the "irregular" I.R.A. led by

Liam Lynch, which a few months later declared De Valera once more President of the Irish Republic, was fought with intense bitterness on both sides; and by men who had become largely dehumanised by the prolonged struggle with the Black-and-Tans. The Free State Government had the advantage, in that its army consisted mainly of trained ex-servicemen, and they had unlimited supplies of arms and ammunition. The Republicans suffered the disability of the lack of any real popular support. A tragic aspect of the struggle was the large number of men, distinguished in the Anglo-Irish War, who were killed either in action, by execution, or "trying to escape". Collins, Liam Lynch, Rory O'Connor, Mellows, Cathal Brugha and Erskine Childers are among this number.

At noon, on April 30, 1923, the Republican Chief of Staff ordered the cessation of offensive operations. On May 24, this was followed by an order to Cease Fire, to conceal all arms and ammunition, and disperse. There was no formal surrender. But the civil war was at an end. Attempts to revive it which have been made from time to time have found no popular backing; except, occasionally, from the exasperated minority in the Six Counties.

The struggle when transferred by De Valera to the plane of political contest met with much greater success.

Partition Consummated

When the civil war ended the Free State Government, now headed by W. T. Cosgrave—Arthur Griffith had died suddenly, shortly before Collins had been killed in action—made approaches for the appointment of a Boundary Commission.

The Northern Ireland Government refused to consider the question. The English Government eventually appointed a representative and nominated one for the Six Counties. These two, with a representative of the Free State, constituted a Boundary Commission.

After a great parade of "investigation" the Commission let it be known that "by a majority" it had decided to act on two principles (1) Northern Ireland had been established for "so long" that changes were undesirable; (2) nothing should be done to worsen the economic position of Northern Ireland. In short, the Treaty-stipulated consideration, "the wishes of the inhabitants", was to be ignored; and the net outcome would be that the Boundary would be altered, if at all, to add territory and population to Northern Ireland.

Even the British Government was staggered by this exhibition of brass-faced Orange bias; accordingly it seized the chance to drive a bargain with the Free State Government, which included the cancellation of the Boundary Clause altogether.

Thus in 1925 Partition was finally consummated.

CHAPTER XXXIV

ECONOMIC WAR: CONCLUSIONS TO DATE

Eamon De Valera returned to power in 1932, and at once opened a struggle to remove, as far as could be done without precipitating a war, all the constitutional and financial ties binding Ireland to England. This policy was replied to by an Economic War, which was ended in 1938 by an Agreement, conceding all De Valera's claims except the vital ones of (1) undoing the Partition; and (2) recognising Ireland's Independence.

The refusal to concede these vital points was the ultimate cause of the Neutrality of *Eire* during World War II; the need to concede these demands—and so to complete the negation of the English Conquest of Ireland—is proved by the whole course of the history surveyed in this book.

De Valera Returns to Power

In 1927, De Valera and the Republicans abandoned their attitude of doctrinaire refusal to "recognise" the Irish Free State and took, under protest, the Oath, and their seats in the *Dáil*. A rump of Republicans (claiming to be the original *Dáil*, the old I.R.A., and *Sinn Fein*) refused to support De Valera in this course. He accordingly, with his supporters, founded a new party, the *Fianna Fáil* (Soldiers of Destiny) and by persistent propaganda, from the view of the urban and rural petit-bourgeoisie, secured, in 1932, a majority position in the *Dáil*.

On becoming Premier he at once notified the English Government that he intended to abolish the Oath of Allegiance and to withhold payment of the Annuities due to the Land Commissioners under the various Land Purchase Acts (1880-1909). The English Government said nothing about the Oath; but said a lot about the annuities (really the instalments due annually as the purchase price of their holdings from the tenants). The Dominions Secretary of the National Government, J. H. Thomas, announced the imposition of special duties on Irish imports into Britain. It was confidently believed that this would so cripple the trade of the Free State that it would be forced to surrender in six months. Actually the "war" lasted for nearly six years, and in that interval more damage was done to the trade of England than to that of the Free State.

The Economic War enabled De Valera to institute a protective system to foster the growth of new industries in the (mainly agricultural) Irish Free State; which growth would, in some measure, compensate for the loss of the industrial area separated from it by Partition.

In January, 1935, the economic war was tempered by concessions, which modified the import duties, on both sides, for the benefit of English exporters of coal and Irish exporters of cattle. Finally the economic war was ended by the Agreements of 1938, negotiated by Neville Chamberlain. The Irish Free State (now *Eire*) paid £10 million in final settlement of all claims of a financial character; and, in return, received a concession of the ports and naval depots retained in English control under the Treaty of 1921-2. The constitutional questions outstanding were not mentioned in the Agreement; and while *Eire* statesmen are entitled to claim that "silence gives consent" the fact remains that the *Eire* constitution of 1936 has never been formally approved (or denounced) by England.

England's constitutional position is weak, here, since by the Statute of Westminster (1931) every Dominion of the British Empire has the right to alter its constitution at will; and the exercise of this right by "Northern Ireland" was at once accepted by the English Government.*
Under this Statute "Dominion status" implied co-equal-

* Dominion Status: Neither *Eire* nor Northern Ireland can be described as a "Dominion" of the British Empire without qualification. The *Eire* Government's official view is that it is a "republic

ity, legislative independence, and "free association" with the British Commonwealth—which, incidentally, carries with it the right of dissociation, including the right to remain neutral in a war waged by England.

De Valera began in 1932 by abolishing the Oath of Allegiance to the King. Then at the first opportunity he got rid of the Governor-Generalship by appointing a party supporter (Donald Buckley, who led a contingent from Maynooth which fought its way into Dublin in Easter Week) on the understanding that he would do nothing whatever in his official capacity.

Then in 1937 a new Constitution was adopted which declared Ireland a "sovereign, independent and democratic state", under the name *Eire*. Its territory was declared to be the whole of Ireland; but the application of the Constitution was limited, temporarily, to the twenty-six counties of the Free State. It included no Governor-General; and no reference to the Crown or the "Commonwealth of Nations" (which is Labour Party humbug for British Empire). Under this Constitution an *Uachtaran* (President) is elected every seven years by direct vote. There are two chambers, a *Dáil* and a Senate, and the *Dáil* appoints (through the President) a *Taoiseach* or Prime Minister who appoints his ministers, not more than two of whom may be members of the Senate. Eamon De Valera has held the office of *Taoiseach* ever since.

The tacit acceptance of this Constitution by Neville Chamberlain and the English Government—while it might conceal an ulterior motive—was and is a tacit recognition, at any rate, that the Irish people claim the right to establish a sovereign, independent State, and that the exercise of that right is obstructed and frustrated by the existence of the Six-County state of "Northern Ireland".

externally associated with" the British Empire, while Northern Ireland is officially a special self-governing "part of the United Kingdom". Nonetheless, they are both in effect "Dominions". [For elucidation of this point see page 437 in Epilogue.]

The Evil of Partition

That Partition is an evil—that it was inflicted upon Ireland expressly to thwart the national aspirations of the Irish people—we have in this book abundantly proved. Forced to abandon the Act of Union—and "Protestant Ascendancy"—the ruling class of England retorted by re-establishing the Pale in a new geographical location.

The excuse for Partition was the pretence that the "Protestants" of N.E. Ulster might be penalised and discriminated against by a Catholic majority. That this was a pure pretence is proved by the abandonment to the Catholic majority of the Twenty-Six Counties of a 6 per cent Protestant minority; and by the enforced inclusion in "Northern Ireland" of a 33 percent Catholic minority which has been insultingly and injuriously discriminated against ever since.

There are many things in the constitution and practice of *Eire* which deserve drastic condemnation from the standpoint of (say) James Connolly, Patrick Pearse, or Theobald Wolfe Tone. But they are matched and surpassed at their worst by the gerrymandered representation and the all-but Fascist administration of Northern Ireland.

Even if this were not so, the war-situation and its outcome shows how very much the enemies of the people of England and of their true interests have been those ruling classes who, the better to be able to exploit the people, have for nearly eight centuries sought to destroy Irish Nationality and to hold Ireland in permanent subjection, directly, or indirectly.

On the ground that the English workers can never be free while they consent to the holding of the Irish people in subjection, it is our case that Partition must be ended to make possible free and fraternal co-operation between England and Ireland.

A free Ireland would have taken its rightful place in

the Liberation War of Humanity as a matter of course. A partitioned and insulted Ireland was morally forced to occupy the less honourable, but necessitated, position of neutral.

To End Partition

Englishmen, during the war, paid in added peril for the crimes committed in Ireland by the rulers of England (and Ireland) for nearly 800 years. But for that evil legacy—for which every honourable Englishman recognises the obligation to make reparation—we could have counted on the invaluable aid a free and united Ireland could give. We must pay our debt—if only to earn, thereby, the right to applaud, as fellow-fighters for Freedom, the men whose deeds and struggles are recorded in this book.

Partition—a crime and an insult in one—was imposed from England. In England the work of undoing Partition must be, and will be, begun.

Partition was imposed by the rulers of England to serve their class ends. The common people of England. impelled by their class needs, must struggle to end Partition as part of the process of winning their own emancipation.

Partition has established vested interests, on either side of its dividing line. It is reinforced on either side by a mass of inculcated prejudices. Because of that it is not possible to end Partition in a merely formal fashion by a simple repeal of the laws which instituted "Northern Ireland". It must be ended by the common agreement of all parties concerned—the Common People in the Six Counties, the Twenty-Six, and in England.

The English democracy has the duty, as well as the privilege, of so cultivating the friendship of the common people on either side of the Boundary that this concrete embodiment of an evil past will fall before the combined assault of the three democracies operating in concert.

Only so shall we fittingly conclude the history set out herein with a return to the beginning on a higher plane—the plane of triumphant democratic advance.

In this effort we can, and will, realise the prophecy of James Connolly: "In our movement North and South will again clasp hands, and again it will be demonstrated, as in '98, that the pressure of a common exploitation will make enthusiastic rebels out of a Protestant working-class, enthusiastic champions of civil and religious liberty out of Catholics, and out of both a united Socialist democracy."

And we can make Patrick Pearse's words also come true: "Let no man be mistaken as to who will be Lord in Ireland, when Ireland is free. The People will be Lord and Master."

PART SIX
EPILOGUE

The settlement imposed on Ireland by Lloyd George's government was presented as a temporary expedient. It has endured near half a century, and it is now clear that it opened a new era of Irish history. The imperialist purpose in Ireland remained the same. But a new system was required in order to achieve it. It is with the "law of motion" of that system that this epilogue is concerned. An attempt is made to show the inevitability of resistance to the partition system, and that the ending of Partition is an essential task of Irish national liberation which it is the duty of English democracy to support. The theme of *Ireland Her Own* is continued up to 1970.

That Partition is far more than a line dividing a country into two can best be illustrated from two main aspects, constitutional and economic. Constitutionally the instrument of partition was the Government of Ireland Act (1920) passed by the Westminster Parliament. The Act was brought into operation piecemeal by Orders in Council in the face of indignant opposition from four-fifths of the Irish people and surly compliance from the remainder. It had no friends in Ireland, not even those who ultimately came to defend it. Its essence was the creation of two parallel legislatures as an alternative to allowing the majority to have its way. These legislatures were both to be wholly subordinated to the Parliament at Westminster, and their local powers were severely limited.

"Northern Ireland" was successfully established. It included most of the population anxious to preserve the Union. But attached to them was a large minority who desired inclusion in an Irish Republic. These formed a majority in a wide belt round the southern and western borders of the new jurisdiction. They were part of the majority of the Irish people, but their majority position was rendered ineffective by imperial decree.

"Southern Ireland" did not materialise. It was still-born. The opposition was too intense and it was all but unanimous. The Irish were however not strong enough or united enough to impose their preferred alternative, an Irish Republic. A compromise was reached. Twenty-six counties, earmarked for "Southern Ireland" became the "Irish Free State" and in this part of Ireland "neo-colonial" relationships were developed.

A comparison of the constitutional positions which were thus established is important for understanding the tactics and difficulties of the national movement and the form the struggle took.

The Government of Ireland Act (1920) continued to apply in six counties and is officially described to this day as the "constitution of Northern Ireland". As a "constitution" it is as solid as a sandbank. Its current edition contains references to several hundred amendments which have resulted from the normal progress of legislation at Westminster. Its first principle was that the English Parliament reserved the right of unlimited interference in Irish affairs.* But by contrast the powers of the Irish to shape their own destiny were narrowly circumscribed. The two Irish Parliaments envisaged in the Act were expressly excluded from legislating on the subject of the Crown, peace and war, armed forces, treaties with foreign powers, treason, alienage, and "trade with any place out of the part of Ireland within their jurisdiction".**

They were to busy themselves making laws "for peace, order and good government" of the areas allotted them. They might by agreement merge their functions, either partially through a "Council of Ireland" or totally in an all-Ireland Parliament. In such case they would receive as a bonus some small additional powers held temporarily in reserve. But the vital attributes of sovereignty were to remain for ever beyond their grasp. The united Ireland

* Sections 6 and 75 specifically safeguard this.
** Section 4.

that the English government was prepared to accept was in all important aspects completely subordinated to Westminster. When the Twenty-six counties became the subject of fresh legislation, the Six retained their status under the 1920 Act, and it is therefore misleading to regard them as constituting a "Dominion" in any sense of the word.

The Irish Free State was described as a Dominion and by a legal fiction extended to all Ireland while its practical functioning was confined to the Twenty-six counties. An impartial American Court held it to be the successor of the British Government and not of the Republic of 1919. That is to say it arose from the Government of Ireland Act as amended by the Free State Agreement Act of 1922. Under this Act nothing in the Free State Constitution must be repugnant to the agreement signed in London in December 1921; and so the constitution was drawn.

Nevertheless imperialism was forced to make real concessions. The Free State Constitution was drafted by Irishmen in Ireland. Formally one of the most democratic in Europe, it guaranteed personal liberty, the inviolability of the zone, freedom of expression, peaceful assembly, religious practice and trade union organisation. It was asserted as a declared principle that all power derived from the people.*

The powers excluded from transfer under the Government of Ireland Act were now vested in the Free State Parliament. But their exercise was rendered subject to limitations. The "co-equal Dominion" as the new state was called,** was obliged to furnish England with military bases and facilities in peace and war. Its legislature must swear fidelity to the English Crown. Its dissatisfied litigants might appeal to the Privy Council. Executive powers were vested in the Crown whose representative

* Article 2.
** Article 1.

439

the Governor-General might, in theory, reserve the Royal Assent to legislation. The oath of fidelity contained an assertion of "common citizenship" with England.

All this may not, in the light of what is now known, have amounted to much. No political Houdini was required to escape from such a box. But there was unfortunately a far weightier matter. The territorial limits of the Free State were not set out in its constitution. Some might believe that this was because the Twenty-six counties were to be added to. Others suspected that it was because they were not. It was provided that if in the month following the establishment of the Free State the Parliament in the Six counties petitioned the Crown to that effect, the area would continue to exist under the Government of Ireland Act with its powers and privileges (and liabilities) unimpaired. So the territory of the Free State was to be decided not by the people of Ireland but by the Crown in response to an address from a Parliament which was the creature of the Crown.

Fidelity to the Crown thus meant the acceptance of Partition—of the right of the king of England to subdivide his own dominions. The civil war, the early stages of which were marked by uprisings in the Six counties, was due to the refusal of republicans to accept this proposition. They asserted indeed the contrary, namely the right of Irish republicans, if they so desired, to invade the Six counties and take them back. In their effort to prevent this, and to protect the compromise on which they had staked their political future, the rulers of the Free State were compelled to overturn their democratic constitution through emergency legislation.

In the period that opened in 1922, therefore, Ireland presented the spectacle of a country divided into two antagonistic states, each apparently ruled by Irishmen each employing draconian repression against a minority within its borders, each in the grip of paralysing economic crisis. Obviously, said imperial commentators, the Irish were unfitted for self-government. Look what they had made of it. But one point must be grasped firmly if subsequent history is to make sense. In each state the repression was directed in favour of the requirements of the English Government and against those who objected to them. It was England's new method of ruling Ireland that bespoke contempt, not Irish self-government, for the Irish had not got it.

If Lloyd George and his successors had made their first principle the self-determination of Ireland, and their second non-intervention in internal Irish affairs, a path of democratic advance could have been found for the whole country. But perhaps, observing the enormous growth of trade unionism, the land seizures and the agricultural and industrial "Soviets" straining against the bounds of a bourgeois revolution, Lloyd George concluded that democracy might go too far and its political consequences rebound too near.

In examining the way in which Partition functioned as the determining feature of the new stage of English imperialism in Ireland, it is useful to contrast it with legislative union. Union swamped Irish democracy. Partition set it against itself. Ireland moreover was now attached to England by a rope made of her own substance. To break free she must tear herself apart. Meanwhile imperialism awaited the time when her people would tire of the struggle and apply for readmission into the United Kingdom. Then the position envisaged in the Government of Ireland Act would be restored. The economic pressures optimists foresaw driving the Six counties into unity with the Twenty-six, were to operate in another direction—that of driving Ireland back into federation. These pressures may now be considered.

Ireland has ample natural resources. In 1923 she had ample labour for their development. But thanks to centuries of foreign exploitation she was starved of capital. Apart from the important commercial centre of Dublin, there was massive investment only in the neighbourhood of Belfast, then the most populous city in the country. For Belfast, dominated by the linen and shipbuilding industries, the supreme need was diversification. This diversification could have arisen ideally from the impulse of developing the remainder of the country. There the great need was an adequate infrastructure, the development of electricity, turf, transport, building materials (especially lime and cement) and certain categories of engineering. The role of Belfast would have been the production of means of production for all Ireland.

Partition destroyed all such prospects. Thus obviously state investment was essential and the state required access to the entire taxable capacity of the nation. But forty percent of this was held at the disposal of the English exchequer. How was the remaining sixty percent to finance recovery at a time when war and revolution had destroyed capital both in industry and agriculture, and delayed the replacement of more?

Recovery would have required more than state investment. It would have required state regulation of capital and commodity movements inwards and outwards. To avoid burdening the books with items capable of manufacture in Ireland, tariffs must be introduced so as to protect and develop native consumer industries. But the principle of common citizenship involved the free movement of capital and labour. Moreover to the extent that the Free State abrogated this principle and took measures to isolate the local economy from that of England, a barrier must be erected across Ireland. The high degree of integration existing in the Irish banking system placed limits on the probable effectiveness of any such effort. At the same time if external regulation was hindered by Partition, so was internal planning. Without regulation of capital movement how was it possible to ensure a balance of agricultural and industrial investment such that manpower displaced by one would be absorbed by the other?

Another problem was the existence of a vast reserve of rural unemployed each side of the border. It was obviously undesirable that valuable manpower should be dissipated by emigration before industry was made available to occupy it. But to retain it there must be immediate land division and substantial internal migration, some of it possibly across the line of the border. Leaving aside such questions as optimum average farm sizes, we need note only the contradiction. If the engineering products required for the industrialisation of the south could not proceed from the diversification of industry in the north, then they must come from England. They must therefore be paid for in commodities able to penetrate the English market. What better than the traditional commodity, cattle? Yet if the ranches were broken up where were the cattle to come from? So the Twenty-six counties produced cattle for the balance of trade, and the Six counties sent ships and linen to the ends of the earth, and thereby earned foreign currency over the disposal of which their local rulers had not the slightest control.

Even if effort had been made to distort it, the Irish economy was still reasonably integrated within the limits of its specialization. But Partition created two local systems each with an inherent imbalance. Forbidden to support each other under a common state policy, the severed parts of Ireland must lean separately on England. Partition thus preserved the Irish market for English manufacture, and Ireland excelled the United States as England's largest customer. The lack of adequate trade contacts abroad encouraged a certain parochialism in the foreign policy of the part of Ireland allowed one. Only gradually were foreign connections built up.

In the Six counties the ruling class was completely blind to the economic possibilities of the national dynamism that still existed in the south. It never claimed that its powers and resources were adequate to solve the problems of recovery. Its policy was to concentrate such means as were available in areas and industries manned by supporters of the Government. The others would be thrown on the mercy of the imperial Government either through relief or emigration. Hence rose the monstrous edifice of religious and political discrimination which is the economic heart of the still continuing crisis in Northern Ireland.

The economic results of Partition were thus no different in kind from those produced by the Union; and this principle extends to the national movement against the partition system.

The Union blocked a badly needed revolution. There sprang up therefore agitations for elements of that revolution, Catholic emancipation, the abolition of tithes, tenant right, the land for the people. There were likewise voluntary movements, for agricultural co-operation, the use of Irish manufactures and the preservation of Gaelic. By these means the classes affected sought to mitigate the consequences of counter-revolution, but they also rallied the opponents of the Union and prepared the public mind for the assault upon it.

Partition also blocked a revolution. As a result there inevitably arose campaigns for democratic rights, the abolition of land annuities, urban and rural housing and above all employment. As in the days of the Union, some were found to discourage such agitations as "socialistic" or to counterpose their effect to the national aim of a united Republic. But far from being a disqualification their "socialistic" character corresponded to the position of the working class as the most numerous class in modern Ireland.

Two alternative means used to be proposed for breaking the Union: Parliament and insurrection. While not necessarily advocated by mutually exclusive movements, the one was favoured by the more comfortable classes, the other by those with little to lose. Under Partition Irish representation at Westminster had been cut to thirteen of which ten were inevitably Unionists. But to some extent the presence in Parliament was replaced by the voice of the Free State in the counsels of the Commonwealth.

At the imperial conference of 1926 it was clear that the bourgeoisie in the Twenty-six counties, who had preferred the settlement to a struggle whose gains might go to other classes, had become dissatisfied with the results of their bargain. They had begun the task of establishing an infrastructure by launching the Shannon electricity scheme; they had passed an important land purchase Act. But the financial obstacles to development were considerable. Kevin O'Higgins proposed what was in effect a new bargain. In return for the ending of Partition by the transference to Dublin of the excepted powers, he would "get the king crowned in Ireland"* and what was more to the point bring Ireland into any war in which Britain was involved.** Nothing came of the plan, though it won the favour of Lord Carson and others. Its rejection shows that the policy makers in Whitehall were not prepared to risk another 1782. Their preferred policy was Partition.

At the other pole Republicans wrestled with their own problems of policy, in the teeth of severe repression. They discussed a fresh resort to arms, possibly an invasion of the Six counties accompanied by local uprisings. Their difficulty was that since the "peace, order and good government" (but not the fundamental sovereignty) of Six counties had become the responsibility of a local legislature, it was almost inevitable that military action must assume the character of civil war. This consideration understandably weakened their mass support.

The year 1926 was one of recovery and regrouping. It was as if the separate strands of which the anti-treaty party was composed began to disentangle themselves. De Valera, the nominal President of the underground Republic, had already forfeited the support of the I.R.A. when

* See De Vere White, *Kevin O'Higgins* pp. 214–217.
** Ibid. p. 226.

445

he first urged participation in the Free State Parliament. The *Sinn Fein* party split on this issue in March 1926. The old leadership kept the funds and De Valera started *Fianna Fáil* without a penny. But the party did not want. For a time it took part in contemporary agitations, but came increasingly under the influence of Irish manufacturers* who felt they were receiving insufficient encouragement from the Free State, and desired a more vigorous fiscal policy. The traditional *Sinn Fein* party was left without any policy but the ending of the partition system. But since that system survived, and remained the source of serious social and political discontents, *Sinn Fein* survived as well. Its numbers shrank until its *Ard Fheis* could be acommodated in a Dublin hotel. By contrast *Fianna Fáil* advanced by leaps and bounds. Its policy was to improve on the treaty settlement in the Twenty-six counties. It was seen by the people as a real alternative. In the election of September 1927 it won fifty-seven seats.

Expulsions and secessions left the Fenian core intact, and many of these "physical force" men had socialist connections. In Ireland every new bourgeois departure seems to spring from the petit bourgeoisie. But this is a class of great complexity and has as many connections with the workers as with the employers. The followers of Connolly and Mellows sought to lead the people of all Ireland in a campaign against the consequences of Partition, anticipating as a result the opening of a general attack on imperialism (which most envisaged in a military form) in which they would win the support of English democracy and the sympathy of the world.

The loose alliance of physical force Republicans, left Socialists and Communists defended the interests of th common people with rare militancy and courage. Suc names as Peadar O'Donnell, Hanna Sheehy-Skeffington

* See for example the names of the proposed directors of th *Fianna Fáil – Irish Press* published in September 1928.

446

George Gilmore and Frank Ryan enliven a dark page of Irish history. The supreme issue in the towns was unemployment. Between 1921 and 1928 over a hundred native factories ceased operations, and thereafter the process accelerated. Unemployed demonstrations were held. In the small farm areas agitations were started against the payment of land annuities. As the great slump gathered way the external trade of the Free State fell from £109 million in 1929 to £69 million in 1932. The number of days lost through strikes, mostly against wage reductions, rose from 54,292 in 1928 to 310,199 in 1931.

If the main body of the working-class movement had been involved in these struggles their outcome might have been different. But a situation of great delicacy had been created, reproducing the general Irish dilemma within the Labour movement. The all-Ireland character of the trade union movement was preserved. But the need for different tactics on the two sides of the border was recognised as early as 1924. The areas responded to different pressures. In the south the employers were weaker and failed to enforce wage reductions comparable with those in Britain and the north. But a mutilated state engaged in industrialisation (however slow) could not expand social services. In the north the unemployed gained benefit from Westminster's social legislation.

All the great mass struggles of the time had an anti-imperialist content. The border and the oath of allegiance were constant targets. But the greater part of the trade unions in the Six counties had headquarters in Britain. In the Twenty-six the Irish Transport Union dominated the field. The prosecution of a vigorous policy against Partition would have brought about the disruption of the movement along the line of the border, a prospect by no means distasteful to the Unionists. In order to avoid the consequences of such a development for the economic struggle the trade unions tended to avoid political questions, or to deal with them in a manner not likely to arouse sectarian controversy in the north. Thus arose the calamitous attitude that questions involving national unity and independence were themselves sectarian, and the movement was under constant danger of slipping into pure economism. This general tendency was facilitated by the mood of many workers who had supported the independence struggle and after making the greatest sacrifices now found themselves economically no better off. Their attitude is depicted in the three "Dublin" plays of Sean O'Casey, glowing with idealism but disgusted with demagogical nationalism.

Under these conditions the product of the mass struggles, initiated before the world economic crisis and intensified as it developed, was the return to power of De Valera in 1932. Agricultural prices fell to record low levels. Emigrants' remittances stopped. In 1932 the migration figures showed the one net inward balance of a century. Drastic repression was employed and the jails filled with defaulting farmers and revolting unemployed.

In the days of the Union the great lesson taught by all agitations was the need for native government. Was there native government in the Free State? In the sense that the Free State was the creature of British Imperialism it was argued that there was not. But the Free State was something to confront England with, and England could no longer be confronted directly by the people. Control of the Free State therefore represented a position to be won by those who were prepared to win it. The masses demanded the rebuilding of the economy to end unemployment, the abolition of the land annuities, the end of the oath of allegiance and of repressive legislation, and the release of the prisoners. *Fianna Fáil* won more seats than any other party and in March 1932 formed a Government with the support of the seven Labour deputies. It was pledged to carry out the popular programme.

The day De Valera was installed he sent his lieutenant Frank Aiken, to arrange the release of prisoners from

448

Arbour Hill. Soon followed his decision to withhold the land annuities, remitting half but collecting the other half to finance reconstruction. The "economic war" declared by the English "National Government" on June 25, 1932, won support for De Valera. To some extent he was excused from taking radical measures against unemployment, which reached 138,000 in 1935. Political measures sufficed as he took the Twenty-six counties along the one road left open. The emergency laws and oath of fidelity were abolished early in 1932. Soon afterwards the Governor-Generalship became a meaningless sinecure. De Valera now turned to the I.R.A. and urged them to disband. Their task was accomplished.

The I.R.A. was weakened and its counsels divided. But disband it did not. It was only the outward symbols of British overlordship in Twenty-six counties that were being ripped down. The partition system remained unchanged. It was this, not the trappings of royalty, that decided the economic fate of the people of Ireland. For a quarter century the assault on the symbols was to continue. It then became clear that independence for part of a nation was no independence at all, and then *Fianna Fáil* ceased to pretend.

The world economic crisis affected the Six counties if anything even more severely than the Twenty-six. The catastrophic slump in farm prices, linen and shipbuilding created an unemployed army estimated at 106,000. Since the Six-county administration was without fiscal authority, the effect of the tariffs imposed by England on imports from the Twenty-six counties was to keep Free State goods out of the North. Apart from hitting the carrying trade, the consequence, reinforced by the retaliatory tariffs imposed by Dublin, was the virtual dereliction of a string of market towns along the northern side of the border: Derry, Strabane, Enniskillen, Clones and Newry. Their population being largely Nationalist, the Unionists viewed their impoverishment with equanimity and for political reasons welcomed their increased dependence on England.

But lacking control over tariffs or foreign trade the Six-county administration was unable to protect its own working-class supporters from the economic blizzard. In the summer of 1932 Catholic and Protestant unemployed joined hands in a struggle for improved outdoor relief. Unity was cemented as a result of common subjection to a system involving payment in kind. There were violent scenes after which old Tom Mann, who had come to help, was deported from one "integral part of the United Kingdom" to another. Employed workers joined in the struggle. As a result of the first combined action of Protestant and Catholic workers since 1919, the unemployed won their demands.

Despite the sharpness of the discontent and the degree of unity achieved in Belfast on an immediate question, the Unionist government survived without difficulty. The Unionists had reinforced their position three years previously by abolishing proportional representation. But this was incidental. Belfast held but a quarter of the population of the Six counties, and unemployment relief was but one issue. To include the country people, unity must extend to democratic questions, as it had done in the Twenty-six counties. But the Northern Ireland Parliament was forbidden even to discuss the most vital democratic question of all, namely whether the majority of the people of Ireland should be entitled to establish a constitution for their country. In the event the English Treasury loosened the purse-strings and while the Twenty-six counties went forward, the Six remained as before, bribed to accept stagnation. It would have required a revolution in the thinking of the average Unionist voter before he would regard the Stormont Government as more than a guarantee that the ultimate decisions would continue to be taken at Westminster.

The effect of the economic war was to diminish sharply both exports from and imports into the Twenty-six counties. The *Fianna Fáil* Government protected the vital cattle trade by means of a bounty on exports, at the same time protecting the home market and aiming at the maximum self-sufficiency. During these years the State financed the development of turf, electricity, sugar and other industries. The State sector subsequently expanded to include transport, and important sections of shipping, insurance and banking. For the first time Irish foreign policy diverged from that of England, and De Valera's championship of Ethiopia in the League of Nations contrasted with the policy of temporisation adopted by the British representative.

The former Treaty party (soon to be known as *Fine Gael*) defended the interests of the merchants, cattle-dealers and large-scale farmers whose future seemed to them to be placed in jeopardy by De Valera's stand. From the midst of these, after the victory of fascism in Germany in June 1933, arose O'Duffy's "blueshirts" on the extreme right of Twenty-six-county politics. Their international orientation was only pro-German in the sense that it was pro-English, and the English ruling class was then supporting Hitler and Mussolini. Their fundamentally anti-National tendency told against them. There were prolonged and often sharp struggles, but finally the Government was compelled to curb their activities, availing itself of the situation to strike simultaneous blows at Republicanism.

What would have been the position if the split of 1926 had been avoided and England and her friends within Ireland had been faced with a *Sinn Fein* Government in the Twenty-six counties is of course a matter of speculation. The position of the Republicans under *Fianna Fáil* was by no means easy. Two opposing tendencies developed. The one, typified by Sean Russell, wished to continue the old policy of preparing for the day when England's difficulty would provide Ireland with another military opportunity. The other, typified best perhaps by Frank Ryan, urged an alliance with the left wing of the Labour movement and a closer identification with anti-imperialist movements internationally. The constant reappearance within the republican movement of this type of right-left bifurcation corresponds to the process of differentiation in the petite bourgeoisie on which it is based.

Some on the extreme left gravitated towards the Revolutionary Workers' Groups which coalesced into the all-Ireland Communist Party in June 1933. The first Secretary was Sean Murray, a County Antrim man who had taken part in one of the Ulster uprisings during the Civil War, emigrated to England, and returned. Others with Frank Ryan had established in 1931 *Saor Eire** for the purpose of securing "the overthrow in Ireland of British imperialism and its ally, Irish capitalism". Fom time to time its statements suggested that this section regarded Irish capitalists as one reactionary mass. Former members of *Saor Eire* in 1934 joined with the Communists and left sections of the Labour Party (since 1930 separated from the T.U.C.) to found the Republican Congress. A number of their leaders resigned from the I.R.A., which then denounced them as traitors and offered physical violence rather than have them march with them at demonstrations. The I.R.A. came to be dominated by its right wing for the greater part of three decades.

Republicans were under the difficulty that they were compelled to support De Valera in the economic war, but were opposed to the constitutional position from which he was waging it, and to his method of financing it. But, as R. J. Connolly shrewdly pointed out, they had not fully understood the nature of the State. The Communist Party advocated united action on an agreed political programme and tactics, which should include a common front against fascism, and the defence of the workers' and

* Free Ireland.

small farmers' immediate interests. This was found unacceptable to a great extent from an objection to urging a state whose legitimacy they rejected to carry out reforms.

Thus, the State placed a duty on drink imported from England. The Republicans sallied forth and smashed the Bass bottles on the quays. Direct action was the slogan. Farmers were urged to withhold payment of land annuities. When they were arrested Republicans gathered to do battle. Repeatedly members of Republican Congress were arrested while protecting the homes of unemployed men who had responded to the slogan of "no work, no rent". The result was a steady stream of victimisations. A Leitrim man, Thomas Gralton, was deported from his own townland. He had become a naturalised American. A schoolteacher in Waterford was dismissed for associating with the Republican Congress. A decisive point was the great Dublin transport strike of March and April 1935 when the I.R.A. decided officially to support the workers. The full force of the State was used against them, showing what the authorities most feared. There were mass arrests. Soon Republicans found they had little more freedom under De Valera than under his predecessors. From this time on, the I.R.A., though in times of quiet its activities might be tolerated, was always illegal or semi-legal. It continued none the less to enjoy greater support than might be expected from its numbers or military capacity, and attracted the most militant and idealistic of the youth. This support was partly sentimental. In part also it was an "insurance policy" against national betrayal.

The general advance of European reaction affected the six counties also. In 1935 after three years of comparative calm, the Unionists were able once more to split the working class. In July Belfast saw the worst anti-Catholic pogroms since 1922. Republicans, Communists and militant workers were imprisoned, often without charge or trial. In 1936 the English National Council for Civil Liberties published a damning indictment of the semi-fascist Six-county State.

In 1937 De Valera, still aiming at drawing the teeth of the Republican opposition, availed himself of the abdication of Edward VIII of England to hold a referendum on a new constitution, as was permissible in British law under the Statute of Westminster of 1931. The new constitution swept away the constitutional basis of the Free State Agreement Act. A new State was proclaimed which rested on the will of the Irish people. This time its territory was defined. It was the whole thirty-two counties. Irish law thus came into direct conflict with English law. The name of the new State was Ireland (in Gaelic, *Eire*). But since the Dublin Parliament was unable to enforce its enactments in the Six-county area, it was to legislate for twenty-six counties only "pending the reunification of the national territory". So in practice there was no change. It is also significant that the reciprocal arrangements between the English and Irish civil services were continued.

The King of England now ceased to be the head of the Executive and an elected President replaced the Governor-General. But in view of the "external association" of Ireland with the countries of the Commonwealth, the King still represented Ireland in foreign relations. Thus Irish diplomats were accredited by the English Crown, passports were made out in the King's name. Ireland was represented in England not by an Ambassador but by a High Commissioner who dealt with the Dominions Office.

Republicans felt that the changes altered only words. Others thought the new position might provide a useful standpoint for future bargaining. But some of the elector feared fresh retaliation. The referendum coincided with a general election. The constitution was accepted, but *Fianna Fáil* once more became dependent on Labour support in the *Dáil*.

The following year, 1938, there was published the report of a Commission of Inquiry into Banking, Currency and Credit, appointed in 1934. It recommended that the Twenty-six counties should continue to use sterling as their currency, and in effect that there should continue to be free movement of capital and labour. The legislative Union had been followed by a financial Union. If there was financial partition, there was to be no currency partition. "We are still part of the United Kingdom as far as credit and currency matters are concerned", said Professor Busteed,* and this was nowhere disputed.

In 1938 De Valera scored a notable victory. He negotiated the evacuation of the bases which English forces had occupied under the Treaty, as part of a package deal which settled the land annuity question and ended the economic war. Two months after the conclusion of the agreement, came the June election in which *Fianna Fáil* recovered its absolute majority. The majority of the people now regarded European war as inevitable. The settlement clearly envisaged the possibility of Irish neutrality. At the same time many had grave doubts over the possibility of maintaining neutrality in a small state with belligerent territory not sixty miles from its capital city.

To the I.R.A. De Valera's diplomatic successes were a challenge. He was approaching the ultimate freedom attainable within the partition system. Was there a danger that the people would accept this as the ultimate in national independence? There were omens in the field of economic policy. On March 18, 1938, three senior civil servants and four University professors presented on Radio Eireann the sole programme that could rest on such acceptance. Its basis was the consolidation of farms and the displacement of population from the land. It was the old imperial recipe and foreshadowed the dreadful rural depopulation of the fifties and sixties. Capital was to be raised by the precise mode of accumulation casti-

* Report of Banting Commission, p. 616.

gated by Marx in 1867.* And indeed, as re-armament breathed feverish vitality into western economy, the tide of emigration had begun already.

Republicans believed that an effort must be made to turn the fight against the Twenty-six-county institutions of Partition, into a fight against Partition itself. But a legal basis had to be found. The second *Dáil*, elected in 1921, had over the past seventeen years maintained a shadowy existence akin to that of the "Irish Republic now virtually established". Sean Russell, now chief of staff, persuaded its survivors to vest its authority in the Army Council. This now became, so to speak, "in law and fact" the "Government of the Irish Republic". On January 11, 1939, an ultimatum was sent to Lord Halifax. England would withdraw from the Six counties or a state of war would ensue. Receiving no acknowledgment the I.R.A. declared war a few days later and over the next year a series of attacks on strategic installations took place on English soil. Wales and Scotland were expressly excluded. They were not regarded as enemy countries.

It is important to appreciate that the young men who carried out "the bombings", which were indeed devoid of military effect, were in no sense of the word fascists. Ireland had sent volunteers to each of the armies engaged in the Spanish Civil War. Those who fought on the Republican side, where many of them lost their lives, were the cream of Irish Republicanism. Some of the survivors took part in the "bombings"**, but none of the supporters of Franco. I.R.A. men regarded the coming war with Germany as a simple inter-imperialist conflict, and it was England that had imposed Partition on Ireland, not Germany. There were of course other Republicans, not involved in the "bombings", who discerned another element in the Anglo-German conflict. George Gilmore hinted that the common struggle against fascism might

* *Capital,* Vol. I. Ch. XXV, Section F.
** e.g. O'Regan and Crompton

lead to the unification of Ireland.* But the aim of the I.R.A. was to further the cause of Irish independence. The injuries and loss of life they caused, and the death and imprisonment some of them suffered, must be charged to the account of imperialism.

Almost immediately after the "bombings" began, the English Government decided to introduce conscription. It was judged impracticable to enforce it in the Six counties, and indeed it was never imposed. To that extent it was admitted that Ireland was one. But the change created new problems for the Irish in Britain. In Irish law, under the Nationality and Citizenship Act, 1935, Irishmen were no longer British subjects. But in English law they remained such and became liable for military service. Up to now the organisations of the Irish community had mostly confined themselves to expressions of solidarity with the independence struggle at home. Dual citizenship created the need for Irish organisations that would also defend the political rights of Irish residents in England, and endeavour to enlist the support of English democrats. In accordance with this need the exiles' branches of the Republican Congress and kindred bodie at this period evolved into the Connolly Club and established the Irish Exiles Advisory Bureau.

England declared war on Germany on September 3, 1939. Next day De Valera announced in the *Dail* that the Twenty-six counties (now known in British law as "Eire")** proposed to remain neutral. The people of the Six counties by contrast had no choice. Their automatic involvement in an English conflict appeared to patriotic Irishmen as a further imperialist aggression against their country, a repetition of 1914. Throughout the entire course of the war massive sections of Irish public opinion held that it was imperialist and no business of theirs.

* Coogan, *Ireland Since the Rising*, p. 267.
** Eire (Confirmation of Agreements) Act, 1938.

There was of course a *prima facie* parallel with 1914. People who thought in formal military terms could be excused for saying that the old antagonists were at it again. But the struggle for markets, spheres of influence and fields of investment had been given a new dimension by the establishment in 1917 of a socialist system whose example threatened the very existence of imperialism. The tyranny of Hitler fascism had been quite deliberately encouraged by English, French and American finance and diplomacy in the hope that it would act as the spearhead of an attack on the Soviet Union, resuming the wars of intervention of 1919–20. On August 23, 1939, the weapon was poised but refused to move. Germany signed the non-aggression pact which threw western Europe into hysteria. The declaration of war on Hitler by England and France was made not because he attacked Poland but because he refused to attack Russia. His next aggression must thus be against themselves.

The political content of Irish neutrality must be estimated against this background. Already on August 26 Germany had been informed of Dublin's intended neutrality. On August 29, Berlin undertook to respect it. Within Ireland De Valera's public statement of September 4 won wide approval. Apart from the Unionists in the north-east and the solitary voice of James Dillon (reflecting the Redmondite tradition he derived from his father John Dillon) all Irish political parties, from *Fine Gael* on the right to the Communist Party of Ireland on the left, were against participation.

No satisfactory study of Irish neutrality has been published, and conclusions must be drawn with caution. The English Government naturally felt disappointed that the bases yielded in expectation of quite another situation were not at once returned when its policy led to a fiasco. That an English invasion of the Twenty-six counties was considered there is plenty of evidence. The absurd pretence that German submarines were being re-

fuelled in south-west Ireland was propaganda made
ready against such an eventuality. But seemingly the fear
of creating a western front and antagonising American-
Irish opinion outweighed the need for the ports.

On the German side there was corresponding satisfaction that England had lost her bases. On the other hand
Ireland was never seriously considered as a theatre of war.
Without command of the seas neither men nor supplies
could be landed there in adequate quantity. The main
consideration was that of avoiding actions likely to provoke or excuse an English invasion. Irish neutrality survived not because of the innate gentlemanliness of the
combatants but because neither side could violate it
without the balance of advantage passing to the other.

There was however a section in Ireland these considerations did not impress, namely the I.R.A. which regarded itself as already "at war" with England. As a
result of some undisclosed intrigue the austere unpolitical
idealist Sean Russell was replaced by Stephen Hayes.
Within days of the opening of the campaign in England,
German initiative established contact in Dublin, and an
I.R.A. envoy set out for Germany. When war broke out
German advice was to make peace with De Valera, and
conduct sabotage operations against maritime installations in the Six counties. The Germans regarded the
I.R.A. merely as useful diversionists whom De Valera
might tolerate providing there were no bombs on his own
doorstep.

But the I.R.A. did not accept the German estimate of
De Valera's neutrality. They regarded it as the only
available means of accepting the partition system without provoking a national revolt. They believed he had
collaborated with Scotland Yard by providing the names
of known Republicans who had left for England. That
just before the war he equipped himself with a "Treason
Act" and an "Offences Against the State Act" for use
against them they knew well. Accordingly it was against

the Twenty-six county regime that their opposition was mainly directed. They could expect little mass support. But in vain the Germans urged them to abandon their "ridiculous street shooting". Without policy there is no discipline. As a result of trying to divorce national revolution from the interests of oppressed classes the I.R.A. entered a period of confusion and demoralisation for which, though Stephen Hayes was blamed, a mistaken policy was responsible.

The jails filled steadily. Later it was decided to establish a concentration camp at the Curragh in County Kildare. Not only members of the dominant wing of the I.R.A. found themselves interned there. Former members of the Republican Congress, and at least one former International Brigader, were rounded up. The two sides discussed and disagreed, night after night.

In the Six counties also there was a wave of arrests. Indeed so many Republicans were taken up that a prison ship, the *Al Rawdah*, was taken across Portaferry bar at high tide and moored in Strangford Lough. There prisoners spent the war under deplorable conditions, many suffering permanent injury to their health. An interesting case is that of the Nationalist M. P. Cahir Healy. Too old and too distinguished for such treatment, and by no stretch of the imagination a Republican, he was arrested by the English Government under "Regulation 18B" and interned in the Isle of Man with the English fascists. A fine poet and brilliant journalist who had belonged to Redmond's party but supported *Dáil Eireann*, he was so much a convinced "fascist" that in 1935 he had shared the plinth at Trafalgar Square with Reginald Bridgeman, Charles Donnelly of the Republican Congress, and E. Wooley of the Communist Party of Great Britain.

A situation in which Six counties of a country were at war and the remaining Twenty-six neutral was naturally fraught with difficulty. It was impracticable to seal the long irregular border passing in places through mountainous country, and in others through the very living rooms of inhabited dwellings. The security frontier thus became the Irish Sea. As a result the Six counties participated to some extent in the isolation imposed on the Twenty-six. But apart from this the two parts of Ireland were subject to opposing tensions, as always with surprisingly similar results.

The volume of imports from across the Channel to the Twenty-six counties fell sharply as a war economy was introduced into England. Increased business with Canada, India and neutral countries did not suffice to make good the loss. There resulted almost immediately serious shortages of grain, coal and oil, fertilisers, engineering and manufactured consumer goods. The grain shortage was met by a policy of compulsory tillage. About a million acres, one-seventeenth of the entire superficies, were ploughed up in the years 1939–44. Nine-tenths of this land was put into corn, one-tenth into potatoes.

There was an immediate effect on employment. The number of males engaged in agriculture rose from 530,899 in 1939 to 555,601 in 1941, but thereafter declined to 526,147 in 1944. The decline after 1941 corresponded to the loss by consolidation of 7,628 holdings of less than 50 acres, and to processes of rationalisation on larger farms.

The industrial infrastructure established during the economic war now stood the country in good stead. The shortage of coal was partially offset by the use of turf. Many were the fires caused by volatile tar in chimneys designed for imported fuel. Petrol was strictly rationed and private motoring virtually ceased. But the country was well provided with draught animals. As a result of the lack of fertilizers and the bringing into cultivation of less productive land, the yields of crops per acre fell by up to 25 percent. To some extent the shortages of engineering and manufactured consumer goods were met from the expansion of native industry. As a result unemployment which stood at 68,828 in September 1939, fell to 35,566 in 1944.

The situation with regard to exports was different. These declined in volume but rose slightly in value, from about £27 million in 1939 to about £30 million in 1944. Since the close of the First World War the Twenty-six counties (unlike the Six) had been running a substantial trade deficit which was balanced by income from investments abroad and emigrants' remittances. The result of the slight trade surplus attained after 1939 was that invisible income accumulated in London. The sterling assets of Irish banks rose from about £100 million in 1939 to some £220 million in 1944. Ireland was compelled to finance the English war effort. Thanks to English price controls the favourable terms of trade which obtained from 1914 to 1918 were not repeated, hence the stagnation of exports, continued emigration and absence of land agitation.* The sterling "dollar pool" ensured that remittances from the U.S.A. were available for English needs.

The Six county administration had no control over defence or foreign trade. English Government policy was to utilize the existing industries for military or dollar-earning purposes. Ships were built for fighting or freight. Linen earned dollars in the U.S.A. Apart from the manufacture of aircraft no important industrial innovations were made. Despite the expansion of employment in shipbuilding to 30,000 workers, Belfast still held over 15,000 unemployed. The Six-county administration did not press hard for war work, presumably from fear of industrialisation in the nationalist areas bordering the Twenty-six counties, and the possible attraction of labour from the south. But its favourable trade balance was of service to the English economy.

* It was suspected that the prices of Irish produce were kept at "bloodsucker levels" to "punish" Eire for her neutrality. The failure to increase imports of food from Ireland was criticised by Lord Templemore in the House of Lords on July 13, 1943.

During the first nine months of the war Chamberlain seems still to have cherished the hope of turning it against the Soviet Union. In September 1939 when Chamberlain was declaiming from the Admiralty about Irish stubbornness in keeping the ports, Germany had only seven divisions in the west, but the allied armies remained quiescent. But when the Russians attempted to remove the threat to their security by attacking the Mannerheim Line in Finland, Chamberlain sent 120 fighters and 40 bombers against them.

On May 10, 1940, Hitler invaded Norway, Denmark, Holland and Belgium. In a speech at Galway De Valera protested against the "grievous wrong" done these small nations and drew an angry riposte from the German ambassador.

After the fall of France on June 25, the Nazis contemplated the invasion of Britain, but appreciated the difficulties involved. They sent assurances to Dublin that no landings in Ireland were contemplated, and allowed it to be known that they supported the reunification of the country. It was at this time that efforts to introduce secret agents reached their maximum. These enterprising individuals were usually quickly apprehended. The most picturesque but tragic effort was the attempt to land Frank Ryan and Sean Russell from a submarine, in which Russell lost his life. It has been speculated that the two men were to work for a detente between De Valera and the I.R.A. with a view to an invasion of the Six counties when England was on her last legs.* On the other side Churchill was endeavouring to draw De Valera into an "All-Ireland Defence Council". He failed because he could give no assurances regarding the ending of Partition. Churchill therefore pressed once more for the return of the ports, but failed to get satisfaction. He solic-

* LaHous however, in the Nürnberg trials, complained that the Nazis got "no satisfaction" from the I.R.A. because "those fellows" were concerned with their own political ends.

ited Roosevelt's good offices, but all he achieved was the American decision to extend its Atlantic security line to the twenty-sixth parallel of longitude the following April.

When in May 1941 manpower shortages led Churchill once more to the subject of conscription in the Six counties, De Valera protested. An intense movement of indignation swept the nationalist areas. Mass meetings were held. It became clear that enforcement would cost more than it would achieve and the proposal was dropped.

It might possibly have been raised again, but for the decisive turn in the fortunes of war that occurred when on June 22, 1941, the Nazis invaded the Soviet Union, and Churchill announced the Anglo-Russian alliance. Imperialist objectives still informed the English war effort, but these were now rendered subordinate to the wider interests of international democracy; not indeed because Churchill wished it, but because survival lay that way.

The most immediate effect of the new situation was felt in Ireland by the Communist movement. The northern branches were desirous of giving unconditional support to the war effort. The southern branches, while sympathetic to that standpoint, felt that this was impracticable in the state of opinion prevailing in the neutral State. The Communist movement therefore divided, the name "Communist Party" being retained by the groups in the Six counties. These grew with great rapidity and their membership soon greatly outnumbered that of the Six-county Labour Party. Other transitional landmarks disappeared in the south. On June 30 Stephen Hayes was kidnapped by members of his Army Council. After being held prisoner for over two months he escaped and went to the police for protection. The result was the public exposure of the state of demoralisation into which the I.R.A. had fallen by ignoring the principle that revolutions are made by the masses. Many believed that the I.R.A. would never again be a force in Irish affairs.

In these conditions the leadership of the progressive movement in Ireland passed to the trade unions. In his efforts to deal with the economic crisis without over-burdening the bourgeoisie, De Valera had introduced a wages standstill order, and was busy with legislation aimed at restricting the bargaining powers of trade unions. The largest union, the Irish Transport and General Workers' Union, whose leadership was in the hands of Larkin's old enemy William O'Brien, the nearest approach to a "right-wing Social Democrat" possible in a country with Ireland's traditions, was prepared to follow the Government in hopes of securing a monopoly in certain fields of organisation. At the end of 1941 when Hitler's armies were deep in the Soviet Union, and some responsible citizens hobnobbed not too discreetly with Germany's secret representatives, trade unionists feared that the State would slip gradually into a form of paternalistic semi-fascism. There was even exaggerated talk of a "Salazar type" dictatorship.

Whether this constituted a real threat or not, successive annual meetings of the Irish T.U.C. showed the gathering of the struggle on the issues of increased wages, trade union rights, the defence of democracy, and opposition to fascism. The Sinclair resolution of July 1942 was defeated by the narrow majority of 47 to 43. A year later the McCullough resolution was passed by 50 to 28. It ran: "This Congress greets with admiration the struggles of the democratic peoples the world over against fascism – the destroyer of trade union rights and democratic liberties of the people – and pledges itself to eternal vigilance against the danger at home and abroad."

The principal opponents of this resolution were the delegates of the Irish Transport and General Workers' Union. In December 1943 this Union moved for the exclusion of James Larkin and his son from membership of the Labour Party. This being defeated the following month, the union disaffiliated and its members in the

Dáil constituted themselves a separate group. So began the disastrous split which weakened Irish Labour at a crucial time. When the British T.U.C. issued the invitation for the World Trade Union Congress to re-establish international connections, the Executive of the Irish T.U.C. declined to participate. But at the 1944 Congress in Drogheda they were overruled despite objections from O'Brien. When the World Congress was held in February 1945 two Irish delegates, Gilbert Lynch and Michael Keyes, attended. But the following month it became clear that those opposed to international connections were preparing to form a breakaway congress. The Irish Council of Trade Unions, dominated by the Transport Union, was established in May. The T.U.C. lost the services of its secretary, and but for James Connolly's old associate Thomas Johnson's stepping forward at the age of seventy to fill the breach the 1945 annual meeting might not have been held. While this further division in the ranks of Irish Labour was wholly deplorable it must be noted that the basis once more lay in the national question and the continuance of Partition. The breakaway movement contained exclusively Irish-based unions whose members were for the most part in the Twenty-six counties. These felt that the English-based unions, the bulk of whose membership resided in the Six counties, were liable to act as vehicles of English political influence. And indeed it was not unknown for London executives to pander to Orange prejudices in the struggle for influence.

The European war ended and Labour swept to power in England on a programme of social reforms and a more enlightened position in international affairs. There was as much jubilation in Dublin as in London. But the Labour Government quickly showed that in all essentials it was as imperialist as its predecessors. Such concessions as were inevitable were reluctantly made, but Herbert

Morrison's lauding of the "jolly old Empire" showed where the new Government stood. The temporarily continuing wartime controls were used to deny Ireland technical products desperately required for her industries. Perhaps the deficiencies could have been repaired if De Valera had adhered to the Marshall plan which was launched in 1947. But the Irish people preferred to continue their neutrality.

Had the Attlee Government shown the slightest inclination to discuss the righting of the wrongs inflicted on Ireland by its predecessors, it is possible that Irish Labour might have led the wave of discontent with *Fianna Fáil* which grew in amplitude from 1945 to 1948. The basic cause of this discontent was, as before, the sacrifices that had to be imposed in order to carry through necessary programmes of capital replacement and new investment. The slight favourable balance of trade was of course swept away. But it was not thought practicable to withdraw sterling balances compulsorily. Such was the continuing entanglement with English finance. The alternative was expressed in a policy of high prices and rising taxation accompanied by low wages and poor social services. A new opposition party was established to the left *of Fianna Fáil*. Called *Clann na Poblachta* it was led by Sean MacBride, the son of Maud Gonne, and attracted many of the supporters of *Saor Eire*, Republican Congress and a new generation of idealistic youth. In the 1948 general election it won only ten seats, but succeeded in placing *Fianna Fáil* in a minority position.

This time Labour did not support *Fianna Fáil* as in the past, and the result was one of the curiosities of Irish politics, the basis for which can be discerned but by no means clearly defined. A coalition was formed. Its components were *Fine Gael* and *Clann na Talmhan* on the right and the two Labour parties with *Clann na Poblachta* on the left. Just what was demagogy and what hard policy in the programme announced will no doubt exercise future historians. Of Labour, O'Casey remarked: "Their backsides were itching for the plush seats of office." Dublin wags called *Clann na Poblachta* the "Kingstown, Queenstown and Sackville Street Republicans".

Contradictory policies lived side by side. Thus the *Fine Gael* premier J. A. Costello in the autumn of 1948 announced the *Clann na Poblachta* plan for withdrawing from the Commonwealth and declaring a Republic. This was of course the logical last step for *Fianna Fáil*. It was no more than placing a crown on De Valera's achievement. But on its basis the prisoners could be released and the gun "disappear" from Irish politics once more. On January 27, 1949, at a great all-party rally at the Mansion House a campaign against partition was announced. How *Fine Gael* saw this matter was revealed in the statement of its Minister for Justice, "the next war will be a holy war". Official pronouncements, while carefully avoiding commitment, managed to convey that if England wanted to do away with Irish neutrality the transference of the excepted powers in the Six counties to Dublin would suffice for the necessary response. This line of policy was of *Cumann na Ngaedheal* pedigree. As has been said, in 1926 Kevin O'Higgins offered concessions of independence in hopes of gaining a *quid pro quo* of national unity. When one reflects that at this period NATO was being established in the euphoria of the largesse distributed throughout Europe by the United States, we can glimpse a hidden perspective which may have motivated the thinking of the coalition parties.

But once more imperialism declined to do business. Nothing short of a gift was acceptable. Accordingly the Republic was declared with great solemnity at Easter 1949. A howl of rage went up at Westminster. The Labour Government introduced the ill-considered Ireland Act which contained two main provisions. First, the

English Government recognised the secession of "Eire". Second, Irish citizens were still not to be regarded as aliens. The remnant of common citizenship was to be preserved. The valuable influx of labour and capital from Ireland was not to be diverted elsewhere by foolish reprisals. The Act need have contained no more. But there were backwoodsmen to be placated. Hence the insulting but constitutionally worthless third provision that the Six counties would not cease to be part of the United Kingdom without the consent of the Parliament at Stormont which was forbidden under its constitution even to discuss the matter! Since no parliament can bind its successors this provision was merely a declaration of policy. What imperialism had, imperialism intended to hold. The real significance of the whole episode was that the declaration of the Republic completed the dismantling of the Free State Agreement Act. Inevitably the next constitutional reforms must affect the Six counties. And to that area inevitably the centre of the national independence struggle must shift.

Without progress towards national reunification public opinion in the Twenty-six counties would accept no detraction from the principle of neutrality. Its resources not differing markedly from those of its predecessor, the record of the Coalition was not markedly superior to that of *Fianna Fáil*. Progress was of course made, particularly in the field of public health. The rejection of Dr Browne's comprehensive health service, which gave rise to the "mother and child scheme" controversy, was however a sign of the times. The promises of the left parties within the Coalition could not be met. In 1951 the Government sought to assist capital accumulation by reducing agricultural subsidies. Unable to carry its left supporters, it appealed to the country and *Fianna Fáil* was returned again in June 1951.

The "Rationalisation" of agriculture could no longer await the advent of rural industrialisation. The plan adumbrated in 1938 went into effect. Under pressure of a price system against which the Government gave no protection the small farmers lost their grip on the soil. The mid-twentieth century witnessed clearances as decisive as the mid-nineteenth. But there were no crowbar brigades. The compulsion was economic and the people left quietly. Whole families departed and some western townlands were left with scarcely an inhabited house. Some land continued to be grazed as conacre. In other places the reeds and thistles grew. The legatees of a culture two thousand years old flooded into the social deserts of the English midlands where life normally consisted of work, worry and drugged sleep and where the sole amenity was drink. Here some of them helped to make tractors to uproot the next wave of migrants. They also came into touch with trade unionism and socialism and built up Irish clubs and societies.

The annual rate of emigration in the quinquennium 1946–51 was given as 8.2 per thousand of average population. The corresponding figure for 1951–56 was 13.4, and for 1956–61 it was 14.8. What this meant for the countryside can be gathered from agricultural statistics. These may continue to treat separately holdings now worked by one farmer. Even so they show a decline of 28,786 in the number of holdings between one and fifty acres in the five years 1955–60. That is to say that about a twelfth of the holdings worked in the Twenty-six counties in 1955 were either consolidated, built on or let run wild by 1960.*

It is estimated that 408,766 persons emigrated in the ten years 1951–61. Possibly in view of the widespread unemployment brought by the recession of the mid-fifties, and the low productivity of the smallest farm units, their departure was no embarrassment to the Department of Finance, especially when their remit-

* The increase in the number of holdings of over fifty acres in the same period was 2,817.

tances from England were brought into the sum. But what of the cost of rearing them? The mass emigration of the fifties showed the beginning of a disquieting trend, the mortgaging of the future by meeting current losses out of capital.

The retrenchment foreshadowed by the Coalition was begun by *Fianna Fáil* but continued by the second Coalition between 1955 and 1957. The genesis of the trade imbalance in the partition of the country has already been noted. Calling one part of Ireland a Republic did not cure it. In 1952 imports stood at £170 million with only £100 million of exports to pay for them. In making up the deficit tourism, personal remittances, net income from foreign investment played their part. There was a net capital influx of £9 million, and foreign holdings were left intact.

By 1955 the situation had deteriorated. The value of imports had risen to £202 million, that of exports to only £108 million. The gap was now £94 million, and this time there appeared in the accounts a figure of £36 million designated, "Banking transactions–changes in net external assets". These assets are linked with the interests of privileged rentier elements within the Twenty-six counties. There will always be a response to the cry of "investments in danger" from these sections, and in 1955 a wide range of import controls was imposed. In subsequent years the foreign reserves were slowly built up, and the accounts were balanced thanks to a steady influx of foreign, mostly English, capital which penetrated every sector of the Irish economy, buying, investing and taking over.

The movement of popular discontent was composed of three strands. The most robust was the trade union movement which pursued its campaign for wage improvement with stolid persistence. The unemployed movement was largely a spontaneous agitation in which the Irish Workers Party (the Twenty-six county successor of the former Communist Party of Ireland) played a formative part. The most significant development was however the revival of *Sinn Fein* and the I.R.A., still under the influence of the honest but non-political ideological progeny of Sean Russell, but containing younger elements receptive to new ideas. The Republicans published a monthly journal and fought local elections. They undertook raids for arms both in England and the Six counties, and those of them who were caught received heavy sentences.

In the Westminster general election of 1955 the Republican candidates, Thomas Mitchell and Philip Clarke were returned for Six-county constituencies, although at the time they were serving ten-year sentences in connection with a raid for arms on Omagh barracks. They were unseated by Court order on the ground that they were convicted felons. In the resultant by-election they were successful again, and the proceedings had to be repeated. The main loser was the old Nationalist party, a survival from Home Rule days, whose worthy but ageing politicians for a time kept the headlines but steadily lost the masses.

On December 12, 1956, the I.R.A. commenced operations on the border. A body not exceeding two hundred was involved. They had woefully inadequate equipment but courage enough for a legion. What did they hope to achieve? Some perhaps considered they were taking up the task left unfinished in 1922. Others were conscious of asserting the principle of revolt once more in their generation. What they expressed historically was the transition to a new epoch when the main struggle against the partition system would centre in the occupied area. Their action released forces inherent in the situation These forces might have more properly been released by the organised Labour movement. But the Labour movement suffered from the political paralysis which was itself a product of partition. As had happened so often

472

before the lead was taken by the petite bourgeoisie. They failed completely in their immediate conscious objective. But in the trial of strength with circumstances they transformed themselves.

The insurgents were under orders not to attack the police or armed forces of the Twenty-six county government. In this they followed the war-time thought of Russell and Ryan. They were prepared to engage members of the well-armed Royal Ulster Constabulary and its associated sectarian B-Specials. But their object was to bring the English Army into action and then create such a national confrontation as Mellows and O'Connor had dreamed of in 1922. Like them they were unsuccessful because the conditions for it did not exist. But it is important to appreciate that they resolutely disclaimed any antagonism to the Six-county Protestants, and declared for religious toleration in a United Irish Republic.

On January 8, 1957, they suffered a serious setback. Their working plan was captured. It listed bridges, B.B.C. transmittors, oil refineries, radar stations, police barracks and other installations they intended to destroy. Such a reverse at the outset inevitably restricted the campaign. The Six-county authorities arrested nearly two hundred prominent Republicans and held them in Crumlin Road jail without charge or trial. Those captured during guerrilla operations were sentenced and joined them there. At the general election in the Twenty-six counties held in May 1957 four *Sinn Fein* deputies were returned, but in accordance with tradition declined to take their seats.

If the Six-county administration reacted with clumsy repression, reactivating the Special Powers Acts which abrogated two-thirds of the provisions of the Universal Declaration of Human Rights, the behaviour of the Tory Government in England was bankruptcy itself. Congenitally incapable of recognising any new stage in Irish history, because they fail to see its independent national movement, they repeated the platitudes of decades. It "would not be proper to intervene". Law and order was "a matter for the Northern Ireland Government". They thus permitted their satraps to descend from foolishness to insanity. Not one reform to meet the real grievances of the Catholic population was proposed while the I.R.A. hammered at the gates. The Tories not only under-estimated the depth of the crisis in Ireland. They failed to appreciate the new degree of organisation of the Irish immigrants and their integration with the Labour movement. The excesses of the B-men, the arbitrary arrests and imprisonments became visible tops revealing the presence of the vast submerged organisation of tyranny. After forty years once more there grew up in England an informed radical opinion friendly to Ireland. The interest of trade unionists was expressed in the campaigns for the acquittal of Mallon and Talbot, young men accused of setting a booby trap which blew up a policeman, and for the release of the untried prisoners.

The I.R.A. campaign made little headway after 1957 and political support dwindled. The Twenty-six county Government rounded up prominent Republicans and once more the Curragh internment camp came into service. The balance of trade went from bad to worse. The deficits of £80 million from 1958 to 1961 increased to £100 million in 1962, £110 million in 1963 and £150 million in 1965. The influx of foreign capital from being a temporary ballast became the financial keel of the economy. In 1961 capital exports roughly balanced capital imports. The excess of imports over exports rose to £13 million in 1962, £22 million in 1963 and £41 million in 1965. Everywhere could be discerned the anglicisation of Irish life, old-established merchants taken over, historic buildings demolished to make way for speculative office blocks, mergers and takeovers every day. The largest native capitalists were fusing their interests with imperialist monopoly. There were pickings for every parasite. The inability of the bourgeoisie to complete the struggle for independence became more glaring every day. The way was being prepared for a revival of socialism.

England was seeking membership of the European Economic Community. Inevitably she must take the Six counties with her. The rough balance of trade enjoyed by the northern area had long disappeared, with the decline of linen and shipbuilding. A series of Reports on the ensuing economic crisis was published. They showed clearly that the Six counties was at a permanent disadvantage as a supplier of the English market which was too remote, i.e., the trouble was Partition. The trade imbalance was being dealt with by the same process of speculative investment and takeover that afflicted the south. Under conditions of membership of the E.E.C. Partition could not of course alone guarantee Britain's predominance in the Irish market. This was to be safeguarded by ownership of Irish industries and commercial outlets. Partition on the other hand retained its importance as a means of weakening the progressive forces which though ranged against the same monopolies were confined to separate jurisdictions. England's conception of Ireland's relation to the common market was thus "integration within integration", an Ireland economically dominated by the same monopolies, but divided politically, integrated in the first place with England, but the whole integrated with the E.E.C. as a single unit dominated from London. In pursuit of this conception the Free Trade agreement between England and the Twenty-six counties was signed in 1964.

This agreement was signed on the understanding that membership of E.E.C. was inevitable. If enthusiasm could have secured it, *Fianna Fáil* would have had the country in within months. The bait dangled before the people was that "the economic border would disappear". But a series of official investigations showed that a number of Irish industries would disappear also. The gain would go to the foreign monopolies. And the political border would remain. Notwithstanding these considerations the movement for "hands across the border" began. There were mutual receptions, and post-prandial compliments were exchanged between *Taoiseach* Lemass and Premier O'Neill. Since some immediate concession was required to prepare Twenty-six county opinion for what seemed obviously to be on the way, the recognition of the Six-county regime, i.e. the amendment of the Constitution of 1937, the "Orange and Green" talks were instituted. There was talk of ameliorating the lot of the Six-county Catholics. But since no firm improvements emerged the result was merely to destroy the authority of the Nationalist Party which up to then had represented them.

The I.R.A. called a halt to the Northern campaign in 1962, in order to organise united resistance to what they described as the "New Act of Union". The Wolfe Tone Commemoration of 1963, the 1916 jubilee in 1966, and the Connolly centenary of 1968 were massively celebrated. They had learned during the struggle that their only friends were on the "left", and the series of commemorations, revealing to a new generation the grandeur and complexity of the Irish revolutionary tradition, made a great impact on all sections of the movement. For the first time the majority of the Republicans came to stand on the left. The formerly unthinkable happened. *Sinn Fein* declared itself a socialist party. The swing to the left was marked in the North by the election of Gerard Fitt to Westminster as a "Socialist Republican" and open supporter of the principles of James Connolly.

Already in the darkest days of the Northern campaign a committee for the protection of Civil Liberties had been set up in Belfast. It was strengthened when as a result of the work of the Connolly Association in London, widespread trade union and Labour support was brought to the demand for the release of internees and prisoners held by the Six-county Government. The initiative in England was of the greatest importance in limiting the freedom to manoeuvre of the Northern Unionists. The decisive event was the calling in Belfast on the initiative of W. McCullough and Elizabeth Sinclair (who had led the fight against fascism during the war) of a remarkable conference. It was held under the auspices of the Belfast Trades Council. For the first time in their lives old Catholic workers told their Protestant trade unionists what it was like to be second-class citizens. A programme of democratic demands was drawn up, and many of these were subsequently adopted by the Northern Ireland Committee of the Irish Congress of Trade Unions (now once more a united body).

Again the spectre had appeared; Catholic and Protestant were combining under the banner of the working class. The movement of the Irish people for democratic rights was winning support among English workers. Hissing and spitting unregarded in the wings was an extremist clergyman, Ian Paisley, who had founded his own breakaway sect so as to be free to pursue his inordinate hatred of Catholicism. At this point he emerged into the glare of the footlights, playing the combined roles, so he hoped and presumably believed, of "roaring Hanna" and Edward Carson.

He attracted to his banner especially those sections who had been threatened as a result of the vast influx of English capital—small shopkeepers, workers whose old occupations were being abolished, Protestants who felt the threat of unemployment after a spell of prosperity. These were people whose interests should direct them against imperialism. But Paisley turned their minds into the past, to by-gone caste favours not in the climate of future times. In doing so he activated the gutter elements who have formed the spearhead of every pogrom since the Battle of the Diamond. He persuaded substantial elements within the Unionist Party that he was an essential safeguard of their position as the chosen vicegerents of the imperial power. Worse than this, he intimidated honest trade unionists and blunted the class-consciousness of workers who were overcoming old prejudices and looking for a new united basis of struggle. He confronted the democratic movement with a difficult tactical situation: to appear to acquiesce in the snail's pace "improvement in community relations" which formed a part of the British plan of integration, or to find more militant action manoeuvred onto sectarian lines. Meanwhile the ruling Unionists availed themselves of the situation to bring even the snail to a halt. The deadlock could only be removed by action from Westminster. But the Labour Government remained sunk in imperturbable complacency. Meanwhile the Catholics had been led to expect something, and groups with mingled reforming and revolutionary aims were developing alongside the old Nationalist Party.

The transition to "direct action" took place in the summer of 1968 when Austin Currie, a young and vigorous member of the Nationalist party at Stormont, led a move to occupy a house in Dungannon that had been let to a single Unionist when hundreds of Catholic families lacked accommodation. The first "Civil Rights" demonstration took place when contingents from Belfast and the surrounding country marched on Dungannon and were held up at the entrance to the town on the grounds that their intended meeting place had been pre-empted by Paisleyites. Despite threatening exchanges the demonstrators dispersed peacefully, thus preserving the position where the Paisleyites remained isolated as the enemies of peace.

The threat posed by such tactics was not to be ignored. Provocation was the answer and the authorities joined in it. A Civil Rights march into the centre of Derry, a city whose two-thirds Nationalist population as a result of gerrymandering returned a two-thirds Unionist council, was banned outright. Indignation reached such fever pitch that the organisers decided to defy the ban and thereby preserve the organised character of the protest. Four English Members of Parliament flew post haste to Derry to witness the use of clubs and water-cannon in an orgy of policy violence and brutality. The world saw on its television screens what Unionism meant to those who lived under its tyranny.

The events in Derry won the Civil Rights movement its widest support. Protestant workers and Liberal intellectuals saw the Catholics engaged in a non-sectarian struggle for basic necessities which it was the duty of the Government to provide. There were joint religious services in Derry which had been "invaded" by the Orange demonstrators. The democratic movement won mass support among Belfast students, who organised demonstrations that were models of discipline and organisation.

The Unionist response was provocation and more provocation. The tactic was to arrange a Paisleyite counter-demonstration and then rely on the Government to ban both. Perhaps under the influence of recent events in Paris, and having but limited political experience or theoretical development themselves, the students allowed themselves to be lured away from their base in the University. "Confrontation" became the watchword, and disturbances in Newry, whither a contingent had ventured, led to the first narrowing of the base of the Civil Rights Movement. A march under student and allied auspices during the first days of 1969 completed the journey from Belfast to Derry after suffering a series of fierce ambushes by Paisleyite mobs who were growing in impudence and establishing secret military formations. The young people showed the highest courage and fortitude. But there were voices raised in criticism of their tactics which it was feared were alienating potential sympathisers on the Protestant side and helping the more extreme Unionists.

By the spring of 1969 Paisleyite demands for a policy of ruthless repression had undermined the stability of the O'Neill administration. Unwilling to seek a democratic alternative when the Westminster Government was so obviously shrinking from its duty of rounding up the fascist bands in defence of the constitution it had itself imposed, O'Neill called a general election on his handling of the situation. The result was on the one hand a strengthening of the right-wing Unionists, on the other the disruption of the old Nationalist Party, and the return of a number of "Civil Rights" members to Stormont.

The atmosphere increasingly resembled that of 1920 and 1935. Mysterious explosions wrecked public installations. Arms were reported to be pouring in. Rumour and counter-rumour became prevalent. When O'Neill resigned, as a prelude to his withdrawal from Irish politics, Chichester-Clark, a sour-faced Orangeman, became Premier. He angered the Paisleyites by promising to continue, if less resolutely, the temporising policies of his predecessor. He had the advantage over O'Neill that he was less purely English in outlook, though he lacked O'Neill's flexibility.

The supreme provocation came in August 1969. Despite widespread appeals to forbid, the Unionist authorities permitted a large Orange demonstration, mostly composed of residents of other areas, to parade through Derry where the Civil Rights demonstrations had been prohibited, thus flaunting before the very faces of the Catholics their status of second-class citizens. Inevitably fighting broke out, in which police and "Specials" joined. The people threw up barricades as the Royal Ulster Constabulary charged with clubs, missiles and deadly gas grenades. There were many casualties, some deaths, and great destruction of property.

These events and the wave of protest they gave rise to, were the signal for what may have been an attempted Paisleyite coup. With every sign of careful preparation behind them, armed bands invaded the Catholic quarter of Belfast, burning houses by the hundred, looting, raking blocks of dwellings with the fire of rifles and machine-guns mounted on police tenders. It is scarcely credible that this could happen without connivance in high places. But though the virulence of this concerted attack exceeded all precedents, 1969 was not 1920 or 1935. The inhabitants of the Falls Road area defended every yard with improvised weapons. Soon they had created a city within a city, its population a hundred thousand strong, walled off from the outside world with barricades manned by sentries, policed by a people's committee, served with news by "Radio Free Belfast", flying over it the Irish National flag.

As the fury mounted the English Government vacillated. In Dublin Premier Lynch moved Irish troops to the border areas, set up huge camps to accommodate the thousands of destitute refugees and informed the United Nations. Four days after he had complacently repeated the parrot phrase "law and order is a matter for the Northern Ireland Government" the English Home Secretary was forced to act, it is said as a result of a direct instruction from the Premier, Wilson. "Law and order" was taken out of the hands of the satrapy, and temporarily vested in the imperialists. The English garrison was reinforced with thousands of fresh troops. Boys in khaki, bewilderment written on their faces, manned the borderland between the two communities. The mask was off. Northern Ireland was after all a colony. On orders from Westminster, Chichester-Clark announced substantial reforms, which nevertheless steadily lost substantiality as the immediate danger passed.

While the Paisleyites, among whom Paisley himself was now emerging as a species of "moderate", had failed ignominiously in the aim of driving out the Catholics from the Six counties and replacing the Chichester-Clark administration by something even more reactionary, they had succeeded in another object. They had fanned the antagonism between Catholic and Protestant to fresh heat and postponed their necessary and inevitable rapprochement. A sense of sullen fear and uneasy resentment descended on all but the most enlightened Protestants. But still it was not "back to 1920". In the shipyard, once a copious reservoir of religious bigotry, the workers pledged themselves to work for communal peace, albeit under a huge Union flag.

There were further repercussions in Dublin. Interest in the issue of Partition was sharply revived. A movement of solidarity with the northern Catholics swept the land. Protestant churchmen entered its ranks. Labour, traditionally weak on national questions, sent deputations to Belfast and London. Throughout Ireland men and women were drawn into political activity for the first time in their lives.

A curious sequel was a fresh split in the Republican movement. This still contained a substantial element who hankered after the old purisms of the forties and fifties. At the *Ard Fheis* in January 1970 these revolted over proposals that *Sinn Fein* should in the new conditions enter the Dublin Parliament to fight in defence of the degree of democracy and national independence so far achieved and for its further extension. The split was in keeping with the petit-bourgeois social basis of the movement, and to some degree ran along the division between town and country. Among some sections there may have been a feeling that the successful defence against counter-revolution in the north should have provided an opportunity for revolution. It is difficult to think so. The initiative in August was in the hands of the reactionaries, but their plans were foiled by the unity and courage of the nationalist people.

The struggle develops in ever more complex forms. Some have attempted to pose the issue of Civil Rights in the Six counties against that of national unity, national independence, even socialism. But it is clear that this struggle, like the parallel struggle of the tenants which involves both Protestants and Catholics in amicable co-operation, has the precise status of the classic tithe war, or the Catholic emancipation campaign. These were struggles for elements of a revolution that had so far been frustrated. It is the form at present being taken by the national liberation struggle and is one of the necessary steps on the road to socialism. Its lesson must be to teach the need for the unity of the people irrespective of religion, and from that will develop the demand for an independent Irish nation, provided of course that Republicans do not hide their aims. It is a struggle to free the initiative of the masses, to end inequalities that poison their mutual relations, and to make possible a united working class.

If the initiative in ending Partition properly belongs in England, as Jackson argued, then the initiative in guaranteeing democratic conditions of development for Irish territory held within the United Kingdom also properly belongs in England. The fault lies in a bad constitution. If this does not provide democratic conditions it must be amended so as to do so. But amendment is acceptable only because of the impracticability *for the moment* of abolishing it in favour of a united Ireland. Any amendment that is acceptable must therefore move in the direction of a united Republic, by providing the facilities necessary for the struggle for this objective. A satisfactory temporary expedient would be the passing of a "Bill of Rights" at Westminster writing into the constitution of Northern Ireland (so-called) the guarantee of civil rights not inferior to those enjoyed in England, but recognising the right to leave the United Kingdom and amalgamate with the rest of Ireland. That right is not at present admitted. The proposal with which Mr Enoch Powell and some Labour men who should know better have flirted, namely the administrative fusion of the Six counties with England, is totally retrogressive. For the only permanent solution of the Irish question is the relinquishment by English Government of all claim to sovereignty in any part of Ireland. If hitherto existing Governments have failed in this duty, a Government of the working class may yet do elementary justice to the interests of a closely neighbouring people.

London
January, 1970   C. Desmond Greaves

INDEX

Abercromby, Lord, 199

Aborigines of Ireland, 25

Act of Indemnity (Carhampton), 133

Act of Settlement, 78

Act of Union (1801), 187–190, 431, *See also* Union

Administration, Irish, 95

Aethelbirt, King of Kent, 32

Agrarian Struggle, unrest and revolt, 102–104, theory of, 305–306

Agreements of 1938, 429

Agricultural Labourers' Union, Whiteboys, 103–104

Agriculture, English markets for Irish products, 205; developments, 1849–1914, 299 to 302

Allen, William Phillip, 288

All-Ireland Communist Party, 452

Alva, Duke of, 71

America, Origins of War of Independence, 94; Declaration of Independence, 100; Wolfe Tone in, 146; and agitation for Repeal of the Union, 235; Fenian Movement, 276 *et seq.*, 333–335; Terence Bellew MacManus' funeral, 280–281; the desertion of Parnell, 356

American Civil War, 248; and Fenianism, 281–282

American Navy (1812), 316

Amnesty, for Fenian prisoners, 307

Amnesty Act, 1798, 184

Amnesty Movement, 1871, 291

Ancient Britons, 157; barbarities of 1798, 170

Ancient Order of Hibernians (A.O.H.), 364, 390; and Orangeism 375; Easter Rising 1916, 396; *See also* Board of Erin

Anglo-Norman feuds, 39–40

Anglo-Spanish war, 48

Annuities, 428–429

Antrim, not planted in 1609, 52; held by Parliament, 1641, 65; poor Catholic farms in, 144; the 1798 rising in, 181–182

Ard Fheis, 446, 482

Ard-Ri (High King), 28–35

Arklow in the rising of '98, 180

Armagh, confiscations in, 51; suppression of Oakboys, 104; bickering of Catholic and Protestant peasants, 134; Peep-of-Day Boys and Defenders, 143; Orange terror in, 155–156; revolt of 40's. freeholders, 214–215

Arms, seized from Volunteers, 130; order for surrender of in Ulster, 157–158; supplied for Ulster resistance, 374, 376; gun-running in Ulster, 379; for Irish Volunteers, 380–381; for Easter rising, 1916, 391–393; for Republican Volunteers, 413; purchased and smuggled for I.R.A. 415

Arms Act, 127, 130

Army, under Strafford, 57; of William III, 82; Orange Order extended to, 212; Fenian penetration in British, 282, 284

Ashe, Thomas, 1916 rising, 397; death during hunger strike, 406

Asquith, Herbert, 390
Athboy, resistance to Militia Act, 132
Athlone, battle of, 83
Attlee, Clement R., 467
Aughrim, battle of, 83
Auxiliaries, 414

Bakunin, 333
Balance of power, 82
Baldwin, Stanley, 421
Balfour, Arthur, Perpetual Coercion Act, 1887, 333; on funeral of Parnell, 357
Balla, Co. Mayo, Land League meeting, 323
Ballina, French landing, 1798, 185
Ballinafad, resistance to Militia Act, 132
Ballot Act, 1872, 309
Ballymena, 181
Ballynahinch, defeat of rebels of '98, 182
Ballynamuck, surrender of the French, 1789, 185
Baltinglass, resistance to Militia Act, 132
Bantry, foundation of, 34
Bantry Bay, French fleet in, 153
"Battle of the Diamond", 144, 224, 478
Beggars, 97
Belfast, Volunteers raised, 106; Courts Martial, 1797, 160; University College proposed, 241; prosperity of, 302; pogroms, 1920–21, 417–418, 422, 453; 1935 pogroms, 453; industries, 442; and Civil Liberties, 476; Labour deputations, 482
Belfast Harbour Board, 302
Belfast Society of United Irishmen, 118–119

Belfast Volunteer Corps, disarmed, 131
Beresford family, 141; opposed at 1826 elections, 214
Beresford John Claudius, 183
Beresford, Marcus, 122
B-Specials, 473–474, 480
"Big Beggar-Man" (O'Connell), 226
Biggar, Joseph Gillis, initiation of Parliamentary obstruction, 300; Coercion Bill, 328
Bill of Rights, 78
Birkenhead, Lord, 422; See also F. E. Smith.
Birrell, Augustine, and the Republicans, 389–390
Black-and-Tans, 360, 414–416
Blackmail, paid by the Pale to Irish, 44
Blanqui, Auguste, 193, 276
Board of Erin, 364, 390
Bog of Allen, 181
Bomba, King of Naples, 279
Bonn, Moritz J., on Irish agrarian standard of living, 361
Boulavogue, Wexford rising begun, '98, 176
Boundary Clause, 422, 424–427
Boundary Commission, 426
Bourgeoisie, English, and Charles I, 54–55
Boycott, Captain, 326–327
Boyne, Battle of the, 82–83
Boys of Wexford, the '98 rising, 174–181
Brehon law, 40, 41
Brian Boroimhe, 35, 240
Bristol, repeopling of Dublin, 38
British Empire, Parnell and, 31
British National Convention, 1792, 120
British T.U.C., 466
Brown, John, 291

Brugha, Cathal, acting President of Dáil, 1918, 411; killed, 426

Brunswick Clubs, 213

Brunswick, Grand Duke of, 170

Buckley, Donald, 430

Budget, Lords v. Commons, 1909, 371

Buonaparte, Napoleon, 150; decision to "double-cross" the Irish, 167

Burke, Thomas Henry, murdered in Phœnix Park, 332

Butlers, Ormond, 46

Butt, Isaac, 286; Home Rule, 309; Crisis in Home Rule Party, 315; death of, 317

Butter-milk, diet-staple, 96

Byrne, Miles, 193–195

Camperdown, Battle of, 155

Canada, and repeal agitation, 235

Cape St. Vincent, Battle of, 154

"Captain Moonlight", 330

Carhampton, Lord, trial of peasants by Court Martial, 132–133

Carlow, opening of the tithe war, 218–219

Carmagnole, 122

Carnarvon, Lord, approach to Parnell, 1883, 337; and Home Rule, 338

Carnot, Lazare Nicolas (1753 to 1823), 147, 200–201

Carrickshork, tithe war, 219

Carrightwohill, tithe war, 223

Carson, Sir Edward, 445, "Revolt" against Home Rule, 304; agitation in Ulster, 373; Ulster gun-running, 380; German hopes of rebellion, 392; and the 1916 executions, 399; on Belfast pogrom, 418

Casement, Roger, attempt to recruit Irish Brigade in Germany, 391–392; landing in Kerry, 393; arrest, 393; executed, 400

Castlepollard, tithe war, 219

Castlereagh, Viscount, 183, 188, 192, 316

Castlerosse, Lord, elections, 1872, 309

Casualties, 1916 rising, 397; Civil War, 425

Catholic Association, founded by Daniel O'Connell, 211 to 216; Act to suppress, 216

Catholic Committee and United Irishmen, 116; Wolfe Tone and, 120–123; and the Union, 191–192; O'Connell's leadership, 210; dissolution of, 210

Catholic Confederation, in the Civil War, 1642, 65; dissolved, 67

Catholic Defence Association, and Tenants' Right League, 270; Pope's Brass Band, 270 to 271

Catholic Emancipation, 114, 210 to 216; and Volunteer Convention, 1783, 112–113; struggle, 121; See also Catholic Relief

Catholic Relief Act, 1793, 124, 208; 1829, 215–216

Catholic Relief Bills, 109, 141, 213

Catholics, exiled into Connacht, 73; land owned by, 79; under the Penal Code, 85–86; debarred from voting, 95; and the Volunteer movement, 106–107; relations with Protestants (1790–1), 114–115; increase of Catholic landowners, 114–115; peers, ecclesiastics, and the "mutinous" laymen, 121; gentry and peasants under martial law, 165 to 166, Wexford rising, 1798, 178; and the Union, 190 to 192; the 1798 rising, 195 *et seq.*; and tithes, 218; curates and Tenants' Right League, 273–274; and Disestablishment, 292; Belfast pogroms, 417–418, 422; and arms regulations, 424; the Civil War, 424–426

Catholics, English, 50; Anti-Parnell campaign, 344

Cattle, English policy and Irish exports, 94

Cattle-lending, 31

Cavan, confiscations in, 51

Cave Hill oath, 146

Cavendish, Lord Frederick, murdered in Phœnix Park, 332

Ceannt, Eamonn, of Provisional Government, 1916, 395; shot, 399

Census, 1851, report, 262

Centenary of '98, 367

Chamberlain, Austen, 422

Chamberlain, Joseph, Kilmainham Compact, 331; approach to Parnell, 1883, 336; and Home Rule, 339; Home Rule Bill, 340–341; *The Times* anti-Parnell campaign, 345 to 348; O'Shea divorce, 353–354

Chamberlain, Neville, 421; Agreements of 1938, 429; Constitution of 1937, 430; Second World War, 463

Charlemont, Lord, Volunteer C.-in-C., 112

Charles I, 54 *et seq.*, 76; and the arrest of Laud and Strafford, 60; subjugation of Ireland, 61–62; the Civil War, 63–68; execution of, 67

Charles II, 67, 70, 77, 78–79, 172

Chartism (Chartists), 119, 209; and O'Connell, 227–229; Repeal agitation, 235; Justice to Ireland, 251; and the *United Irishman*, 252; discredited, 253–254

Chesterfield, Lord, on Whiteboys and landlords, 104

Chichester-Clark, James, Major, 480, 481, 482

Chief Secretary, 95

Childers, Erskine, 426

Children, sale of, 74–75; effects of Penal Code on, 89

Christianity, early influences from Europe, 24

Church, in Gaelic Ireland, 32 to 33; and the feudal system, 36; Anglo-Norman Conquest, 36, 38; under the Tudors, 43; under the Penal Code, 85 to 86; English revolution, 57 to 59

Churchill, Lord Randolph, approach to Parnell, 1883, 337; Home Rule, 338

Churchill, Sir Winston, on O'Shea divorce, 349; Second World War, 463–464

Cinel, 28, 29

Citizen Army, 378, 387–88; and the Irish Volunteers, 388; 1916 rising, 396

"Citizen Soldiers", 129

Civil Liberties, 476

Civil List, 96

Civil Rights demonstrations, 478–480, 483

Civil War (1641–9), 63–68

Civil War, 1798, 169

488

Civil War, Irish, 422–426

Clan na Gael, 280

Clann na Poblachta, 467, 468

Clann Rickard, 42

Clare, 1829 election and emancipation, 215–216

Clare, Earl of, 141, 183; and the Catholic Committee, 121

Clarence, Duke of (son of Edward III), Viceroy, Statute of Kilkenny, 40–42

Clarke, Thomas James, Republican leader, 385; and I.R.B. chiefs, 390; and 1916 rising, 391; of Provisional Government, 395; shot, 398

Clarke, Philip, 472

Class struggle, nature of, in England and Ireland, 151 to 152

Class war, 1798, 170–171

Classes, in Ulster resistance to Home Rule, 374–375

Clearance and plantation, 49 to 51

Clerkenwell explosion, 284

Cloncurry, Lord, 173

Clonmel, New Model Army defeated, 71

Clones, 449

Clontarf, Battle of, 1014, 35

Clontarf, monster meeting, 237

Clubs, in the Irish Confederation, 249

Cobden, Richard, and Ecclesiastical Titles Bill, 271

Cockayne, informer against Jackson, 138–139, 142

Coercion Act, 1832, 223; effect of, 328–329

Coercion Act, Perpetual, 1887, 333

Coercion Bill, 251, 327–329

Coinage, control of, 101

Coinmed, 42

Colbert, Con, shot, 399

Coleraine (Derry), confiscations in, 51; restoration of, 52

Collins, Michael, at grave of Thomas Ashe, 406; "life on the run" 1918–21, 408; building a General Staff, 408; plan for escape of De Valera, 411; Director of Intelligence, Anglo-Irish war, 413; negotiations for the Treaty, 420; C.-in-C. of Free State Army, 425; killed, 426

Commercial Restraints Act, 205

Commission, House of Lords, on resistance to Militia Act, 133–134

Commission, Special, on Parnell and *The Times* (1888 to 90), 333, 346–348

Communards, 279

Commune Council of Paris, executed, 200

Commune, Paris, 1871, 333

Communist Party of Ireland, 458, 572

Communists, 276

Condon, O'Mara, 288

Confederate Clubs, 251

Confederates, and arrests of Mitchell and Meagher, 255; rising of 1848, 255–257

Confederation, The Irish, foundation, 247–248

Confiscations, 49–51, 73–74, 84

Congested Districts Board (C.D.B.), 360

Connacht, 73; threat of plantation, 56; disposition of estates, 1665, 79; land hunger in, 134; Orange terror in, 155–156

Connachta, 29–30

Connolly Association, 476

Connolly Club, 457

Connolly, James, 295, 306, 411, 446, 466, 476; on Board of Erin, 364, 375; Socialist Republican Party, 368–369; Labour War, 1913, 376–378; and the 1914 War, 386; substitute for Larkin, 389; impatience of, 390; and S.L.P., 390; and I.R.B. plan for Easter rising, 1916, 391; Easter Rising, 391; member of Provisional Government, 1916, 395; shot, 399; on Partition, 433; Centenary, 1968, 476

Connolly, R. J., 452

Connolly-Larkin Agitations, 358

Conscription, resistance to, 404, 408

Constitution of 1937, 430

Convention, 407

Convention Act, and the Volunteers, 127–129

Convention, Catholic, 1792, 121 to 124; and the Convention Act, 127

Convention, French National, 122

Convention Parliament, 80

Convention of Volunteers, 1782, 109–110

Coogan, *Ireland Since the Rising*, 457

Co-operative creameries, 360

Coote, Sir Charles, leader of Parliamentary army, 65; besieged in Derry, 67

Cork, foundation of, 34; held by King's Party, 1641, 65; captured by Marlborough, 83; Courts Martial, 1797, 160; disturbances repressed, 1798, 170; University College proposed, 241

Cork, County, tithe war, 220

Corn Law, 114

Corn Laws, repeal of, 1846, 244

Cornwallis, Lord, Viceroy, on vengeance after the '98, 182

Cosgrave, W. T., M. P. for Kilkenny, 1918, 409; head of Free State Government, 426

Costello, J. A., 468

Council of Ireland, 438

Court of Star Chamber, and plantation of Ulster, 56; declared unconstitutional, 1640, 60

Courts Martial, after 1916 rising, 398–400

Covenant, Ulster, 373–374

Cowper, Earl, Viceroy, 331

Coyne and livery, 41–42

Crawfurd, Sharman, 269

Crimes Act, 1883, 337; 1885, 339

Cromwell, Oliver, 54–75; landing in Dublin, 1649, 68; and the Levellers, 70; conquest and settlement of Ireland, 70–72

"Croppy", 176, 198

"Croppy" priests of Wexford, 178

Crozier, General, 419

Crumlin Road jail, 473

Cullen, Cardinal, 273, 279; head of Catholic hierarchy, 271; the MacManus funeral, 281

Cumann na mBan, 387

Cumberland, Duke of, head of the Orange Order, 212

Curfew Order, 1920, 414

Curragh incident, 1914, 376, 379

Curran, John Philpot, defence of Hamilton Rowan, 137 to 138; defence of *Press* newspaper, 163–164; after the '98, 183; and Lord Norbury, 194

Curran, Sarah, 194

Currie, Austin, 478

Cusack, M. F., *Speeches and Public Letters of the Liberator*, 229

Dáil Eireann, 410–412, 428, 430; and Government of Ireland Act, 417; and the Treaty, 420 to 422; after Partition, 454, 466; Second, 456

Dairy products, 97

Daly, Edward, shot, 398

Danes, invasion by, 33–35

Davis, Thomas Osborne, 230 to 232, 246, 277, 293, 363; and O'Connell, 1844, 239–240; and William Smith O'Brien, 240–241; death of, 242; compared with John Mitchel, 248; and Fenian faith, 293; on uselessness of piecemeal "reform", 362

Davitt, Michael, 305–306, 318; Land League, 303, 318–320; life of, 320; with Fenians in U.S.A., 321; land agitation, 322–323; trial abandoned, 323; on Parnell and famine relief, 324; elections, 1880, 324–325; re-imprisoned, 329; Kilmainham Compact, 331; loyalty to Parnell, 335; Land Act, 334; franchise reform, 337; and Special Commission, 347

de Burgh, Hugo, 41

de Burke, Richard, Ri-mor, 41–42

de Burke, William, 42

Declaration of Irish Right, 1782, 109–110

Defenders, 197; and United Irishmen, 133–136; acquisition of arms and Peep-of-Day Boys, 135–136; renewed activity, 143–144; a tenants' protection league, 145; joined to United Irishmen, 156; assisted by Lord Edward Fitzgerald, 172; in Wexford, 1798, 174

Deirbhfine, 27

de Lamartine, Alphonse, 253

Derry, confiscations in, 51; restoration of, 52; held by Parliament, 1641, 65; Siege, 67, 80–81; dereliction of, 449; Civil Rights demonstrations, 478–480

Desmond, Earl of, 42

De Valera, Eamon, President of Sinn Fein, 407, 445–446; returned for Clare, 409; under life sentence, 409; President of the Dáil, 411; truce, 416, 420; Civil War, 426; return to power, 428–430, 448–449; Oath of Allegiance, 430; as Taoiseach, 430; after return to power, 451, 452, 453, 454, 455, 468; Irish neutrality, 457–459, 467; All-Ireland Defence Council, 463, 464; economic crisis, 465

Devlin, Joseph, 375

Devoy, John, 285, 286, 294, 365; and Michael Davitt, 321; favours New Departure, 335; Easter rising, 1916, 391; and the Treaty, 423

Dillon, James, 458

Dillon, John, 409, 458; suspended, 1881, 329; the 1916 executions, 399

Dillon, John Blake, 230

Dingle, landing of Papal expedition, 1579, 48

Directory, National, 168

Directory, Secret of United Irishmen, 172–174

491

Discussion Clubs, 367

Disestablishment, 290, 292

Disraeli, and Irish vote, 1880, 324

Dissenters, 58, 87

Distilling, 97, 300

Doheny, Michael, in Fenian movement, 276–277

Dominion Status, 430

Donegal, confiscations in, 51

Doon, Co. Limerick, tithe war, 220

Down, not planted in 1609, 52; held by Parliament, 1641, 65; the 1798 rising, 181–182

"Drapier Letters", 101–102

Drennan, William, 129, 137, 138

Drogheda, sack of, 70

Drummond, Thomas, and the tithe war, 224–225

Dublin, foundation of, 34; sack of, 37; special appanage of the English Crown, 38; held by King's Party, 1641, 65; surrendered to Parliament, 1647, 66; landing of Cromwell, 68; Land League meeting, 1879, 323; Easter Monday, 1916, 394–395; after Partition, 441, 463, 468, 482

Dublin Artillery, Tandy's, 107, 128

Dublin Metropolitan Police, 362

Dublin Society of United Irishmen, 118–119; suppressed, 138

Dublin Volunteer Corps, disarmed, 130

Duffy, Charles Gavan, 230, 249 to 252, 261; on T. O. Davis, 232; on Monster Repeal meetings, 234; on trial of O'Connell and others, 1844, 238; on death of T. O. Davis, 242; and Lalor's plan, 250–251;

and transportation of Mitchel, 255; failure of prosecution against, 256; Tenants' Right League, 266–274; restarting the *Nation*, 268; on William Keogh, 271–272; emigration, 274

Duncan, Adam (1st Viscount), Battle of Camperdown, 155

Dungannon, Convention of Ulster Volunteers, 1782, 109

Dwyer, Michael, 193, 316

Dynamite War, 333–335

Ecclesiastical Titles Bill, 271, 273

Economic conditions (1690 to 1778), 96–99

Economic development outside the Pale, 45

Economic War, 428–433

Economy, Ireland's place in England's, 205

Economy, Gaelic, 25

Education, under the Penal Code, 89

Edward III, 40

Edward VIII, 453

Eire (Confirmation of Agreements) Act, 1938, 457

Elections, General, 1826, 214; 1832, 222; 1852, 272; 1869, 308; 1874, 309; 1880, 324; 1885, 338–339; 1886, 342; 1895, 358; 1906, 370; 1910, 371; 1918, 403, 408–409; 1921, 411–413

Elections, Irish Municipal, 1920, 411

Elections, Irish Rural Districts, 1920, 411

Elective offices in Gaelic political structure, 28

Elizabeth I, 18, 48

Emigration, during the famine, 245; its consequences, 265;

during American Civil War, 282; and the Land Acts, 261; effect of stoppage of, 423

Emmet Club, 249

Emmet, Robert, 254, 281; attempted insurrection, 1803, 187, 192–195

Emmet, Thomas Addis, 192; and Wolfe Tone, 146; the 1798 rising, 171; after the '98, 184

Enclosures of waste land, 103

Encumbered Estates Act, 261, 263–265, 269, 351

Engels, Friedrich, and the Fenians, 290–291

English National Council for Civil Liberties, 454

Enniskillen: defence of, 80; resistance to Militia Act, 132; dereliction of, 449

Epidemics, following famine, 1845–7, 243

Eric (bloodfine), 27

Erne, Lord, 326

Estates, distribution of, 1665, 79

Europe, situation, 1795–8, 149 to 153; failure of potato crops, 1845–7, 243

European Economic Community, 475

Evictions, statistics, 1845–52, 262; 1877–80, 320; 1880, 325

Executions, after 1916 rising, 398–400

Exports, and American War of Independence, 105; during the Great Famine, 244

Faery Queen by Edmund Spenser, 51

Fairs, 45

Family, Gaelic, 26–27

Famine, of 1595, 49; "Hungry Forties", 209; the "Great Starvation", 1846–7, 243 to 245; of 1879, 318–320

Fascism, Orange Society the first "Fascist" body, 145

Federal plan, 235

"Felon-setting", 277–278

Fenians, 261, 265; The Fenian Brotherhood, 275–283; revolutionary affiliations of, 276 to 277; crisis of Fenianism, 283–288; outcome of the movement, 290–296; the tradition, 292–296; inspiration of Home Rule Party, 207 et seq.; capture of gunboat, 1880, 325; the 1916 rising, 398; the Fenian dead, 404 to 405

Fermanagh, confiscations in, 51; resistance to Militia Act, 132

Fermanagh Mail, and Tenants' Right League, 270

Feudalisation of Gaelic nation, 44

Fianna (Gaelic Boy Scouts), 365

Fianna Fáil, 428, 446, 448, 449, 451, 454, 455, 467, 469, 471, 475

Fine (Gaelic economic unit), 26 et seq.; and slaves, 31

Fine Gael, 451, 458, 467, 468

Fitt, Gerard, M. P., 476

Fitzgerald, Lord Edward, 122, 168, 181, 184, 281 and the rising of 1798, 171–174

Fitzgeralds, Desmond, 42, 46

Fitzgeralds, Kildare, 42

Fitzgibbon family, 141

Fitzgibbon, John, Chancellor, 147

Fitzwilliam, Earl, Viceroy, 141 to 143

Flags, 179

Flaith (head of Geilfine), 26 et seq.

Fleetwood, Gen. Charles, 72

Flogging, abolition of, in Army and Navy, 313

Flood, Henry, and Convention of 1783, 110–113

Foley, Catherine, 222

Food, early Gaelic, 25; of 18th century peasants, 97; production of, during the Great Famine, 244

Forster, William Edward, Chief Secretary, Coercion, 1881, 330; resignation, 331

Fort George, prisoners interned after the '98, 185

Forward, on 1916 rising, 301

Fox, Charles James, 122, 313; and declaration of Irish right, 110; sympathy with France, 137; break with the Duke of Portland, 140; cousin of Lord Edward Fitzgerald, 172

France, and American War of Independence, 105; overthrow of monarchy, 120; National Convention, 122; war declared by England, 126; assistance offered to United Irishmen, 139; "The French are in the Bay", 146–160; Revolution, 149–150; attempts to invade Ireland, 1796–7, 153–155; Fleet in Bantry Bay, 153, 155; and the 1798 rising, 172; 1798 expeditions, 185–186

Franchise, 95–96; Franchise Reform, 338; Franchise Act, 1885, 338

Franco, Francisco, 456

Franklin, Benjamin, 100, 130

Freeholders, forty-shilling, revolt of, 214–215; Disfranchisement Act, 1829, 215

Freeman's Journal, editor on trial, 238

Free men, 30

Free State, 440, 442, 448

"Free State" and "Republic", 422

Free State Agreement Act, 1922, 439, 469

Free State Parliament, 439, 446

Free trade, demanded, 1779, 108; in land, 261, 263, 302

Fuidhir, 31

Gaelic Athletic Association, 365

Gaelic League, 358, 365, 406; efforts to revive language, 363 et seq.

Gaelic Republicans and war, 1914, 386

Gaels, origins, 24–25; society, 24–28; political structure, 28–30; unity and opposition, 30–32

Gaeltacht, 45, 48, 89

Galloglaich (foreign soldiers), 34–35

"Gallow glasses", 35

Galway, surrender of, 1691, 83; University College proposed, 241; the 1916 rising, 397; De Valera's speech at, 463

Garibaldi, Joseph, and the Pope, 278–280

Garrett Mor, Earl of Kildare, 46

Garrett Og, Earl of Kildare, 46–47

Garryowen, 199

Geilfeine (true family), 26–27

Geography, 23–24

George III, and reform proposals, 141; the Act of Union, 189

George IV, 212

George V, 371

Geraldines, the Earls of Kildare, 42, 44, 46 *et seq.*, 172

Geraldine Thomas ("Silken" Thomas Fitzgerald, son of Garrett Og), 47

German Peasants' War, 71

Germany, "Young Germany", 231; I.R.B. and, 386; and the Easter rising, 1916, 391–393

Gettysburg, 282

Gilmore, George, 447, 456

Ginnell, Laurence, M.P., 399

Gladstone, William Ewart and Ecclesiastical Titles Bill, 271; Disestablishment, 290, 292; Land Act, 1870, 303–305; Home Rule Bills, 203; Irish grievances, 207; Amnesty to Fenians, 207; Elections, 1874, 209; Elections, 1880, 325; Coercion Bill, 327–329; procedure resolution, 1881, 329; Phœnix Park murders, 333; conversion to Home Rule, 336–340; approach to Parnell, 1883, 337; Franchise reform, 337; Elections, 1885, and Home Rule, 339; first Home Rule Bill, 340–341; Election defeat, 1886, 342; the O'Shea divorce, 353; the Parnell Party split, 355; retirement, 358

Glamorgan, Lord, 66

Glasnevin, 281, 357

God Save Ireland, 289

Godkin, Rev. James, *Land War in Ireland*, 267–268

Gonne, Maud, 467

Gordon Riots, 254

Gorey, meeting of Wexford magistrates, 1798, 176

Gormanstown, Lord, 65

Gosforth, Lord, protest against Orange terror, 156

Government of Ireland Act, 1920, 437, 438–439, 441

Grahame of Claverhouse ("Bonnie Dundee"), 80

Graigue, opening of tithe war at, 218

Grain, 96; production of, during the famine, 244; decline in acreage, 299

Grass-farmers, 98

Grattan, Henry (1750–1820), 91, 93, 187, 197, 216; his revolution, 100–113; leadership of Patriot opposition, 107 to 110; Declaration of Irish Right, 110; and Henry Flood, 110–113; horror of democracy, 111; Wolfe Tone on, 118; on social changes in the Volunteers, 128; sympathy with France, 137; desertion of Tone, 140; after the '98, 183

Grattan, Henry, junior, 130, 241

Grattan's Parliament, 310, 340, 367, 368

Greville-Nugent, 308

Griffith, Arthur, and Sinn Fein, 367–368; denunciation of Larkin, 377; criticism of Redmond's war policy, 309; Vice-President of Sinn Fein, 407; negotiations for the Treaty, 420; Free State leader, 425; death, 426

Habeas Corpus Act, Irish, 109; suspended, 152, 156, 256

Halifax, Lord Edward F.L. Wood, 456

Hanover, throne of, 212

Hardy, Thomas, 140

Harrell, Assistant Commissioner of Dublin Police, and Irish Volunteers, 380–381

Harrington, Timothy, 356

Harvey, Beauchamp Bagenal, 175, 179; hanged, 182

Hayden-Moonan, *Short History of the Irish People*, 33, 45, 51, 88

Hayes, Stephen, 460, 464

Healy, Timothy, 364, 409; and Parnell, 1890, 355

Healy, Cahir, M.P., 460

Hedge-schoolmasters, 89–90

Heine, Heinrich, 231

"Hell or Connacht", 144

Henrietta Maria, Queen of Charles I, 59, 66

Henry II, and Diarmuid MacMorrogh, 35, 36 *et seq.*; and claim of Strongbow to High Kingship of Ireland, 37–38

Henry VII, 42–44, 46

Henry VIII, 39, 44, 46

Henry, Mitchell, on the Gaelic League, 365–366

Hesse, Grand Duke of, 170

Heuston, Sean, shot, 399

Hibernian Rifles, Easter rising, 1916, 396

Hill, Christopher, *English Revolution*, 54–55

Hitler, Adolf, 59, 169, 415, 451, 458, 463, 465

Hoche French flagship, sunk, 186

Hoche, Lazar, Jacobin general, meeting with Wolfe Tone, 147; attempt to invade Ireland, 153–155; death, 167, 201

Holland, negotiations with Tone for invasion of Ireland, 154–155

Holmes, Robert, defence of Mitchel, 254–255

Home Government Association for Ireland, 308–309

Home Rule, agitation, 307–317; "Moderate", 324; the O'Shea divorce, 353–354; "killing it with kindness", 358–359; crisis, 1912–14, 370–381; Tory opposition, 372–373; postponement, 404

Home Rule Act (1914), Royal Assent given, 383; Act suspended, 383, 416

Home Rule Bills, 1885, 1893, 1910, 304; First, 1885, 333, 340 to 341; Second, 1893, 358; Third, 1910, 358

Home Rule Confederation, Parnell elected President, 317

Home Rule League, established, 309

Home Rule Party, 309–310; Parliamentary obstruction, 310–313; crisis, 314–315; Parnell and Butt, 315–317; in 1880 elections, 324–325; Kilmainham Compact, 331; maximum power, 333

Hompesch Dragoons, 170

Hope, Jamie, 162, 195

House of Lords, verdict and sentence on O'Connell and others quashed by, 1844, 238

Housing, 207

Howth, arms running, 392

Humbert, General, landing at Ballina, 1798, 185

Hunger Strikes, 406

"Hungry Forties", 209

Hutton, John Wolfe Tone, 122–123

Iarfine, 27

Inchiquin, Lord (Murrough O'Brien), 65, 71, 240

Indemnity, Act of, 1798, 155 to 156

Independence, demand for, 404

Independence, legislative, demanded, 1780; 109

Independent, and Dublin Labour War, 377; and 1916 rising, 400

Industrial Revolution, 205, 211

Innfine, 27

Insurrection, moral, 250

Insurrection Act, 1798, 156; the case of William Orr, 161 to 163; terrorism, 169

Intelligence service, English, paralysed, 413

International, First, 333

International Working Men's Association, 276–277, 290, 307

Invasions, Anglo-Norman, 1169, 24, 36–42; Danish, 795–1014, 33–35; Tudor, 42–53; Cromwellian, 54–75

Investments, by Anglo-Irish landlords, 95

Invincibles, 333 *et seq.*

Ireton, General Henry, 72

Irish Agricultural Organisation Society (I.A.O.S.), 360

Irish Brigade, for defence of the Pope, 279

Irish Brigades, in American Civil War, 281

Irish Catholic on 1916 executions, 400

Irish chiefs and English lords, 48–49

Irish Exiles Advisory Bureau, 457

Irish Felon, 256

Irish Freedom, I.R.B. journal,
389; printed in Belfast, 390

Irish Free State, 465

Irish Home Rule League: See Home Rule League

Irish National Assembly, 1918, 410

Irish National League: See National League

Irish National Land League: See Land League

Irish People, 293–295; established, 282–283; raided, 284

Irish Republic, "virtually established", 284

Irish Republican Army (I.R.A.), 413 *et seq.*, 445, 452, 453, 455, 474; and the Treaty, 423; urged to disband, 449; Irish independence, 456, 457; "at war" with England, 459, 460, 463; demoralisation within, 470; revival and Northern campaign, 472, 474, 476

Irish Republican Brotherhood (I.R.B.), activities after Parnell, 364; and Irish Volunteers, 379; and World War I, 385; and the Treaty, 423; *See also* Fenians

Irish Self-Determination League, 419

Irish Society, the, 52

Irish Transport and General Workers' Union, Labour War, 1913, 376–377; Second World War, 465–466

Irish Tribune, suppressed, 256

Irish T.U.C., 465–466

Irish Volunteers, 365, 369, 381; split, 1914, 384–388; Republicans and Redmondites, 388; and Sinn Fein, 407

Irish Worker, and the struggle with authority, 389; printed in Glasgow, 390

Irish Workers Party, 471
Italy, "Young Italy", 231

Jackson, Rev. William, arrest of and suppression of United Irishmen, 138 *et seq.;* trial and death, 1795, 142
Jacobin Society, French, and United Irishmen, 120
"Jacobin" Societies, English and Scottish, 119–120
Jacobins, Ulster, 201
Jacob's Biscuit Factory, 377–378
James I, clearance and plantation, 49–51
James II, 77, 78–84
Jemappes, French victory at, 128
Jervis, Sir John, 154
Jenks, Edward, *History of Politics,* 32–33
Johnson, Thomas, 466
Jones, Ernest, defence of the Manchester Martyrs, 288
Jones, General Michael, capture of Dublin, 1647, 66
Juries, packed by Strafford, 57
"Justice to Ireland", 251

Kavanagh, Father Francis, 178
Kearns, Father Moses, 178
Kelley, Colonel, "Head Centre" of I.R.B. in Ireland, the 1867 rising, 287–288, 291
Kells, 181
Kenmare, Lord, 309
Kent, Thomas, shot, 399
Keogh, John, demand for redress for Catholics, 120 *et seq.;* Defenders and Peep-of-Day Boys, 135; loyalty to Wolfe Tone, 140; support for Tone's French mission, 146; and Daniel O'Connell, 210

Keogh, William, and Tenants' Right League, 270; Pope's Brass Band, 270–272; appointed Solicitor-General for Ireland, 272; Lord Chief Justice of Ireland, 274; a classic crook, 275; trials of Luby and others, 286
Kerry, Bishop of, and Fenians, 277
Kerry, Elections of 1872, 309
Keyes, Michael, 466
Kickham, Charles Joseph, 282; arrest and trial, 285–286; on clericalism, 294; and land agitation, 292
Kildare, and Emmet's conspiracy, 193
Kildare, support for 1916 rising, 396
Kildare, disturbances repressed, 1798, 170
Kildare, Earls of, Lords Deputy from 1468–1533, 46
Kildare, Earls of, 44
Killiecrankie, battle of, 81
Kilkenny, Articles of, 72
Kilkenny, disturbances repressed, 1798, 170
Kilkenny, support for 1916 rising, 396
Kilkenny, tithe war, 219
Kilkenny, Statute of, 40–42
Kilkenny, formation of Catholic Confederation, 65
Killaloe, Bishop of, 419
Kilmainham Compact, 1882, 318, 331; effect of Phœnix Park murders, 332
Kilmainham Gaol, Land League workers imprisoned, 330
Kilmurray, tithe war, 222
Kilwarden, Lord, 194
King's County, disturbances repressed, 1798, 170

498

King's County, 50

King's Party in 1641 rising, 65

Kinsale, landing of Papal forces, 1580, 48

Kinsale, captured by Marlborough, 83

Kinship society, 25

Labouchere, Henry, 347

Labour, agricultural, 206–207

Labour, forced, for repair of roads, 104

Labour Movement, English, judgment on 1916 rising, 401

Labour Party, 1906 elections, 370

Labour war, 376–378

Labourers, agricultural, 18th century conditions, 97–98

Ladies' Land League, 330

Laighin, 29

Lake, General, Military Commander for Ulster, 157 et seq.; defeated by the French, 1798, 185

Lalor, James Fintan, 276, 282, 293, 321; his idea of moral insurrection, 249–250; the Irish Felon, 256; theory of agrarian struggle, 305–306; Faith of a Felon, 306

Land, Gaelic tenure, 26–28; ownership in 18th century, 97; tenure, 206–207; free trade in, 261–263, 302; struggle for, 1870–1909, 303–305

Land Acts (1870–1909), 303, 308, 318, 329, 330, 336, 337, 359 to 362

Land Commissions, Cromwell's settlement, 72–73

"Land-grabbers", 266

Land Hunger, 423

Land League, 303, 305–306, 318; and 1879 famine, 323; and Land Act, 1881, 330; Kilmainham Compact, 331

Land purchase, 360

Land Purchase Acts, 428

Land tax, 371

Land war, Parliament and, 323 to 327

Landlords, 48; confiscation and plantation by English, 49 to 51; absentees, 50; and the Catholic Confederation, 65; Irish Catholic, 73; agrarian unrest, 102–105; landlordism, 206–207; the Great Famine, 244; the three F's, 265; and 1869 elections, 308; the 1879 famine, 323; Land Act, 1881, 330, 336; monopoly broken, 335; Wyndham Act, 359–360

Language, efforts to revive Gaelic, 365

Larkin, James, Socialist Labour revival, 369; Labour war, 376–378; to America, 1914, 389; and the Toiler, 398; and Labour Party, 465

Larkin, Michael, 288

Laud, William, Archbishop of Canterbury, 55–59, 76

Law, Andrew Bonar, and executions, 1916, 399; the Treaty, 421–422

Lawless, William, 173

Leadbeater, Mary, on the 1798 rising in Carlow, 198

Leaseholds, 96, 134

Lecky, William, 198; on proclamation of March, 1798, 169 "Left"-ism, 333–336

Leinster, disposition of estates, 1665, 79; Directory, 168; Duke of, 122, 172

Lemass, Sean F., 476

Lenin, Vladimir Ilich, 369, 402

Levellers, 68–70, 77, 87

Lewines, Edward John, negotiation with Dutch Government, 149

Lewis, House of Lords Select Committee, 207

Liberals, and Workers, 338

Liberal-Unionist split, 1885, 331

Liebknecht, Karl, 387

Limerick, foundation of, 34; resistance to Cromwell, 71; defence of, 1690, 83; Treaty of, 84; Courts martial, 1797, 160; disturbances repressed, 1798, 170; tithe war, 220

Linen, Charter of Monopoly granted by Strafford, 57; English policy and Irish manufacture, 95; American War of Independence, 105

Lisburn, pogrom against Catholics, 417

Lloyd George, David, leader of the Radical Left, 1906, 370 et seq.; postponement of Home Rule, 403–404; the Convention, 407–408; proposals for conscription, 408; "Police measures" in Ireland, 1920, 414–415; Truce, 416, 420; Government of Ireland Act, 1920, 416–417; the Treaty, 420–422, 437, 441

Loan, called for by Dáil, 412

Local Government Reform, 338

London, City of, Revocation of Ulster Charter, 56

London, Corporation of, planting of County Coleraine (Londonderry), 52

London Corresponding Society, English "Jacobin" democratic society, 117, 158–159

London-Irish Confederates, 254

Longueville, Lord, 171

Lord Deputy, 39–40

Lorraine, Duke of, 71

Louis XIV, 78, 82

Louis XVI, dethroned and beheaded, 120, 126

Louis Napoleon, 279, 291

Louth, held by King's party, 1641, 65; Defenders versus Peep-of-Day Boys, 136; revolt of 40s. freeholders, 214

Luby, Thomas Clarke, 305; editor of the Irish People, 282; arrest and trial, 285 to 286; on clericalism, 294 to 295; elections, 308

Ludlow, Edmund, 72

Luttrell family, 132–133

Luttrell, Henry, 83

Lynch, Gilbert, 466

Lynch, Jack, 481

Lynch, Liam, 426

MacArdle, Dorothy, The Irish Republic, 410

MacBride, John, shot, 399

MacBride, Sean, 467

MacCabe, Archbishop of Dublin, "Moderate" Home Rule, 324

McCaffery, John, rising of 1867, 287

MacCarthy, Justin, Kilmainham Compact, 331; leader of anti-Parnell Party, 356

MacCracken, Henry Joy, leader of the '98 in Antrim, 181, 195

McCullough, W., 477

MacDermott (MacDiarmada), Sean, editor Irish Freedom, 389; and I.R.B. Chiefs, 390; Provisional Government, 395; shot, 399

MacDonagh, Thomas, 389; Provisional Government, 1916, 395; shot, 398

MacDonald, Ramsay, on 1916 rising, 401

MacGuinness, Joe, 409

Mac Mahon, Marshal, 279

MacManus, Terence Bellew, funeral of, 280–281

MacMurrogh, Diarmuid, Ri-Mor in Laighin, 35; expelled from office, 35; swears fealty to Henry II, 35; invades Ireland with Strongbow, 37; claims Ard Ri-ship of Ireland, 37

MacMurroughs, the, 50

MacNally, Leonard, 194

MacNeill, Eoin, and Easter rising, 1916, 393–394, 396

MacNevin, William James, after the '98, 184

Macready, General, 420

MacWilliam, Burkes, sept of, 42

Maguires, the, 61

Mallin, Michael, shot, 399

Mallow, monster meeting, 234

Manchester Guardian, on 1916 executions, 399

Manchester Martyrs, 289

Manchester Rescue, 284, 288–289

Mann, Tom, 450

Marat, Jean Paul (1743–93), 122

Markets, Irish, and Industrial Revolution, 205

Markievicz, Madame, unifying influence of, 387; in 1916 rising, 396

Marlborough, (John Churchill) Duke of, capture of Cork and Kinsale, 83

Marseillaise, 122

Marshall Plan, 467

Marston Moor, battle of, 66

Martial law in Ulster, 157

Martin, John, 256, 289; Parliamentary candidate, 1869, 308; elected for Co. Meath, 309; death of, 310

Marx, Karl, *Eighteenth Brumaire*, 266–267; on Europe and American Civil War, 282; and Repeal question, 290 to 291; on demand for amnesty, 307; *Capital*, 456

Mary, daughter of James II, joint monarch with William III, 78

Mary the Catholic, Queen, 50

Maryborough, 50

Massey, General, rising of 1867, 288

Maxwell, Sir John, 398, 400

Maynooth, stronghold of Thomas, Earl of Kildare, surrender of, 47; Catholic seminary, 197; and Sinn Fein, 408

Mazzini, Giuseppe, 231

Meagher, Thomas Francis, "Meagher of the Sword", 246; deputation to France, 253; prosecution of, 253; and transportation of Mitchel, 255; transported, 257; American Civil War, 281

Meath, held by King's Party, 1641, 65; the 1916 rising, 396 to 397

Melbourne, Lord, 268; and the tithe war, 224

Mellows, Liam, 446, 473; 1916 rising, 397; supply of arms, 415; the civil war, 424; death of, 426

Middlemen, 102, 206; influence of, 135; eliminated, 261

Midhe (Meath), 30

Militia Act, 127, 131–133

Militia English, mutinies, 152

Militia, North Cork, 175, 177

Mill, John Stuart, on Rockism and Whiteboyism, 268

Milton, John, and massacre of Ulster Protestants, 1641, 61

Mitchel, John, 293, 390; on death of Thomas Davis, 242; leader-writer on *The Nation*, 246; and the American Civil War, 248–249; leaves *The Nation*, 250; and Lalor, 251; establishment of *The United Irishman*, 252; prosecution of, 254; transportation of, 255

Mitchel, Thomas, 472

Mitchelstown, meeting attacked by police, 1887, 343

Molyneux, William, 101

Monaghan, revolt of 40s. free-holders, 214

Monarchy, Absolute, in England, 43

Monastic communities, and Danish invasion, 34

Money-lending, 115; Land Act and, 336

Monk, General, George, 67, 69

Monmouth, James, Duke of, Revolt of the West, 77

Monster meetings in Repeal crisis, 233–234

Montefiore, Dora, 378

Moore, Sir John, 181; condemnation of repression, 183

Morrison, Herbert, 464–465

"Morrough of the Burnings" (Lord Inchiquin), 65

Mount Norris, Lord, 176

Muir, Thomas, 120

Mullaghmast, Monster meeting, 234

Mullinahone, tithe war, 223

Muman (Munster), 29

Municipal Reform, 338

Munro, Henry, leader of the '98 in Down, 182

Munro, Robert, commander of Parliamentary army, 65

Munster, clearance and plantation, 50; disposition of estates (1665), 79

Murphy, Father John, rising of 1798, 177–178

Murphy, Father Michael, 178

Murphy, W. M., 377, 400

Mussolini, Benito, 414–415, 451

Mutiny Act, 1782, 110

Mutiny Bill, 1780, 108–109

Napoleon III, 278

Naseby, battle of, 66

Nation, 295; establishment of, and its writers, 230–231; Repeal propaganda, 233 *et seq.*; editor on trial, 237; and W. Smith O'Brien, 240–241; opposition to O'Connell, 246; and the famine, 248; Mitchel resigns, 250–251; raided by police, 256; restarted, 1850, 268; after Duffy's departure, 277

"National" agitation, 209

National Anthem of Ireland, 289

National Convention of 1914, 388

National League, formation of, 1882, 336; elections, 1885, 339; Plan of Campaign, 1886, 342 to 344; suppressed, 343

National Reform League, 290

National Volunteer Force, 379

National Volunteers (Redmondite), 388

Nationalism, and Socialism, 369; character of Parliamentary, 384–385

Nationalist Party, effect of O'Shea divorce suit, 353 *et seq.;* the Party split, 355 to 356; decline, 358, 362–364; Redmond and the First World War, 382–384; the 1918 elections, 408–409

Nationality and Citizenship Act, 1935, 457

Nationality, Irish, and the Penal Code, 87–90

Natives, Servitors, and Undertakers, 51

NATO, 468

Navigation Acts, (1650–51, 1660), 93–94, 205

Navy, English, mutinies, 152, 154; Orange Order extended to, 212

Navy and Army Mutiny Bill, 1877, 313

Neilson, Samuel, founder of *Northern Star,* 119, 173

Nelson, Horatio, Battle of Cape St. Vincent, 154; Battle of the Nile, 187

Neutrality, 1939–45, 428, 457 to 466

New Departure, Land League and Nationalist agitation, 321–322

New Model Army, 68–70, 87

New Ross, 180

Newcastle West, tithe war, 223

Newry, 449, 479

Newtownbarry, tithe war, 219

Nile, Battle of, 188

Njal Saga, 35

"No Popery", 87, 179, 271, 424

Nonconformists, 58–59

Nonconformist-Liberals, and the O'Shea divorce, 353 to 355

Norbury, Lord, 194

Nore, naval mutiny, 1797, 158

North, Lord, 109

Northern Ireland, 422, 437; Parliament and arms regulations, 424; the Civil War, 424–427; Dominion status, 429, 439

Northern Star, 119; office attacked, 131; prosecution of, 138; suppressed, 160; replaced by *Press* newspaper, 163

Oakboys, 104

Oath of Allegiance, 422, 428 to 430

O'Brien, James Bronterre, 228

O'Brien, Michael, 288

O'Brien, William, 409; editor of *United Ireland:* The Plan of Campaign, 1886, 342–344; leader of Irish Transport and General Workers' Union, 465; Irish T.U.C. Congress, 1944, 466

O Brien, William Smith, 250, 251, 275; *Tanist* of the Repeal Association, 240; and insurrection, 251; prosecuted, 253; deputation to France, 253; and transportation of Mitchel, 255; 1848 rising, 256 to 257; transported, 257; and Fenians, 278

O'Casey, Sean, 448, 468

O'Connell, Daniel, 273, 286; Catholic Emancipation, 210 to 216; Clare by-election, 1829, 215–216; tithe war, 219, 222, 227; transition to Repeal agitation, 226–232; his political standpoint, 226–227; the Chartists, 227–229; and the *Nation,* 230–231; crisis of Repeal agitation, 233–242; monster meetings, 233–234; trial, 237–239; change of front, 239–242; the end, 245 to 247; and John Mitchel, 252

O'Connell, John, 240, 246–247, 251

O'Connor, Arthur, 163, 168, 228; the 1798 rising, 171 et seq., 184

O'Connor, Feargus, Chartist leader, 172, 228, 254; leader of Repeal Party, 251

O'Connor, Rory, the Civil War, 424; shot, 426

O'Connor, Ruraidhe, Ri-Mor in Connacht and Ard-Ri, 35, 38

O'Connor, T. P., returned to Parliament, 339

O'Donnell, F. Hugh, Libel action of, 345

O'Donnell, Peadar, 446

O'Donovan-Rossa, Jeremiah, the Phœnix conspiracy, 275 to 276; business manager of the Irish People, 282; arrest and trial, 284; elected for Tipperary, 308; quarrel with Devoy, 321; Dynamite War, 333; Patrick Pearse's speech at his grave, 404–405

O'Dwyer, Dr., Bishop of Limerick, and 1916 executions, 400

O'Hanrahan, Michael, shot, 398–399

O'Hegarty, P. S., on I.R.B., 364–365

O'Higgins, Kevin, 445, 468

Old Retainers, 31

O'Leary, John, 305, 335; on I.R.B., 277; editor of the Irish People, 382; arrest and trial, 284; on the first year of the Irish People, 295; and the Land league, 321

O'Mahoney, John, Fenian, 276 to 277; American Civil War, 282; "deposed", 286

"One-hearth dwellings", 207 to 209

O'Neill septs, 46, 51, 61; resistance to Cromwell, 71

O'Neill, Owen Roe, 63–68, 230; Catholic Confederate Council, 67; negotiations with General Monk, 67, 69 to 70

O'Neill, Terence Marne, 476, 480

Opposition in Gaelic Society, 30 et seq.

Orange Society (Orange Lodges, Orangemen), 126; foundation, 142–145; the first "Fascists", 145; terror in Ulster, 155–159; the 1798 rising, 174 et seq.; barbarities of, 188; the Union, 190–192; malice of, 196; Tories and Whigs, 211–213; provided with arms, 1848, 254; and Disestablishment, 292; and Capt. Boycott, 327; and Home Rule, 374–375, 384; Boundary Clause and Civil War, 424

O'Reily, John Boyle, Fenian, 296; and Michael Davitt, 321; a moderating influence, 335

Orkney, Countess of, 84

Ormond, James Butler, 12th Earl and 1st Duke of, leader of the King's party, 1641, 66–68

O'Rourkes, the, feud with Diarmuid MacMorrogh, 35

Orr, William, the case of, 161 to 163

O'Shea, Capt., negotiation of Kilmainham Compact, 331; and Joseph Chamberlain, 341; and the anti-Parnell

504

campaign, 347; the divorce, 1889, 349, 350–353

O'Shea, Katherine, 350–353

"Ostentatious consumption" in Gaelic economy, 25

Paine, Thomas (1737–1809), *Rights of Man*, 119; *Age of Reason*, 119

Paisley, Ian, 477–481

Pale, the, 38, 44–45, 47; reinstituted by Partition, 431

Pallaskenry, tithe war, 223

Parliament Act, 1911, 370–372

Parliament, Dublin, and Treaty of Limerick, 84; the Penal Code, 85–86

Parliament, English, Renunciation of right to legislate for Ireland, 111–112; and the Land War, 323–326

Parliament, Irish, Strafford's, 56, 60; and English Parliament, 95–96; and American War of Independence, 105; "To consider Irish grievances", 1782, 110; principles of election and composition, 119

Parliament, Kilkenny, 1367, 40 to 42

Parliament, Long, 60

Parliament, Pale, 40

Parliament, "Patriot", Dublin, 1689, 81

Parnell, Charles Stewart (1846 to 91), elected for Co. Meath, 1875, 310; in House of Commons, 311; organised obstruction, 312–313; crisis in Home Rule Party, 314–315; and Isaac Butt, 315–317; Land League, 303–304, 318, 320, 224 *et seq.*; Famine, 323; elections, 1880, 324; evictions speech at Ennis, 325; indicted

for sedition, 327; Coercion Bill, 328–329; suspended, 329; Land Act, 1881, 330; arrested, and in Kilmainham Gaol, 331; Kilmainham Compact, 331; Phœnix Park murders, 332; "Uncrowned King", 333 to 349; agrarian agitation, 335; and English political leaders, 1883, 337; Joseph Chamberlain, 338; Crimes Act, 339; Act to assist Irish tenants, 339; balance of power, 1885, 339; and William O'Brien, 342; tribute to, 344; and Tories, 344–346; *The Times*, 344–346; Special Commission, 346–348; vindicated, 348–349; the O'Shea divorce, 349 *et seq.*; the Party split, 1890, 355–356; defeated at by-election, 356; death of, 357; effect of death on the Parliamentary Party, 362 to 364; and Redmond, 383

Parnellism, invented by C. G. Duffy, 249

Partition, 403, 416–417, 422, 431 to 433

Peace of Amiens, 192

Pearse, Patrick Henry, 364, 386, 411, 431; on the 1798 rising, 201; on Wolfe Tone and Thomas Davis, 231; and Redmond, 380; Gaelic Republican, 386; the 1916 rising, 393; President of Provisional Government, 395; shot, 398, 400; speech at grave of Rossa, 404–405; "the people will be Lord and Master", 433

Pearse, William, shot, 399

Peasants, Agrarian unrest and revolts, 102–105; resistance

to Militia Act, 131–132; alien to Dublin Castle, 133; Catholic and Protestant bickering, 134; tithe war, 219 *et seq.;* the Great Famine, 243 to 245

Peasants, French, 266–267

Peep-of-Day Boys, 134–136, 143 to 145

Pembroke, Richard, Earl: *See* "Strongbow"

Penal Code, 85–90, 125, 168, 178, 197

People's Charter, 227

Perry, Anthony, 175

Phillipstown, 50

Phœnix Conspiracy, 275–276

Phœnix Park Assassinations, 332, 333 *et seq.;* attempt to implicate Parnell, 344

Pigott, Richard, forger, 346–347

Pilot, editor on trial, 238

Pitt, William (1759–1806), 308; war on French Republic, 126; Irish policy, 126–127; secret service, 139; alliance with Moderate Whigs, 141; the French Revolution, 151; class war and French war, 151–153; naval mutinies, 1797, 159; secret informers, 168 to 169; Act of Union, 187–190

Plantations, the First English, 1171, 38; confiscation and, 49 to 51; of Ulster, 51–53; Cromwellian, 72

Pledge, anti-tithe, 221

Plunket, Sir Horace, 360

Plunkett, Count, 409

Plunkett, Joseph, of Provisional Government, 1916, 395; shot, 398

Plunkett, Lawyer (Irish Lord Chancellor), 122

Poblacht na hEireann (Republic of Ireland) proclaimed, Easter, 1916, 395

Pogroms in Belfast, 1920–21, 417–418, 422

Police, 224–225, 362, 411, 415 to 416

Poor Law Commission, *Report,* 1847, 262

Pope: *See* Vatican

"Pope in Danger", 279

Pope's Brass Band, 266, 270 to 272, 286

Portland, Duke of, in Pitt's administration, 140–141

"Potato-ground", 97

Potatoes, 207; diet-staple, 97 to 98; failure of crops, 1845–7, 243 *et . seq.;* decline in acreage, 299–300

Poultry, 300

Poverty, extent of, 207–209

Powell, Enoch, 484

Poyning's Law, 96

Press newspaper, 163–164

Preston, Thomas, C.-in-C. of Catholic Confederation, 65 *et seq.*

Prison Bills, 1877, 313

Prisoners' Aid Society, 406

Protection, for Irish manufactures, 114

Protestant Ascendancy, 86–87

Protestants, massacre of, 1641, 61–62; land owned by, 1667, 79; "Gentry", 114; Peep-of-Day Boys, 134–135; Fitzwilliam's viceroyalty, 141 to 142, 143; Wexford rising, 1798, 178–179; the tithe war, 217–218; Repeal agitation, 235; Encumbered Estates Act, 269; "No Popery", 1851, 271; Disestablishment, 290, 292; Partition, 431

Provisional Government, for Ulster, 374

Provisional Government, Easter, 1916, 395

Queen's Country, 50; disturbances repressed, 1798, 170

Railways, Irish, 360

Rakes of Mallow, 199

Raleigh, Sir Walter, 50–51

Rand, Louise, 378

Rathcormack, tithe war, 220; massacre, 1834, 223

Reading-rooms, Repeal, 213, 233, 241, 246

Redmond, John, 390; United Irish Party, 1900, 362; the Curragh incident, 376; Ulster gun running, 380; First World War, 382–384; National Convention, 388; on the 1916 rising, 398; and Partition, 407; death of, 407

Redmond, Father Michael, 178

Reform Bill, Flood's, 113; of 1832, 217, 227

Reform, Parliamentary, and United Irishmen, 117

Reformation, Protestant, and the Irish Church, 50; nature of, in England 58–59

Reformism, agrarian, 335

Relief, during the Great Famine, 244

Religion, in the English revolution, 57–59; and the Nationalist Party, 363–364

Reilly, Thomas Devin, 251–252, 255

Rent, 30, 97–98

"Rent", Key-idea of Catholic Association, 211

Renunciation Act, 1783, 112

Repeal agitation, International and, 290–291

Repeal Association, 235, 240 to 242, 245–246

"Repeal Year", 232

Republic, agitation for, 209; proclaimed, Easter, 1916, 306, 395; declared established, 411; and "Free State", 421 *et seq.*

Republicans, 368–369; and First World War, 385–386; the 1918 elections, 408–409; "military" operations, 412

Republican Congress, 453, 460, 467

Resident Magistrate ("R.M."), 219

Restoration, 1660, 75

Revolt of the 40s. freeholders, 214–215

Revolution, English, 1640, 54 to 55

Revolution, French, 149 *et seq.*, 211; effect on Wolfe Tone, 115–116; and United Irishmen, 120; and Volunteers, 128; and Ulster, 200–201

Reynolds, John, 140, 146

Reynolds, Thomas, informer, 168–169, 184

Ribbon Lodges, 104, 339

Ribbonism, 264, 268–269, 275, 293

Richard II, defeated by the Wicklow clans, 42

Richardson, General, commander of Ulster Volunteers, 380

Right *versus* Might, 102

Right to Secede, 247

Rights of Man, in Ireland, 118 to 120

Ri, 28–29

Ri-Mor, 29, 32, 34–35, 38

Rising, 1641, 60–61, 63–68
Rising of 1798, 161–186, 196 *et seq.*
Rising of 1848, 252–257
Rising of 1867, 286–288
Rising of Easter week, 1916, 304; preparations for, 391 to 394; Easter Monday, 394 to 395; Easter week, 396–402; judgments on, 401–402
Ri-tuatha, 29
Robespierre, Maximilien, executed, 200
Roche, Father Philip, 178
Rockism, 268
Roosevelt, Franklin, 464
"Rossa": *See* Jeremiah O'Donovan
Round Towers, 34
Rowan, Archibald Hamilton, 129, 137–140, 146
Royal Irish Constabulary (R.I.C.), 362; and "military" operations of Republicans, 412–413, 414–415
Royal Ulster Constabulary, 473, 480
"Rundale" villages, 206
Rupert, Prince, 70
Radicals, English, 119
Rae, John, 240
Russell, Sir Charles, 347
Russell, Lord John, Ecclesiastical Titles Bill, 270–271
Russell, Sean, 451, 456, 459, 463, 472, 473
Russell, Thomas, 115, 161; and United Irishmen, 118; support for Wolfe Tone's French mission, 146; hanged, 195
Rutland Island, attempted French landing, 1798, 186
Ryan, Frank, 447, 452, 463, 473

Sadleir, John, 271–275
St. Augustine, 32

St. Patrick, 32
St. Ruth, General, 83
Sala, George Augustus, 347
Sale of estates after the famine, 264
Salic Law, 212
Salisbury, Lord, Prime Minister, 1886, 342
Sáorstat Eireann (Irish Free State), 411, 421, 452, 467
Sarsfield Club, 249
Sarsfield, Patrick, 82–83
Scotland, The Kirk and Archbishop Laud, 59; assistance to Royalists, 67
Scrope, Charles Poulett, 268
Sea-ports, established by Danes, 34
Searchlight, editor shot, 398
Sedition (Treason-Felony) Act, 253
Senate, 430
Separatism, 250, 364
Sept, 25 *et seq.*, 30 *et seq.*
Servitors, Natives and Undertakers, 51
Settlement, Cromwellian, 72 to 75
Seven Bishops, Trial of the, 80
Shaw, Bernard, on 1916 executions, 399
Sheares, Henry, 173, 184
Sheares, John, 173, 184
Short History of the Irish People by Hayden and Moonan, 33, 45, 51, 88
Sinclair, Elizabeth, 477
Sinn Fein, 358, 365, 367, 388 to 389, 398; and Labour, 377; and Irish Volunteers, 379; emergence of the Party, 405 to 407; and Conscription, 408; the 1918 elections, 408 to 409; party split, 1926, 446, 451, 482; revival, 472; gen-

eral election, 1957, 473; Socialist Party, 476

Skeffington, Francis Sheehy, executed, 397

Skeffington, Hanna Sheehy, 446

Slaves, 31

Sligo, resistance to Militia, 132

Smallholders, reduction of, 262

Smith, F. E., prosecution of Roger Casement, 400–401

Social order, Gaelic, 23–35

Socialism, 276; and Nationalism, 369; Gladstone's "Socialism", 340

Socialist Republican Party, 368–369; and First World War, 386; propaganda, 389

Society of United Irishmen: See United Irishmen

Soldier's Song, 289

Solemn League and Covenant, Scottish, 59

South African Government Bill, 1877, 313

Spain, 48, 105, 154

Spanish Civil War, 456

Special Powers Act, 473

Speculators and the Cromwellian Settlement, 74

Spenser, Edmund, View of the State of Ireland (1595), 49, 51

Spithead, naval mutiny, 1797, 158

Squireens, and peasant feuds, 135

Stalin, Joseph V., 369

Starvation, the Great, 243 et seq.

State, territorial, and the Church, 32–33

Statistics, of poverty, 207–209; holdings and farms, 1841–51, 262; crops and livestock, 1849–1914, 299–300; crops

and values, 1876–79, 320; tenant purchasers, 1870–1910, 359–360

Statute of Kilkenny, 40–42

Steelboys, 104–105

Stephens, James, Phœnix Conspiracy, 275–276; Fenian movement, 276–277; and American Civil War, 282; establishment of the Irish People, 283; arrest and escape, 284–285; goes to America, 286–287; deposed, 285

Strabane, 449

Strafford, Earl of, 55–57, 76; and Scottish revolt, 59; impeachment of, 60; trial and execution, 60–61

Strangers, in Gaelic society, 30

"Strongbow" (Earl of Pembroke), 37–38

Stuarts, compared with Tudors, 55

Submission of 1171, 37–39

Subsistence tillage, 97

Sullivan, Alexander M., 289; and The Nation, 277–278; and Marshal MacMahon, 279 to 280; 1869 elections, 308; Home Government Association, 309; anti-Parnell, 364

Sullivan, Timothy D., "God Save Ireland", 289

Swift, Jonathan (1667–1745), Modest Proposal, 98–99, 102; Champion of the Irish "Colony", 101–102; Drapier's Letters, 101–102

Tandy, James Napper, 146; "Tribune of the Plebs" and Volunteers, 107; demand for free trade, 1779, 108; and United Irishmen, 118; revival of Volunteers, 1792, 128;

Louth Defenders, 136; escape to Continent, 136; attempt at invasion 1798, 186
Tanist, 29
Taoiseach, 29, 430, 476
Tara, monster meeting, 234
Tara, Hill of, 29
Tariffs, on wool, 94
Teeling, Bartholomew, hanged, 185
Teeling, Luke, 185
Ten Hours Bill, 235
Tenancies, auction of, 102
Tenant League, 250
Tenants' Protection Associations, 269
Tenants' Protection Society, Whiteboys, 103
Tenants' Right Bill, betrayed, 272–274
Tenants' Right League, 261, 266, 268–270
Tenants' Right Principles, defined, 269
Terrorism, by Whiteboys, 103 to 104; in Ulster, 1797–8, 155; counter-revolutionary, 169 to 171; in Wexford, 174–175; vengeance after the '98, 182 et seq.; persistence of, 266 to 268; after Coercion Act, 1881, 330; Phœnix Park and after, 333–336; by Black-and-Tans, 415
The Times, Boycott's letter to, 327; anti-Parnellite propaganda, 333, 344 et seq.
Thomas, J. H., 429
Thomastown, tithe war, 223
"Thorough" conspiracy, 55–57
Thurles, tithe war, 219
Tilly, Count John, 71
Tipperary, disturbances repressed, 1798, 170; tithe war, 221–222; rising of 1848, 256 to 257
Tipperary Bank, failure of, 274
Tithe Commutation Act, 1837, 223–224
Tithe Composition Act, 221
Tithe war, 217–225
Toiler, editor shot, 398
Tone, Matthew, hanged, 185
Tone, Theobald Wolfe (1763 to 98), 114, 115, 118, 181, 195, 200, 231, 281, 290, 293, 363, 386, 404, 431; United Irishmen, 116–117; aims, 117, 121; on 1782 revolution, 118; on overthrow of French monarchy, 120; and the Catholic Committee, 120–123; on Irish Bar and Catholic question, 1792, 123–124; revival of Volunteers, 127–128; Defenders and Peep-of-Day Boys, 135 to 136; on the Whigs, 137; voluntary exile, 142; efforts for French landing, 146–160; and Buonaparte, 167; friend of T. A. Emmet, 146, 171; success of French mission, 185; taken prisoner, 186; suicide, 186; 1963 Commemoration, 476
Tooke, Horne, 140
Torture, inflicted by Orange Yeomanry in Ulster, 157–159
Tory Island defeat of French, 1798, 186
Trade, and Danish invasion, 34
Trade, foreign, development at, 45
Trade, Irish, restraints upon, 94–95; demand for free export trade, 107
Trade Unions, and Repeal agitation, 235; English and Parnell, 349; Irish, 368

Trades Councils in Lalor's scheme, 250

"Transplanters", 74

Treason, under Statute of Kilkenny, 41

Treaty of Limerick, 1691, 84

Treaty, Peace, between Charles I and Catholic Confederation, 1646, 66; of 1649, 67

Treaty, secret, between Charles I and Catholic Confederation, 66

Tribune, New York, 291

"Tribute" to Daniel O'Connell, 216

Tricolour, Irish, 253

Troops, English, to "crush rebellion", 1798, 169, 182

Truce, 1921, 414, 416–418

Tuam, Archbishop of, and land agitation, 322

Tuath, 28, 34

Tuileries, storming of, 122

Tynan, P. J., on Phœnix Park murders, 334

Tyrconnel, Richard Talbot, Earl of ("Lying Dick" Talbot), C.-in-C. and Lord Lieutenant, 79–80

Tyrconnell, Earl of, estates confiscated, 51

Tyrone, confiscations in, 51

Tyrone, Earl of, estates confiscated, 51

Uachtaran (President), 430

Ulaidh, 29

Ulster, plantation of, 51–53, 56; massacre of Protestants, 1641, 61; disposition of estates, 1665, 79; the Volunteers, 105 *et seq.;* Defenders and Peep-of-Day Boys, 135–136; political unity disrupted, 143; dragooning of, 155–159; United Irishmen, 200–201; tenants, property, 208; land in, 303; and Home Rule, 372 to 376; gun-running, 379–380; and the First World War, 382–384; Home Rule Bill, 1914, 383

Ulster Custom, 269

Ulster Freemasons, 140

Ulster Volunteers, 379–380

Ultramontanes, 279

Undertakers, Servitors and Natives, 51

Unemployment, in feudal system, 37

Unfree, 30

Uniform of "National Guard", 1792, 128

Union, Act of, 187–201; agitation for repeal, 209, 226–242; repeal crisis, 233–242; failure of, 290; *See* Repeal

"Unionists", 342

United Irish League, and Irish Volunteers, 379

United Irish Party, formed under John Redmond, 1900, 362–363

United Irishman, established, 252; suppressed, 256; programme for Sinn Fein, 367

United Irishmen, 93, 228, 275, 290, 404; rise of, 114–125; declared purposes, 116; demands, 119–120; war upon, 126–145; a "Jacobin" conspiracy, 126–127; and French Republic, 128; address to Volunteers, 128–129; and Defenders, 133–136; suppressed, 136–142; sympathy with French, 137; influence in Ulster, 143; a liberating force, 145; French landing, 152; naval mutinies, 158; case of

William Orr, 161–163; the '98, 161–186; Secret Directory, 171; their achievement, 195–200

United Land and Labour League, 349

United Nations, 481

United States of America, "Colour bar", 87

Unity, Gaelic, 30 et seq.

Universities, proposals for, 241

Valmy, 122, 128

Vatican, authority to Henry II to become Lord of Ireland, 36; and expeditions to Ireland, 1579–80, 48; Balance of Power, 82; Battle of the Boyne, 83; and Parnell, 344, 363–364

Viceroy, 95

Vicksburg, 282

Victor Emmanuel, King of Sardinia, 278

Victoria, Queen, efforts of Orange Order to prevent her accession, 212

View of the State of Ireland by Edmund Spenser, 49

Villiers-Stuart, opposition to Berresfords, 1826 election, 214

Vinegar Hill, the '98 rising, 181; the 1916 rising, 397

Volunteers (1778–82), 93, 105 to 107, 197; and United Irishmen, 116–117, 197; Convention Act, 127–129; suppression of, 130–131; "Citizen soldiers", 137

Volunteers, Republican, raids for arms, 413

Volunteers, Ulster, 374

Wages, agricultural, 207

Wakefield, Edward, 199; on landlordism, 206; *Survey of Ireland*, 208–209

Wales, Prince of, 311

Wallenstein, Albrecht, 71

Wallscourt, tithe war, 221–222

War, 1914–8, 304, 381, 382 et seq.

War, 1939–45, Eire's neutrality, 428, 431–432

War, Anglo-Irish, 410–420

War, economic, 428–433

War against French Republic, 126 et seq.

War of Independence, American, 94, 105, 109

Wars of the Roses, 42–43

Washington, George, 100, 109, 128

"Waste" land, enclosures, 103

Waterford, foundation of, 34; captured by Diarmuid, 37; resistance to Cromwell, 71; revolt of 40s. freeholders, 214

Waterford, Marquis of, 122

Wealth, early Gaelic, 25

Wellesley, Lord, Viceroy, 212

Westmeath, revolt of 40s. freeholders, 214

Westport, Land League inaugurated, 222

Wexford, foundation of, 34; captured by Diarmuid, 37; clearance and settlement, 50; massacres by Cromwell, 71; resistance to Militia Act, 132; the 1798 rising, 174 et seq.; the 1916 rising, 397

Whig Revolution (1688), 76–7

Whigs, 76; and Catholic Relief Bill, 109; Grattanite, 114 to 115; sympathy with France, 137; Portland and Fox factions, 140; and Catholic Irish, 141; Tone's contemp for, 148–149; Orangeism and Tories, 211–213; and Repeal agitation, 235

White, De Vere, *Kevin O'Higgins*, 445

Whiteboy Acts, 136

Whiteboy Conspiracy, 103–105

Whiteboys, 135, 197, 213, 228, 264, 265, 268; Protestant leaders, 115; "Freemasonry" of, 133; join United Irishmen, 156; in Wexford in '98, 174; and the tithe war, 218

Wicklow, clearance and settlement in, 50; the 1798 rising, 174 *et seq.*; Emmet's conspiracy, 1803, 193; arms running, 392

Wicklow clans, defeat of Richard II, 42

Wild Geese, 253

William of Orange, King William III, 78–84, 212

William IV, 212

Williams, Dalton, 256

Williams-Wynn, Sir Watkin, 157

Wilson, Harold, 481

Wilson, Sir Henry, assassinated, 425

Wolfe Tone Club, 249

Women, in 1916 rising, 396

Wool, export of cloth forbidden, 57; export of raw wool subsidised, 57; English policy and Irish trade, 94

Woolstonecraft, Mary, *Vindication of the Rights of Woman*, 119

Workers, and Liberal Party, 338

Workers' Republic, 390

World, on Biggar's obstructions in Parliament, 311

World Trade Union Congress, 466

Wyndham, George, 304

Wyndham Land Act, 1903, 359

Yeomanry, barbarities of, 157, 160, 198

Youghal, foundation of, 34

Young Arthur, on squireens, 198–199

"Young Ireland", 231, 246, 305; and O'Brien, 240–241

Partition Border

Briefly,
ABOUT THE EDITOR

C. DESMOND GREAVES has been editor of
The Irish Democrat, published in London,
since 1948. Before that date his publications
were confined to verse and to such matters as
patent specifications and scientific translations.
Since then he has produced a steady stream of
articles and pamphlets on Irish affairs and
Anglo-Irish relations. He is author of the standard life of James Connolly—*The Life and Times
of James Connolly* (Lawrence and Wishart,
London, 1961), and has just completed a second book on *The Life and Times of Liam Mellows.*